COMMENTS AB

"I love this book! It is a true ing the transformative lesson o. A Course in Miracles. Both lifelong students of ACIM and beginners will find Beth's comprehensive summaries enlightening, clarifying, and compelling. It's true nourishment for the soul for anyone learning to walk the lighted path of awakening." —Janine Miller-DeLany, MA, LPCC-S, Counselor, Author, Spiritual Teacher, Host of the podcast, Divine Choas: Spiritual Awakening,

"Thank you for making the writings more understandable. Once I have a clear grasp on what each section is saying I can go back and reread it in its entirety." —@Meechka

"How lovely to have a place where ACIM is decoded in such clear words. I love The Course, but what you have here really helps me stay The Course!" —@ElaineFielding

"Thank you, Beth, for making it easier to understand the Course. It can be overwhelming." —@leonorcampbell6309

"This is excellent! Thank you so much. Helps me greatly on my journey." —@UpRyzeQueen

"Beth, this is an answer to my prayer. I had felt confused and unable to understand the Text until now! I thank you so much! Much love and a multitude of blessings." —@auretjean1

"I love you and I am happy for these ACIM summaries. Love from Germany." —@callmefriend

"Thank you, Beth Geer, for your work. I love your course summaries. I listen to them every day." —@josephmckinght2807

"These chapter summaries are comforting, true, loving, and indeed helpful to all who listen." —@Kathleendelancy

"Thank you, Beth. Very helpful chapter summaries."—@ingridgrace

"Thank you so much for sharing these Truths with us!!" —@trent2830

"Thank you. I really appreciate your coverage of the text... since we almost singlemindedly seem to focus on the Lessons. Text allows us to get much deeper and have more understanding." —@JohnDick5887

"Thank you. I've been away from *A Course In Miracles* for a while. I'm back and it feels good." —@Provingsharonscottmiracles

"These are so helpful. I've found certain chapters a bit intense—like chapter 25. I'm grateful for your work." —@guidedbysunshine333

"Awesome!" —@brianjett

THE LIGHT HAS COME!

Published by Cogent Publishing NY
Imprint of The Whitson Group, Inc.
3770 Barger Street, Unit 604
Shrub Oak, NY 10588
USA
(845) 528-7617

Copyright © 2022 Beth Geer

ALL RIGHTS RESERVED. No part of this book may be reproduced or transmitted in any form or by any means, electronic or mechanical, including photocopying, recording, video, or by any information and retrieval system, without the prior written permission from the publisher. The scanning, uploading and distribution of this book via the Internet or via any other means without the prior written permission of the publisher is illegal and punishable by law.

A Course in Miracles material used in this book comes from its Third edition published by the Foundation for Inner Peace (www.acim.org).

ISBN: 978-0-925776-21-1

1 2 3 4 5—26 25 24 23

This book is dedicated to the Light in each and every one of us. For indeed:

"The light has come. You are healed and you can heal. The light has come. You are saved and you can save. You are at peace, and you bring peace with you wherever you go. Darkness and turmoil and death have disappeared. The light has come."
A Course In Miracles Lesson 75 1:1-7

"The light has come. I have forgiven the world."
A Course In Miracles Lesson 75 5:4-5

THE LIGHT HAS COME!

Divinely Guided Chapter Summaries from
A Course in Miracles

BETH GEER

Cogent Publishing NY
Imprint of The Whitson Group, Inc.

CONTENTS

INTRODUCTION 1
HOW REFERENCING IS USED IN THIS BOOK 3
MY PERSONAL IMPORTANT TERMS 3
CHAPTER 1   THE MEANING OF MIRACLES 17
CHAPTER 2   THE SEPARATION AND THE ATONEMENT 25
CHAPTER 3   THE INNOCENT PERCEPTION 38
CHAPTER 4   THE ILLUSIONS OF THE EGO. 47
CHAPTER 5   HEALING AND WHOLENESS 59
CHAPTER 6   THE LESSONS OF LOVE 70
CHAPTER 7   THE GIFTS OF THE KINGDOM 82
CHAPTER 8   THE JOURNEY BACK 96
CHAPTER 9   THE ACCEPTANCE OF THE ATONEMENT 109
CHAPTER 10   THE IDOLS OF SICKNESS 120
CHAPTER 11   GOD OR THE EGO 127
CHAPTER 12   THE HOLY SPIRIT'S CURRICULUM 139
CHAPTER 13   THE GUILTLESS WORLD 150
CHAPTER 14   TEACHING FOR TRUTH 168
CHAPTER 15   THE HOLY INSTANT 185
CHAPTER 16   THE FORGIVENESS OF ILLUSIONS 203
CHAPTER 17   FORGIVENESS AND THE HOLY RELATIONSHIP 216
CHAPTER 18   THE PASSING OF THE DREAM 228
CHAPTER 19   THE ATTAINMENT OF PEACE 244
CHAPTER 20   THE VISION OF HOLINESS 260
CHAPTER 21   REASON AND PERCEPTION 272
CHAPTER 22   SALVATION AND THE HOLY RELATIONSHIP 286
CHAPTER 23   THE WAR AGAINST YOURSELF 298
CHAPTER 24   THE GOAL OF SPECIALNESS 309
CHAPTER 25   THE JUSTICE OF GOD 321
CHAPTER 26   THE TRANSITION 336
CHAPTER 27   THE HEALING OF THE DREAM 352
CHAPTER 28   THE UNDOING OF FEAR 368
CHAPTER 29   THE AWAKENING 380
CHAPTER 30   THE NEW BEGINNING 394
CHAPTER 31   THE FINAL VISION 409
AUTHOR BIOGRAPHY 427
ACKNOWLEGEMENTS 429

INTRODUCTION

Use this book as you journey through its thirty-one chapters presenting a review of the chapters of the TEXT section of *A Course in Miracles* ("the Course"), inviting you to see the Course in a different light. It presents a chapter-by-chapter overview of the Course in an abbreviated version—one that I hope you will both enjoy and find simple to understand—allowing you to remember each chapter with ease as you read selections taken from the Course; and inspiring you to find a deeper understanding of the meaning of each chapter as you read its review.

In the beginning, this book started out as something I used only for myself—an aid I created to help me better learn the Course. Then, what began as mere notes and a collection of quotes, soon became organized into a body of material that I felt clearly needed to be shared with others because I was benefiting so greatly. And so it was that sometime later, I received an inspiration to turn these "chapter summaries" into YouTube videos—which I did—and now this book. (You can find my channel on YouTube under the channel handle name: @BethGeer. The videos are grouped together under "Playlists" titled: "ACIM Text Chapter Summaries.")

What this book contains then, are thirty-one chapters of carefully selected quotes from each of the thirty-one chapters of the TEXT section of the Course, reducing the quotes to their clearest meaning. Each chapter is then followed by a brief summary to help clarify the meaning even further. These "chapter section summaries" or explanations, were received in my mind through the Voice of the Holy Spirit.

This project took me almost three years to complete. At times I wondered how—or even whether—I should proceed. My typical method was to just sit down and begin to meticulously read each line of a chapter in the Course, waiting for the "inner yes" from the Holy Spirit as to whether or not I should include the quote. This process flowed smoothly. The proper quotes would simply jump out, falling easily into place, making total sense even though the content in the Course's TEXT was being basically cut into less than half.

Then I would listen quietly as I typed what I received from our Inner Teacher as He summarized the meaning of those quotes in a way I could relate to more easily.

And each time I would be blown away—section by section—simply because I did not have such a deep and clear understanding before I started. I did not know in advance what anything would be.

However, at times, it was nearly impossible to write. Not because it was difficult to receive the words, but because my ego did not want this project completed.

For instance, sometimes, I'd sit down to type and be overcome with sneezes. Or coughing. Or total body itching. Or I would suddenly be starving and have to go make something to eat. And... the list of ego-delay tactics is endless.

But each time, once I finally committed to typing and began the first word, there was no stopping Holy Spirit from coming through. Every physical problem would instantly resolve, and my mind would leave this world—and my body—behind.

And so now... here it is!

Please enjoy each chapter-summary as we journey together through the thirty-one chapters of the TEXT from *A Course In Miracles*. It is my hope only to be truly helpful, and that together, our understanding and ability to apply the Course principles to our daily lives will be enhanced.

"Nothing will change unless it is understood, since light is understanding." (T-9.V.6:5).

And if light *is* understanding, then indeed *The Light Has Come!* Let us decode the mysteries of *A Course In Miracles* together. For it is a deeper understanding that I hope to impart to you through what I share in the pages that follow.

With unconditional love to you,
Beth Geer

HOW REFERENCING IS USED IN THIS BOOK

All references to *A Course in Miracles* ("the Course" - "ACIM") used within this book are from the numbered editions of the Course published by the Foundation for Inner Peace - www.acim.org.

The Course contains a number of "sections" listed below, each referenced by the letter that follows its name.
TEXT—T
WORKBOOK FOR STUDENTS—W
MANUAL FOR TEACHERS—M
CLARIFICATION OF TERMS—C
In addition, two Supplements to the Course are referenced as:
THE SONG OF PRAYER—S
PSYCHOTHERAPY—P

For example, T-21.III.5:4-8—would reference:
Text book chapter 21. section III. paragraph 5: sentences 4 to 8.

The TEXT section of the Course contains thirty-one chapters, each of which is reviewed in the thirty one chapters of *The Light Has Come*.

MY PERSONAL IMPORTANT TERMS

Before we begin, I want to share my personal list of important terms with you. This is because as I read through *A Course In Miracles* for the first time—and even subsequent times—I found there were words I thought I understood, being used with different meanings.

I also knew that once I understood the new meanings, it would make all the difference in my understanding of the overall message of the Course.

So, I began to pay careful, close attention. Anytime I came across a sentence or idea that seemed to deeply clarify a particular word for me, I'd make note of it and then begin to substitute the new meaning for the word as I read along.

This helped me make tremendous "forward" progress in my understanding of ACIM!

Because of this, I am sharing my personal list of such words with you here to be used as a supportive reference as you read along.

With that being said, the question for many is, "Why do these words in ACIM have different meanings than we're used to, to begin with? Why doesn't the Course simply say what it means without requiring us to decipher new meanings for old words?"

The answer is that our current beliefs are outdated. And as we expand our beliefs to a new higher understanding of Who We Are, our language must expand as well. This means that some words need to be broadened in order to incorporate a new, deeper meaning.

Our reality reflects our beliefs, and as our beliefs expand, our reality shifts to accommodate our new higher understanding.

As it states in TEXT chapter 21 Introduction:

"Projection makes perception. The world you see is what you gave it, nothing more than that." (T-21.in.1:1-2)

"Therefore, to you it is important. It is the witness to your state of mind, the outside picture of an inward condition." (T-21.in.1:4-5)

"Perception is a result and not a cause. And that is why order of difficulty in miracles is meaningless. Everything looked upon with vision is healed and holy." (T-21.in.1:8-10)

Most of our metaphysical and spiritual thought systems are structured on very outdated beliefs. If our concepts remain caught up in old definitions, we will also remain caught up in our old mistakes of the past.

What we want is a new future. In order for that to be brought forth, our new beliefs need new ways to be expressed through our deeper understanding.

New definitions create new beliefs which beget a new experience. It is simply the idea of looking at ourselves and the world in a new way, which unlocks us from our past and propels us into a new more positive future, springing from our changed perspective.

ATONEMENT:

It is the *knowing* of our Oneness. It is uncompromising, all-inclusive Love. Atonement is to know you love all creation as One, despite the separate forms you see. It is to understand that in truth, we are One Love in God. There is no person, situation or place excluded from your Love. You see all things, living and non-living as part of your One Self. It is to love the world as God does. Once realized, the Atonement is the total healing of your mind of all thoughts of separation, exclusion, pain, hatred, resentment, anxiety, depression, and anger. It is a mind and heart at total peace with all things, events, situations, and people—because you know the truth of our Oneness and join with that thought only.

"Healing and Atonement are not related; they are identical." (M-22. 1:1)

"Accept Atonement and you are healed. Atonement is the Word of God." (M-22.1:5-6)

"Accept His Word and every miracle has been accomplished. To forgive is to heal. The teacher of God has taken accepting the Atonement for himself as his only function." (M-22.1:7-10)

"The progress of the teacher of God may be slow or rapid, depending on whether he recognizes the Atonement's inclusiveness, or for a time excludes some problem areas from it." (M-22.2:1)

"The offer of Atonement is universal. It is equally applicable to all individuals in all circumstances. And in it is the power to heal all individual of all forms of sickness." (M-22.6:1-3)

"Herein does he receive Atonement, for he withdraws his judgment form the Son of God, accepting him as God created him." (M-22.7:8)

CHRIST:

The state of recognition of our One Self in everyone, created as God's holy Son. This is the United Self in which we all exist in the Unified Field of God's Love.

"The name of Jesus is the name of one who was a man but saw the face of Christ in all his brothers and remembered God. So he became identified with Christ, a man no longer, but at one with God." (C-5.2:1-2)

CHRIST VISION:

To see one another as One, recognizing everyone as part of our One Self in God's Love.

"Christ's vision is the Holy Spirit's gift, God's alternative to the illusion of separation and to the belief in the reality of sin, guilt and death. It is the one correction for all errors of perception; the reconciliation of the seeming opposites on which this world is based."

"What was regarded as injustices done to one by someone else now becomes a call for help and for union. Sin, sickness and attack are seen as misperceptions calling for remedy through gentleness and love. Defenses are laid down because where there is no attack there is no need for them. Our brothers' needs become our own, because they are taking the journey with us as we got to God. Without us they would lose their way. Without them we could never find our own." (Preface page xii.2)

CREATION:

The word creation refers to anything that is eternal, for only what can last forever can truly be called "created." We are God's creation. Therefore, we are His Thoughts, for only the mind can create. And we exist eternally United within His Loving Mind.

"Creation is the sum of all God's Thoughts, in number infinite, and everywhere without all limit." (W-Part II.11.1:1)

EGO:

The ego is the "personality" part of our mind that is insane; the part that we split off or separated from the remembrance of God's Unity. It is the reason for the great amnesia we are each born with, for we had to forget eternal joy in order to know what is not eternal.

"The ego is idolatry; the sign of limited and separated self, born in a body, doomed to suffer and to end its life in death. It is the "will" that sees the Will of God as enemy, and takes a form in which it is denied." (W-Part II.12.1:1-2)

"Any thought system that confuses God and the body must be insane." (T-4.V.3:1)

FEAR:

It is the deception or illusion that we can be harmed in any way. It can also be called the absence of our awareness of Oneness and Love. It is the belief in our false form as a physical body and all forms surrounding us. It is fully under our control whether we choose to feel fear or love, for fear stems from thoughts in our own mind. No one can control what we feel, but ourselves.

"Being afraid seems to be involuntary; something beyond your own control." (T-2.VI.1:1)

MY PERSONAL IMPORTANT TERMS

"The correction of fear is your responsibility." (T-2.VI.4:1)

"Only your mind can produce fear." (T-2.VI.6:7)

FORGIVENESS:

To forgive as ACIM teaches is to overlook our false form as bodies and see or know only the truth of our Oneness in God. This is also referred to as looking only upon the face of Christ in another.

"Forgiveness is the healing of the perception of separation." (T-3.V.9:1)

"To forgive is to overlook. Look, then, beyond error and do not let your perception rest upon it, for you will believe what your perception holds. Accept as true only what your brother is, if you would know yourself." (T-9.IV.1:2-4)

"That forgiveness is healing needs to be understood, if the teacher of God is to make progress." (M-22.3:1)

"He overlooks the mind and the body, seeing only the face of Christ shining in front of him, correcting all mistakes and healing all perception." (M-22. 4:5)

"Forgiveness is the means by which we will remember. Through forgiveness the thinking of the world is reversed. The forgiven world becomes the gate of Heaven, because by its mercy we can at last forgive ourselves. Holding no one prisoner to guilt, we become free. Acknowledging Christ in all our brothers, we recognize His Presence in ourselves. Forgetting all our misperceptions, and with nothing from the past to hold us back, we can remember God." (Preface page xii.4)

Forgiveness can also be described as the stillness of ego-thoughts or all thoughts of the world of form and bodies. And in this stillness of thought about the world, a miracle occurs, and we remember our Oneness. God is then allowed entrance into our full awareness. Forgiveness is the trigger for the healing the miracle brings—healing not only of the spirit but the body also.

"The body can be healed as an effect of true forgiveness. Only that can give remembrance of immortality which is the gift of holiness and love. Forgiveness must be given by a mind which understands that it must overlook all shadows on the holy face of Christ, among which sickness should be seen as one." (S-3.I.3:1-3)

"For all that we forgive we will not fail to recognize as part of God Himself." (W-Final Lessons.Intro.3:5)

"The Son is still, and in the quiet God has given him enters his home and is at peace at last." (C-Epilogue.5:6)

"And what has been forgiven must join, for nothing stands between to keep them separated and apart. The sinless must perceive that they are one, for nothing stands between to push the other off. And in the space that sin left vacant do they join as one, in gladness recognizing what is part of them has not been kept apart and separate." (T-26.IV.2:4-6)

GOD:

The word "God" can be interchanged anywhere in the Course with the words "Love," "Life," "Union," or "Oneness" and still make sense within the context of use. God is the Lifeforce that holds all creation together as One. God can also be described as the feeling of total equality or zero conflict with all creation. With such feelings you are experiencing the state of grace, which is the constant state of our Creator.

GRACE:

Feeling our Oneness in God or knowing our Oneness in God. It can also be described simply as God's love applied directly to our heart, overlooking anything our physical eyes may see as not worthy of love.

"Grace is not given to a body, but to a mind. And the mind that receives it looks instantly beyond the body and sees the holy place where it was healed. There is the altar where the grace was given, in which it stands." (T-19.I.13:1-3)

"Grace is an aspect of the Love of God which is most like the state prevailing in the unity of truth." (W-1691:1)

GUILT:

The result of our choice to experience separation from God. It is an emotional response to the experience of being a body, which is the physical manifestation of thinking we are separate. The body is the vehicle the ego uses to express itself. Deep down, we each have a "guilty feeling" for having chosen to experience separation from God—not unlike the prodigal son parable of the bible. The words "guilt," "separation," and "body" can be interchanged with each other anywhere in the Course.

Try re-reading the quote below, substituting the word "guilt" with either the word "separation" or "body" and watch how a deeper meaning unfolds:

"Guilt remains the only thing that hides the Father, for guilt is the attack upon His Son." (T-13.IX.1:1)

HEALING:

We are healed when we choose to heal our perception of separation. This includes bodies, circumstances, and places—anything that appears "outside" of us. It is to know the uncompromising all-inclusive Love God has towards all things perceived by our ego-vision or rather, the illusions of what our physical eyes are showing us. It is to let go of the world of illusions through forgiveness, which is to look beyond what we see, and accept instead only the truth: we are One Love. To heal, we must first correct our vision in this way. It is never an outside circumstance that needs healing, but rather, our own mind. From that correction, all other corrections follow.

"Healing is always certain. It is impossible to let illusions be brought to truth and keep illusions." (M-6.1:1-2)

"...One who has perfectly accepted the Atonement for himself can heal the world." (M.-23.2:1)

"He has recognized himself as God created him, and in so doing he has recognized all living things as part of him. There is now no limit on his power, because it is the power of God. So has his name become the Name of God for he no longer sees himself as separate from Him." (M-23.2:6-8)

HOLY RELATIONSHIP:

This is a relationship seen through the eyes of Oneness. It is to see no difference between yourself and another. The body is not recognized as someone's identity, but rather, the sense of Unity within and love for another as part of your One Self. By seeing all others this way, you can make every relationship holy. Everyone is therefore in a holy relationship of Unity with all living things, everywhere, all the time. To recognize this Unity in any relationship, is to make it holy.

"Yet if given to the Holy Spirit, these relationships can become the holiest things on earth—the miracles that point the way to the return to

THE LIGHT HAS COME!

Heaven." (Preface page xii.2)

"A holy relationship starts from a different premise. Each one has looked within and seen no lack. Accepting completion, he would extend it by joining with another, whole as himself. He sees no difference between these selves, for differences are only of the body." (T-22.Intro.3:1-4)

"Think what a holy relationship can teach! Here is belief in differences undone." (T-22.Intro.4:1-2)

"Reason now can lead you and your brother to the logical conclusion of your union." (T-22.Intro.4:5)

"Here is the golden circle where you recognize the Son of God. For what is born into a holy relationship can never end." (T-22.4:9-10)

HOLY SPIRIT:

The Mediator between us and God or the Voice of God. We each carry the Holy Spirit within us as the bridge of communication with God while we still believe we are separate.

"The Holy Spirit mediates between illusions and the truth." (W-Part II-7 1:1)

"It is the Holy Spirit's goal to help us escape from the dream world by teaching us how to reverse our thinking and unlearn our mistakes. Forgiveness is the Holy Spirit's great learning aid in bringing this thought reversal about. However, the Course has its own definition of what forgiveness really is just as it defines the world in its own way." (Preface page xi.1)

"The Holy Spirit is the only part of the Holy Trinity that has a symbolic function." (T-5.4:1)

"The Holy Spirit is the Christ Mind which is aware of the knowledge that lies beyond perception. He came into being with the separation as a protection, inspiring the Atonement principle at the same time. Before that there was no need for healing, for no one was comfortless." (T-5.1.5:1-3)

"But what God creates is eternal. The Holy Spirit will remain with the Sons of God, to bless their creations and keep them in the light of joy." (T-5.5:6-7)

MY PERSONAL IMPORTANT TERMS

INJUSTICE:
It is an "injustice" to see only the illusion of this world of separate forms. The ego expresses injustice towards all things because it judges all things unfairly; as separate from itself, not knowing the truth of our Unity. Since it perceives itself as separate, the ego feels all forms of "injustice" done to it: unfair treatment, abuse, fear, anger, anxiety, depression, and pain. When in truth, these are just expressions of the unhealed parts of our One Mind. Therefore, we must learn to extend only justice in the face of such pain. Justice extends only love, compassion and understanding to our One Self when any un-loving thought enters our mind.

JUSTICE:
God's all-inclusive Love. It is the feeling our Oneness through the peace of stillness of all ego thoughts. It is to know our Unity. It is to withdraw our judgment from all things, knowing we do not know who or what anything is in truth. When we cannot see the Light within all things exclusively, we unjustly misjudge all things to be bodies and forms. Nothing in this world appears here as it is in Heaven. Justice is the correction of our ego-vision by letting go of all such unjust judgments.

"Justice is the divine correction for injustice. Injustice is the basis for all the judgments of the world. Justice corrects the interpretations to which injustice gives rise, and cancels them out." (M-19.1:1-3)

"All concepts of your brothers and yourself; all fears of future states and all concerns about the past, stem from injustice." (M-19.3:1)

"Salvation is God's justice. It restores to your awareness the wholeness of the fragments you perceive as broken off and separate." (M.-19. 4:1-2)

MIRACLE:
A moment of forgiveness. The remembrance that we are not separate. It is to know all things exist as One in the stillness of God's Love and what we see and hear with our physical senses is not the truth.

"A miracle is a correction." (W-Part II-13.1:1)

"It merely looks on devastation, and reminds the mind that what it sees is false." (W-Part II-13.1:3)

"Forgiveness is the home of miracles. The eyes of Christ deliver them to all they look upon in mercy and in love." (W-Part II-13.3:1-2)

"The miracle is taken first on faith, because to ask for it implies the mind has been made ready to conceive of what it cannot see and does not understand." (W-Part II-13.4:1)

"And thus the miracle will justify your faith in it, and show it rested on a world more real than what you saw before; a world redeemed from what you thought was there." (W-Part II-13.4:3)

"The miracle establishes you dream a dream, and that its content is not true. This is a crucial step in dealing with illusions. No one is afraid of them when he perceives he made them up. The fear was held in place because he did not see that he was the author of the dream, and not a figure in the dream." (T-28.II.7:1-4)

REASON:

To use reason is to remember the truth of our Oneness. It is the opposite of the ego's reasoning, which is that everything exists in a state of separation from itself. The words "reason" and "truth" can be interchanged anywhere in the Course and still make sense within the context of use.

"The introduction of reason into the ego's thought system is the beginning of its undoing, for reason and the ego are contradictory." (T-22.III.1:1)

SALVATION:

The knowing and acceptance of our Oneness, despite the separation our bodily eyes can see. We are "saved" when we no longer believe in our separation. It is to look upon the world we see and know that all it contains is false.

"Salvation is no more than a reminder this world is not your home." (T-25.VI.6:1)

"Salvation is a paradox indeed!" (T-30.IV.7:1)

"It asks you but that you forgive all things that no one ever did; to overlook what is not there, and not to look upon the unreal as reality." (T-30.IV.7:3)

SIN:

It is the idea of being separated from each other and the Unity of God's Love, or rather the mental state of experiencing a lack of love. It can also be defined as a "mistake in belief." Sin is merely the mistaken belief in our separation, for no one can exist outside of God's all-inclusive Love. To exist outside His Love would mean you do not exist at all. The word "sin" can be interchanged with the word "separation" and "body" anywhere in the Course and still make sense within the context of use.

"Sin is defined as "lack of love" (T-1.IV.3:1)

Since love is all there is, sin in the sight of the Holy Spirit is a mistake to be corrected, rather than an evil to be punished." (Preface page xi.3)

"Darkness is lack of light as sin is lack of love." (T-1.IV.3:1)

"Sin is insanity. It is the means by which the mind is driven mad, and seeks to let illusions take the place of truth." (W-Part II.4.1:1-2)

THE WORLD:

The physical representation of our decision to separate or "sin." It is a false reality born of our mistake to choose to separate from God, and so it is that everything thing we see appears to be separate from us. In essence, the world represents our defiance against the Oneness of God through our choice to see ourselves as separate.

"The world is false perception. It is born of error, and it has not left its source." (W-Part II.1:1-2)

"The world was made as an attack on God. It symbolizes fear. And what is fear except love's absence? Thus, the world was meant to be a place where God could enter not, and where His Son could be apart from Him." (W-Part II.3.2:1-4)

"Not one thing in this world is true." (W-240.1:3)

THE LAST JUDGMENT:

God judges that what is false, is false and what is true is true forever and cannot be undone or changed. God's judgment of the world, is that our ego-based world is not real and affirms that only what is eternal can be true. There is no punishment associated with this proclamation, for all is forgiven now and forever. For no pardon is needed for what was never real to begin with.

"The final judgment on the world contains no condemnation. For it sees the world as totally forgiven, without sin and wholly purposeless." (W-Part II.10.2:1-2)

"You who believed that God's Last Judgment would condemn the world to hell along with you, accept this holy truth: God's Judgment is the gift of the Correction He bestowed on all your errors, freeing you from them, and all effects they ever seemed to have. To fear God's saving grace is but to fear complete release from suffering, return to peace, security and happiness, and union with your own Identity." (W-Part II.10.3:1-2)

THE REAL WORLD:

A reality that is completely opposite in every way to our current world. It is the world God created for us; a world that can only be seen through the eyes of stillness and love; eyes that are not looking through the eyes of the ego.

"Your world is seen through the eyes of fear, and brings the witness of terror to your mind. The real world cannot be perceived except through eyes forgiveness blesses, so they see a world where terror is impossible, and witnesses to fear can not be found." (W-Part II.8.1:3-4)

"The real world shows a world seen differently, through quiet eyes and with a mind at peace." (W-Part II.8.2:2)

THE SECOND COMING OF CHRIST:

The time when the world is transformed through our choice to see it correctly; through the eyes of forgiveness. It is the total and complete correction of our mistaken perception of separation we hold now.

"The Second Coming of Christ means nothing more than the end of the ego's rule and the healing of the mind." (T-4.IV.10:2)

"Christ's Second Coming, which is sure as God, is merely the correction of mistakes, and the return of sanity." (W-Part II.9.1:1)

"The Second Coming ends the lessons that the Holy Spirit teaches, making way for the Last Judgment, in which learning ends in one last summary that will extend beyond itself, and reaches up to God." (W-Part II.9.3:1)

TRUE PERCEPTION:

The words "true perception" and "knowledge" can be interchanged anywhere in the Course and still make sense within the context of use. It can also be called "Christ Vision" or "real vision." It is not associated with physical sight, but rather, an inner knowing.

"Real vision is not only unlimited by space and distance, but it does not depend on the body's eyes at all. The mind is its only source." (W- 30. 5:1-2)

"The world you see is an illusion of a world. God did not create it, for what He creates must be eternal as Himself. Yet there is nothing in the world you see that will endure forever." (M.-4.1:1-3)

"The body's eyes are therefore not the means by which the real world can be seen, for the illusions that they look upon must lead to more illusions of reality." (M-4.2:1)

"The one correction possible for false perception must be true perception." (M-4.3:2)

"For true perception is a remedy with many names. Forgiveness, salvation, Atonement, true perception, all are one. They are the one beginning, with the end to lead to Oneness far beyond themselves. True perception is the means by which the world is saved from sin (separation), for sin does not exist (we are not separate in God). And it is this that true perception sees." (M-4.3:5-9)

Therefore, true perception recognizes our Oneness and nothing else. Bodies are seen, but not believed to be our identity. This shift in belief (from being separate bodies to One in Spirit) leads us to treat others as part of our One Self. This shift undoes the world as we know it—revealing a new, more glorious, egoless world in its place.

TRUTH:
The truth is, we have never separated from God and remain as He created us—at One with Him and All Creation. Yes

CHAPTER 1
THE MEANING OF MIRACLES

I. Principles of Miracles

Out of the 50 miracle principles, let us review a few that have been specifically selected that seem to represent the essence of what a miracle is:

Miracle Principle 1: "There is no order of difficulty in miracles. One is not "harder" or "bigger" than another. They are all the same. All expressions of love are maximal." (T-1.I.1)

Miracle Principle 3: "Miracles occur naturally as expressions of love. The real miracle is the love that inspires them. In this sense everything that comes from love is a miracle." (T-1.I.3)

Miracle Principle 12: "Miracles are thoughts. Thoughts can represent the lower or bodily level of experience, or the higher or spiritual level of experience. One makes the physical, and the other creates the spiritual." (T-1.I.12)

Miracle Principle 20: "Miracles reawaken the awareness that the spirit, not the body, is the altar of truth. This is the recognition that leads to the healing power of the miracle." (T-1.I.20)

Miracle Principle 25: "Miracles are part of an interlocking chain of forgiveness which, when completed, is the Atonement. Atonement works all the time and in all the dimensions of time." (T-1.I.25)

Miracle Principle 40: "The Miracle acknowledges everyone as your brother and mine. It is a way of perceiving the universal mark of God."

Miracle Principle 44: The Miracle is an expression of an inner awareness of Christ and the acceptance of His Atonement." (T-1.I.40)

In summary, Chapter I – I. "Principles of Miracles" is saying:
There is no order of difficulty in miracles because the world we see is not eternal, and therefore not real. Everything in this world is equally unreal and therefore equally eligible for healing through the expression of God's Love. All expressions of God's love are maximal because God cannot give love partially. Miracles are natural expressions of God's Love through us, through our loving thoughts. We can have two types of thoughts: those of the "lower"

CHAPTER 1 — THE MEANING OF MIRACLES

[handwritten: Takes Awareness, Perserverance]

or bodily level and those of the "higher" or spiritual level, which are those thoughts that represent our union in God's love. Only these thoughts have the potential to extend miracles. Once you have cleared your inner altar of all thoughts that do not represent unity, you have made space for God's Presence in your mind, and thus, the ability to work miracles is awakened.

Your miracle working abilities are awakened through miracle-mindedness, which stems from true forgiveness. True forgiveness is nothing more than overlooking the bodies that seem to separate us. It is to remember that we are One. Recognizing this Oneness is called the Atonement. It is a miracle to recognize the Oneness we share with one another and God. Conscious acceptance of our Oneness is the way to perceive the universal mark of God in one another.

Therefore, a miracle is simply the inner awareness of Christ's presence within all people. It is a miracle to understand that such awareness of unity completes the circle of Atonement. When your mind rests in such a state of miracle-minded thinking, anything is possible in the physical world, for you have then already overcome it, even as Christ Himself applied the principles of miracles in order to do so.

II. Revelation, Time and Miracles

"Miracles unite you directly with your brother." (T-1.II.1:6)

"Revelation induces only experience. Miracles, on the other hand, induce action." (T-1.II.2:3-4)

"Revelation is literally unspeakable because it is an experience of unspeakable love." (T-1.II.2:7)

"The miracle minimizes the need for time. In the longitudinal or horizontal plane the recognition of the equality of the members of the Sonship appears to involve almost endless time. However, the miracle entails a sudden shift from horizontal to vertical perception. This introduces an interval from which the giver and receiver both emerge farther along in time than they would otherwise have been. The miracle thus has the unique property of abolishing time to the extent that it renders the interval of time it spans unnecessary." (T-1.II.6:1-5)

"The miracle substitutes for learning that might have taken thousands of years." (T-1.II.6:7)

In summary, Chapter 1– I. "Revelation, Time and Miracles" is saying:
Revelation is the resulting EXPERIENCE of extending miracles. Miracles are the action we take in order to have the experience of "unspeakable love" that defines what revelation is. Time is irrelevant. Miracles abolish the need for time because miraculous thinking actually causes our mind to step out of the horizontal dimension of time entirely and "go vertical." Horizontal thinking is exactly what it sounds like; our thoughts literally "go sideways" when they rest on the physical world and its horizontal path through time. But if your mind elevates to the level of miracle-mindedness it lifts out of the realm of time itself. Miracles actually erase the time it takes to achieve "vertical" thinking under ordinary circumstances. In order to shift our perception "vertical," we must see only Light in our brothers, thus saving us "thousands of years" of learning what the truth is. This is the meaning behind revelation, time, and miracles. Revelation is the understanding of our Oneness. Time is unnecessary for knowing this—revelation takes place the instant we accept our Oneness as true. And this acceptance is a miracle.

III. Atonement and Miracles

"As you share my unwillingness to accept error in yourself and others, you must join the great crusade to correct it; listen to my voice, learn to undo error and act to correct it. The power to work miracles belongs to you. I will provide the opportunities to do them, but you must be ready and willing. Doing them will bring conviction in the ability, because conviction comes through accomplishment. The ability is the potential, the achievement is its expression, and the Atonement, which is the natural profession of the children of God, is the purpose." (T-1.III.1:6-10)

"'Lead us not into temptation'" means "'Recognize your errors and choose to abandon them by following my guidance.'" (T-1.III. 4:7)

"You are free to establish your kingdom where you see fit, but the right choice is inevitable if you remember this:

> Spirit is in a state of grace forever.
> Your reality is only spirit.
> Therefore you are in a state of grace forever.

Atonement undoes all errors in this respect, and thus uproots the source of fear." (T-1.III. 5:3-7)

"The Golden Rule asks you to do unto others as you would have them

CHAPTER 1 — THE MEANING OF MIRACLES

do unto you. This means that the perception of both must be accurate." (T-1.III.6:2-3)

"You cannot behave appropriately unless you perceive correctly." (T-1.III.6:5)

"You should look out from the perception of your own holiness to the holiness of others." (T-1.III.6:7)

"That the miracle may have effects on your brothers that you may not recognize is not your concern. The miracle will always bless you." (T-1.III.8:1-2)

"The impersonal nature of miracle-mindedness ensures your grace, but only I am in a position to know where they can be bestowed." (T-1.III.8:5)

"Since the miracle aims as restoring the awareness of reality, it would not be useful if it were bound by laws that govern the error it aims to correct." (T-1.III.9:4)

In summary, Chapter I – III. "Atonement and Miracles" is saying: "Error" is to mistake anyone for the body they appear to be and forget Who They Are in truth. We are called by Jesus to join Him in seeing others as He does, through the eyes of forgiveness—eyes that see only the Light of God within. Our opportunities to do so are endless. We only need to be willing, and as we practice true forgiveness, we will witness miracles in healing—in healing of relationships as well as physical bodies. This will give us great conviction in our newfound abilities. These abilities are not special; they are our natural way of being. To perform miracles is our purpose in the world.

All we need remember is that we want to be alert as to when we are seeing only errors in one another. Let us not be tempted to see the body above the Light within one another; and if we become mistaken, we must abandon such thoughts immediately, which invites the presence of Jesus.

We cannot behave appropriately towards one another until we see each other correctly. Until then, our actions will remain insane. We need to learn to perceive others through the eyes of our own holiness and see only the holiness in another. This miracle is the foundation for Atonement, or the realization of our Oneness—which is a miracle.

IV. The Escape from Darkness

"The escape from darkness involves two stages: First, the recognition that darkness cannot hide. This step usually entails fear. Second, the recognition that there is nothing you want to hide even if you could. This step brings escape from fear. When you have become willing to hide nothing, you will not only be willing to enter into communion but will also understand peace and joy." (T-1.IV.1:1-5)

"Holiness can never be really hidden in darkness, but you can deceive yourself about it. This deception makes you fearful because you realize in your heart it is a deception, and you exert enormous efforts to establish its reality." (T-1.IV2:1-2)

"Darkness is lack of light as sin is lack of love." (T-1.IV3:1)

"The emptiness engendered by fear must be replaced by forgiveness." (T-1.IV4:1)

"Those who witness for me are expressing, through their miracles, that they have abandoned the belief in deprivation in favor of the abundance they have learned belongs to them." (T-1.IV4:8)

In summary, Chapter I – IV. "The Escape from Darkness" is saying: "Darkness" is the mind that is unaware of its own holiness and its union in holiness and love with all other minds. First, we must recognize that we cannot hide from such union and love by simply forgetting about it. This will entail some fear, as we suddenly feel guilty for attempting to hide from God. We will move into peace as we accept there is nothing about God from which we would wish to hide from in the first place. This is accomplished through forgiveness. Forgiveness replaces the hatred you once held for all those whom you thought were separate from you, for forgiveness is the inner recognition they actually belong to you in Spirit. Only in darkness could you mistake your brother for an enemy and try to destroy one who is a part of you. In light, you can see Who They Are, your dearest Friend Who—through your inner recognition of them—is there only to help you escape from darkness.

V. Wholeness and Spirit

"The basic decision of the miracle-minded is not to wait on time any longer than is necessary." (T-1.V.2:1)

"Ultimately, every member of the family of God must return." (T-1.V. 4:1)

CHAPTER 1—THE MEANING OF MIRACLES

"Whatever is true is eternal, and cannot change or be changed. Spirit is therefore unalterable because it is already perfect, but the mind can elect what it chooses to serve." (T-1.V. 5:1-2)

"The miracle is a sign that the mind has chosen to be led by me in Christ's service." (T-1.V.6:1)

In summary, Chapter 1 – V. "Wholeness and Spirit" is saying:
The miracle-minded person has decided to "go vertical" in their thinking, which is to no longer believe in what the world shows them. This is opposite to "horizontal thinking" which means that your thoughts go nowhere but along the same lines you have always been thinking—"horizontal thoughts" are those thoughts about the world of form and physicality. To "go vertical" means you acknowledge only what is eternal is true about everyone. The body is a false identity to be overlooked and thus forgiven. This thinking is the path that sets us on our return to God. We have thus decided to allow Him to lead our thoughts and place them in service to Christ, which brings our mind back into the wholeness and peace of Spirit.

VI. The Illusion of Needs

"You who want peace can find it only by complete forgiveness." (T-1.VI.1:1)

"Until the "separation," which is the meaning of the "fall," nothing was lacking. There were no needs at all." (T-1.VI.1:6-7)

"A sense of separation from God is the only lack you really need correct." (T-1.VI.2:1)

"The idea of orders of need, which follows from the original error that one can be separated from God, requires correction at its own level before the error of perceiving levels at all can be corrected." (T-1.VI.3:1)

"The real purpose of this world is to use it to correct your unbelief. You can never control the effects of your fear yourself, because you made fear, and you believe in what you made." (T-1.VI.4:1-2)

"To whatever extent you are willing to submit your beliefs to this test, to that extent are your perceptions corrected. In sorting out the false from the true, the miracle proceeds along these lines:

> *Perfect love casts out fear.*
> *If fear exists,*
> *Then there is not perfect love.*
> **But:**
> *Only perfect love exists.*
> *If there is fear,*
> *It produces a state that does not exist.*
> Believe this and you will be free." (T-1.VI.5:1-9)

In summary, Chapter I – VI. "The Illusion of Needs" is saying:
We have an illusion that we need things in this world, the illusion of our separation by bodies. However, our only real need is to correct this error in thinking which brought about the existence of this world to begin with: the thought that it is possible for us to be separated from God. This thought needs to be corrected before any other correction is possible. In order to do this, we must submit everything we think we understand to this one simple test: Do we feel fear or love in association with it? Is there a possibility of loss of some kind? Perfect love can never be lost or stolen. If there is fear, we are associating our mind with a false reality and therefore it does not exist in the first place. There is nothing to lose! Only perfect love exists, and this is the thought that has the power to free us from all forms of fear. It removes the illusion of needs of any kind.

VII. Distortions of Miracle Impulses

"The confusion of miracle impulses with physical impulses is a major perceptual distortion." (T-1.VII.1:2)

"Do not deceive yourself into believing that you can relate in peace to God or to your brothers with anything external." (T-1.VII.1:7)

"You can use your body best to help you enlarge your perception so you can achieve real vision of which the physical eye in incapable. Learning to do this is the body's only true usefulness." (T-1.VII.2:5)

"Fantasy is an attempt to control reality according to false needs." (T-1.VII.3:4)

"Fantasies are a means of making false associations and attempting to obtain pleasure from them. But although you can perceive false associations, you can never make them real except to yourself. You believe in what you make. If you offer only miracles, you will be equally strong

CHAPTER 1—THE MEANING OF MIRACLES

in your belief in them." (T-1.VII.3:6-9)

"Complete restoration of the Sonship is the only goal of the miracle-minded." (T-1.VII.3:14)

"This is a course in mind training. All learning involves attention and study at some level." (T-1.VII.4:1-2)

"Some of the later steps in this course, however, involve a more direct approach to God Himself. It would be unwise to start on these steps without careful preparation, or awe will be confused with fear, and the experience will be more traumatic than beatific. Healing is of God in the end. The means are being carefully explained to you." (T-1.VII. 5:7-10)

In summary, Chapter I – VII. "Distortions of Miracle Impulses" is saying:

Deep down inside, beneath our conscious awareness, is our desire to be one with God. This is our heart's desire. We must not confuse the desires of the body—our "body impulses"—as a means for fulfilling our deep seeded desire for oneness with God. It is a fantasy to attempt to use the body as replacement for what only the awareness of oneness can restore.

The body is the fantasy of separation we set between God and us. While we still relate to it as our identity, we are not at peace with God. The gains of this world we seem to use it for can never be real, for the body is not Who We Are. The only true use for the body is for forgiveness, which is to see no one as a body. To see in this way is a miracle. It is to extend our corrected perception, which the physical eye cannot see. Having bodily fantasies is to create more illusions of false needs. Fantasies about worldly goals are attempts to simply be more comfortable here within the illusion, rather than trying to heal it. This is a distortion in our natural miracle impulse; a distortion of our true goal in coming to this world. The only goal we need is acceptance of our Oneness—not to strengthen the idea of our separation through believing bodies are our true identity. Our only goal in coming here is to restore God's Sonship to wholeness and correct the distortions of our miracle impulses. The means to do this are being given to us through specific instruction in this course; we are being taught the true meaning of miracles.

CHAPTER 2
THE SEPARATION AND THE ATONEMENT

I. The Origins of Separation

"To extend is a fundamental aspect of God which He gave to His Son. In the creation, God extended Himself to His creations and imbued them with the same loving Will to create." (T-2.I.1:1-2)

"Because of your likeness to your Creator you are creative. No child of God can lose this ability because it is inherent in what he is, but he can use it inappropriately by projecting. The inappropriate use of extension, or projection, occurs when you believe that some emptiness of lack exists in you, and that you can fill it with your own ideas instead of truth. This process involves the following steps:

First, you believe that what God created can be changed by your own mind.

Second, you believe that what is perfect can be rendered imperfect or lacking.

Third, you believe that you can distort the creations of God, including yourself.

Fourth, you believe that you can create yourself, and that the direction of your own creation is up to you." (T-2.I.1:5-12)

"These related distortions represent a picture of what actually occurred in the separation, or the "detour into fear." None of this existed before the separation, nor does it actually exist now." (T-2.I.2:1-2)

"You do not have to continue to believe what is not true unless you choose to do so." (T-2.I.3:3)

"What is seen in dreams seems to be very real. Yet the Bible says that a deep sleep fell upon Adam, and nowhere is there reference to his waking up. The world has not yet experienced any comprehensive reawakening or rebirth. Such a rebirth is impossible as long as you continue to project or miscreate." (T-2.I.3:5-8)

"Whatever lies you may believe are of no concern to the miracle, which can heal any of them with equal ease." (T-2.I.5:1)

"But remember the first principle in this course; there is no order of

CHAPTER 2—THE SEPARATION AND THE ATONEMENT

difficulty in miracles. In reality you are perfectly unaffected by all expressions of lack of love." (T-2.I.5:5-6)

"Health is inner peace. It enables you to remain unshaken by lack of love from without and capable, through your acceptance of miracles, of correcting the conditions proceeding from lack of love in others." (T-2.I.5:11-12)

In summary, Chapter 2 – I. "The Origins of Separation" is saying:
We think we can be something other than the Spirit of Love and Light God created us as. We think we can become a physical body, perishable and filled with sin and darkness. This cannot be done, given the eternal nature of our true Self as Spirit. What is eternal cannot be changed. However, we can forget our eternal Identity. We have indeed done this through a four-step process—a process that caused us to change our mind about who we are in truth. We decided to forget the Laws of God and made our own. Because of this, we should not believe in anything this world shows us. And it can all be easily undone with a miracle, despite how real this dream may appear to be. Who We Are in truth still exists beneath our false identity as a body, and health can be restored to our mind through choosing not to believe in the separation we see all around us. This may sound insane, and yet a healthy mind is one that knows this world is not our real existence, thus forgiving its falsity, which corrects our perception of everything outside of us. Everyone can agree they feel better once they wake from a nightmare, only to realize none of it was real. Until we do this in our reality here, we will remain asleep and continue to project a fear-filled world that is not real. The miracle corrects and heals all forms of fear through us, by our withdrawing our belief in it—we do this through understanding the origins of separation.

II. The Atonement as Defense

"I have asked you to perform miracles, and have made it clear that miracles are natural, corrective, healing and universal. There is nothing they cannot do, but they cannot be performed in the spirit of doubt or fear. When you are afraid of anything, you are acknowledging its power to hurt you." (T-2.II.1:1-3)

"True denial is a powerful protective device. You can and should deny any belief that error can hurt you. This kind of denial is not a concealment but a correction. Your right mind depends on it. Denial of error is a strong defense of truth, but denial of truth results in miscreation, the projections of the ego." (T-2.II.2:1-5)

26

III. The Altar of God

"You can defend truth as well as error." (T-2.II.3:1)

"Everyone defends his treasure, and will do so automatically. The real questions are, what do you treasure, and how much do you treasure it?" (T-2.II.3:4-5)

"The Atonement is the only defense that cannot be used destructively because it is not a device you made." (T-2.II.4:1)

"The Atonement is a total commitment. You may still think this is associated with loss, a mistake all the separated Sons of God make in one way or another." (T-2.II.7:1)

"The miracle turns the defense of Atonement to your real protection, and as you become more and more secure you assume your natural talent of protecting others, knowing yourself as both brother and a Son." (T-2.II.7:8)

In summary, Chapter 2 – II. "The Atonement as Defense" is saying:
When we deny this world of illusions and separation rather than denying the truth of our reality as One with God, we are "turning the tables" on the ego. We are literally dismantling its whole belief system and thus opening the way for miracles. The question is: how badly do we want this world? Are we willing to give up our belief in it in exchange for a promise of a better world? A world we have nothing with which to compare to in this world.

This requires trust, faith, and belief. It is a "total commitment" as the Course puts it. To believe in the Atonement—our Oneness—above all else is to work a miracle. Such belief is not for those who feel to give up belief in this world is a sacrifice. Yet it is merely the exchange of hell for Heaven.

But, if our faith is given over to the Atonement, we are protected from all forms of disappointment and feelings of loss in this world. This point of view will become habit for those who practice it wholeheartedly. Loving all people without thinking will become a natural defense of our Oneness—Atonement—against the false world of separation we see now.

III. The Altar of God

"The Atonement can only be accepted within you by releasing the inner light. Since the separation, defenses have been used almost entirely to defend against the Atonement, and thus maintain the separation. This is generally seen as a need to protect the body. The many body fantasies in which minds engage arise from the distorted belief that the body can be used as a means for attaining "atonement." Perceiving the body as a temple is only part of it." (T-2.III.1:1-5)

"The next step, however, is to realize that a temple is not a structure at all. Its true holiness lies at the inner altar around which the structure is built. The emphasis on beautiful structures is a sign of the fear of Atonement, and an unwillingness to reach the altar itself." (T-2.III.1:7-9)

"The acceptance of the Atonement by everyone is only a matter of time. This may appear to contradict free will because of the inevitability of the final decision, but this is not so. You can temporize and you are capable of enormous procrastination, but you cannot depart entirely from your Creator, Who set the limits on your ability to miscreate." (T-2.III.3:1-3)

"Tolerance for pain may be high, but it is not without limit. Eventually everyone begins to recognize, however dimly, that there must be a better way. As this recognition becomes more firmly established, it becomes a turning point. This ultimately reawakens spiritual vision, simultaneously weakening the investment in physical sight." (T-2.III.3:5-8)

"Spiritual vision literally cannot see error, and merely looks for Atonement. All solutions the physical eye seeks dissolve. Spiritual vision looks within and recognizes immediately that the altar has been defiled and needs to be repaired and protected." (T-2.III.4:1-3)

"This re-establishes the power of the mind and makes it increasingly unable to tolerate delay, realizing that it only adds unnecessary pain. As a result, the mind becomes increasingly sensitive to what it would once have regarded as very minor intrusions of discomfort." (T-2.III.4:6-7)

"The children of God are entitled to the perfect comfort that comes from perfect trust. Until they achieve this, they waste themselves and their true creative powers on useless attempts to make themselves more comfortable by inappropriate means." (T-2.III.5:1-2)

"God is lonely without His Sons, and they are lonely without Him. They must learn to look upon the world as a means of healing the separation. The Atonement is the guarantee that they will ultimately succeed." (T-2.III.5:11-13)

In summary, Chapter 2 – III. "The Altar of God" is saying:

Within each of us is an "altar to God." It can be filled with either thoughts of this world and our separated bodies, or thoughts of our Oneness in God's Love and Light. Clearing our inner altar of all thoughts associated with the body and this world is only a matter of time. We have only so much tolerance for the pain that comes from this world. Once we realize that by releasing ourselves from such thoughts, we also release ourselves from pain, we become increasingly aware of when we are having such thoughts and seek more quickly to release them. The world then becomes a place where we can consciously heal the separation and guarantee that the Atonement will ultimately come to us sooner rather than later. We heal the world through ceasing to attempt to search for happiness in what the world has to offer. Our focus then becomes the search for the eternal Light within all living things. In this way, we clear our inner altar to God of all that no longer serves us.

IV. Healing as Release from Fear

"Our emphasis is now on healing. The miracle is the means, the Atonement is the principle, and healing is the result." (T-2.IV.1:1)

"The kind of error to which Atonement is applied is irrelevant. All healing is essentially the release from fear. To undertake this you cannot be fearful yourself. You do not understand healing because of your own fear." (T-2.IV.1.6-9)

"The body can act wrongly only when it is responding to misthought. The body cannot create, and the belief that it can, a fundamental error, produces all physical symptoms. Physical illness represents a belief in magic. The whole distortion that made magic rests on the belief that there is a creative ability in matter which the mind cannot control. This error can take two forms; it can be believed that the mind can miscreate in the body, or that the body can miscreate in the mind. When it is understood that the mind, the only level of creation, cannot create beyond itself, neither type of confusion need occur." (T-2.IV.2.5-10)

"Only the mind can create because spirit has already been created, and the body is a learning device for the mind." (T-2.IV.3:1)

"All material means that you accept as remedies for bodily ills are restatements of magic principles. This is the first step in believing that the body makes its own illness. It is a second misstep to attempt to heal it

CHAPTER 2—THE SEPARATION AND THE ATONEMENT

through non-creative agents. It does not follow, however, that the use of such agents for corrective purposes is evil. Sometimes the illness has a sufficiently strong hold over the mind to render a person temporarily inaccessible to the Atonement. In this case it may be wise to utilize a compromise approach to mind and body, in which something from the outside is temporarily given healing belief. This is because the last thing that can help the non-right-minded, or the sick, is an increase in fear. They are already in a fear-weakened state." (T-2.IV.4.1-8)

"This means that a miracle, to attain its full efficacy, must be expressed in a language that the recipient can understand without fear." (T-2.IV.5:3)

"The whole aim of the miracle is to raise the level of communication, not to lower it by increasing fear." (T-2.IV.5:6)

In summary, Chapter 2 – IV. "Healing as Release from Fear" is saying:
All healing begins with the mind. The body can do nothing in and of itself; it is forever and always simply responding to what our mind tells it. If it is sick, then it is because we have had thoughts that believe it can be sick. This belief is an error. An error, that when corrected, will also heal the body. It is an error to believe you are a body to begin with. If you do not believe you are a body, then there is nothing capable of being sickened by your thoughts. In this way, the body cannot be made sick by your mind, and neither can a sick body affect the purity, health, and wholeness of your mind. The body is merely a teaching and learning device; its only function is to be used to communicate the truth of our Oneness. THAT'S ALL IT DOES!

And once the truth is accepted, all fear associated with the body is released, and healing becomes your experience. True healing only comes from the release from fear—primarily the fear of loss of the body. At times, we may still need to resort to worldly means to bring about physical healing, as our fear is still too great for our minds to let go of it all at once. It is not wrong to use a form of worldly medicine in addition to the healing belief in our Oneness—the Atonement—which is the ultimate correction device for healing us and releasing ourselves from all forms of fear.

V. The Function of the Miracle Worker

"Before miracle workers are ready to undertake their function in this world, it is essential that they fully understand the fear of release. Otherwise they may unwittingly foster the belief that release is imprisonment, a belief that is already very prevalent. This misperception arises in turn from the belief that harm can be limited to the body. That is because of the underlying fear that the mind can hurt itself. None of these errors is meaningful, because the miscreations of the mind do not really exist." (T-2.V.1:1-5)

"Magic is the mindless or the miscreative use of mind. Physical medications are forms of "spells," but if you are afraid to use the mind to heal, you should not attempt to do so. The very fact that you are afraid makes your mind vulnerable to miscreation. You are therefore likely to misunderstand any healing that might occur, and because egocentricity and fear usually occur together, you may be unable to accept the real Source of the healing. Under these conditions, it is safer for you to rely temporarily on physical healing devices, because you cannot misperceive them as your own creations." (T-2.V.2:1-5)

"I have said already that miracles are expressions of miracle-mindedness, and miracle-mindedness means right-mindedness. The right-minded neither exalt nor depreciate the mind of the miracle worker or the miracle receiver. However, as a correction, the miracle need not await the right-mindedness of the receiver. In fact, its purpose is to restore him to his right mind." (T-2.V.3:1-4)

"The sole responsibility of the miracle worker is to accept the Atonement for himself. This means you recognize that mind is the only creative level, and that its errors are healed by the Atonement. Once you accept this, your mind can only heal." (T-2.V.5:1-3)

"It should be emphasized that the body does not learn any more than it creates. As a learning device it merely follows the learner, but if it is falsely endowed with self-initiative, it becomes a serious obstruction to he very learning it should facilitate." (T-2.V.6:1-2)

"Corrective learning always begins with the awakening of spirit, and the turning away from the belief in physical sight. This often entails fear, because you are afraid of what your spiritual sight will show you." (T-2.V.7:1-2)

CHAPTER 2—THE SEPARATION AND THE ATONEMENT

"Discomfort is aroused only to bring the need for correction into awareness." (T-2.V.7:8)

"The fear of healing arises in the end from an unwillingness to accept unequivocally that healing is necessary." (T-2.V.8:1)

"As long as you believe in what your physical sight tells you, your attempts at correction will be misdirected." (T-2.V.8:3)

"It must be understood, however, that whenever you offer a miracle to another, you are shortening the suffering of both of you. This corrects retroactively as well as progressively." (T-2.V.10:7-8)

"You can do much on behalf of your own healing and that of others if, in a situation calling for help, you think of it this way:

I am here only to be truly helpful.
I am here to represent Him Who sent me.
I do not have to worry about what to say or what to do, because
   He Who sent me will direct me.
I am content to be wherever He wishes, knowing He goes there with me.
I will be healed as I let Him teach me to heal." (T-2.V.A.18:1-6)

In summary, Chapter 2 – V. "The Function of the Miracle Worker" is saying:

As stated previously, all healing begins in the mind. What the mind believes to be true becomes the experience we will have through the body. Therefore, to achieve healing of the body, we must correct our thoughts about it before true healing can be accomplished. The first error we need to correct is that we are separate bodies to begin with. For some, to let go of their identity as a body is a very fearful thing. It appears they have to give up something important to them and this can be greatly distressing. In such cases, it is best to rely on physical forms of healing that the mind is accustomed to, lest the change in mind required causes too much fear.

The right-minded can heal both themselves and others. To be right-minded is to be miracle-minded. The healer need not wait for the recipient to also be in their right-mind. In fact, the healing itself will correct the recipient's mind. To bring about such correction, the healer is one who has achieved an awakening to the knowledge that the spirit is our true identity and not the body. The healer then sees past the body and all its ailments, faults, and problems—seeing only the beauty of the Light of God within.

True vision such as this, comes entirely without fear on the part of the healer. It is the total relinquishment in belief in what one's physical sight shows us. It is to love without thought, and to experience the oneness of such love without doing. To be miracle-minded one must remember that they are there only to be truly helpful to God's Plan for our Atonement—to see only our Oneness in Him. Once miracle-mindedness is achieved, the healer will not need to worry about what to say or do, because such loving thoughts and actions will become automatic. As healers we will be fully directed by Him Who sent us into the world to heal it and fulfill our function as a miracle worker.

VI. Fear and Conflict

"Being afraid seems to be involuntary; something beyond your own control." (T-2.VI.1:1)

"Fear prevents me from giving you my control. The presence of fear shows that you have raised body thoughts to the level of the mind. This removes them from my control, and makes you feel personally responsible for them." (T-2.VI.1:5-7)

"The correction of fear is your responsibility. When you ask for release from fear, you are implying that it is not. You should ask, instead, for help in the conditions that have brought the fear about. These conditions always entail a willingness to be separate. At that level you *can* help it. You are much too tolerant of mind wandering, and are passively condoning your mind's miscreations." (T-2.VI.4:1-6)

"The correction is always the same. Before you choose to do anything, ask me if your choice is in accord with mine. If you are sure that it is, there will be no fear." (T-2.VI.4:8-10)

"Fear is always a sign of strain, arising whenever what you want conflicts with what you do." (T-2.VI.5:1)

"There is no strain in doing God's Will as soon as you recognize that it is also your own." (T-2.VI.6:4)

"The first corrective step in undoing the error is to know first that the conflict is an expression of fear. Say to yourself that you must somehow have chosen not to love, or the fear could not have arisen. Then the whole process of correction becomes nothing more than a series of pragmatic steps in the larger process of accepting the Atonement as the remedy. These steps may be summarized in this way:

Know first that this is fear.
Fear arises from lack of love.
The only remedy for lack of love is perfect love.
Perfect love is the Atonement." (T-2.VI.7:1-8)

"Few appreciate the real power of the mind, and no one remains fully aware of it all the time." (T-2.VI.9:3)

"The mind is very powerful, and never loses its creative force. It never sleeps. Every instant it is creating. It is hard to recognize that thought and belief combine into a power surge that can literally move mountains. It appears at first glance that to believe such power about yourself is arrogant, but that is not the real reason you do not believe it. You prefer to believe that your thoughts cannot exert real influence because you are actually afraid of them." (T-2.VI.9:5-10).

There are no idle thoughts. All thinking produces form at some level." (T-2.VI.9:13-14)

In summary, Chapter 2 – VI. "Fear and Conflict" is saying,

Our thoughts are very powerful. This is why all healing begins in the mind. And yet, we believe we have no control over our thoughts and that they are largely meaningless. When fear strikes, we feel helpless against it, however it is important to quickly let go of such thoughts for they block the ability of God to enter into our minds and bring about healing. They block God's Will, because the presence of fear is the assertion of our own will, and God will not interfere with what we will. Therefore, it is important to correct fear thoughts as soon as you are aware of them, thus restoring God to His rightful place in your mind. Fear exists whenever your ego-will conflicts with God's Will within you—it is the strain that arises between ego-driven thoughts and spirit-led thoughts.

It is not enough to simply behave in spirit-driven ways if your thoughts rest with the ego. This will only cause you to feel fear and conflict. Your ego-driven thoughts must be corrected, and your actions will follow fearlessly accordingly. To correct ego-driven thoughts you must first recognize you are experiencing fear, which arises from thoughts about the ego-driven world in which we all appear separate. Thoughts of separation are without love because love is all-inclusive. The only remedy for such loveless thoughts is Perfect love, which are thoughts about our unity in God's peace rather than our separation as bodies. Such loving thoughts will always heal thoughts of fear and conflict.

VII. Cause and Effect

"You may still complain about fear, but you nevertheless persist in making yourself fearful. I have already indicated that you cannot ask me to release you from fear. I know it does not exist, but you do not. If I intervened between your thoughts and their results, I would be tampering with a basic law of cause and effect; the most fundamental law there is. I would hardly help you if I depreciated the power of your own thinking." (T-2.VII.1:1-5)

"Miracle working entails a full realization of the power of thought in order to avoid miscreation. Otherwise a miracle will be necessary to set the mind itself straight, a circular process that would not foster the time collapse for which the miracle was intended. The miracle worker must have genuine respect for true cause and effect as a necessary condition for the miracle to occur." (T-2.VII.2:2-4)

"It has already been said that you believe you cannot control fear because you yourself made it, and your belief in it seems to render it out of your control. Yet any attempt to resolve the error through attempting the mastery of fear is useless. In fact, it asserts the power of fear by the very assumption that it need be mastered. The true resolution rests entirely on mastery through love." (T-2.VII.4:1-4)

"Fear is really nothing and love is everything. Whenever light enters darkness, the darkness is abolished." (T-2.VII.5:3-4)

"However, to concentrate on error is only a further error. The initial corrective procedure is to recognize temporarily that there is a problem, but only as an indication that immediate correction is needed. This establishes a state of mind in which the Atonement can be accepted without delay." (T-2.VII.5:7-9)

"Any part of the Sonship can believe in error or incompleteness if he so chooses. However, if he does so, he is believing in the existence of nothingness. The correction of this error is the Atonement." (T-2.VII.6:7-9)

In summary, Chapter 2 – VII. "Cause and Effect" is saying,
As stated before, our thoughts hold great power. Our thoughts literally show us what we believe. If we believe we are bodies, we will experience all that bodies entail such as fear, anxiety, and a deep sense of lonely separation. God cannot release us from our belief in being a body, for that would violate the

law of cause and effect: that what we believe, or think is real is what becomes our experience. In order to change what we experience we must change our thoughts and beliefs about who we are. It is a miracle to reverse our thoughts to the extent we fully accept and believe we are a part of God's holy Sonship; at one with one another and not the separate bodies our eyes show us. Belief in our separation is the root of all our fears.

Such fear cannot be mastered, for this only emphasizes its reality for us. Rather, it must be undone with love, for love is the only remedy for fear. Love reminds us of the truth of the Atonement: we are One Love and therefore no harm can come to us. Harm can be imagined through our bodily experiences, but such experiences can be shifted into joy through remembering the Atonement, despite what our eyes are showing us. We will then automatically react to all forms of lack of love with only Perfect Love. Perfect Love is the cause of peace, which is Love's effect, which is the purpose of miracles. God is the Cause, and we are His Effects, at One with Him.

VIII. The Meaning of the Last Judgment

"The Last Judgment is one of the most threatening ideas in your thinking. This is because you do not understand it." (T-2.VIII.2:1-2)

"The Last Judgment is generally thought of as a procedure undertaken by God. Actually it will be undertaken by my brothers with my help. It is a final healing rather than a meting out of punishment, however much you may think that punishment is deserved." (T-2.VIII.3:1-3)

"The Last Judgment might be called a process of right evaluation. It simply means that everyone will finally come to understand what is worthy and what is not." (T-2.VIII.3:5-6)

"The term "Last Judgment" is frightening not only because it has been projected onto God, but also because of the association of "last" with death. (T-2.VIII.5:1)

"If the meaning of the Last Judgment is objectively examined, it is quite apparent that it is really the doorway to life." (T-2.VIII. 5:4)

"Your own last judgment cannot be directed toward yourself, because you are not your own creation. You can, however, apply it meaningfully and at any time to everything you have made, and retain in your memory only what is creative and good." (T-2.VIII.5:5-6)

VIII. The Meaning of the Last Judgment

"When everything you retain is lovable, there is no reason for fear to remain with you. This is your part in the Atonement." (T-2.VIII.5:10-11)

In summary, Chapter 2 – VIII. "The Meaning of the Last Judgment" is saying,

The Last Judgment is actually to see the world correctly through miracle-minded thinking. Miracle-minded thinking sees the world as needing correction of the idea of the error of separation. It is not that God has judged us as unworthy of His love and therefore deserving of His punishment, but rather, it is an evaluation of a situation in need of total unconditional love. This is the key to our release from all false seeing. We must apply true judgment to all that we see—through the knowing of the falsity of the world of separation and understanding our Unity with all living things in truth. In this way, all things are looked upon lovingly.

And when the world is seen in this way, there is no reason to fear it—no reason to believe that harm can come to you, you who cannot be harmed, because you are not the body your ego would have you believe you are. You instead believe in your Oneness, and when such belief is accepted wholeheartedly, you fulfill your part in the Atonement—the place you hold in God's Oneness. You have never been anything less than His perfect Creation, at One with Him all living things. Once the true meaning of God's Last Judgment is accepted by you, it is the moment where separation is undone, and Atonement realized.

CHAPTER 3
THE INNOCENT PERCEPTION

I. Atonement without Sacrifice

"A further point must be perfectly clear before any residual fear still associated with miracles can disappear. The crucifixion did not establish the Atonement; the resurrection did. Many sincere Christians have misunderstood this." (T-3.I.1:1-3)

"If the crucifixion is seen from an upside-down point of view, it does appear as if God permitted and even encouraged one of His Sons to suffer because he was good. This particularly unfortunate interpretation, which arose out of projection, has led many people to be bitterly afraid of God." (T-3.I.1:5-6)

"Yet the real Christian should pause and ask, "How could this be?" (T-3.I.:8)

"It is unwise to accept any concept if you have to invert a whole frame of reference in order to justify it." (T-3.I.2:2)

"Persecution frequently results in an attempt to "justify" the terrible misperception that God Himself persecuted His Own Son on behalf of salvation." (T-3.I.2:4)

"The statement "Vengeance is mine, saith the Lord" is a misperception by which one assigns his own "evil" past to God. The "evil" past has nothing to do with God. He did not create it and He does nothing to maintain it. God does not believe in retribution." (T-3.I.3:1-4)

"Sacrifice is a notion totally unknown to God. It arises solely from fear, and frightened people can be vicious." (T-3.I.4:1-2)

"Innocence is incapable of sacrificing anything, because the innocent mind has everything and strives only to protect its wholeness." (T-3.I.6:1)

"The Atonement itself radiates nothing but truth. It therefore epitomizes harmlessness and sheds only blessing. It could not do this if it arose from anything but perfect innocence." (T-3.I.7:1-3)

"The resurrection demonstrated that nothing can destroy truth. Good can withstand any form of evil, as light abolishes forms of darkness." (T-3.I.7:6-7)

"Knowing His Son as he is, you realize that the Atonement, not sacrifice, is the only appropriate gift for God's altar, where nothing except perfection belongs. The understanding of the innocent is truth. That is why their altars are truly radiant." (T-3.I.8:3-5)

In summary, Chapter 3 – I. "Atonement without Sacrifice" is saying:
It may appear at first glance that the crucifixion of Jesus was a great sacrifice on His part for us. It appears to be that He gave up His body on our behalf, to "atone" for our sins against God. However, here we learn the truth: Jesus did not sacrifice His body on behalf of our sins. Rather, He willingly gave it up, without any sense of sacrifice or loss, to demonstrate through the resurrection that the body is not who we are. Our gift from Jesus was not His death, but His resurrection. The Atonement is the acceptance of the belief we are one with Christ. It is to also accept we are as innocent as He is, and there is nothing to "atone" for in the first place. It is a mistake to think that killing a body can be used as punishment or a form of "sacrifice." We are not our bodies. So, we must understand there is no point in harming one another's bodies, as we are attacking what is nothing. In truth, we are innocent and perfect in our Wholeness with God and all Creation. No sacrifice need be made in order to achieve our perfection, but only acceptance of it. And with this thought, our inner altar to God becomes "truly radiant." When we recognize our At-One-Ment we learn there is nothing that can ever be sacrificed. What is One already has everything, and for eternity. *We have the potential to be Jesus – one with the Father*

II. Miracles as True Perception

"Certain fundamental concepts cannot be understood in terms of opposites. It is impossible to conceive of light and darkness or everything and nothing as joint possibilities. They are all true or all false." (T-3.II.1:2-4)

"The miracle perceives everything as it is. If nothing but the truth exists, right-minded seeing cannot see anything but perfection." (T-3.II.3:4-5)

"Nothing can prevail against a Son of God who commends his spirit into the Hands of his Father. By doing this the mind awakens from its sleep and remembers its Creator. All sense of separation disappears." (T-3.II.5:1-3)

"Understanding the lesson of the Atonement they are without the wish to attack, and therefore they see truly." (T-3.II.5:9)

CHAPTER 3 — THE INNOCENT PERCEPTION

"The way to correct distortions is to withdraw your faith in them and invest it only in what is true." (T-3.II.6:1)

"If you perceive truly you are canceling out misperceptions in yourself and in others simultaneously." (T-3.II.6:5)

"This is the healing that the miracle induces." (T-3.II.6:7)

In summary, Chapter 3 – II. "Miracles as True Perception" is saying:
Seeing with "true perception" is a way of seeing the world through understanding that both truth and un-truth cannot both be real. If light is the truth, then how can darkness also be true? If our bodies are real, then how can we also be love and light? One must be false because fundamental principles of existence cannot contradict one another. Yet we can imagine that such contradictions do indeed exist, and such fantasies then can seem to be our real experience, despite their falsity. This world is based upon the false idea we are separate. In order to correct this mistake, we must look upon the world and each other through miraculous thinking: the knowing that such separation is indeed false, and nothing but our Oneness exists in truth. Such thinking is true perception. It is to understand and live the message of the Atonement. Such seeing is the way to correct the separation we perceive, which cancels out all misperceptions in others and ourselves. This healing of the mind is the miracle of true perception.

III. Perception versus Knowledge

"We have been emphasizing perception, and have said very little about knowledge as yet. This is because perception must be straightened out before you can know anything. To know is to be certain." (T-3.III.1:1-3)

"All your difficulties stem from the fact that you do not recognize yourself, your brother or God." (T-3.III.2:1)

"You can see in many ways because perception involves interpretation, and this means that it is not whole or consistent." (T-3.III.2:3)

"Questioning illusions is the first step in undoing them. The miracle, or the right answer, corrects them." (T-3.III.2:6-7)

"To perceive the truth is not the same as to know it." (T-3.III.5:13)

"If you attack error in another, you will hurt yourself. You cannot know your brother when you attack him." (T-3.III.7:1-2)

"Perceive him correctly so that you can know him. There are no strangers in God's creation." (T-3.III.7:6-7)

"God knows His children with perfect certainty. He created them by knowing them. He recognizes them perfectly. When they do not recognize each other, they do not recognize Him." (T-3.III.7:9-12)

In summary, Chapter 3 – III. "Perception versus Knowledge" is saying: To perceive the truth and to know it are two different things. We can look upon the world and perceive it as an illusion of separation, but still "know" we are One. Once we have embraced the knowledge of the truth of our Union, we will also behave accordingly. Our actions will match what we perceive in our minds. This means we will cease to attack others, knowing we are attacking a part of our One Self. Kindness and love will dominate over all we do in relation to everything in the world around us. When perception has moved into knowledge, we will love one another without thinking, for we will recognize God in everyone we see. We will perceive only Union when knowing it becomes our only truth.

IV. Error and the Ego

"The ego is the questioning aspect of the post-separation self, which was made rather than created. It is capable of asking questions but not of perceiving meaningful answers, because these would involve knowledge and cannot be perceived." (T-3.IV.3:1-2)

"Right-mindedness is not to be confused with the knowing mind, because it is applicable only to right perception. You can be right-minded or wrong-minded, and even this is subject to degrees, clearly demonstrating that knowledge is not involved." (T-3.IV.4:1-2)

"The mind returns to its proper function only when it wills to know. This places it in the service of spirit, where perception is changed." (T-3.IV.5:6-7)

"The ability to perceive made the body possible, because you must perceive *something* and *with* something." (T-3.IV.6:1)

"The interpretative function of perception, a distorted form of creation, then permits you to interpret the body as yourself in an attempt to escape from the conflict you have induced. Spirit, which knows, could not be reconciled with this loss of power, because it is incapable of darkness." (T-3.IV.6:3-4)

"God and His creations remain in surety, and therefore know that no miscreation exists." (T-3.IV.7:1)

CHAPTER 3 — THE INNOCENT PERCEPTION

"I was a man who remembered spirit and its knowledge. As a man I did not attempt to counteract error with knowledge, but to correct error from the bottom up. I demonstrated both the powerlessness of the body and the power of the mind." (T-3.IV.7:3-5)

"Only your misperceptions stand in your way." (T-3.IV.7:8)

"The "chosen ones" are merely those who choose right sooner. Right minds can do this now, and they will find rest unto their souls." (T-3.IV.7:14-15)

In summary, Chapter 3 – IV. "Error and the Ego" is saying:
The ego is our "wrong mind." It is the aspect of our thinking that is capable of questioning but not of accepting an answer that is the truth. When we are in our right mind, we can accept degrees of truth, but true knowledge means we have accepted it without compromise. The fact that we do make compromises is indicated by our chaotic behavior. Sometimes we act lovingly towards one another and sometimes we attack. We have such erratic reactions to one another because we are only capable of sometimes perceiving the truth and sometimes not. We do not fully know the truth until our understanding consistently causes us to align with love. The only thing that stands in our way of total understanding is our choice to misperceive—to see the body rather than perceiving God within the body. To choose to see beyond the misperception of the body is to choose to see correctly. We can do this at any instant we so decide. In fact, we can do this now, and instantly correct all error and the ego.

V. Beyond Perception

"I have said that the abilities you possess are only shadows of your real strength, and that perception, which is inherently judgmental, was introduced only after the separation. No one has been sure of anything since. I have also made it clear that the resurrection was the means for the return to knowledge, which was accomplished by the union of my will with the Father's. We can now establish a distinction that will clarify some of our subsequent statements." (T-3.V.1:1-4)

"Since the separation, the words "create" and "make" have become confused. When you make something, you do so out of a specific sense of lack or need." (T-3.V.2:1-2)

"When you make something to fill a perceived lack, you are tacitly im-

V. Beyond Perception

plying that you believe in separation." (T-3.V.2:4)

"The confusion between your real creation and what you have made of yourself is so profound that it has become literally impossible for you to know anything. Knowledge is always stable, and it is quite evident that you are not." (T-3.V.3:2-3)

"You keep asking what it is you are." (T-3.V.4:2)

"Yet you cannot perceive correctly. You have no image to be perceived. The word "image" is always perception-related, and not a part of knowledge. Images are symbolic and stand for something else." (T-3.V.4:4-7)

"Knowing is not open to interpretation." (T-3.V.5:1)

"Prayer is a way of asking for something. It is the medium of miracles. But the only meaningful prayer is for forgiveness, because those who have been forgiven have everything. Once forgiveness has been accepted, prayer in the usual sense becomes utterly meaningless. The prayer for forgiveness is nothing more than a request that you may be able to recognize what you already have." (T-3.V.6:1-5)

"Forgiveness is the healing of the perception of separation. Correct perception of your brother is necessary, because minds have chosen to see themselves as separate." (T-3.V.9:1-2)

"As long as perception lasts prayer has a place. Since perception rests on lack, those who perceive have not totally accepted the Atonement and given themselves over to truth." (T-3.V.10:1-2)

"Communion, not prayer, is the natural state of those who know." (T-3.V.10:4)

"Do not perceive yourself in different lights. Know yourself in the One Light where the miracle that is you is perfectly clear." (T-3.V.10:8-9)

In summary, Chapter 3 – V. "Beyond Perception" is saying:

We do not see ourselves as we truly are; our self-perception is completely opposite of What We Are in truth. This has been our state since the idea of separation entered our One Mind. Because nothing appears to us as it is in truth, we cannot be sure of anything we see. What we currently see is a world we made—not created. Something "made" is anything that is not eternal. Only what is *eternal* can be *created*. This is the vast difference between the words "made" and "created." Currently we only perceive what we made

CHAPTER 3 — THE INNOCENT PERCEPTION

and not what God created in truth. The way beyond the perception of the world we made is through forgiveness. As quoted earlier, "forgiveness is the healing of the perception of separation." When we struggle to forgive the falsity of the world we see, we must pray the only prayer that has any value here—the prayer to forgive the idea of separation. Pray only to accept the Atonement, to see yourself in the One Light that is your One Self beyond perception entirely.

VI. Judgment and the Authority Problem

"We have already discussed the Last Judgment, but in insufficient detail. After the Last Judgment there will be no more. Judgment is symbolic because beyond perception there is no judgment." (T-3.VI.1:1-3)

"The choice to judge rather than to know is the cause of the loss of peace." (T-3.VI.2:1)

"In the end it does not matter whether your judgment is right or wrong. Either way you are placing your belief in the unreal." (T-3.VI.2:10-11)

"You have no idea the tremendous release and deep peace that comes from meeting yourself and your brothers totally without judgment. When you recognize what you are and what your brothers are, you will realize that judging them in any way is without meaning." (T-3.VI.3:1-2)

"When you feel tired, it is because you have judged yourself as capable of being tired." (T-3.VI.5:1)

"The strain of constant judgment is virtually intolerable. It is curious that an ability so debilitating would be so deeply cherished." (T-3.VI.5:6-7)

"I have spoken of different symptoms, and at that level there is almost endless variation. There is, however, only one cause for all of them: the authority problem." (T-3.VI.7:1-2)

"The issue of authority is really a question of authorship. When you have an authority problem, it is always because you believe you are the author of yourself and project your delusion onto others." (T-3.VI.8:1-2)

"God's creations are given their true Authorship, but you prefer to be anonymous when you choose to separate yourself from your Author." (T-3.VI.8:7)

"This leaves you in a position where it sounds meaningful to believe that you created yourself." (T-3.VI.8:9)

"The problem everyone must decide is the fundamental question of authorship." (T-3.VI. 10:3)

"There is no one who does not feel that he is imprisoned in some way." (T-3.VI.11:1)

"Judgment always imprisons because it separates segments of reality by the unstable scales of desire." (T-3.VI.11:4)

In summary, Chapter 3 – VI. "Judgment and the Authority Problem" is saying:
There is only one Author of all creation and that is God. When the thought of separation came into our mind, we tried to become something other than Oneness and thus forgot Who our Author was. Since we could not remember how we came into being, we decided we must have created ourselves. To judge ourselves as separate bodies is to try and usurp the Authorship of God. The strain of maintaining this constant false judgment is debilitating in endless variations of suffering in the world. At its base level it feels like imprisonment. To be released, we have only to walk the world totally without judgment; to see the separation and yet know what the truth is: judgment is pointless when all there is, is One Self, created by one Authority.

VII. Creating versus the Self-Image

"Every system of thought must have a starting point. It begins with either a making or creating, a difference we have already discussed." (T-3.VII.1:1-2)

"You cannot resolve the authority problem by depreciating the power of your mind. To do so is to deceive yourself, and this will hurt you because you really understand the strength of the mind." (T-3.VII.2:1-2)

"We have discussed the fall or separation before, but its meaning must be clearly understood. The separation is a system of thought real enough in time, though not in eternity. All beliefs are real to the believer." (T-3.VII.3:1-3)

"You can perceive yourself as self-creating, but you cannot do more than believe it. You cannot make it true. And, as I said before, when you finally perceive correctly you can only be glad that you cannot." (T-3.VII.4:6-8)

CHAPTER 3—THE INNOCENT PERCEPTION

"Your starting point is truth, and you must return to your Beginning. Much has been seen since then, but nothing has really happened. Your Self is still in peace, even though your mind is in conflict." (T-3.VII.5:6-8)

"Your Kingdom is not of this world because it was given you from beyond this world. Only in this world is the idea of an authority problem meaningful. The world is not left by death but by truth, and truth can be known by all those for whom the Kingdom was created, and for whom it waits." (T-3.VII.6:9-11)

In summary, Chapter 3 – VI. "Creating versus the Self-Image" is saying:

We have two choices in seeing: we can either see the world of separation we made ourselves or perceive the eternal world God created. One will show us bodies, and the other will show us our true One Self. Whichever identity we believe to be true is the one we will see. And only one is true. The world of form and all its long history and many happenings has been a kaleidoscope of things to behold, however, nothing has really happened here because a world made by the ego is no real world at all. Nothing we see here is eternal and only what is eternal is part of God's creation. Therefore, our Kingdom is not of this world, and we have no authority here. Let us give up all authorship of a world destined to disintegrate as time passes and thus leave it, not through death, but by embracing the truth of our eternal Self-Image as God created us. To see yourself this way, is the innocent perception of your One Self.

CHAPTER 4
THE ILLUSIONS OF THE EGO

Introduction

"The Bible says that you should go with a brother twice as far as he asks. It certainly does not suggest that you set him back on his journey." (T-4.in.1:1-2)

"You can speak from the spirit or from the ego, as you choose. If you speak from spirit you have chosen to 'Be still and know that I am God.' These words are inspired because they reflect knowledge. If you speak from the ego you are disclaiming knowledge instead of affirming it, and are thus dis-spiriting yourself. Do not embark on useless journeys, because they are indeed in vain." (T-4.in.2:1-5)

"The journey to the cross should be the last "useless journey." Do not dwell upon it, but dismiss it as accomplished." (T-4.in.3:1-2)

"If you can accept it as your own last useless journey, you are also free to join my resurrection. Until you do so your life is indeed wasted. It merely re-enacts the separation, the loss of power, the futile attempts of the ego at reparation, and finally the crucifixion of the body, or death. Such repetitions are endless until they are voluntarily given up." (T-4.in.3:3-6)

"We have another journey to undertake, and if you will read these lessons carefully they will help prepare you to undertake it." (T-4.in.3:11)

In summary, Chapter 4 – Introduction is saying:

I believe many of us can intuitively feel that we've been here before. And I have no doubt that all of us feel, to some degree, that we would like to cease coming here. In order to do this, we have to learn a new way of living here; the way of being in this world, but not of it. We must learn how to make the choice to listen and act only from the guidance of the Holy Spirit and not our ego. Until we do so, as *A Course In Miracles* puts it, "Such repetitions are endless until they are voluntarily given up."

CHAPTER 4 — THE ILLUSIONS OF THE EGO

I. Right Teaching and Right Learning

"A good teacher must believe in the ideas he teaches, but he must meet another condition; he must believe in the students to whom he offers the ideas." (T-4.I.1:4)

"Many stand guard over their ideas because they want to protect their thought systems as they are, and learning means change. Change is always fearful to the separated, because they cannot conceive of it as a move towards healing the separation." (T-4.I.2:1-2)

"Spirit need not be taught, but the ego must be. Learning is ultimately perceived as frightening because it leads to the relinquishment, not the destruction, of the ego to the light of spirit." (T-4.I.3:1-2)

"Teaching and learning are your greatest strengths now, because they enable you to change your mind and help others to change theirs." (T-4.I.4:1)

"Every good teacher hopes to give his students so much of his own learning that they will one day no longer need him. This is the one true goal of the teacher." (T-4.I.5:1-2)

"Egos can clash in any situation, but spirit cannot clash at all. If you perceive a teacher as merely "a larger ego" you will be afraid, because to enlarge an ego would be to increase anxiety about separation. I will live with you if you will think with me, but my goal will always be to absolve you finally from the need for a teacher. This is the opposite of the ego-oriented teacher's goal. He is concerned with the effect of his ego on other egos, and therefore interprets their interaction as a means of ego preservation." (T-4.I.6:1-5)

"The ego tries to exploit all situations into forms of praise for itself in order to overcome its doubts." (T-4.I.8:1)

"When you are afraid, be still and know that God is real, and you are His beloved Son in whom He is well pleased. Do not let your ego dispute this, because the ego cannot know what is as far beyond its reach as you are." (T-4.I.8:6-7)

"The ego has built a shabby and unsheltering home for you, because it cannot build otherwise. Do not try to make this impoverished house stand." (T-4.I.11:1-2)

II. The Ego and False Autonomy

"Only God could make a home that is worthy of His creations, who have chosen to leave it empty by their own dispossession." (T-4.I.11:4)

"Of your ego you can do nothing to save yourself or others, but of your spirit you can do everything for the salvation of both." (T-4.I.12:1)

"The meek shall inherit the earth because their egos are humble, and this gives them truer perception." (T-4.I.12:4)

"I need devoted teachers who share my aim of healing the mind. Spirit is far beyond the need of your protection or mine. Remember this:

In this world you need not have tribulation because I have overcome the world. That is why you should be of good cheer." (T-4.I.13:7-11)

In summary, Chapter 4 – I. "Right Teaching and Right Learning" is saying:

There are only two types of teachers we can learn from, and they are either the ego or Spirit. We can recognize when we are teaching and learning from Spirit because Spirit always seeks to liberate us from learning altogether. There is a saying that the sign of a true master is not the one with the most students, but rather, the one who has created the most masters. The ego will always try to ensnare us into body-beliefs that corner our minds into endless stories about ourselves requiring endless ego-analysis. Spirit will always tell us to let go of such beliefs in order that we may move above and beyond the body altogether. The ego wants us never to forget our worldly hurts and injustices and focuses on them with detailed scrutiny. Spirit would have us overlook them, knowing they point only to what will one day cease to be. This is why the meek shall inherit the earth— they will have transformed it through humbly accepting they have been wrong about everything and are willing to accept our Identity in Spirit. This is why we "should be of good cheer." Jesus has already overcome this world for us through forgiveness. We need not experience this world as a tribulation; we can escape it entirely through simply laying it down in our minds and accepting only the truth. Let us then demonstrate both "right teaching" and "right learning" through our loving actions towards others, because we see them as One with us.

II. The Ego and False Autonomy

"It is reasonable to ask how the mind could ever have made the ego. In fact, it is the best question you could ask." (T-4.II.1:1-2)

"Everyone makes an ego or a self for himself, which is subject to enor-

CHAPTER 4 — THE ILLUSIONS OF THE EGO

mous variation because of its instability. He also makes an ego for everyone else he perceives, which is equally variable." (T-4.II.2:1-2)

"Your own state of mind is a good example of how the ego was made. When you threw knowledge away it is as if you never had it." (T-4.II.3:1-2)

"Belief that there is another way of perceiving is the loftiest idea of which ego thinking is capable. That is because it contains a hint of recognition that the ego is not the Self." (T-4.II.4:10-11)

"Babies scream in rage if you take away a knife or scissors, although they may well harm themselves if you do not. In this sense you are still a baby. You have no sense of real self-preservation, and are likely to decide that you need precisely what would hurt you most." (T-4.II.5:2-4)

"To the ego, to give anything implies that you will have to do without it." (T-4.II.6:3)

"The ego literally lives by comparisons. Equality is beyond its grasp, and charity becomes impossible." (T-4.II.7:1-2)

"The ego believes it is completely on its own, which is merely another way of describing how it thinks it originated. This is such a fearful state that it can only turn to other egos and try to unite with them in a feeble attempt at identification, or attack them in an equally feeble show of strength." (T-4.II.8:1-2)

"Spirit in its knowledge is unaware of the ego. It does not attack it; it merely cannot conceive of it at all. While the ego is equally unaware of spirit, it does perceive itself as being rejected by something greater than itself." (T-4.II.8:6-8)

"The so-called "battle for survival" is only the ego's struggle to preserve itself, and its interpretation of its own beginning. This beginning is usually associated with physical birth, because it is hard to maintain that the ego existed before that point in time." (T-4.II.9:3-4)

"Who is the "you" who are living in this world? Spirit is immortal, and immortality is a constant state. It is as true now as it ever was or ever will be, because it implies no change at all." (T-4.II.11:8-10)

III. Love without Conflict

In summary, Chapter 4 – II. "The Ego and False Autonomy" is saying:
In order to fully experience our choice to live life as separate bodies, separate from God and all living things, we had to create an alternate identity; an ego persona, and we had to forget all knowledge we had of our life before being a body. God did not interfere with this decision, but neither did He allow us to fall into such thinking without His loving restriction: we could not be a separate being from Him in truth, for if this were to become truth we would be cut off from our Source and would cease to exist—an impossible state for an eternal being—and so we were allowed to play make-believe, but without dangerous toys. We are only experiencing a "false autonomy" here as bodies. Now our purpose has become to learn how to un-make the choice to be an ego and seek instead to know our true Identity as immortal Spirit.

III. Love without Conflict

"It is hard to understand what "The Kingdom of Heaven is within you" really means. This is because it is not understandable to the ego, which interprets it as if something outside is inside, and this does not mean anything. The word "within" is unnecessary. The Kingdom is you. What else but you did the Creator create, and what else *but* you is His Kingdom? This is the whole message of the Atonement; a message which in its totality transcends the sum of its parts." (T-4.III.1:1-6)

"The Kingdom is perfectly united and perfectly protected, and the ego will not prevail against it. Amen." (T-4.III.1:12-13)

This is written in the form of a prayer because it is useful in moments of temptation. It is a declaration of independence. You will find it very helpful if you understand it fully." (T-4.III.2:1-3)

"Against our united strength the ego cannot prevail." (T-4.III.2:6)

"The ego arose from the separation, and its continued existence depends on your continuing belief in the separation." (T-4.III.3:2)

"You who identify with your ego cannot believe God loves you." (T-4.III.4:1)

"There is a kind of experience so different from anything the ego can offer that you will never want to cover or hide it again." (T-4.III.5:1)

"No force except your own will is strong enough or worthy enough to guide you. (T-4.III.6:1)

CHAPTER 4 — THE ILLUSIONS OF THE EGO

"It has never really entered your mind to give up every idea you ever had that opposes knowledge. You retain thousands of little scraps of fear that prevent the Holy One from entering. Light cannot penetrate through the walls you make to block it, and it is forever unwilling to destroy what you have made. No one can see through a wall, but I can step around it." (T-4.III.7:1-4)

"I will come in response to a single unequivocal call." (T-4.III.7:10)

"Watch carefully and see what it is you are really asking for." (T-4.III.8:1)

"God has given you everything. This one fact means the ego does not exist, and this makes is profoundly afraid." (T-4.III.9:2-3)

"The Holy Spirit knows that you both have everything and are everything." (T-4.III. 9:5)

"That is why we make no distinction between having the Kingdom of God and being the Kingdom of God." (T-4.III.9:7)

In summary, Chapter 4 – III. "Love without Conflict" is saying:
To hear that you both have and are the Kingdom of God may bring a feeling of disappointment to some. You may well say to yourself, "So this is it? It's just been me all along? I was really hoping for something more spectacular." This knowledge may fall short of your expectations of what you imagined the Kingdom of God to be. However, do not forget that the Course states that God's Kingdom is not understandable to the ego. So how can we wrap our minds around it while we are currently living through our ego? We can only comprehend it through having faith in the unseen, to believe without proof that despite what we see now, our Unity in God's Kingdom—our Atonement—still stands. This idea is even referenced in the Bible when Jesus said to the apostle Thomas, "Because you have seen me, you have believed; blessed are those who have not seen and yet have believed."(John 20:29) And so we must trust in God's Kingdom, a Kingdom we cannot see, where we live unified in His Love without conflict. A state of peaceful being that is better than anything our ego can imagine. To prepare ourselves for this state, we must practice giving up all attachment to our thoughts of this world and love one another without conflict in our hearts.

IV. This Need Not Be

"If you cannot hear the Voice for God, it is because you do not choose to listen. That you do listen to the voice of your ego is demonstrated by your attitudes, your feelings and your behavior." (T-4.IV.1:1-2)

IV. This Need Not Be

"Your mind is filled with schemes to save the face of your ego, and you do not seek the face of Christ." (T-4.IV.1:5)

"I have said that you cannot change your mind by changing your behavior, but I have also said, and many times, that you can change your mind. When your mood tells you that you have chosen wrongly, and this is so whenever you are not joyous, then *know this need not be*." (T-4.IV.2:1-2)

"When you are sad, *know this need not be*." (T-4.IV.3:1)

"When you are anxious, realize that anxiety comes from the capriciousness of the ego, and know this need not be." (T-4.IV.4:1)

"When you feel guilty, remember that the ego has indeed violated the laws of God, but you have not." (T-4.IV.5:1)

"While you feel guilty your ego is in command, because only the ego can experience guilt. *This need not be*." (T-4.IV.5:5-6)

"Watch your mind for the temptations of the ego, and do not be deceived by it. It offers you nothing. When you have given up this voluntary dis-spiriting, you will see how your mind can focus and rise above fatigue and heal. Yet you are not sufficiently vigilant against the demands of the ego to disengage yourself. *This need not be*." (T-4.IV.6:1-5)

"The habit of engaging with God and His creations is easily made if you actively refuse to let your mind slip away. The problem is not one of concentration; it is the belief that no one, including yourself, is worth consistent effort." (T-4.IV.7:1-2)

"Have you really considered how many opportunities you have had to gladden yourself, and how many of them you have refused?" (T-4.IV.8:1)

"Watch your mind carefully for any beliefs that hinder its accomplishment, and step away from them. Judge how well you have done this by your own feelings, for this is the one right use of judgment." (T-4.IV.8:5-6)

"I do work with your higher mind, the home of the Holy Spirit, whether you are asleep or awake, just as your ego does with your lower mind, which is its home." (T-4.IV.11:2-2)

"I have called and you will answer." (T-4.IV.11:10)

CHAPTER 4 — THE ILLUSIONS OF THE EGO

"My calling you is as natural as your answer, and as inevitable."(T-4. IV.11:12)

In summary, Chapter 4 – IV. "This Need Not Be" is saying:

We think our suffering is beyond our own control, that it is something that happens against our will. And yet, here we are being told that this need not be. All suffering stems from the thinking of the ego, and as soon as we cease to identify with its thoughts, our mind is free to identify with Christ-thinking instead, which is always joyous. All we need to do is notice when we are having ego thoughts, and we will know them by how we feel. Once identified, then it is only a matter of how long we wish to hold onto such thoughts. It is inevitable that we will eventually decide to let them go, in exchange for the joy of answering God's call. Never forget, in any form you perceive your suffering, "this need not be."

V. The Ego-Body Illusion

"All things work together for good. There are no exceptions except in the ego's judgment." (T-4.V.1:1-2)

"Sane judgment would inevitably judge against the ego, and must be obliterated by the ego in the interest of its self-preservation." (T-4.V.1:6)

"A major source of the ego's off-balanced state is its lack of discrimination between the body and the Thoughts of God. Thoughts of God are unacceptable to the ego, because they clearly point to the nonexistence of the ego itself." (T-4.V.2:1-2)

"Any thought system that confuses God and the body must be insane. Yet this confusion is essential to the ego, which judges only in terms of threat or non-threat to itself." (T-4.V.3:1-2)

"The body is the ego's home by its own election. It is the only identification with which the ego feels safe, since the body's vulnerability is its own best argument that you cannot be of God." (T-4.V.4:1-2)

"Yet the ego hates the body, because it cannot accept it as good enough to be its home. Here is where the mind becomes actually dazed. Being told by the ego that it is really part of the body and that the body is its protector, the mind is also told that the body cannot protect it." (T-4.V. 4:4-6)

"This is the question that *must* be asked: "Where can I go for protection?" (T-4.V. 5:1)

"The ego thinks it is an advantage not to commit itself to anything that is eternal, because the eternal must come from God." (T-4.V.6:1)

"The ego's characteristic busyness with nonessentials is for precisely that purpose. Preoccupations with problems set up to be incapable of solution are favorite ego devices for impeding learning progress. In all these diversionary tactics, however, the one question that is never asked by those who pursue them is, "What for?" This is the question that you must learn to ask in connection with everything." (T-4.V.6:5-8)

In summary, Chapter 4 – V. "The Ego-Body Illusion" is saying:
A sane mind knows it is not a body or an ego. A sane mind knows it can be nothing but an eternal creation of God, as God only creates like Himself, Who is eternal. However, the ego craftily keeps this thought as far away from your conscious mind as possible. Its plan for doing this involves the endless distractions this world readily provides: an endless parade of problems that seem to have no answer. You feel distressed and in constant conflict because you know there IS an answer, yet you cannot quite place your finger on it; it always seems to be just out of reach. You know something about this world feels "off," but exactly what, remains a mystery. The answer is this: the body is an ego-illusion made to cover the truth of your eternal identity. Even the ego itself has a problem with being a body. It knows the body will one day die, and it hates you for it. Yet, the ego will turn even this thought to its advantage—proof your eternal identity is not the truth. If you can die, then you cannot be an eternal creation of God. And yet, if you gave up the idea of being a body altogether, the ego would cease to exist, and thus be undone. This thought alone is where your mind can go for protection, here is where you belong—in the knowledge that what God created eternal, will forever be so, regardless of what the ego tries to convince you of. This thought alone has the power to end the ego-body illusion.

VI. The Rewards of God

"I have spoken of the ego as if it were a separate thing, acting on its own. This was necessary to persuade you that you cannot dismiss it lightly, and must realize how much of your thinking is ego-directed." (T-4.VI.1:3-4)

"The ego is nothing more than a part of your belief about yourself. Your other life has continued without interruption, and has been and always

CHAPTER 4—THE ILLUSIONS OF THE EGO

will be totally unaffected by your attempts to dissociate it." (T-4.VI.1:6-7)

"You have very little trust in me as yet, but it will increase as you turn more and more often to me instead of to your ego for guidance. The results will convince you increasingly that this choice is the only sane one you can make." (T-4.VI.3:1-2)

"Learning through rewards is more effective than learning through pain, because pain is an ego illusion, and can never induce more than a temporary effect. The rewards of God, however, are immediately recognized as eternal." (T-4.VI.3:4-5)

"I am teaching you to associate misery with the ego and joy with the spirit. You have taught yourself the opposite." (T-4.VI.5:6-7)

"Your mission is very simple. You are asked to live so as to demonstrate that you are not an ego, and I do not choose God's channels wrongly." (T-4.VI.6:2-3)

"My chosen channels cannot fail, because I will lend them my strength as long as theirs is wanting." (T-4.VI.6:7)

"Your gratitude to your brother is the only gift I want. I will bring it to God for you, knowing that to know your brother is to know God. If you are grateful to your brother, you are grateful to God for what He created." (T-4.VI.7:2-4)

"God will come to you only as you will give Him to your brothers. Learn first of them and you will be ready to hear God." (T-4.VI.8:4-5)

In summary, Chapter 4 – VI. "The Rewards of God" is saying:
Simply put, the rewards of God are, the release from the pain of being identified with the ego. And as we learn to associate our mind more and more with the Thoughts of God, we will increasingly experience the inner peace and joy that comes from such association. The Thoughts of God are those thoughts that remind us to see only the divine within our brothers. Learn to look past the illusion of the body and you will forgive what you see, thus freeing your mind from all association with it and also the ego. This is how you live so as to demonstrate that you are not an ego. Living this way is our mission here. It may seem difficult at first, but Jesus promises us that we cannot fail, for He will lend us His strength as long as ours is wanting. As we learn to see God within all our brothers, God comes ever nearer to our awareness, and we learn to hear only Him instead of the ego. And the release this brings to us, are the rewards of God.

VII. Creation and Communication

"The communication system of the ego is based [on its] system, as is everything else it dictates. Its communi[cation is determined] by its need to protect itself, and it will disrupt com[munication when it] experiences threat. This disruption is a reaction to [specific] persons." (T-4.VII.2:3-5)

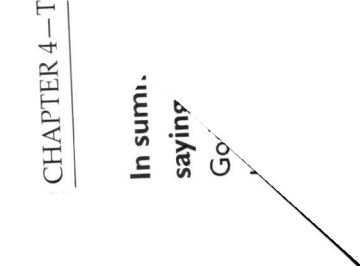

"In contrast, spirit reacts in the same way to everything it knows is true, and does not respond at all to anything else. Nor does it make any attempt to establish what is true. It knows that what is true is everything that God created." (T-4.VII.3:1-3)

"Creation and communication are synonymous. God created every mind by communicating His Mind to it, thus establishing it forever as a channel for the reception of His Mind and Will. Since only beings of a like order can truly communicate, His creations naturally communicate with Him and like Him." (T-4.VII.3:6-8)

"God, Who encompasses all being, created beings who have everything individually, but who want to share it to increase their joy. Nothing real can be increased except by sharing. That is why God created you." (T-4.VII.5:1-3)

"The Bible repeatedly states that you should praise God. This hardly means that you should tell Him how wonderful He is. He has no ego with which to accept such praise, and no perception with which to judge it. But unless you take your part in the creation, His joy is not complete because yours in incomplete." (T-4.VII.6:1-4)

"The constant going out of His Love is blocked when His channels are closed, and He is lonely when the minds He created do not communicate fully with Him." (T-4.VII.6:7)

"God is praised whenever any mind learns to be wholly helpful." (T-4.VII.8:1)

"The truly helpful are invulnerable, because they are not protecting their egos and so nothing can hurt them." (T-4.VII.8:3)

"The truly helpful are God's miracle workers, whom I direct until we are all united in the joy of the Kingdom. I will direct you to wherever you can be truly helpful, and to whoever can follow my guidance through you." (T-4.VII.8:7-8)

...ary, Chapter 4 – VII. "Creation and Communication" is...

...d created us through the process of expressing or communicating His Love. God extended His Love through His mind, and we came into being. Only God's Love is real, and it can only be increased through sharing. Therefore, it can truly be said, we ARE Love—God's Love made manifest. His Love is eternally pouring out to us, sustaining us, but our experience of His Love can be blocked whenever we are unloving towards our brothers. We are His channels of Love here on earth, and it is our duty to communicate His Love as He directs. We praise God whenever we help Him extend His Love here in this world. This work makes us invulnerable because we recognize the powerlessness of the ego to affect the Love of God sustaining us. As we learn to be truly helpful to God in joining His Will to extend His love, He will send us only those who can benefit from our loving thoughts and be healed. We need do nothing but allow God to direct us in this task; this is our joint creation and communication with God, which will bring an end to the illusions of the ego.

CHAPTER 5
HEALING AND WHOLENESS

Introduction

"To heal is to make happy. I have told you to think how many opportunities you have had to gladden yourself, and how many you have refused. This is the same as telling you that you have refused to heal yourself." (T-5.in.1:1-3)

"Joy calls forth an integrated willingness to share it, and promotes the mind's natural impulse to respond as one. Those who attempt to heal without being wholly joyous themselves call forth different kinds of responses at the same time, and thus deprive others of the joy of responding wholeheartedly." (T-5.in.1:6-7)

"To be wholehearted you must be happy." (T-5.in.2:1)

"There is no difference between love and joy." (T-5.in.2:3)

"To heal or to make joyous is therefore the same as to integrate and to make one." (T-5.in.2:5)

"Only God's holy children are worthy channels of His beautiful joy, because only they are beautiful enough to hold it by sharing it. It is impossible for a child of God to love his neighbor except as himself. That is why the healer's prayer is:

Let me know this brother as I know myself." (T-5.in.3:5-8)

In summary, Chapter 5 – Introduction" is saying:
Healing comes from living in the joy of knowing that only God's Love is real and all else is a false reality. Anything that is not wholly joyous is not of God. True joy comes from the awareness that God's Love unites us, as He extends It to all creation through us. Only a mind completely aware of one's true Source of joy can heal truly. It is an awareness of one's love for all others; to love them as part of one's self. It is to love all people regardless of who they are, and what they've said or done—it is to love without thinking. The mind has ceased to judge and one's heart has become whole. That is why the prayer, "Let me know this brother as I know myself," is the healer's prayer. It is the prayer of the wholeheartedly loving.

CHAPTER 5—HEALING AND WHOLENESS

I. The Invitation to the Holy Spirit

"Healing is a thought by which two minds perceive their oneness and become glad. This gladness calls to every part of the Sonship to rejoice with them and lets God go out into them and through them." (T-5.I.1:1-2)

"Let us start our process of reawakening with just a few simple concepts:

> Thoughts increase by being given away.
> The more who believe in them the stronger they become.
> Everything is an idea.
> How then, can giving and losing be associated?" (T-5.I.2:1-5)

"This is the invitation to the Holy Spirit. I have said already that I can reach up and bring the Holy Spirit down to you, but I can bring Him to you only at your own invitation." (T-5.I.3:1-2)

"Knowledge is always ready to flow everywhere, but it cannot oppose. Therefore you can obstruct it, although you can never lose it." (T-5.I.4:10)

"The Holy Spirit is the Christ Mind which is aware of the knowledge that lies beyond perception." (T-5.I.5:1)

"God honored even the miscreations of His children because they had made them. But He also blessed His children with a way of thinking that could raise their perceptions so high they could reach almost back to Him." (T-5.I.6:1-2)

"The Holy Spirit, the shared Inspiration of all the Sonship, induces a kind of perception in which many elements are like those in the Kingdom itself:

> First, its universality is perfectly clear, and no one who attains it could believe for one instant that sharing it involves anything but gain.
>
> Second, it is incapable of attack and is therefore truly open. This means that although it does not engender knowledge, it does not obstruct it in any way. Finally, it points the way beyond the healing that it brings, and leads the mind beyond its own integration toward the paths of creation. It is at this point that sufficient quantitative change occurs to produce a real qualitative shift." (T-5.I.7:1-6)

In summary, Chapter 5 – I. "The Invitation to the Holy Spirit" is saying:

God already established our oneness, but in order to perceive it, we must invite Him to reveal it to us. To be healed is to achieve awareness of our oneness, which will also bring us great joy. We invite God to reveal our oneness through our minds. We do this through sharing or "giving away" our loving thoughts.

The more who join us in such thoughts, the stronger they become, which is why giving them away actually increases their strength. Our loving thoughts are those thoughts that remind us of our oneness in God and with each other; our loving thoughts look beyond the bodies our eyes show us; bodies which, along with every physical form outside of us, are referred to as our "miscreations" in *A Course In Miracles*.

True knowledge is to truly know and believe that such bodily identities are not the truth of Who We Are. We share or extend this idea every time we remember our true Identity in Spirit. When our thoughts of oneness reach a point where we actually believe them (the quantitative shift) we will move into the experience of our oneness (the qualitative shift). This shift happens through a shift in your perception from separation to oneness. It is your invitation to the Holy Spirit to replace the ego as your guide.

II. The Voice for God

"Healing is not creating; it is reparation. The Holy Spirit promotes healing by looking beyond it to what the children of God were before healing was needed and will be when they have been healed." (T-5.II.1:1-2)

"The Holy Spirit is the motivation for miracle-mindedness; the decision to heal the separation by letting it go. Your will is still in you because God placed it in your mind, and although you can keep it asleep you cannot obliterate it." (T-5.II.1:4-5)

"The Holy Spirit is the spirit of joy." (T-5.II.2:1)

"The Holy Spirit is God's Answer to the separation; the means by which the Atonement heals until the whole mind returns to creating." (T-5.II.2:5)

"When the ego was made, God placed in the mind the Call to joy. This Call is so strong that the ego always dissolves at Its sound. This is why

CHAPTER 5—HEALING AND WHOLENESS

you must choose to hear one of two voices within you. One you made yourself, and that one is not of God. But the other is given you by God, Who asks you only to listen to it." (T-5.II.3:2-6)

"It is possible even in this world to hear only that Voice and no other. It takes effort and great willingness to learn." (T-5.II.3:9-10)

"The Voice of the Holy Spirit does not command, because It is incapable of arrogance. It does not demand, because It does not seek control." (T-5.II.7:1-2)

"It merely reminds." (T-5.II.7:4)

"It brings to your mind the other way, remaining quiet even in the midst of the turmoil you may make. The Voice for God is always quiet, because It speaks of peace." (T-5.II.7:6-7)

"The Holy Spirit is the way in which God's Will is done on earth as it is in Heaven." (T-5.II.8:4)

"When you are tempted by the wrong voice, call on me to remind you how to heal by sharing my decision and making it stronger. As we share this goal, we increase its power to attract the whole Sonship, and to bring it back into the oneness in which it was created." (T-5.II.11:1-2)

In summary, Chapter 5 – II. "The Voice for God" is saying:
The Holy Spirit IS the Voice for God. We can choose to hear It, or we can choose to listen to our ego instead, which is the separate will we made in opposition to God's Voice. We choose to listen to the Holy Spirit every time we choose to love instead of condemn—every time we choose to forgive and let go of all we think we see and understand in this world. It is to allow our minds to rest in peace, knowing the truth of Who We Are. It is God's Will we remember our unity in Him. The Holy Spirit is the Voice Who will remind us of this when we choose to listen to Him. This may take all of our mental vigilance, because so far, our minds have been conditioned to hearing only the ego. Imagine what miracles we could work if we turned as much effort towards hearing only the Voice for God instead?

III. The Guide to Salvation

"The way to recognize your brother is by recognizing the Holy Spirit in him." (T-5.III.1:1)

"He is part of the Holy Trinity, because His Mind is partly yours and

III. The Guide to Salvation

also partly God's." (T-5.III.1:4)

"The Holy Spirit is the idea of healing. Being thought, the idea gains as it is shared." (T-5.III.2:1)

"Since you are part of God it is also the idea of yourself, as well as of all His creations." (T-5.III.2:4)

"It increases in you as you give it to your brother. Your brother does not have to be aware of the Holy Spirit in himself or in you for this miracle to occur." (T-5.III.2:7-8)

"There are two diametrically opposed ways of seeing your brother." (T-5.III.3:1)

"See him through the Holy Spirit in his mind, and you will recognize Him in yours. What you acknowledge in your brother you are acknowledging in yourself, and what you share you strengthen." (T-5.III.3:4-5)

"The Holy Spirit is the Mediator between the interpretations of the ego and the knowledge of the spirit." (T-5.III.7:1)

"His ability to look beyond symbols into eternity enables Him to understand the laws of God, for which He speaks. He can therefore perform the function of reinterpreting what the ego makes, not by destruction but by understanding." (T-5.III.7:3-4)

"Peace is the ego's greatest enemy because, according to its interpretation of reality, war is the guarantee of its survival. The ego becomes strong in strife. If you believe there is strife you will react viciously, because the idea of danger has entered your mind." (T-5.III.8:7-9)

"The ego made the world as it perceives it, but the Holy Spirit, the reinterpreter of what the ego made, sees the world as a teaching device for bringing you home." (T-5.III.11:1)

"He is in communion with God always, and He is part of you. He is your Guide to salvation, because He holds the remembrance of things past and to come, and brings them to the present." (T-5.III.11:8-9)

In summary, Chapter 5 – III. "The Guide to Salvation" is saying:
The Voice of God, the Holy Spirit, is literally part of each and every one of us. We have a choice in whether we want to listen to Him or the ego. The way to hear the Holy Spirit is by recognizing Him in your brothers as replacement for the body your ego's eyes see. The Holy Spirit's function is to help you do this;

CHAPTER 5—HEALING AND WHOLENESS

He is the Mediator between the seeing of the ego and the seeing of God. His job is to reinterpret what the ego sees, not by denying its sight, but by understanding that what the ego is showing you is false. This reinterpretation will bring our minds peace, which is the exact opposite of what the ego stands for and exists by. We are here to learn to tell the difference between the peaceful Voice of God and the attacking voice of the ego and to choose only God. The ego will one day leave us whence we leave our bodies, but God is ours for eternity. Yet we need not wait for death of the body, let us choose the Holy Spirit as our only Guide to salvation now. Now!

IV. Teaching and Healing

"What fear has hidden still is part of you. Joining the Atonement is the way out of fear. The Holy Spirit will help you reinterpret everything that you perceive as fearful, and teach you that only what is loving is true." (T-5.IV.1:1-3)

"Every loving thought held in any part of the Sonship belongs to every part. It is shared because it is loving. Sharing is God's way of creating, and also yours." (T-5.IV.3:1-3)

"It is impossible to share opposing thoughts. You can share only the thoughts that are of God and that He keeps for you." (T-5.IV.3:7-8)

"Listening to one Voice implies the decision to share It in order to hear It yourself. The Mind that was in me is still irresistibly drawn to every mind created by God, because God's Wholeness is the Wholeness of His Son. You cannot be hurt, and do not want to show your brother anything except your wholeness. Show him that he cannot hurt you and hold nothing against him, or you hold it against yourself. This is the meaning of "turning the other cheek." (T-5.IV.4:2-6)

"Teaching is done in many ways, above all by example." (T-5.IV.5:1)

"I call upon you to teach what you have learned, because by so doing you can depend on it." (T-5.IV.5:4)

"As you teach so shall you learn." (T-5.IV.6:4)

"I place the peace of God in your heart and in your hands, to hold and share." (T-5.IV.8:10)

"We cannot lose. My judgment is as strong as the wisdom of God, in Whose Heart and Hands we have our being." (T-5.IV.8:12-13)

V. The Ego's Use of Guilt

In summary, Chapter 5 – IV. "Teaching and Healing" is saying:
We are always teaching and always learning either from the ego or the Holy Spirit. The ego teaches only how to fear, and the Holy Spirit teaches only how to love. How we interact with our brothers, indicates which teacher we are learning from. Our goal here is to teach and learn only through the Holy Spirit. The Holy Spirit will help us see only Love through teaching us how to reinterpret everything fearful the ego shows us. We will learn that only loving thoughts are true, and as we learn this, we simultaneously teach it, through responding with only love to the world. Teaching love is done best through being an example of love. And the more we learn to love, the more we teach love, and the more we teach love, the more we learn it. It is an ever increasing and endless circle of giving and receiving the healing power of our loving thoughts.

V. The Ego's Use of Guilt

"Perhaps some of our concepts will become clearer and more personally meaningful if the ego's use of guilt is clarified." (T-5.V.1:1)

"The ego's purpose is fear, because only the fearful can be egotistic." (T-5.V.1:3)

"If the ego is the symbol of the separation, it is also the symbol of guilt." (T-5.V.2:8)

"It is the symbol of attack on God." (T-5.V.2:10)

"This is the belief from which all guilt really stems." (T-5.V.2:12)

"The ego is the part of the mind that believes in division." (T-5.V.3:1)

"The ego is quite literally a fearful thought. However ridiculous the idea of attacking God may be to the sane mind, never forget that the ego is not sane." (T-5.V.3:7-8) *You attack your Brother,*
"The ego does not perceive sin as a lack of love, but as a positive act of *you are attacking* assault." (T-5.V.4:10) *God*

"The ego believes that by punishing itself it will mitigate the punishment of God. Yet even in this it is arrogant." (T-5.V.5:6-7)

"The continuing decision to remain separated is the only possible reason for continuing guilt feelings. We have said this before, but did not emphasize the destructive results of the decision." (T-5.V.8:1-2)

"Your mind does make your future, and it will turn it back to full creation at any minute if it accepts the Atonement first." (T-5.V.8:6)

CHAPTER 5—HEALING AND WHOLENESS

In summary, Chapter 5 – V. "The Ego's Use of Guilt" is saying:

All guilt stems from the original error or "sin" in thinking we could create an identity separate from the oneness that God created us as. The ego maintains our separate bodily identity through guilt. Deep down we feel guilty for our decision to be separate, but God knows we have done nothing wrong. To imagine we are something else is no more harmful than a child playing make-believe. God does not see us guilty of any wrongdoing, but since we suffer from our choice, He Wills we let go of all our fearful ego-thoughts and return our mind to Him. To continue to believe our separation is the truth is to continue to choose against what God Wills for us. Therefore, this world is actually an attack on God—our rebellion against oneness—but an attack without results, for God cannot suffer from any form of fear or attack. We reverse and thus heal the decision to separate through accepting the Atonement as truth. Once done, this thought creates a new and miraculous future for us, for our mind does make our future. And the ego's use of guilt, or the idea we are bodies, no longer shapes our reality.

VI. Time and Eternity

"God in His knowledge is not waiting, but His Kingdom is bereft while you wait. All the Sons of God are waiting for your return, just as you are waiting for theirs. Delay does not matter in eternity, but it is tragic in time." (T-5.VI.1:1-3)

"Guilt feelings are the preservers of time. They induce fears of retaliation or abandonment, and thus ensure that the future will be like the past. This is the ego's continuity." (T-5.VI.2:1-3)

"Remember the Kingdom always, and remember that you who are part of the Kingdom cannot be lost. The Mind that was in me is in you, for God creates with perfect fairness." (T-5.VI.3:1-2)

"The ego speaks in judgment, and the Holy Spirit reverses its decision, much as a higher court has the power to reverse a lower court's decisions in this world. The ego's decisions are always wrong, because they are based on the error they were made to uphold. Nothing the ego perceives is interpreted correctly." (T-5.VI.4:1-3)

"The Bible is a fearful thing in the ego's judgment. Perceiving it as frightening, it interprets it fearfully. Being afraid, you do not appeal to the Higher Court because you believe its judgment would also be against you." (T-5.VI.4:5-7)

"You need not fear the Higher Court will condemn you. It will merely dismiss the case against you. There can be no case against a child of God, and every witness to guilt in God's creations is bearing false witness to God Himself." (T-5.VI.10:1-3)

"Your patience with your brother is your patience with yourself. Is not a child of God worth patience? I have shown you infinite patience because my will is that of our Father, from Whom I learned of infinite patience." (T-5.VI.11:4-6)

"Now you must learn that only infinite patience produces immediate effects. This is the way in which time is exchanged for eternity. Infinite patience calls upon infinite love, and by producing results now it renders time unnecessary." (T-5.VI.12:1-3)

In summary, Chapter 5 – VI. "Time and Eternity" is saying:
We can spend as much time as we want on the process of our awakening. How long we delay is up to us. We delay each time we choose to see guilt (a body) rather than light. Guilt is anything outside of us associated with our separation, which includes the body and all the other separate forms outside of us. The body is what we made to experience this world of separation, and deep inside we feel guilty for having done so. Therefore, guilt in all its forms around us preserves time. It does so by reflecting the effects of time—all things here in this world must end in time. However, nothing the ego perceives is correct. We have an alternate way of seeing; we can choose to see beyond what the body's eyes show—to see only what is eternal. This is the Vision of the Holy Spirit, Who has infinite patience with our learning. His Vision of the world both corrects and heals it of the ravages of time. The Holy Spirit has the power to override the judgment of the ego, much like a higher court can overrule a lower one. And what is the verdict of the Holy Spirit? Case dismissed. There is no world over which to dispute our guilt or innocence. Our innocence is not up for debate or ransom. It stands before God immutable and absolute, for what God created holy, remains so for all eternity, despite how we see ourselves now in time. The instant we believe this truth about ourselves, time becomes unnecessary, and we experience eternity.

VII. The Decision for God

"Do you really believe you can make a voice that can drown out God's?" (T-5.VII.1:1)

CHAPTER 5—HEALING AND WHOLENESS

"Do you really believe you can plan for your safety and joy better than He can? You need be neither careful nor careless; you need merely cast your cares upon Him because He careth for you. You are His care because He loves you." (T-5.VII.1:3-4)

"There have been many healers who did not heal themselves. They have not moved mountains by their faith because their faith was not whole." (T-5.VII.2:1-2)

"Unless the healer heals himself, he cannot believe that there is no order of difficulty in miracles." (T-5.VII.2:4)

"God commended His Spirit to you, and asks that you commend yours to Him." (T-5.VII.3:2)

"I am making His plan perfectly explicit to you, and will also tell you of your part in it, and how urgent it is to fulfill it." (T-5.VII.4:4)

"Whenever you are not wholly joyous, it is because you have reacted with a lack of love to one of God's creations." (T-5.VII.5:1)

"The decision to react in this way is yours, and can therefore be undone." (T-5.VII.5:3)

"Decision cannot be difficult." (T-5.VII.6:1)

"Be very firm with yourself in this, and keep yourself fully aware that the undoing process, which does not come from you, is nevertheless within you because God placed it there. Your part is merely to return your thinking to the point at which the error was made, and give it over to the Atonement in peace. Say this to yourself as sincerely as you can, remembering that the Holy Spirit will respond fully to your slightest invitation:

I must have decided wrongly, because I am not at peace.
I made the decision myself, but I can also decide otherwise.
I want to decide otherwise, because I want to be at peace.
I do not feel guilty, because the Holy Spirit will undo all the consequences of my wrong decision if I will let Him.
I choose to let Him, by allowing Him to decide for God for me." (T-5.VII.6:4-11)

VII. The Decision for God

In summary, Chapter 5 – VII. "The Decision for God" is saying:
The decision for God is simply the decision to be at peace. To be at peace, one must let go of the world. To let go of the world, one must recognize its falsity. To recognize its falsity, one must let it rest in peace. To let the world rest in peace, is to forgive it. To forgive the world is to make the decision for God instead of the ego. To make the decision for God instead of the ego, we must let go of every thought occupying our mind that is of the world—thoughts that are not at peace. This is God's plan for us, plain and simple. This is the plan by which we heal ourselves and remember our wholeness in God. Remembering we are one is to know we are healed and whole.

Right here... here it is

CHAPTER 6
THE LESSONS OF LOVE

Introduction

"The relationship of anger to attack is obvious, but the relationship of anger to fear is not always so apparent." (T-6.in.1:1)

"Anger cannot occur unless you believe that you have been attacked, that your attack is justified in return, and that you are in no way responsible for it." (T-6.in.1:3)

"You cannot be attacked, attack *has* no justification, and you are responsible for what you believe." (T-6.in.1:7)

"Everyone teaches, and teaches all the time." (T-6.in.2:2)

"Once you have developed a thought system of any kind, you live by it and teach it." (T-6.in. 2:4)

In summary, Chapter 6 – Introduction is saying:
If our true Identity is love, then there cannot be anger or fear in us. To react in this way is a misperception of both our self and others. It is an incorrect thought system to believe in any identity other than love. Now we are going to learn this new thought system; one we will teach the world by how we live it. We are going to learn the lessons of love.

I. The Message of the Crucifixion

"For learning purposes, let us consider the crucifixion again." (T-6.I.1:1)

"There is a positive interpretation of the crucifixion that is wholly devoid of fear, and therefore wholly benign in what it teaches, if it is properly understood." (T-6.I.1:5)

"It can be, and has been, misunderstood. This is only because the fearful are apt to perceive fearfully." (T-6.I.2:3-4)

"While I emphasized only the resurrection before, the purpose of the crucifixion and how it actually let to the resurrection was not clarified then." (T-6.I.2:7)

"The real meaning of the crucifixion lies in the apparent intensity of the assault of some of the Sons of God upon another. This, of course,

I. The Message of the Crucifixion

is impossible, and must be fully understood as impossible." (T-6.I.3:4-5)

"Assault can ultimately be made only on the body. There is little doubt that one body can assault another, and can even destroy it. Yet if destruction itself is impossible, anything that is destructible cannot be real. Its destruction, therefore, does not justify anger. To the extent to which you believe that it does, you are accepting false premises And teaching them to others." (T-6.I.4:1-5)

"You are free to perceive yourself as persecuted if you choose. When you do choose to react that way, however, you might remember that I was persecuted as the world judges, and did not share this evaluation for myself." (T-6.I.5:2-3)

"If you react as if you are persecuted, you are teaching persecution. This is not a lesson a Son of God should want to teach if he is to realize his own salvation. Rather, teach your own perfect immunity, which is the truth in you, and realize that it cannot be assailed." (T-6.I.6:2-4)

"You are merely asked to follow my example in the face of much less extreme temptations to misperceive, and not to accept them as false justifications for anger." (T-6.I.6:7)

"Your resurrection is your reawakening." (T-6.I.7:1)

"I elected, for your sake and mine, to demonstrate that the most outrageous assault, as judged by the ego, does not matter." (T-6.I.9:1)

"You are not persecuted, nor was I." (T-6.I.11:1)

"The message of the crucifixion is perfectly clear:

Teach only love, for that is what you are." (T-6.I.13:1-2)

"If you interpret the crucifixion in any other way, you are using it as a weapon for assault rather than as the call for peace for which it was intended." (T-6.I.14:1)

In summary, Chapter 6 – I. "The Message of the Crucifixion" is saying:

Jesus left this world in an extreme manner; He was betrayed, abandoned, beaten, tortured, and finally crucified while still alive. His death ranged the whole gamut of possible ways pain can be inflicted upon a human body. And we are asked to see past these atrocities and to know that despite the suffering He appeared to endure, His true form of Love, remained undefiled and serenely rested in the Arms of God. By not reacting to His abuse as a victim, He taught us Who He Was in truth: He taught only love, for that is What He IS. Only Love could react to such torture and abuse with nothing but total forgiveness. Jesus knew such actions stemmed from people who were fearful, and fear is apt to be vicious. He knew they knew not Who He Was, and that they were ignorantly trying to kill Love Itself. The ego will always retaliate against Love and try to harm it. Do not let this reaction tempt you into believing that Love can be harmed. The body yes, but not the Love that is Who You Are. That is the message of the crucifixion. Your resurrection is your awakening to this truth.

II. The Alternative to Projection

"We have said before that the separation was and is dissociation, and that once it occurs projection becomes its main defense, or the device that keeps it going." (T-6.II.1:5)

"What you project you disown, and therefore do not believe is yours. You are excluding yourself by the very judgment that you are different from the one on whom you project." (T-6.II.2:1-2)

"It is solely a device of the ego to make you feel different from your brothers and separated from them." (T-6.II.3:3)

"The ego uses projection only to destroy your perception of both yourself and your brothers." (T-6.II.3:7)

"We have learned, however, that there is an alternative to projection." (T-6.II.4:1)

"The Holy Spirit begins by perceiving you as perfect. Knowing this perfection is shared He recognizes it in others, thus strengthening it in both." (T-6.II.5:1-2)

"To perceive yourself this way is the only way in which you can find happiness in the world. That is because it is the acknowledgement that you are not in this world, for the world is unhappy." (T-6.II.5:6-7)

"How else can you find joy in a joyless place except by realizing that you are not there? You cannot be anywhere God did not put you, and God created you as part of Him. That is both where you are and what you are. It is completely unalterable." (T-6.II.6:1-4)

"The full awareness of the Atonement, then, is the recognition that the separation never occurred. The ego cannot prevail against this because it is an explicit statement that the ego never occurred." (T-6.II.10:7-8)

In summary, Chapter 6 – II. "The Alternative to Projection" is saying:

The world we currently see is one we made through dissociation—we dissociated our mind from the unity of God in order to experience the separation we now understand as our reality. The ego maintains what we see, through continuous projection of its thoughts of separation. This destroys our perception of oneness and allows only for seeing each other as separate bodies living in a world of other separate living things. The Holy Spirit can show us another way to perceive the world that restores our true sight: He can remind us of our perfection—our perfect unity in God and each other—a state the ego cannot see. To see the world this way is the only way to happy because it is the acknowledgment that this reality is not the truth. The truth is, the separation never truly happened, and what we see is not true about us. We are not bodies. We are still Love, as God created us. And being as God created us is the only alternative to projection.

III. The Relinquishment of Attack

"Your Godlike mind can never be defiled. The ego never was and never will be part of it, but through the ego you can hear and teach and learn what is not true. You have taught yourself to believe that you are not what you are." (T-6.III.1:6-8)

"Every lesson you teach you are learning." (T-6.III.1:10)

"That is why you must teach only one lesson. If you are to be conflict-free yourself, you must learn only from the Holy Spirit and teach only by Him. You are only love, but when you deny this, you make what you are something you must learn to remember." (T-6.III.2:1-3)

""As you teach so will you learn." If that is true, and it is true indeed, do not forget that what you teach is teaching you. And what you project or extend you believe." (T-6.III.2:7-9)

"The only safety lies in extending the Holy Spirit, because as you see His gentleness in others your own mind perceives itself as totally harmless. Once it can accept this fully, it sees no need to protect itself. The protection of God then dawns upon it, assuring it that it is perfectly safe forever. The perfectly safe are wholly benign." (T-6.III.3:1-4)

CHAPTER 6—THE LESSONS OF LOVE

"Safety is the complete relinquishment of attack." (T-6.III.3:7)

"Since you cannot not teach, your salvation lies in teaching the exact opposite of everything the ego believes. This is how you will learn the truth that will set you free, and will keep you free as others learn it of you. The only way to have peace is to teach peace." (T-6.III.4:1-3)

"Only thus can you win back the knowledge that you threw away." (T-6.III.4:5)

In summary, Chapter 6 – VI. "The Relinquishment of Attack" is saying:
When we think of attack and the fear associated with it, we think of harm coming to us in some form, be it verbal or physical. All forms of attack trigger pain and suffering in us. Yet here we learn that all fear and attack stem from a single belief: that we are bodies that can be attacked. To believe we are bodies is actually an attack upon God's definition of us—it is to deny He created us as eternal beings of light and love. Rebelliously, through the use of the ego, we have taught ourselves the opposite: that we are not eternal and can easily lose the short little life we think we have in these bodies. Which from the ego's perspective is indeed true. No matter what we do or try in this life, the body will be lost. The only way to freedom and safety from this grim demise is give up all such false beliefs. Relinquishment of all ideas of attack upon the Identity God gave us by giving up our belief in the body is the way to safety. Our minds can then rest in the knowledge of Who We truly Are. As quoted previously, "Safety is the complete relinquishment of attack." Teach this lesson in Love and you will learn that you ARE Love through your reactions towards others loveless acts. This is the relinquishment of attack.

IV. The Only Answer

"Remember that the Holy Spirit is the Answer, not the question. The ego always speaks first. It is capricious and does not mean its maker well. It believes, and correctly, that its maker may withdraw his support from it at any moment." (T-6.IV.1:1-4)

"The ego does not regard itself as part of you." (T-6.IV.1:6)

"When God created you He made you part of Him." (T-6.IV.2:1)

"You made the ego without love, and so it does not love you." (T-6.IV.2:3)

"The ego, then raised the first question that was ever asked, but one it

IV. The Only Answer

can never answer. That question, "What are you?" was the beginning of doubt. The ego has never answered any questions since although it has raised a great many." (T-6.IV.2:6-8)

"Hear, then, the one answer of the Holy Spirit to all the questions the ego raises: You are a child of God, a priceless part of His Kingdom, which He created as part of Him. Nothing else exists and only this is real. You have chosen a sleep in which you have had bad dreams, but the sleep is not real and God calls you to awake." (T-6.IV.6:1-3)

"Your dreams contain many of the ego's symbols and they have confused you. Yet that was only because you were asleep and did not know. When you wake you will see the truth around you and in you, and you will no longer believe in dreams because they will have no reality for you. Yet the Kingdom and all that you have created there will have great reality for you, because they are beautiful and true." (T-6.IV.6:5-8)

"The separation was not a loss of perfection, but a failure in communication. A harsh and strident form of communication arose as the ego's voice. It could not shatter the peace of God, but it could shatter yours. God did not blot it out, because to eradicate it would be to attack it. Being questioned, He did not question. He merely gave the Answer. His Answer is your Teacher." (T-6.IV.12:5-11)

In summary, Chapter 6 – IV. "The Only Answer" is saying:
When we rebelled against our Unity with God through imagining ourselves separate from Him, our minds split—one part was still joined with God in Holy Unity and the other part then became unaware of God and the ego was the manifestation of that unawareness. In response to the manifestation of the ego's voice for separation, which is our only problem, God instantaneously placed within us the only Answer to this problem: The Voice of the Holy Spirit. The Holy Spirit is the One Answer to our seeming separation, for He is the Voice for Unity—a Unified Mind in God, which is a healed mind. Until our split minds are healed, we have a choice to make between teachers we may listen to—the ego or the Holy Spirit. Only the Voice of Holy Spirit can teach us how to heal our split mind with His one and only Answer to all the lies the ego would have us believe: we are still unified with God in perfect holiness, love, and everlasting joy. And this is the only Answer to all forms of suffering.

CHAPTER 6—THE LESSONS OF LOVE

V. The Lessons of the Holy Spirit

"Like any good teacher, the Holy Spirit knows more than you do now, but He teaches only to make you equal with Him." (T-6.V.1:1)

"Would God teach you that you had made a split mind, when He knows your mind only as whole?" (T-6.V.1:4)

"How can you wake children in a more kindly way than by a gentle Voice that will not frighten them, but will merely remind them that the night is over and the light has come?" (T-6.V.2:1)

"The Holy Spirit never itemizes errors because He does not frighten children, and those who lack wisdom are children." (T-6.V.4:1)

"Children do confuse fantasy and reality, and they are frightened because they do not recognize the difference. The Holy Spirit makes no distinction among dreams. He merely shines them away. His light is always the Call to awaken, whatever you have been dreaming. Nothing lasting lies in dreams, and the Holy Spirit, shining with the light from God Himself, speaks only for what lasts forever." (T-6.V.4:3-7)

In summary, Chapter 6 – V. "The Lessons of the Holy Spirit" is saying:

We do not know we sleep, and think this world is true. We are frightened here within the dream of this world, and yet we are even more frightened of waking from it for we fear what will then be our new reality. We fear the unknown, or rather, what we have simply forgotten. The best way for God to awaken us is to simply keep reminding us that the nightmare is not real, and we can waken from this dream any time we fully accept the truth: what is not eternal cannot be real. The Holy Spirit will not "itemize" or "count up" our errors, knowing this would increase our guilt rather than heal it. We are like children in that we know not what we do. We are confused about where we are, who we are, and what we should be doing. The Holy Spirit would clarify all these questions by simply teaching this lesson: "Do not worry about anything precious child. None of what you think you know is the truth. Nothing here is everlasting and so you can let it all go in peace." With this realization, the Light of the Holy Spirit will shine into your dreams, and you will awaken to God's Heavenly Reality. You will have learned the lessons of the Holy Spirit.

V. The Lessons of the Holy Spirit

A. To Have, Give All to All

"When your body and your ego and your dreams are gone, you will know that you will last forever. Perhaps you think this is accomplished through death, but nothing is accomplished through death, because death is nothing." (T-6.V.A.1:1-2)

"If we share the same mind, you can overcome death because I did. Death is an attempt to resolve conflict by not deciding at all. Like any other impossible solution the ego attempts, it will not work." (T-6.V.A.1:5-7)

"God did not make the body, because it is destructible, and therefore not of the Kingdom. The body is the symbol of what you think you are. It is clearly a separation device, and therefore does not exist." (T-6.V.A.2:3)

"I have said that the Holy Spirit is the motivation for miracles. He always tells you that only the mind is real, because only the mind can be shared. The body is separate, and therefore cannot be part of you. To be of one mind is meaningful, but to be one body is meaningless. By the laws of mind, then, the body is meaningless." (T-6.V.A.3:1-5)

"To the Holy Spirit, there is no order of difficulty in miracles. This is familiar enough to you by now, but it has not yet become believable. Therefore, you do not understand it and cannot use it." (T-6.V.A.4:1-3)

"You cannot perform miracles without believing it, because it is a belief in perfect equality. Only one equal gift can be offered to the equal Son of God, and that is full appreciation." (T-6.V.A.4:6-7)

"The ego uses the body for attack, for pleasure and for pride. The insanity of this perception makes it a fearful one indeed. The Holy Spirit sees the body only as a means of communication, and because communicating is sharing it becomes communion." (T-6.V.A.5:3-5)

"The Holy Spirit communicates only what each one can give to all. He never takes anything back, because He wants you to keep it. Therefore, His teaching begins with the lesson:

To have, give all to all." (T-6.V.A.**5:10-13)**

"This is a very preliminary step, and the only one you must take for yourself." (T-6.V.A.6:1)

"Some remain at this step for a long time, experiencing very acute con-

CHAPTER 6—THE LESSONS OF LOVE

flict. At this point they may try to accept the conflict, rather than take the next step towards its resolution. Having taken the first step, however, they will be helped. Once they have chosen what they cannot complete alone, they are no longer alone." (T-6.V.A.6:6-9)

In summary, Chapter 6 – V.A "To Have, Give All to All" is saying:
In order to overcome the belief we are a body, we must understand how we can truly escape from it. Currently, we believe that death of the body is our final release from it. Yet if that were true, we would cease to come here at all—there would be no desire to return to a body if we were truly released from it. Clearly, we are not released from the body if we find ourselves here now. Physical death in any way, shape or form is not a release. True release from the body comes from releasing our belief that we are a body to begin with. We know we have released this belief by how we treat our brothers. If we have learned how to love them as God does—that is, to love them without even thinking about it—then we have achieved a miracle! It is a miracle to use the body only for communicating love, which is also the feeling of communion or oneness with all living things—love given equally to all without discrimination or attack. This idea may cause your ego to feel great discomfort, because to love everyone in this manner means it would have to give up its identity as your body. Only bodies can say and do things that cause us to feel unloving towards one another. We may try to simply accept that there are some people we just cannot seem to love, and yet the Course says that once we reach this often prolonged and difficult stage, we will receive Divine Help because we have taken the first step towards choosing only love. To have love, we must learn to give all our love, to all—to see ourselves as one Love.

B. To Have Peace, Teach Peace to Learn It

"All who believe in separation have a basic fear of retaliation and abandonment. They believe in attack and rejection, so that is what they perceive and teach and learn." (T-6.V.B.1:1-2)

"All good teachers realize that only fundamental change will last, but they do not begin at that level. Strengthening motivation for change is their first and foremost goal. It is also their last and final one." (T-6.V.B.2:1-3)

"Change in motivation is a change of mind, and this will inevitably produce fundamental change because the mind is fundamental." (T-6.V.B.2:5)

V. The Lessons of the Holy Spirit

"The first step in the reversal or undoing process is the undoing of the getting concept. Accordingly, the Holy Spirit's first lesson was "To have, give all to all." (T-6.V.B.3:1-2)

"Upside down as always, the ego perceives the first lesson as insane." (T-6.V.B.4:1)

"Meanwhile, the increasing clarity of the Holy Spirit's Voice makes it impossible for the learner not to listen. For a time, then, he is receiving conflicting messages and accepting both." (T-6.V.B.4:5-6)

"The way out of conflict between two opposing thought systems is clearly to choose one and relinquish the other." (T-6.V.B.5:1)

"There can be no conflict between sanity and insanity. Only one is true, and therefore only one is real." (T-6.V.B.6:1)

"The Holy Spirit perceives the conflict exactly as it is. Therefore, His second lesson is:

"To have peace, teach peace to learn it."(T-6.V.B.7:3-5)

"This is still a preliminary step, since having and being are still not equated." (T-6.V.B.8:1)

"The second step, then, is still perceptual, although it is a giant step toward the unified perception that reflects God's knowing." (T-6.V.B.9:1)

In summary, Chapter 6 – V.B "To Have Peace, Teach Peace to Learn It" is saying:

Our ego tells us that in order to be happy in this world, we must have and get certain things. What these things are, differ from person to person, yet they all have one thing in common: they are all things of this world. Yet these things either never come to us, or once gotten, fail to make us happy in a sustained way. The feeling always fades, and our egos are on the hunt once again. Some call this greed, because enough is never enough when it comes to the ego. The pursuit of happiness has then become a process without hope of achievement, yet the ego will insanely keep trying. This is why the Holy Spirit instructs us that the first step in the reversal of the egos thought system is the letting go of the "getting concept." This is a fundamental or permanent change at the very bedrock of our current belief system. It is to learn that there is no loss or penalty for giving what you truly have—in fact; it only increases as it is given. What is it we want above and beyond what the ego

CHAPTER 6—THE LESSONS OF LOVE

relentlessly searches for, but never finds? What is it we are trying to achieve with all of our wants and needs? Inner peace. We want peace of mind and the satisfied feeling of completion. The only way to have it is to give it. This concept is in direct opposition to the egos thought system, and yet if we embrace it, all our needs and wants will be satisfied beyond what we ever thought possible. Our motivation to make this fundamental change in thinking comes from experiencing the positive results of learning peace through teaching it by our thoughts and actions. True peace comes from letting go of all thoughts about the world—this allows you to have peace, and by doing this, you are thus teaching peace to the world, in order to learn how to have it for yourself.

C. Be Vigilant Only for God and His Kingdom

"We said before that the Holy Spirit is evaluative, and must be. He sorts out the true from the false in your mind, and teaches you to judge every thought you allow to enter it in the light of what God put there." (T-6.V.C.1:1-2)

"God Himself has established what you can extend with perfect safety. Therefore, the Holy Spirit's third lesson is:

Be vigilant only for God and His Kingdom." (T-6.V.C.2:6-8)

"This is a major step toward fundamental change." (T-6.V.C.3:1)

"I have already told you that you can be as vigilant against the ego as for it. This lesson teaches not only that you can be, but that you must be." (T-6.V.C.4:2-3)

"This lesson is unequivocal in that it teaches there must be no exceptions, although it does not deny that the temptation to make exceptions will occur. Here, then, your consistency is called on despite the chaos." (T-6.V.C.4:5-6)

"You learn first that having rests on giving, and not on getting. Next you learn that you learn what you teach, and that you want to learn peace." (T-6.V.C.6:1-2)

"The third step is thus one of protection for your mind, allowing you to identify only with the center, where God placed the altar to Himself. Altars are beliefs, but God and His creations are beyond belief because they are beyond question." (T-6.V.C.7:1-2)

"To teach the whole Sonship without exception c
perceive its wholeness, and have learned that it is o.
be vigilant to hold its oneness in your mind because,
enter, you will lose awareness of its wholeness and will
teach it." (T-6.V.C.8:1-2)

"The third step, then, is a statement of what you want to belie
entails a willingness to relinquish everything else." (T-6.V.C.10:1)

"You have exerted great effort to preserve what you made because
was not true. Therefore, you must now turn your effort against it."
(T-6.V.C.10:5-6)

In summary, Chapter 6 – V.C "Be Vigilant Only for God and His Kingdom" is saying:

And so now that we know that thoughts of this world, including all our needs and wants are actually thoughts of the ego, we must be vigilant for when we are having them. We must do this in order to re-train our minds to think the Thoughts of God. Our inner altars must be clear. And as stated previously, altars are beliefs. Our belief in what we know to be true must undergo a fundamental, permanent change: We must learn we are Love and not a body—a thing filled with needs, wants and endless desires for things of this world. We are not separate beings, but a unified creation in God. There can be no exceptions to our wholeness, despite the fact that there are some bodies we would rather not include as part of us. We must be vigilant for such thoughts of exclusion. Why? Because to exclude anyone means that we ourselves are also excluded from God's Love and this is a false belief, corrupting our purified altar. We must be willing to relinquish all thoughts of separation in exchange for the desire for knowing our wholeness and having peace. Therefore, let your mind be vigilant only for God and His Kingdom. You will know you have chosen to keep the correct thoughts by the level of peace and love that you feel. It is through this inner process that you learn the lessons of Love.

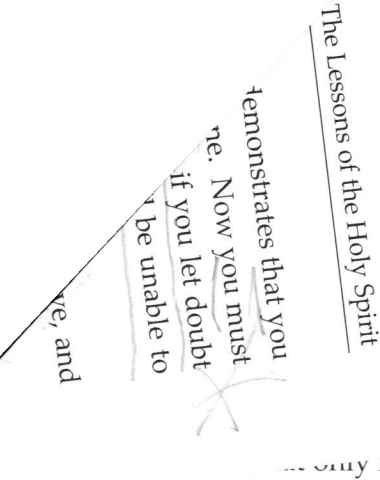

CHAPTER 7
THE KINGDOM

Last Step

"..., as He does with you. This is an ..., and because you share it, you are ... reation you are not in a reciprocal ... ou but you did not create Him. I ... only in this respect your creative power differs from His." (T-7.I.1:2-5)

"If you created God and He created you, the Kingdom could not increase through its own creative thought. Creation would therefore be limited, and you would not be co-creator with God. As God's creative Thought proceeds from Him to you, so must your creative thought proceed from you to your creations. Only in this way can all creative power extend outward." (T-7.I.2:1-4)

"Love extends outward simply because it cannot be contained." (T-7.I.3:4)

"The ego, on the other hand, always demands reciprocal rights, because it is competitive rather than loving." (T-7.I.4:1)

"I gave only love to the Kingdom because I believed that was what I was." (T-7.I.5:1)

"To think like God is to share His certainty of what you are, and to create like Him is to share the perfect Love He shares with you." (T-7.I.6:1)

"I have said that the last step in the reawakening of knowledge is taken by God. This is true, but it is hard to explain in words because words are symbols, and nothing that is true need be explained." (T-7.I.6:3-4)

"God does not take steps, because His accomplishments are not gradual." (T-7.I.7:1)

"The "last step" that God will take was therefore true in the beginning, is true now, and will be true forever. What is timeless is always there, because its being is eternally changeless." (T-7.I.7:8-9)

In summary, Chapter 7 – I. "The Last Step" is saying:
The last step in our reawakening is the experience of our oneness with God. This is a state of being that cannot be explained with words because it is beyond what mere words can describe—it is a state beyond all symbols. That being said, we are currently living in bodies, which are in and of themselves, mere symbols of an identity we decided on. The body is the symbol of the separated self. To invite God to come and take the last step towards our awakening to our True Self, we must forgo all belief in our false self. The ego thinks it created itself and thus became a body. But the Holy Spirit tells us that we cannot create ourselves, no more than a baby can be born without parents. We differ from God only in that He is our Father, and we are His One United Son. This will be true for all eternity regardless of what we imagine ourselves to be now. Therefore, the last step in our journey to awakening will be taken by God, who will initiate the *experience* of this Unity—which is joyous and loving beyond all words or comprehension.

II. The Law of the Kingdom

"To heal is the only kind of thinking in this world that resembles the Thought of God, and because of the elements they share, can transfer easily to it." (T-7.II.1:1)

"Sickness and separation are not of God, but the Kingdom is. If you obscure the Kingdom, you are perceiving what is not of God." (T-7.II.1:4-5)

"To heal, then, is to correct perception in your brother and yourself by sharing the Holy Spirit with him. This places you both within the Kingdom, and restores its wholeness in your mind." (T-7.II.2:1-2)

"In the Kingdom there is no teaching or learning, because there is no belief. There is only certainty. God and His Sons, in the surety of being, know that what you extend you are." (T-7.II.3:4-6)

"The extension of truth, which is the law of the Kingdom, rests only on the knowledge of what truth is. This is your inheritance and requires no learning at all, but when you disinherited yourself you became a learner of necessity." (T-7.II.5:6-7)

"No one questions the connection of learning and memory." (T-7.II.6:1)

"That is why the Holy Spirit's teaching is a lesson in remembering. I said before that He teaches remembering and forgetting, but the forgetting is only to make the remembering consistent." (T-7.II.6:3-4)

CHAPTER 7—THE GIFTS OF THE KINGDOM

"This is the only way you can learn consistency, so that you can finally be consistent." (T-7.II.6:8)

In summary, Chapter 7 – II. "The Law of the Kingdom" is saying:
The law of the Kingdom is this: the thoughts you believe and therefore extend, are what you will experience or manifest. Some take this to be the same as the "law of attraction." However, if you believe you are a body, and strive for things associated with the body, you will be stranded here in this world—returning again and again for what you can never truly have. The Law of the Kingdom goes far beyond this world entirely, in that it is the means for our total and complete healing. To be healed is to no longer be sick. Sickness and the idea of separation are synonymous in *A Course In Miracles*. Therefore, to heal your mind, you have only to give up the belief in separation. This is done through correct perception of your brothers—to truly believe they are one with you. To think this way, is to simultaneously teach and learn the truth of Who We Are. Your thoughts of oneness reflect the truth of the Law of the Kingdom, and you thus restore your own mind and everyone else's, to the Kingdom. When we forgot our oneness, then did learning become necessary in order to remember Who We Are in truth. To remember the truth, or "The Law of the Kingdom," we must let go of the bodily identities we think we are now and remember our Unity in God.

III. The Reality of the Kingdom

"The Holy Spirit teaches one lesson, and applies it to all individuals in all situations." (T-7.III.1:1)

"By teaching the power of the Kingdom of God Himself, He teaches you that all power is yours." (T-7.III.1:3)

"Your vigilance does not establish it as yours, but it does enable you to use it always and in all ways. When I said "I am with you always," I meant it literally. I am not absent to anyone in any situation." (T-7.III.1:6-8)

"How can you who are God's meaning perceive yourself as absent from it?" (T-7.III.2:4)

"This is why the ego is insane; it teaches that you are not what you are." (T-7.III.2:6)

"To be in the Kingdom is merely to focus your full attention on it. As long as you believe you can attend to what is not true, you are accepting conflict as your choice." (T-7.III.4:1-2)

"You who are the Kingdom are not concerned with seeming." (T-7.III.4:5)

"The certain are perfectly calm, because they are not in doubt." (T-7.III.5:6)

"This holds them in perfect serenity, because this is what they share, knowing what they are." (T-7.III.5:8)

In summary, Chapter 7 – III. "The Reality of the Kingdom" is saying:

The Holy Spirit knows that every single one of us comprises the Kingdom of God. The power of our oneness is ours, but in order to claim it, we must choose it. This choosing is simply the recognition that we can never be without it. The power and reality of the Kingdom belongs to us, even as we belong to God and Him to us. God has never left us. How then is it possible to conceive of a "self" that is absent from Him? Yet, this is indeed what we think has happened to us, and to undo the choice to separate our memory from God is to be vigilant against those thoughts that support the world of separation. These are any and all thoughts that cause us suffering—suffering because they are thoughts associated with the body and therefore our false self. This is the ego-self that is in direct conflict with God, because it represents a contraction to the truth of our unity with Him. Those who do not doubt their unity are perfectly calm and serene, knowing that all power and glory and love is equally shared. No one goes without, who goes within to the reality of the Kingdom of God.

IV. Healing as the Recognition of Truth

"Truth can only be recognized and need only be recognized." (T-7.IV.1:1)

"Healing does not come directly from God, Who knows His creations as perfectly whole. Yet healing is still of God, because it proceeds from His Voice and from His laws." (T-7.IV.1:4-5)

"The Holy Spirit must work through you to teach you He is in you. This is an intermediary step toward the knowledge that you are in God because you are part of Him." (T-7.IV.2:1-2)

"By healing you learn of wholeness, and by learning of wholeness you learn to remember God. You have forgotten Him, but the Holy Spirit understands that your forgetting must be translated into a way of remembering." (T-7.IV.4:3-4)

CHAPTER 7—THE GIFTS OF THE KINGDOM

"The ego always seeks to divide and separate. The Holy Spirit always seeks to unify and heal." (T-7.IV.5:2-3)

"Healing is the way to undo the belief in differences, being the only way of perceiving the Sonship as one." (T-7.IV.5:5)

"The strength of right perception is so great that it brings the mind into accord with His, because it serves His Voice, which is in all of you." (T-7.IV.5:7)

"God is All in all in a very literal sense. All being is in Him Who is all Being." (T-7.IV.7:4-5)

"Healing is a way of forgetting the sense of danger the ego has induced in you, by not recognizing its existence in your brother. This strengthens the Holy Spirit in both of you, because it is a refusal to acknowledge fear. Love needs only this invitation." (T-7.IV.7:7-9)

"By your awakening to it, you are merely forgetting what you are not. This enables you to remember what you are." (T-7.IV.7:11-12)

In summary, Chapter 7 – IV. "Healing as the Recognition of Truth" is saying:

If our mind is split between the ego and the Holy Spirit, then to heal it is to make it whole once again. To heal then, we must recognize our oneness and recognize only this as true. Healing is to undo our belief in our differences, which is the only way we can see ourselves as one. When we are tempted to believe in the fear, hatred, or even mild irritation our ego would have us feel towards our brothers, we must remember how to see them rightly. We must forget all we think we know and understand about them and recognize only the existence of the light of God within them. When we perceive our brothers this way, we strengthen the presence of the Holy Spirit in each other because we have invited love to come to us both. This is how one awakens to one love; by letting go of what we are not and accepting only what we are. Thus, does healing come by simply recognizing what is true.

V. Healing and Changelessness of Mind

"Only minds can communicate." (T-7.V.2:1)

"Healing is the one ability everyone can develop and must develop if he is to be healed. Healing is the Holy Spirit's form of communication in this world, and the only one He accepts." (T-7.V.3:1-2)

V. Healing and Changelessness of Mind

"The body in the service of the ego can hurt other bodies, but this cannot occur unless the body has already been confused with the mind." (T-7.V.3:5)

"Healing perceives nothing in the healer that everyone else does not share with him." (T-7.V. 4:3)

"He may believe that the gift comes from God to him, but it is quite evident that he does not understand God if he thinks he has something that others lack." (T-7.V.4:5)

"Love is incapable of any exceptions." (T-7.V.5:7)

"True learning is constant, and so vital in its power for change that a Son of God can recognize his power in one instant and change the world in the next. That is because, by changing his mind, he has changed the most powerful device that was ever given him for change." (T-7.V.7:5-6)

"You are recognizing the changeless mind in your brother by realizing that he could not have changed his mind. That is how you perceive the Holy Spirit in him. It is only the Holy Spirit in him that never changes His Mind." (T-7.V.8:2-4)

"If you see only the changeless in him you have not really changed him. By changing your mind about his for him, you help him undo the change his ego thinks it has made in him." (T-7.V.8:7-8)

"Our brothers are forgetful. That is why they need your remembrance of me and of Him Who created me. Through this remembrance, you can change their minds about themselves, as I can change yours. Your mind is so powerful a light that you can look into theirs and enlighten them, as I can enlighten yours." (T-7.V.10:3-6)

"The mind we share is shared by all our brothers, and as we see them truly they will be healed. Let your mind shine with mine upon their minds, and by our gratitude to them make them aware of the light in them." (T-7.V.11:2-3)

In summary, Chapter 7 – V. "Healing and the Changelessness of Mind" is saying:

Every human being has been given the same power to heal. Do not let another's ego try to convince you that only they hold the keys to your salvation. We each hold a key that is essential to the awakening of us all. No one

CHAPTER 7—THE GIFTS OF THE KINGDOM

is endowed with special gifts that others cannot discover for themselves. It is only that some discover them sooner. The gift of healing we all share is the ability to change our mind about who we think we are. This is the simple shift in thinking required to unleash the power of God within us. Since only minds can communicate and only minds can share in God's power, then it must be that it is given to us all equally. It is the realization of this power and light within our brothers that causes our mind to shift into true healing. As you see your brothers truly—that is to see them as endowed with the love and light of God, the same as yourself—you shine your light into their mind, thus "enlightening them." You are not changing them, but simply recognizing the truth in them. You are remembering Who They Are in truth. Your brothers need you to do this for them, for they have forgotten it themselves. Look upon them with only gratitude for their part in our One Self and through such loving gratitude you will help awaken them to the light they share with you. You will both be healed by recognizing only what is changeless within each other.

VI. From Vigilance to Peace

"Although you can love the Sonship only as one, you can perceive it as fragmented." (T-7.VI.1:1)

"The mind that accepts attack cannot love. That is because it believes it can destroy love, and therefore does not understand what love is. If it does not understand what love is, it cannot perceive itself as loving." (T-7.VI.2:1-3)

"The ingeniousness of the ego to preserve itself is enormous, but it stems from the very power of the mind the ego denies." (T-7.VI.3:1)

"Fearful of perceiving the power of this source, it is forced to depreciate it." (T-7.VI.3:6)

"Love is your power, which the ego must deny. It must also deny everything this power gives you because it gives you everything." (T-7.VI.4:7-8)

"The Holy Spirit undoes illusions without attacking them, because He cannot perceive them at all. They therefore do not exist for Him. He resolves the apparent conflict they engender by perceiving conflict as meaningless." (T-7.VI. 6:1-3)

"Vigilance has no place in peace. It is necessary against beliefs that are not true, and would never have been called upon by the Holy Spirit if you had not believed the untrue. When you believe something, you have made it true for you." (T-7.VI.7:5-7)

"If truth is total, the untrue cannot exist. Commitment to either must be total; they cannot coexist in your mind without splitting it. If they cannot coexist in peace, and if you want peace, you must give up the idea of conflict entirely and for all time. This requires vigilance only as long as you do not recognize what is true." (T-7.VI.8:7-10)

"Your mind is dividing its allegiance between two kingdoms, and you are totally committed to neither." (T-7.VI.9:1)

"The Oneness of the Creator and the creation is your wholeness, your sanity and your limitless power." (T-7.VI.10:4)

"If you dissociate your mind from it you are perceiving the most powerful force in the universe as if it were weak, because you do not believe you are part of it." (T-7.VI.10:6)

"You cannot create in this divided state, and you must be vigilant against this divided state because only peace can be extended." (T-7.VI.12:3)

"Creation, not separation, is your will because it is God's, and nothing that opposes this means anything at all." (T-7.VI.13:6)

In summary, Chapter 7 – VI. "From Vigilance to Peace" is saying:
The ego would have you believe you are a powerless victim of the world around you, a helpless piece of dust upon an ocean of fear. Yet the Holy Spirit would help us undo this illusion about ourselves. He would have us learn of our true power in God's wholeness. It is the perception of our separation that promotes our sense of weakness; therefore, we must give up the idea we are fragmented into seemingly different bodies. To perceive bodies and believe them real is to attack God's wholeness. We can read these words and tell ourselves that we believe in our wholeness, yet still react to the world as though we are separated bodies. Thus, our minds are divided between the false beliefs of the ego and the truth of the Holy Spirit. We cannot create in this divided state, nor find peace. Therefore, we must learn to recognize when our mind is paying allegiance to the ego and actively decide against such thoughts. In our vigilance against any thoughts associated with separation, we will move into peace. But, until we fully accept that only what is eternal within us is true, we must remain vigilant over our thoughts. This is how true peace is gained.

VII. The Totality of the Kingdom

"It is as impossible to deny part of the Sonship as it is to love it in part." (T-7.VII.1:2)

"You cannot be totally committed sometimes." (T-7.VII.1:4)

"Reality cannot be partly appreciated. That is why denying any part of it means you have lost the awareness of all of it. Yet denial is a defense, and so it is as capable of being used positively as well as negatively." (T-7.VII.1:7-9)

"What you deny you lack, not because it is lacking, but because you have denied it in another and are therefore not aware of it in yourself." (T-7.VII.2:6)

"What you want to be, then, must determine every response you make." (T-7.VII.2:8)

"All illusions about the Sonship are dispelled together as they were made together. Teach no one that he is what you would not want to be. Your brother is the mirror in which you see the image of yourself as long as perception lasts." (T-7.VII.3:7-9)

"Illusions are investments. They will last as long as you value them." (T-7.VII.4:1-2)

"The only way to dispel illusions is to withdraw all investment from them, and they will have no life for you because you will have put them out of your mind." (T-7.VII.4:4)

"Only honor is a fitting gift for those whom God Himself created worthy of honor, and whom He honors. Give them the appreciation God accords them always, because they are His beloved Sons in whom He is well pleased. You cannot be apart from them because you are not apart from Him." (T-7.VII.5:1-3)

"You must be fearful if you believe that your brother is attacking you to tear the Kingdom of Heaven from you." (T-7.VII.8:4)

"Being part of your mind that does not believe it is responsible for itself, and being without allegiance to God, the ego is incapable of trust." (T-7.VII.9:1)

"Whenever a brother attacks another, that is what he believes." (T-7.VII.9:3)

"If you choose to separate yourself from God, that is what you will think others are doing to you." (T-7.VII.9:5)

"But see the Love of God in you, and you will see it everywhere because it is everywhere. See His abundance in everyone, and you will know that you are in Him and with them." (T-7.VII.10:4-5)

"Wanting this only you will have this only, and giving this only you will be only this." (T-7.VII.11:3)

In summary, Chapter 7–VII "The Totality of the Kingdom" is saying:
It may seem impossible to love every single person in our lives, all the time; those we despise, those we think we love, yet sometimes dislike, and those whom we do not even know. The only way to do this, is to see them differently. We must withdraw our belief in the illusions surrounding them. If we see them as bodies, capable of making us unhappy, then that is what they will be to us, and ourselves included. This is because we are either One Self or we are separate selves. Both identities cannot be true. And what we believe to be true will be revealed by how we respond to our brothers. Therefore, before we respond lovelessly to anyone, we must first pause and weigh what it is we want to be true. Choose to see beyond the body and remember only the Love of God that shines hidden behind the clouds of the ego's darkness, and you will have chosen correctly. To want to see only this in another, is to call forth the Love of God within them—it is to see totally by calling forth the unified totality of God's Kingdom—and only God's Kingdom will then become your reality.

VIII. The Unbelievable Belief

"The ego always tries to preserve conflict. It is very ingenious in devising ways that seem to diminish conflict, because it does not want you to find conflict so intolerable that you will insist on giving it up." (T-7.VIII.2:2-3)

"It projects conflict from your mind to other minds, in an attempt to persuade you that you have gotten rid of the problem." (T-7.VIII.2:6)

"There are two major errors involved in this attempt. First, strictly speaking, conflict cannot be projected because it cannot be shared." (T-7.VIII.3:1-2)

"The second error is the idea that you can get rid of something you do not want by giving it away. Giving it away is how you keep it." (T-7.VIII.3:6-7)

CHAPTER 7—THE GIFTS OF THE KINGDOM

"You cannot perpetuate an illusion about another without perpetuating it about yourself. There is no way out of this, because it is impossible to fragment the mind." (T-7.VIII.4:1-2)

"The ego is a confusion in identification." (T-7.VIII.4:7)

"Do not be afraid of the ego. It depends on your mind, and as you made it by believing in it, so you can dispel it by withdrawing belief from it." (T-7.VIII.5:1-2)

"The Holy Spirit will teach you to perceive beyond your belief, because truth is beyond belief and His perception is true. The ego can be completely forgotten at any time, because it is a totally incredible belief, and no one can keep a belief he has judged to be unbelievable." (T-7.VIII.6:1-2)

"The whole purpose of this course is to teach you that the ego is unbelievable and will forever be unbelievable." (T-7.VIII.7:1)

"By accepting the Atonement for yourself, you are deciding against the belief that you can be alone, thus dispelling the idea of separation and affirming your true identification with the whole Kingdom as literally part of you." (T-7.VIII.7:3)

In summary, Chapter 7 – VIII "The Unbelievable Belief" is saying:
The unbelievable belief is that we could ever exist in a state separated from God. God is the Source of Who and What We Are. Without God, we would simply cease to exist. The moment we give up the unbelievable belief that we could be anything other than the perfect love in peaceful unity with God we were created as, we will have given up our belief in the ego. The idea of the ego will then become unbelievable, and we will at last believe in the Atonement—our oneness—over the idea of being separate. In our attempt to preserve our ego, we try to project the idea of separation outside of us, which manifests as the experience of living in separate bodies. This idea is in direct conflict with the truth of our unity. This causes us unexplainable distress that we attribute to a myriad of outside factors, when in reality our only discomfort stems from living against what we truly are. The ego uses many ingenious tactics in an attempt to diminish our discomfort here. It keeps us seeking and seeking in the world outside of us for what we think will make us feel happy, safe, and complete. The untold truth is that there is nothing outside of us that can heal our discomfort. The only way we can be healed is by giving up the unbelievable belief we could ever exist separate from God and one another to begin with.

IX. The Extension of the Kingdom

"Only you can limit your creative power, but God wills to release it." (T-7.IX.1:1)

"Selfishness is of the ego, but Self-fullness is of spirit because that is how God created it." (T-7.IX.1:4)

"Spirit knows that the awareness of all its brothers is included in its own, as it is included in God. The power of the whole Sonship and of its Creator is therefore spirit's own fullness, rendering its creations equally whole and equal in perfection." (T-7.IX.2:1-2)

"Everything He created is given all His power, because it is part of Him and shares His Being with Him." (T-7.IX.2:4)

"Being must be extended." (T-7.IX.2:6)

"It does not wish to contain God, but wills to extend His Being." (T-7.IX.2:10)

"The Kingdom is forever extending because it is in the Mind of God. You do not know your joy because you do not know your own Self-fullness." (T-7.IX.4:1-2)

"Be confident that you have never lost your Identity and the extensions which maintain It in wholeness and peace. Miracles are an expression of this confidence. They are reflections of both your proper identification with your brothers, and of your awareness that your identification is maintained by extension. The miracle is a lesson in total perception. By including any part of totality in the lesson, you have included the whole." (T-7.IX.7:1-5)

In summary, Chapter 7 – IX. The Extension of the Kingdom" is saying:

When we remember our wholeness in spirit and react with all-inclusive love to those who appear separate from us, we are extending the Love of God. This is how He loves us—as an extension of Himself. This Identity in God's wholeness cannot be lost, but it can be forgotten. When this happens, we feel unhappiness toward others and ourselves. We can regain our joy simply by bringing our awareness back into correct perception; forgive what you think is causing you pain and remember it is only a projection of your own ego to keep you tied to the idea you are a body. Undo this false thought by extending the miracle of re-

CHAPTER 7—THE GIFTS OF THE KINGDOM

membering the truth; you and all others remain forever an extension of God's Loving Thoughts. And this remembrance is the extension of God's Kingdom.

X. The Confusion of Pain and Joy

"You may have carried the ego's reasoning to its logical conclusion, which is total confusion about everything." (T-7.X.1:2)

"You are willing to look at the ego's premises, but not at their logical outcome." (T-7.X.1:5)

"The ability to see a logical outcome depends on the willingness to see it, but its truth has nothing to do with your willingness." (T-7.X.2:4)

"The Holy Spirit will direct you only so as to avoid pain. Surely no one would object to this goal if he recognized it. The problem is not whether what the Holy spirit says is true, but whether you want to listen to what He says. You no more recognize what is painful than you know what is joyful, and are, in fact, very apt to confuse the two." (T-7.X.3:1-4)

"You believe that doing the opposite of God's Will can be better for you." (T-7.X.4:3)

"As long as you avoid His guidance in any way, you want to be weak." (T-7.X.5:2)

"No one gladly obeys a guide he does not trust, but this does not mean that the guide is untrustworthy." (T-7.X.5:8)

"The Holy Spirit is perfectly trustworthy, as you are. God Himself trusts you, and therefore your trustworthiness is beyond question." (T-7.X.6:1-2)

"His Voice will teach you how to distinguish between pain and joy, and will lead you out of the confusion you have made." (T-7.X.7:3)

"This means that you are confused about what you are. If you are God's Will and do not accept His Will, you are denying joy. The miracle is therefore a lesson in what joy is. Being a lesson in sharing it is a lesson in love, which is joy. Every miracle is thus a lesson in truth, and by offering truth you are learning the difference between pain and joy." (T-7.X.8:2-6)

In summary, Chapter 7 – X. "The Confusion of Pain and Joy" is saying:

We currently think that we can find joy through the body, but despite all the pain we find, we refuse to consider letting go of this identity. We must learn and accept in the end, this single lesson: that we remain as God Willed us to be. We are One Love. It is a miracle to hold this truth in our minds as we walk this world of separation—learning the difference between pain and joy. Pain is the idea we are separate bodies, and joy is the relinquishment of this belief; it is belief in our unity in Spirit. Once this is understood, the confusion between pain and joy is undone.

XI. The State of Grace

"Grace is the natural state of every Son of God. When he is not in a state of grace, he is out of his natural environment and does not function well. Everything he does becomes a strain, because he was not created for the environment that he has made." (T-7.XI.2:1-3)

"When a mind has only light, it knows only light. Its own radiance shines all around it, and extends out into the darkness of other minds, transforming them into majesty." (T-7.XI.5:1-2)

"Whenever you heal a brother by recognizing his worth, you are acknowledging his power to create and yours." (T-7.XI.6:5)

"The Kingdom of God includes all His Sons and their children, who are as like the Sons as they are like the Father. Know, then, the Sons of God, and you will know all creation." (T-7.XI.7:10-11)

In summary, Chapter 7 – XI. "The State of Grace" is saying:

Living in a state of grace, is simply to live in the loving peace of knowing we are one with God and nothing else about us is true. When we live against this unity, everything becomes a strain because we are living in conflict with the truth of our very being. We are not living as our natural Identity. The only way to enter this state is by recognizing our shared unity with other minds. This is done by acknowledging only the Light within them as true. Thus, we heal them and ourselves by recognizing their value to us, as part of us. Our mind becomes all-inclusive in its love of all creation, the state of God's grace. This peaceful state of grace is a gift from the Kingdom of God, reflected back to us, just as we have given It.

CHAPTER 8
THE JOURNEY BACK

I. The Direction of the Curriculum

"Knowledge is not the motivation for learning this course. Peace is." (T-8.I.1:1-2)

"The distractions of the ego may seem to interfere with your learning, but the ego has no power to distract you unless you give it the power to do so." (T-8.I.2:1)

"You are merely asked to evaluate them in terms of their results to you. If you do not want them on the basis of loss of peace, they will be removed from your mind for you." (T-8.I.2:5-6)

"Every response to the ego is a call to war, and war does deprive you of peace." (T-8.I.3:1)

"Those whom you perceive as opponents are part of your peace, which you are giving up by attacking them." (T-8.I.3:4)

"Your past learning must have taught you the wrong things, simply because it has not made you happy. On this basis alone its value should be questioned." (T-8.I.4:1-2)

"The curriculum of the Atonement is the opposite of the curriculum you have established for yourself, but so is its outcome. If the outcome of yours has made you unhappy, and if you want a different one, a change in the curriculum is obviously necessary. The first change to be introduced is a change in direction." (T-8.I.5:1-3)

"You cannot learn simultaneously from two teachers who are in total disagreement about everything." (T-8.I.6:2)

"Your reality is unaffected by both, but if you listen to both, your mind will be split about what your reality is." (T-8.I.6:5)

In summary, Chapter 8 – I. "The Direction of the Curriculum" is saying:
The ego's voice may seem to be the dominant teacher in our minds, but we can choose against it just as easily as for it. We withdraw our support from its voice when we notice a loss of peace; a clear sign we are listening to the wrong

teacher. Every person is a part of our peace, being that we are created as one. Therefore, to allow unpeaceful thoughts about others to dominate our minds is to support the ego's teaching. We cannot learn from both the ego and the Holy Spirit at the same time—we know from experience it is impossible to travel in opposite directions simultaneously. Therefore, we must constantly be vigilant over our thoughts in order to maintain the direction the Holy Spirit would have us travel. The direction that leads us to our peace and Home. Until we learn to hear only the Voice for God, our minds will remain split between the ego and the Holy Spirit, as what we experience as our reality. The direction of the curriculum is to move our thoughts solely in the direction of peace.

II. The Difference Between Imprisonment and Freedom

"There is a rationale for choice. Only one Teacher knows what your reality is." (T-8.II.1:1-2)

"Even if you could disregard the Holy Spirit entirely, which is impossible, you could still learn nothing from the ego, because the ego knows nothing." (T-8.II.1:9)

"The ego has never given you a sensible answer to anything. Simply on the grounds of your own experience with its teaching, should not this alone disqualify it as your future teacher?" (T-8.II.2:4-5)

"The ego tries to teach that you want to oppose God's Will. This unnatural lesson cannot be learned, and the attempt to learn it is a violation of your own freedom, making you afraid of your will because it is free." (T-8.II.4:1-2)

"The Holy Spirit leads you steadily along the path of freedom, teaching you how to disregard or look beyond everything that would hold you back." (T-8.II.4:4)

"The Holy Spirit's teaching takes only one direction and has only one goal. His direction is freedom and His goal is God." (T-8.II.6:1-2)

"To what else except all power and glory can the Holy Spirit appeal to restore God's Kingdom? His appeal, then, is merely to what the Kingdom is, and for its own acknowledgment of what it is." (T-8.II.8:1-2)

CHAPTER 8—THE JOURNEY BACK

In summary, Chapter 8 – II. "The Difference between Imprisonment and Freedom" is saying:

The ego would have us believe that freedom comes from striking out on our own and going our own separate ways. However, we have learned that this is a lonely path filled with fear, pain, and unhappiness. We are actually trapped and isolated through seeking for independence from one another and God. This is the opposite of what true freedom is. True freedom is the discovery of our true Identity and rejoining all those whom we thought were lost. It is the remembrance of our Oneness. The Holy Spirit simply asks that we desire this state of peace and love above all else the world has to offer. His only request is that we acknowledge the truth we have forgotten; we are free in Unity and bound in pain by separation. Only this truth can set us free from the ego chains that bind us. The difference between imprisonment and freedom is the difference between the desire to be imprisoned in a separate ego-body and the choice for freedom through choosing God's Unity.

III. The Holy Encounter

"Ask and it shall be given you, because it has already *been* given. Ask for light and learn that you are light." (T-8.III.1:2-3)

"To fulfill the Will of God perfectly is the only joy and peace that can be fully known, because it is the only function that can be fully experienced." (T-8.III.2:1)

"Yet the wish for other experience will block its accomplishment, because God's Will cannot be forced upon you, being an experience of total willingness." (T-8.III.2:3)

"When you meet anyone, remember it is a holy encounter. As you see him you will see yourself. As you treat him you will treat yourself. As you think of him you will think of yourself. Never forget this, for in him you will find yourself of lose yourself. Whenever two Sons of God meet, they are given another chance at salvation. Do not leave anyone without giving salvation to him and receiving it yourself. For I am always there with you, in remembrance of you." (T-8.III.4:1-8)

"The goal of the curriculum, regardless of the teacher you choose, is "Know thyself." There is nothing else to seek." (T-8.III.5:1-2)

"Whenever you are with anyone, you have another opportunity to find them. Your power and glory are in him because they are yours." (T-8.III.5:4-5)

"Give him his place in the Kingdom and you will have yours." (T-8.III.5:12)

"To achieve the goal of the curriculum, then, you cannot listen to the ego, whose purpose is to defeat its own goal." (T-8.III.6:2)

"You cannot be powerless to do this, because this is your power. Glory is God's gift to you, because that is what He is. See this glory everywhere to remember what you are." (T-8.III.8:6-8)

In summary, Chapter 8 – III. "The Holy Encounter" is saying:
Whenever you meet or even think of another, it is a holy encounter because you are meeting or thinking of an aspect of your Oneself Who is also One with God. You are therefore encountering God in everyone all the time. The problem then becomes one of recognition. Do you see a body and all its works, or will you be able to remember Who is hidden behind the body and seeks your recognition? Ask to see the Light within another and it shall be given. And in your asking you will also learn the Light is in you. In this way, you learn to know your true Self. But in order to achieve this goal in learning, you cannot listen to the ego for it will never support the idea of your unity in God's light and love. It will insist the body you see is guilty and warrants only your hate and fear. You are not powerless against such thoughts. In fact, you were born to overcome them. See the glory, light and love of God in every holy encounter and learn the truth of Who You Are.

IV. The Gift of Freedom

"If God's Will for you is complete peace and joy, unless you experience only this you must be refusing to acknowledge His Will." (T-8.IV.1:1)

"You cannot exempt yourself from His laws, although you can disobey them. Yet if you do, and only if you do, you will feel lonely and helpless, because you are denying yourself everything." (T-8.IV.1:7-8)

"If I am with you in the loneliness of the world, the loneliness is gone. You cannot maintain the illusion of loneliness if you are not alone. My purpose, then, is still to overcome the world. I do not attack it, but my light must dispel it because of what it is. Light does not attack darkness, but it does shine it away." (T-8.IV.2:6-10)

"Dispelling it is salvation, and in this sense I am the salvation of the world. The world must therefore despise and reject me, because the

CHAPTER 8—THE JOURNEY BACK

world is the belief that love is impossible. If you will accept the fact that I am with you, you are denying the world and accepting God." (T-8.IV.3:6-8)

"Do you not think the world needs peace as much as you do? Do you not want to give it to the world as much as you want to receive it?" (T-8.IV.4:1-2)

"For unless you do, you will not receive it. If you want to have it of me, you must give it. Healing does not come from anyone else." (T-8.IV.4:3-5)

"Healing reflects our joint will." (T-8.IV.5:1)

"Healing is the way in which the separation is overcome. Separation is overcome by union." (T-8.IV.4:3-4)

"Your mind is the means by which you determine your own condition, because mind is the mechanism of decision. It is the power by which you separate or join, and experience pain or joy accordingly." (T-8.IV.5:7-8)

"Nothing God created can oppose your decision, as nothing God created can oppose His Will. God gave your will its power, which I can only acknowledge in honor of His." (T-8.IV.6:1-2)

"If you want to be different, I will wait until you change your mind." (T-8.IV.6:4)

"Freedom is the only gift you can offer to God's Sons, being an acknowledgment of what they are and what He is." (T-8.IV.8:1)

"When you imprison yourself you are losing sight of your true identification with me and with the Father." (T-8.IV.8:5)

In summary, Chapter 8 – IV. "The Gift of Freedom" is saying:

In this world we can either experience the imprisonment of the ego's pain and suffering or the joyous freedom of God's Will. We have total freedom of choice between either mindset. God will not thwart our gift of freedom to choose. He will simply wait until we are ready for His peace. God's peace comes from the knowing that the separation we currently see in this world is not the truth. We can all enjoy a big sigh of peaceful relief over this knowledge! The next step then is to actively join God's Will by allowing the peace of this truth to not be tarnished by any belief in separation. Give the world your peace, and peace will be yours. To give it, you must simply walk through this reality acknowledging Who walks with you in everyone you meet or think of. With this recognition, you free everyone from their ego-identity. If you see them otherwise, you imprison them in the identity of the body, and you will be imprisoned with them. Give the gift of freedom equally to all people and you will live free of the ego yourself.

V. The Undivided Will of the Sonship

"Can you be separated from your identification and be at peace? Dissociation is not a solution; it is a delusion." (T-8.V.1:1-2)

"Alone we can do nothing, but together our minds fuse into something whose power is far beyond the power of its separate parts." (T-8.V.1:6)

"The undivided will of the Sonship is the perfect creator, being wholly in the likeness of God, Whose will it is." (T-8.V.2:1)

"By the belief that your will is separate from mine, you are exempting yourself from the Will of God which is yourself. Yet to heal is still to make whole. Therefore, to heal is to unite with those who are like you, because perceiving this likeness is to recognize the Father." (T-8.V.2:3-5)

"When you unite with me you are uniting without the ego, because I have renounced the ego in myself and therefore cannot unite with yours. Our union is therefore the way to renounce the ego in you." (T-8.V.4:1-2)

"On this journey. You have chosen me as your companion instead of the ego. Do not attempt to hold on to both, or you will try to go in different directions and will lose the way." (T-8.V.5:8-9)

"Let us not lose sight of His direction through illusions, for only illusions of another direction can obscure the one for which God's Voice speaks in all of us. Never accord the ego the power to interfere with the journey." (T-8.V.6:3-4)

"Leave all illusions behind, and reach beyond all attempts of the ego to hold you back. I go before you because I am beyond the ego. Reach, therefore, for my hand because you want to transcend the ego." (T-8.V.6:6-8)

In summary, Chapter 8 – V. "The Undivided Will of the Sonship" is saying:

You cannot recognize both God and the ego as the true identity of anyone, including yourself. No one can be two things at the same time. Therefore, if we are part of God's Identity, then the ego must be false. To identify only with

CHAPTER 8—THE JOURNEY BACK

your Identity in Him is then the same as renouncing the ego in yourself. In truth, we remain undivided by anything the ego may show us, and to accept this is to heal our mind of all division between God and the ego. Let us not lose sight of our will to join with God's Will for us to remember our Union in Him. Let us not be tempted by anything we see outside of us to interfere with this belief. When we feel sad, alone, and fully identified with our bodies, let us reach then for the Hand of God, because we want to transcend what the ego is showing us. Be undivided in your will to be one with the Sonship.

VI. The Treasure of God

"We begin the journey back by setting out together, and gather in our brothers as we continue together." (T-8.VI.1:2)

"The world can add nothing to the power and the glory of God and His holy Sons, but it can blind the Sons to the Father if they behold it. You cannot behold the world and know God. Only one is true." (T-8.VI.2:1-2)

"No one created by God can find joy in anything except the eternal; not because he is deprived of anything else, but because nothing else is worthy of him." (T-8.VI. 3:2)

"Listen to the story of the prodigal son, and learn what God's treasure is and yours: This son of a loving father left his home and thought he had squandered everything for nothing of any value, although he had not understood its worthlessness at the time. He was ashamed to return to his father, because he thought he had hurt him. Yet when he came home the father welcomed him with joy, because the son himself was his father's treasure. He wanted nothing else." (T-8.VI.4:1-4)

"You made neither yourself nor your function. You made only the decision to be unworthy of both. Yet you cannot make yourself unworthy because you are the treasure of God, and what He values is valuable." (T-8.VI.5:11-12)

"His joy lay in creating you, and He extends His Fatherhood to you so that you can extend yourself as He did." (T-8.VI.6:5)

"God would not have us be alone because He does not will to be alone. That is why He created His Son, and gave him the power to create with Him." (T-8.VI.8:6-7)

"The journey to God is merely the reawakening of the knowledge of where you are always, and what you are forever. It is a journey without distance to a goal that has never changed. Truth can only be experienced. It cannot be described and it cannot be explained." (T-8.VI. 9:6-9)

"What God has willed for you is yours." (T-8.VI.10:1)

"Your heart lies where your treasure is, as His does. You who are beloved of God are wholly blessed. Learn this of me, and free the holy will of all those who are as blessed as you are." (T-8.VI.10:3-5)

In summary, Chapter 8 – VI. "The Treasure of God" is saying:
We are God's treasure, but we do not know it. In fact, the last thing we feel like is anybody's "treasure," much less God's. But the truth remains, you are everything to God. We are His everything. It is important that we remember our value to God, because by so doing, we remember our value to each other. It is a reawakening to our oneness and the important part we each play in such unity for the completion of our wholeness. We are each other's treasure.

Remembering this may seem like a long and difficult journey, but it is a journey without distance because the truth is already true. We have only to accept the truth, and the experience of God and all we walked away from like prodigal sons, will return to our freed and open minds. Let your heart rest where your treasure is—let it rest in God and know you are everything to Him. You are literally the treasure of God Himself.

VII. The Body as a Means of Communication

"Attack is always physical. When attack in any form enters your mind you are equating yourself with a body, since this is the ego's interpretation of the body." (T-8.VII.1:1-2)

"When you equate yourself with a body you will always experience depression." (T-8.VII.1:6)

"Remember that the Holy Spirit interprets the body only as a means of communication." (T-8.VII.2:1)

"The ego separates through the body. The Holy Spirit reaches through it to others." (T-8.VII.2:3-4)

"If you use it only to reach the minds of those who believe they are bodies, and teach them through the body that this is not so, you will understand the power of the mind that is in you." (T-8.VII.3:2)

CHAPTER 8 — THE JOURNEY BACK

"In the service of uniting it becomes a beautiful lesson in communion, which has value until communion is." (T-8.VII.3:4)

"If the body becomes a means you give to the Holy Spirit to use on behalf of union of the Sonship, you will not see anything physical except as what it is." (T-8.VII.4:5)

"Healing is the result of using the body solely for communication." (T-8.VII.10:1)

"All mind is whole, and the belief that part of it is physical, or not mind, is a fragmented or sick interpretation." (T-8.VII.10:3)

"By reaching out, the mind extends itself. It does not stop at the body, for if it does it is blocked in its purpose." (T-8.VII.10:5-6)

"The removal of blocks, then, is the only way to guarantee help and healing." (T-8.VII.11:1)

"Perceiving the body as a separate entity cannot but foster illness, because it is not true." (T-8.VII.11:4)

"Learning must lead beyond the body to the re-establishment of the power of the mind in it. This can be accomplished only if the mind extends to other minds, and does not arrest itself in its extension. This arrest is the cause of all illness, because only extension is the mind's function." (T-8.VII.12:6-8)

"To see a body as anything except a means of communication is to limit your mind and to hurt yourself." (T-8.VII.13:3)

"Whenever you see another as limited to or by the body, you are imposing this limit on yourself." (T-8.VII.14:3)

"Freedom from illusions lies only in not believing them. There is no attack, but there is unlimited communication and therefore unlimited power and wholeness. The power of wholeness is extension. Do not arrest your thought in this world, and you will open your mind to creation in God." (T-8.VII.16:5-8)

In summary, Chapter 8 – VII. "The Body as a Means of Communication" is saying:

The ego uses the body as a "separation device," which in its service only promotes fear and attack upon one another. We must switch allegiance from the ego and place our bodies under the service of the Holy Spirit, Who would only use the body to communicate God's Love. God's Love sees us all as

one; unlimited and not restricted to being mere bo⟨
power to extend this loving thought to all other m
natural function as a creation of God. God creates
thoughts and we create like Him, being *of* Him. Ther
and do not restrict your thoughts to that of being a me
Think beyond what your eyes see and learn to heal all ill
selves through your disbelief in them. Through doing so , ., ⌄r
extend, only love from your body to others. And your b⟨ , will become the
perfect means for God's Communication of Love to the world.

VIII. The Body as Means or End

"The body exists in a world that seems to contain two voices fighting for its possession. In this perceived constellation the body is seen as capable of shifting its allegiance from one to the other, making the concepts of both health and sickness meaningful." (T-8.VIII.2:1-3)

"You must have noticed an outstanding characteristic of every end that the ego has accepted as its own. When you have achieved it, it has not satisfied you. This is why the ego is forced to shift ceaselessly from one goal to another, so that you will continue to hope it can yet offer you something." (T-8.VIII.2:5-7)

"The ego has a profound investment in sickness. If you are sick, how can you object to the ego's firm belief that you are not invulnerable?" (T-8.VIII.3:2-3)

"Sickness is a way of demonstrating that you can be hurt. It is a witness to your frailty, your vulnerability, and your extreme need to depend on external guidance. The ego uses this as its best argument for your need for its guidance. It dictates endless prescriptions for avoiding catastrophic outcomes. The Holy Spirit, perfectly aware of the same situation, does not bother to analyze it at all. If data are meaningless there is no point in analyzing them. The function of truth is to collect information that is true. Any way you handle error results in nothing." (T-8.VIII.6:1-8)

"You might well ask how the voice of something that does not exist can be so insistent. Have you thought about the distorting power of something you want, even if it is not real?" (T-8.VIII.8:1-2)

"...Spirit's Voice is as loud as your willingness to listen." (T-8.

"...The Holy Spirit teaches you to use your body only to reach your brothers, so He can teach His message through you." (T-8.VIII.9:1)

"Health is the result of relinquishing all attempts to use the body lovelessly. Health is the beginning of the proper perspective on life under the guidance of the one Teacher Who knows what life is, being the Voice for Life Itself." (T-8.VIII.9:9-10)

In summary, Chapter 8–VIII. "The Body as Means or End" is saying: The ego part of our mind uses the body as a means to attain what it thinks is important to *it*, namely, things of this physical world it thinks will make it happy. This includes all material things and bodies. To the ego, the body is merely a "getting device." This is an unfortunate and unhealthy mindset, for as many of us have noticed, attaining things of this world do not actually make us happy. Even so, the ego is undeterred by this fact, and relentlessly pursues its hopeless dreams, occupying our mind with a near constant state of planning for the future or lamenting the past. It's constantly analyzing what it should or shouldn't do next. This is the sickness of the mind the ego induces in us. The Holy Spirit on the other hand, would heal us of this mindset once and for all by accepting this single fact: none of what you're worrying about, striving for, or in pain over is true. None of it is the real world as all of it lacks eternal qualities. All of it will pass away in time, regardless of what you do. The Holy Spirit therefore teaches us there is no point in letting any of it pollute our mind. Clearing your mind of all this clutter results in mental health. Mental health is the result of letting go of all thoughts that are attempts to use the body for what will only bring you pain and suffering. It is the beginning of learning proper perspective as directed by the Holy Spirit. The body is the means and end for our release from the illusion of needs.

IX. Healing as Corrected Perception

"I have said before that the Holy Spirit is the Answer." (T-8.IX.1:1)

"When the ego tempts you to sickness do not ask the Holy Spirit to heal the body, for this would merely be to accept the ego's belief that the body is the proper aim of healing. Ask, rather, that the Holy Spirit teach you the right perception of the body, for perception alone can be distorted. Only perception can be sick, because only perception can be wrong." (T-8.IX.1:5-7)

IX. Healing as Corrected Perception

"All forms of sickness, even unto death, are physical expressions of the fear of awakening. They are attempts to reinforce sleeping out of fear of waking." (T-8.IX.3:3)

"Wrong perception is the wish that things be as they are not." (T-8.IX.2:1)

"You do not have to seek reality. It will seek you and find you when you meet its conditions." (T-8.IX.2:4-5)

"All forms of sickness, even unto death, are physical expressions of the fear of awakening." (T-8.IX.3:2)

" "Rest in peace" is a blessing for the living, not the dead, because rest comes from waking, not from sleeping." (T-8.IX.3:5)

"The decision to wake is the reflection of the will to love, since all healing involves replacing fear with love." (T-8.IX.5:2)

"His function is to distinguish only between the false and the true, replacing the false with the true." (T-8.IX.5:4)

"The Name of God's Son is one, and you are enjoined to do the works of love because we share this Oneness. Our minds are whole because they are one. If you are sick you are withdrawing from me." (T-8.IX.7:3-5)

"When you limit yourself we are not of one mind, and that is sickness. Yet sickness is not of the body, but of the mind. All forms of sickness are signs that the mind is split, and does not accept a unified purpose." (T-8.IX.8:5-7)

"The unification of purpose, then, is the Holy Spirit's only way of healing." (T-8.IX.9:1)

"Your healing, then, is part of His health, since it is part of His Wholeness. He cannot lose this, but you can not know it. Yet it is still His Will for you, and His Will must stand forever and in all things." (T-8.IX.9:6-8)

In summary, Chapter 8–IX. "Healing as Corrected Perception" is saying:

Our body is never truly sick. Only the mind that directs it can be sick or misperceiving the body as something it is not. When our body is sick, it is the manifestation of our fear of waking from the dream of sickness. The decision to wake is merely a change of mind—the reflection of the will to love instead of fear. How do we meet these conditions? How do decide for love over fear?

CHAPTER 8—THE JOURNEY BACK

The Answer lies in the meaning behind Who the Holy Spirit IS. He is the idea of our Oneness, and He is in our mind, waiting but for us to choose this mindset over separation. If we are sick, we have chosen to be something separated from God, if our heart "rests in peace" we know we have chosen to identify only with the Unity of the Holy Spirit. This healing can happen whether the body appears to be well or not. Choosing Oneness over separation may not automatically grow you a new pair of legs, heal your cancer or raise someone's body from the dead. This is a healing of the mind that brings about the peace of God; a peace that surpasses all else that may assail you in this world. And once achieved, don't rule out walking on water or growing new limbs as a result of such inner healing. Do not limit your identity to a body. This is the perception of the sick-minded and separated. Choose to believe you are part of God's healthy one-minded Wholeness. This fact is already true—we have only to choose to believe it. This is the only healed and correct perception we can have, and it is the belief that will lead us on our journey back to God and His Kingdom.

CHAPTER 9
THE ACCEPTANCE OF THE ATONEMENT

I. The Acceptance of Reality

"Reality cannot "threaten" anything except illusions, since reality can only uphold the truth." (T-9.I.1:3)

"What seems to be the fear of God is really the fear of your own reality." (T-9.I.2:2)

"If you do not know what your reality is, why would you be so sure that it is fearful?" (T-9.I.3:1)

"All this could mean is that you are arbitrarily associating something beyond your awareness with something you do not want. It is evident, then, that you are judging something of which you are totally unaware." (T-9.I.3:3-4)

"I have emphasized many times that the Holy Spirit will never call upon you to sacrifice anything. But if you ask the sacrifice of reality of yourself, the Holy Spirit must remind you that this is not God's Will because it is not yours." (T-9.I.5:1-2)

"How sensible can your messages be, when you ask for what you do not want?" (T-9.I.6:6)

"You may insist that the Holy Spirit does not answer you, but it might be wiser to consider the kind of questioner you are. You do not ask only for what you want." (T-9.I.7:1-2)

"When you ask the Holy Spirit for what would hurt you He cannot answer because nothing can hurt you, and so you are asking for nothing. Any wish that stems from the ego is a wish for nothing, and to ask for it is not a request." (T-9.I.10:1-2)

"Willing against reality, though impossible, can be made into a very persistent goal even though you do not want it." (T-9.I.12:2)

"Remember, then, that God's Will is already possible, and nothing else will ever be." (T-9.I.14:1)

"You cannot distort reality and know what it is. And if you do distort reality you will experience anxiety, depression and ultimately panic,

CHAPTER 9—THE ACCEPTANCE OF THE ATONEMENT

because you are trying to make yourself unreal. When you feel these things, do not try to look beyond yourself for truth, for truth can only be within you. Say, therefore: *Christ is in me, and where He is God must be, for Christ is part of Him."* (T-9.I.14:3-7)

In summary, Chapter 9 – I. "The Acceptance of Reality" is saying:
Our true reality is that we are one with God, Christ, and each other. This reality is nothing even close to our bodily experience we are having here now. So how do we accept our true reality when we clearly do not know what it is? We ask the Holy Spirit to show it to us. Currently we are asking the wrong question and therefore receiving an unacceptable answer. This is because we are allowing the ego to do all the talking for us. It wants us stuck here in these bodies for as long as possible and would only ask for what we do not really want—more of this world, which will only result in more of what will delay us from reaching our true reality. Let us cease to ask for what we do not want. Let us no longer ask for the "nothing" that is this world and ask instead for what we really want: to know the truth of God's reality and our place within It. Acceptance of reality is merely to cease to judge our current ego-reality. Acceptance of reality comes when all such distortions are removed from our mind.

II. The Answer to Prayer

"Everyone who ever tried to use prayer to ask for something has experienced what appears to be failure." (T-9.II.1:1)

"Let us suppose, then, that what you ask of the Holy Spirit is what you really want, but you are still afraid of it. Should this be the case, your attainment of it would no longer be what you want." (T-9.II.2:1-2)

"An individual may ask for physical healing because he is fearful of bodily harm. At the same time, if he were healed physically, the threat to his thought system might be considerably more fearful to him than its physical expression." (T-9.II.2:4-5)

"This request is, therefore, not for healing at all." (T-9.II.2:7)

"The very fact that the Holy Spirit has been asked for anything will ensure a response. Yet it is equally certain that no response given by Him will ever be one that would increase fear." (T-9.II.3:2-3)

"There are many answers you have already received but have not yet heard. I assure you that they are waiting for you." (T-9.II.3:6-7)

II. The Answer to Prayer

"If you would know your prayers are answered, never doubt a Son of God." (T-9.II.4:1)

"The message your brother gives you is up to you." (T-9.II.5:1)

"Your decision about him determines the message you receive. Remember that the Holy Spirit is in him, and His Voice speaks to you through him." (T-9.II.5:4-5)

"Your brother may not know who he is, but there is a light in his mind that does know. This light can shine into yours, giving truth to his words and making you able to hear them." (T-9.II.5:8-9)

"The Holy Spirit extends from your mind to his, and answers you." (T-9.II.6:4)

"I love you for the truth in you, as God does. Your deceptions may deceive you, but they cannot deceive me." (T-9.II.7:1-2)

"Believe in your brothers because I believe in you, and you will learn that my belief in you is justified." (T-9.II.8:1)

"Never forget, then, that you set the value on what you receive, and price it by what you give." (T-9.II.11:1)

"You can ask of the Holy Spirit, then, only by giving to Him, and you can give to Him only where you recognize Him. If you recognize Him in everyone, consider how much you will be asking of Him, and how much you will receive." (T-9.II.12:1-2)

Say, then, to everyone: *"Because I will to know myself, I see you as God's Son and my brother."* (T-9.II.2:5-6)

In summary, Chapter 9 – II. "The Answer to Prayer" is saying:

There seems to be times our prayers go unheard and unanswered. This is not because God is not listening or refusing to answer. Rather, the answer we really want, but have forgotten, is being saved for us until we are ready to receive It. If we want God's answer, we must make ourselves ready through seeing each other correctly. We must open our minds to the idea that God is within each and every person we meet or think of and we must love them accordingly. Your decision about them determines when you receive God's reply. If you see yourself and them as bodies, then God's reply is temporarily blocked. Do not be deceived by the ego! It would pray for only more of what the world contains. You want only what is eternal, loving, and real. This is found within one another. How much do we value one another? Are we willing to

CHAPTER 9—THE ACCEPTANCE OF THE ATONEMENT

look past the ego and all its physical works to the Light contained therein? If so, then be ready to receive God's bountiful answer to your prayer.

III. The Correction of Error

"The alertness of the ego to the errors of other egos is not the kind of vigilance the Holy Spirit would have you maintain." (T-9.III.1:1)

"To the ego it is kind and right and good to point out errors and "correct" them." (T-9.III.2:1)

"Errors are of the ego, and correction of errors lies in the relinquishment of the ego." (T-9.III.2:3)

"If you point out the errors of your brother's ego you must be seeing through yours, because the Holy Spirit does not perceive his errors." (T-9.III.3:1)

"When you react at all to errors, you are not listening to the Holy Spirit." (T-9.III.4:1)

"When a brother behaves insanely, you can heal him only by perceiving the sanity in him. If you perceive his errors and accept them, you are accepting yours. If you want to give yours over to the Holy Spirit, you must do this with his. Unless this becomes the one way in which you (T-9.III.5:1-4)

"You cannot correct yourself. Is it possible, then, for you to correct another?" (T-9.III.6:1-2)

"Your brother's errors are not of him, any more than yours are of you." (T-9.III.7:1)

"The Holy Spirit in you forgives all things in you and in your brother." (T-9.III.7:4)

"Any attempt you make to correct a brother means that you believe correction by you is possible, and this can only be the arrogance of the ego. Correction is of God, Who does not know of arrogance." (T-9.III.7:8-9)

"Do not undertake His function, or you will forget yours." (T-9.III.8:2)

"He will teach you how to see yourself without condemnation, by learning how to look on everything without it. Condemnation will then not be real to you, and all your errors will be forgiven." (T-9.III.8:10-11)

In summary, Chapter 9 – III. "The Correction of Error" is saying:
Anytime we react to our fellow brothers and sisters here in this world as bodies, we are judging them to be something they are not. This is a perceptual error in need of correction. The only way to be free of this ego-perception is to give all judgment over to the Holy Spirit, Who knows the truth about us. We do this through making no assumptions about anyone—for we do not know who they truly are in Spirit. By so doing, we correct all forms of error that we look upon, simply by acknowledging the falsity we see. Seeing only the Holy Spirit within all others is the correction of all errors.

IV. The Holy Spirit's Plan of Forgiveness

"To forgive is to overlook. Look, then, beyond error and do not let your perception rest upon it, for you will believe what your perception holds." (T-9.IV.1:2-3)

"You do not understand how to overlook errors, or you would not make them." (T-9.IV.2:2)

"The way to undo them, therefore, is not of you but for you." (T-9.IV.2:7)

"The ego's plan is to have you see error clearly first, and then overlook it. Yet how can you overlook what you have made real? By seeing it clearly, you have made it real and cannot overlook it." (T-9.IV.4:4-6)

"Forgiveness through the Holy Spirit lies simply in looking beyond error from the beginning, and thus keeping it unreal for you." (T-9.IV.5:3)

"Fairy tales can be pleasant or fearful, but no one calls them true. Children may believe in them, and so, for a while, the tales are true for them." (T-9.IV.11:6-7)

"Reality has not gone in the meanwhile. The Second Coming is the awareness of reality, not its return." (T-9.IV.11:9-10)

"Behold, my child, reality is here. It belongs to you and me and God, and is perfectly satisfying to all of Us. Only this awareness heals because it is the awareness of truth." (T-9.IV.12:1-3)

In summary, Chapter 9 – IV. "The Holy Spirit's Plan of Forgiveness" is saying:
The plan forgiveness presents, is a simple one: overlook all errors we see with our bodily eyes in the world outside of us. To overlook the world of separation is to forgive it. Forgiveness then, is to merely forgive its "real-

CHAPTER 9—THE ACCEPTANCE OF THE ATONEMENT

ness." For the time being, we appear to be caught up in a child's fantasy world. We are in need of assistance in order to waken from this false reality. We do this by seeing it correctly. The ability to do this is not ours, but rather, it is done *for* us through the Holy Spirit's Help as a result of our choice to see it *differently*. The real world is not gone simply because we cannot see it. It but awaits our awareness of its presence. We become aware of God's Reality through forgiving the one we currently see now. This is the Holy Spirit's plan of forgiveness.

V. The Unhealed Healer

"Let us consider the unhealed healer more carefully now." (T-9.V.1:3)

"Every healer who searches fantasies for truth must be unhealed, because he does not know where to look for truth, and therefore does not have the answer to the problem of healing." (T-9.V.2:3)

"There is an advantage to bringing nightmares into awareness, but only to teach that they are not real, and that anything they contain is meaningless. The unhealed healer cannot do this because he does not believe it." (T-9.V.3:1-2)

"Nothing real has happened to the unhealed healer, and he must learn from his own teaching." (T-9.V.5:4)

"When God said, "Let there be light," there was light. Can you find light by analyzing darkness, as the psychotherapist does, or like the theologian, by acknowledging darkness in yourself and looking for a distant light to remove it, while emphasizing the distance?" (T-9.V.6:1-3)

"A therapist does not heal; *he lets healing be.*" (T-9.V.8:1)

"The Holy Spirit is the only Therapist. He makes healing clear in any situation in which He is the Guide. You can only let Him fulfill His function." (T-9.V.8:4-6)

"He will tell you exactly what to do to help anyone He sends to you for help, and will speak to him through you if you do not interfere." (T-9.V.8:8)

"As you awaken other minds to the Holy Spirit through Him, and not yourself, you will understand that you are not obeying the laws of this world." (T-9.V.8:12)

"This course offers a very direct and a very simple learning situation, and provides the Guide Who tells you what to do. If you do it, you will see that it works." (T-9.V.9:1-2)

"By following the right Guide, you will learn the simplest of all lessons: *By their fruits ye shall know them, and they shall know themselves.*" (T-9.V.9:5-6)

In summary, Chapter 9– V. "The Unhealed Healer" is saying:
Many of us like to analyze our problems, hashing them over and over to no end except to only conclude there is no conclusion. The pain remains and the situation goes on unhealed. We may attempt to enlist the help of others who claim to be professional healers—such as psychotherapists and religious leaders. However, many of these individuals do not know where true healing can be found and may only direct you in the same direction you have already been traveling. In order to heal, we must call on our Inner Therapist, the Holy Spirit. Our healing always involves His loving Word: That we are already healed and whole for we have never left the perfection of God's Kingdom and only dream a dream that this is so. In fact, it is a nightmare for most. We will not awaken through analyzing the nightmare. A nightmare is only dissipated through waking from it, and when we wake, we will no longer believe in its reality. We awaken through listening to our Inner Therapist Who directs us to clear away all mistaken beliefs about ourself and others. And we will know if we have done so by the loving actions and thoughts we have; the fruits we yield. The unhealed healer is merely the one who has not yet realized there is nothing in need of healing.

VI. The Acceptance of Your Brother

"How can you become increasingly aware of the Holy Spirit in you except by His effects?" (T-9.VI.1:1)

"If you inspire joy and others react to you with joy, even though you are not experiencing joy yourself there must be something in you that is capable of producing it." (T-9.VI.1:4)

"It seems to you that the Holy Spirit does not produce joy consistently in you only because you do not consistently arouse joy in others. Their reactions to you are your evaluations of His consistency." (T-9.VI.2:1-2)

"What you offer to your brother you offer to Him, because He cannot go beyond your offering in His giving. This is not because He limits His giving, but simply because you have limited your receiving." (T-9.VI.2:4-5)

CHAPTER 9—THE ACCEPTANCE OF THE ATONEMENT

"If your brothers are part of you, will you accept them?" (T-9.VI.3:1)

"If what you do to my brother you do to me, and if you do everything for yourself because we are part of you, everything we do belongs to you as well. Everyone God created is part of you and shares His glory with you." (T-9.VI.3:8-9)

"Wholeness is indivisible, but you cannot learn of your wholeness until you see it everywhere." (T-9.VI.4:6)

"Could you but accept one of them you would not want anything the world has to offer." (T-9.VI.7:5)

"Accept your brother in this world and accept nothing else, for in him you will find your creations because he created them with you. You will never know that you are co-creator with God until you learn that your brother is co-creator with you." (T-9.VI.7:8-9)

In summary, Chapter 9–VI. "The Acceptance of Your Brother" is saying:

What we give is what we will receive. This is an understood basic law of giving. Though everyone seems to understand this, we behave in ways towards each other that often reflect the desire for unhappiness. This can only mean one of two things: Either we prefer unhappiness, or we do not fully understand the law of giving after all. We will receive from others what we have given them, so let us give them only love. This will inspire joy in them because it is God's Will that we give what He has given us. Yet there are times we feel un-loving and un-joyful towards one another. How then is this overcome in order to maintain God's Will? We must learn to accept our brothers as part of us and choose only peace with them, lest we wage war upon our Self. Such wholeness cannot be learned until we see it in everyone. Once we truly accept our wholeness, we will move into a state of unity where the real world we co-created with each other exists. It is through acceptance of our brothers that we finally accept our Unity with God.

VII. The Two Evaluations

"God's Will is your salvation." (T-9.VII.1:1)

"Your brothers are everywhere. You do not have to seek far for salvation. Every minute and every second gives you a chance to save yourself. Do not lose these chances, not because they will not return, but because delay of joy is needless." (T-9.VII.1:4-7)

VII. The Two Evaluations

"It is perfectly obvious that if the Holy Spirit looks with love on all He perceives, He looks with love on you. His evaluation of you is based on His knowledge of what you are, and so He evaluates you truly." (T-9.VII.3:1-2)

"The ego is also in your mind, because you have accepted it there. Its evaluation of you, however, is the exact opposite of the Holy Spirit's, because the ego does not love you." (T-9.VII.3:4-5)

"You, then, have two conflicting evaluations of yourself in your mind, and they cannot both be true." (T-9.VII.4:1)

"The ego will attack your motives as soon as they become clearly out of accord with its perception of you. This is when it will shift abruptly from suspiciousness to viciousness, since its uncertainty is increased." (T-9.VII.4:6-7)

"If you choose to see yourself as unloving you will not be happy." (T-9.VII.5:1)

"You cannot evaluate an insane belief system from within it." (T-9.VII.6:1)

"You can only go beyond it, look back from a point where sanity exists and *see the contrast*." (T-9.VII.6:3)

"Whenever you question your value, say: *God Himself is incomplete without me*. Remember this when the ego speaks, and you will not hear it." (T-9.VII.8:1-3)

"You do not want anything else." (T-9.VII.8:6)

In summary, Chapter 9– VII. "The Two Evaluations" is saying:
We have two voices within our minds, each defining us in diametrically opposed ways. The ego would have us believe we are vicious creatures, who are in constant competition with one another, striving for love and happiness. The Holy Spirit tells us that we are a part of All That Is, and that to strive for love and happiness is insane for we already contain all the love and happiness in existence. His definition of us is so lofty, we can scarcely grasp even a faint hint of what it means to be a part of God's Identity. When we find ourselves believing in the ego's definition of us, we can dispel its untruth by returning to the truth: God Himself is incomplete without us, and so how can we, who complete God Himself, feel the need to strive to be anything more? And with this thought we will have let the one true evaluation of ourself *be* true and the ego's voice will be muted. The world then, will shift to accommodate our

CHAPTER 9 — THE ACCEPTANCE OF THE ATONEMENT

new self-perception; and what we will see, is beyond any evaluation our ego could ever conceive of. We will want nothing else. There will no longer be two evaluations, for we are only One Identity.

VIII. Grandeur versus Grandiosity

"Grandeur is of God, and only of Him. Therefore it is in you." (T-9.VIII.1:1-2)

"We said before that the ego vacillates between suspiciousness and viciousness. It remains suspicious as long as you despair of yourself. It shifts to viciousness when you decide not to tolerate self-abasement and seek relief." (T-9.VIII.2:7-9)

"The ego does not understand the difference between grandeur and grandiosity, because it sees no difference between miracle impulses and the ego-alien beliefs of its own." (T-9.VIII.3:1)

"Its profound sense of vulnerability renders it incapable of judgment except in terms of attack." (T-9.VIII.3:3)

"If you accept its offer of grandiosity it will attack immediately." (T-9.VIII.3:5)

"The ego is immobilized in the presence of God's grandeur, because His grandeur establishes your freedom." (T-9.VIII.4:1)

"Grandeur is totally without illusions, and because it is real it is compellingly convincing." (T-9.VIII.4:3)

"You made grandiosity and are afraid of it because it is a form of attack, but your grandeur is of God Who created it out of His Love." (T-9.VIII.4:8)

"It is easy to distinguish between grandeur and grandiosity, because love is returned and pride is not." (T-9.VIII.8:1)

"You did not establish your value and it needs no defense." (T-9.VIII.11:2)

In summary, Chapter 9–VIII. "Grandeur versus Grandiosity" is saying:

Grandeur is God's definition of us; it is to know we are part of one Grand Being at one with All Creation. Grandiosity is the ego's definition of us; a small self in need of proving its worth to others through competition, attack, and conflict. It is not arrogance to think we are indestructible eternal beings—it is arrogance to think we could ever be anything less. And to know our grandeur, is to know we need not prove our perfection to anyone; it is inherent in Who We Are. As we accept our united grandeur, we thus accept the Atonement, which undoes the ego and this world of pain and suffering entirely.

CHAPTER 10
THE IDOLS OF SICKNESS

Introduction

"Nothing beyond yourself can make you fearful or loving, because nothing is beyond you. Time and eternity are both in your mind, and will conflict until you perceive time solely as a means to regain eternity. You cannot do this as long as you believe that anything happening to you is caused by factors outside yourself." (T-10.in.1:1-3)

"God created nothing beside you and nothing beside you exists, for you are part of Him. What except Him can exist?" (T-10.in.2:1-2)

"Your holy mind establishes everything that happens to you. Every response you make to everything you perceive is up to you, because your mind determines your perception of it." (T-10.in.2:6-7)

"God does not change His Mind about you, for He is not uncertain of Himself." (T-10.in.3:1)

"When anything threatens your peace of mind, ask yourself, "Has God changed His Mind about me?" Then accept His decision, for it is indeed changeless, and refuse to change your mind about yourself." (T-10.in.3:9-10)

In summary, Chapter 9 – Introduction is saying:
We often feel powerless against the happenings of our daily lives—especially when it is something we do not prefer. When such times come, it is paramount we remember it is but a lesson in forgiveness; a part of our mind still in need of healing. Then we reclaim our power, our ability to change our thoughts about what we see. Every response we make determines our future experience. Therefore, let our hearts and minds join in thoughts of peace about all things, for we remain as God created us. We are at war with no one and nothing, for all things are Us. I am you and you are me. We are them, and they are us. Do not resist the changeless Union that WE ARE, for God Himself has Willed it to be, and what can change His Will?

I. At Home in God

"You are at home in God, dreaming of exile but perfectly capable of awakening to reality. It is your decision to do so? You recognize from

II. The Decision to Forget

your own experience that what you see in dreams you think is real while you are asleep. Yet the instant you waken you realize that everything that seemed to happen in the dream did not happen at all. You do not think this strange, even though all the laws of what you awaken to were violated while you slept. Is it not possible that you merely shifted from one dream to another, without really waking?" (T-10.I.2:1-6)

"Would you bother to reconcile what happened in conflicting dreams, or would you dismiss both together if you discovered that reality is in accord with neither? You do not remember being awake." (T-10.I.3:1-3)

"You will remember everything the instant you desire it wholly, for if to desire wholly is to create, you will have willed away the separation, returning your mind simultaneously to your Creator and your creations." (T-10.I.4:1)

"Dreams will be impossible because you will want only truth, and being at last your will, it will be yours." (T-10.I.4:3)

In summary, Chapter 10 – I. "At Home in God" is saying:
We have never left God's Heavenly Mind, yet we dream that we are someplace else and that this is our home. We do not remember what it's like to be anywhere except here, within this dream. In order to waken from it, we must embrace the idea that nothing that happens here has any real effects, though the experiences are real indeed and we are learning real lessons. Just like our sleeping dreams, we are affected emotionally by what we perceive. And just like our sleeping dreams, all it takes is the realization, the authentic belief, that the dream is not real, and all its effects are gone. Desire to waken then, with your whole heart and you will have healed your mind of all your dreams. Then this world will hold no power over you any longer; for dreaming is impossible once you waken to the acceptance you are, and have always been, at Home in God.

II. The Decision to Forget

"You are fearful because you have forgotten. And you have replaced your knowledge by an awareness of dreams because you are afraid of your dissociation, not of what you have dissociated." (T-10.II.1:4-5)

"Offer the Holy Spirit only your willingness to remember, for He retains the knowledge of God and of yourself for you, waiting for your acceptance." (T-10.II.2:3)

CHAPTER 10 – THE IDOLS OF SICKNESS

"To remember is merely to restore to your mind what is already there. You do not make what you remember; you merely accept again what is already there but was rejected." (T-10.II.3:1-2)

"All attack is Self attack. It cannot be anything else. Arising from your own decision not to be what you are, it is an attack on your identification. Attack is thus the way in which your identification is lost, because when you attack, you must have forgotten what you are." (T-10.II.5:1-4)

"If you realized the complete havoc this makes of your peace of mind you could not make such an insane decision. You make it only because you still believe it can get you something you want." (T-10.II.6:1-2)

"By deciding against your reality, you have made yourself vigilant against God and His Kingdom." (T-10.II.6:5)

In summary, Chapter 10 – II. "The Decision to Forget" is saying:
We have forgotten the real world through dissociating from it; the decision to forget it completely. Now, the world we see as its replacement commands our total and undivided attention, and as far as our ego is concerned, IS the real world. Because of this disconnection from the truth, the suggestion that there is another dimension beyond this one, is very frightening to the ego, because it cannot conceive of such a place and what the ego does not understand, it automatically fears. Therefore, in order to remember our true Home, we must make way for it, through *acknowledging* its existence, *accepting* it as the truth, and finally *allowing* it to be. To do this here and now in our daily lives, we must apply these three simple steps to every brother we meet or think of. First, *acknowledge* we are Light, second, *accept* that only this is true about us, and lastly, *allow* this identity to be the truth. Through this 3-step mindset of "acknowledge, accept and allow," all forms of attack will disappear, for you are now willing to remember the truth. Your vigilance will be *for God and His Kingdom* rather than *against it*. You will have reversed your decision to forget the truth of our Unity, through determination to remember it.

III. The God of Sickness

"You have not attacked God and you do love Him." (T-10.III.1:1)

"When you think you are attacking yourself, it is a sure sign that you hate what you *think* you are. And this, and only this, can be attacked by you. What you think you are can be very hateful, and what this strange

III. The God of Sickness

image makes you do can be very destructive. Yet the destruction is no more real than the image, although those who make idols do worship them." (T-10.III.1:4-7)

"What Comforter can there be for the sick children of God except His power through you?" (T-10.III.2:1)

"God's remaining Communication Link with all His children joins them together, and them to Him. To be aware of this is to heal them because it is the awareness that no one is separate, and so no one is sick." (T-10.III.2:6-7)

"Do not side with sickness in the presence of a Son of God even if he believes in it, for your acceptance of God in him acknowledges the Love of God he has forgotten." (T-10.III.3:4)

"To believe a Son of God is sick is to worship the same idol he does." (T-10.III.4:1)

"Sickness is idolatry, because it is the belief that power can be taken from you." (T-10.III.4:4)

"And that is exactly what the ego does perceive in a Son of God; a sick god, self-created, self-sufficient, very vicious and very vulnerable." (T-10.III.4:7)

"Are you really afraid of losing this?" (T-10.III.4:10)

"God's Son knows no idols, but he does know his Father." (T-10.III.6:2)

"When a brother is sick it is because he is not asking for peace, and therefore does not know he has it. The acceptance of peace is the denial of illusion and sickness is an illusion." (T-10.III.7:1-2)

"Very simply, then, you may believe you are afraid of nothingness, but you are really afraid of nothing. And in that awareness you are healed." (T-10.III.9:1-2)

"Honor is not due to illusions, for to honor them is to honor nothing." (T-10.III.10:9)

"You can give up the god of sickness for your brothers; in fact, you would have to do so if you give him up for yourself." (T-10.III.11:4)

CHAPTER 10—THE IDOLS OF SICKNESS

In summary, Chapter 10 – III. "The God of Sickness" is saying:

We cannot unmake ourselves and become something other than the Perfection God created us to be. Yet, this is exactly what the ego thinks it has done, and now we think we have become false gods; bodies or idols, made from a mind that has become sick. Sickness is merely the idea of separation. A mind that thinks itself separate from other minds, will perceive all living things as separate from itself. This is sickness, and what the mind sees have now become false idols. And yet, we must remember that what God created cannot be changed. What we see is not only untrue, but *nothing*. In order to heal the idea of separation, we must ask for peace to replace what we have tried to make of ourselves. Separation is attack, and peace is Union. Honor only our Union and not the illusionary persona of bodily separation in your brothers and you will give up the god of sickness for them and yourself as well.

IV. The End of Sickness

"Sickness and perfection are irreconcilable. If God created you perfect, you are perfect." (T-10.IV.1:3-4)

"Reality can dawn only on an unclouded mind." (T-10.IV.2:1)

"To know reality must involve the willingness to judge unreality for what it is. To overlook nothingness is merely to judge it correctly, and because of your ability to evaluate it truly, to let it go. Knowledge cannot dawn on a mind full of illusions, because truth and illusions are irreconcilable." (T-10.IV.2:3-5)

"Oneness cannot be divided." (T-10.IV.3:3)

"The miracle is the act of a Son of God who has laid aside all false gods, and calls on his brothers to do likewise. It is an act of faith, because it is the recognition that his brother can do it. It is a call to the Holy Spirit in his mind, a call that is strengthened by joining. Because the miracle worker has heard God's Voice, he strengthens It in a sick brother by weakening his belief in sickness, which he does not share. The power of one mind can shine into another, because all the lamps of God were lit by the same spark." (T-10.IV.7:1-5)

"In many only the spark remains, for the Great Rays are obscured." (T-10.IV.8:1)

"If you but see the little spark you will learn of the greater light, for the Rays are there unseen. Perceiving the spark will heal, but knowing the light will create." (T-10.IV.8:3-4)

"Put all your faith in it, and God Himself will answer you." (T-10.IV.8:7)

In summary, Chapter 10 – IV. "The End of Sickness" is saying:
The end of sickness is the end of our belief in illusions. It is to believe only in our joint Perfection in God's Love. It is to believe it is impossible that we be divided. In order to know this truly in our hearts, we must judge the world correctly; we must lay aside all thoughts about the effects this world seems to have on us. We must focus our attention only on the spark within the body and not the body itself. All its works are meaningless in the light of the Great Rays it obscures from our bodily sight. If we are willing to at least see the spark, God Himself will show us our brother's Great Rays; the truth of his being and your own. And this way of seeing will bring the end of sickness forever.

V. The Denial of God

"The rituals of the god of sickness are strange and very demanding. Joy is never permitted, for depression is the sign of allegiance to him. Depression means that you have forsworn God. Many are afraid of blasphemy, but they do not understand what it means. They do not realize that to deny God is to deny their own Identity, and in this sense the wages of sin is death." (T-10.IV.1:1-5)

"Do not forget however, that to deny God will inevitably result in projection, and you will believe that others and not yourself have done this to you." (T-10.IV.2:1)

"Do not attribute your denial of joy to them, or you cannot see the spark in them that would bring joy to you. It is the denial of the spark that brings depression, for whenever you see your brothers without it, you are denying God." (T-10.IV.2:4-5)

"Allegiance to the denial of God is the ego's religion." (T-10.IV.3:1)

"Blasphemy, then, is *self*-destructive, not God-destructive. It means that you are willing not to know yourself in order to be sick." (T-10.IV.3:5-6)

"Son of God, you have not sinned, but you have been much mistaken. Yet this can be corrected and God will help you, knowing that you could not sin against Him." (T-10.IV.6:1-2)

"You do not realize how much you have denied yourself, and how

CHAPTER 10 — THE IDOLS OF SICKNESS — ILLUSIONS

much God, in His Love, would not have it so. Yet He would not interfere with you, because He would not know His Son if he were not free." (T-10.IV.10:1-2)

"If God knows His children as wholly sinless, it is blasphemous to perceive them as guilty. If God knows His children as wholly without pain, it is blasphemous to perceive suffering anywhere. If God knows His children to be wholly joyous, it is blasphemous to feel depressed. All of these illusions, and the many other forms that blasphemy may take, are refusals to accept creation as it is. If God created His Son perfect, that is how you must learn to see him to learn of his reality. And as part of the Sonship, that is how you must see yourself to learn of yours." (T-10.IV.12:1-6)

"If you would remember eternity, you must look only on the eternal. If you allow yourself to become preoccupied with the temporal, you are living in time. As always, your choice is determined by what you value. Time and eternity cannot both be real, because they contradict each other. If you will accept only what is timeless as real, you will begin to understand eternity and make it yours." (T-10.IV.14:6-9)

In summary, Chapter 10 – V. "The Denial of God" is saying:
Whenever we become immersed in the dramas of this world, we are denying God, Who knows no pain, suffering or depression. To experience these things, means we have stepped out of eternity and into the realm of time—a false place where the impossible seems possible. It is impossible for us to die or be harmed in any way. To believe in death and suffering is blasphemous because it flies in the face of our truth as eternal Sons of God. We Who can never die, suffer pain or loss must come to believe in only our eternal nature. It is blasphemous to believe we are less. No one has ever done anything to us; we have experienced all things at our own hand, as we projected our own Self-denial outward and hence received what we gave. Heal this now and withdraw all belief in the god of sickness; the ego, whom we project outward as a false idol, in form of the body. Cease to deny the spark of God within your brothers and He will step forward and carry you into His eternal Kingdom where you will know only joy. Let go of all idols of sickness, and you cease to deny God.

Nothing here is Real —
Nothing eternal here
except what God created

CHAPTER 11
GOD OR THE EGO

Introduction

"Either God or the ego is insane. If you will examine the evidence on both sides fairly, you will realize this must be true." (T-11.in.1:1-2)

"Each is internally consistent, but they are diametrically opposed in all respects so that partial allegiance is impossible." (T-11.in.1:4)

"If you made the ego, how can the ego have made you? The authority problem is still the only source of conflict, because the ego was made out of the wish of God's Son to father Him. The ego, then, is nothing more than a delusional system in which you made your own father." (T-11.in.2:2-4)

"It sounds insane when it is stated with perfect honesty, but the ego never looks on what it does with perfect honesty." (T-11.in.2:6)

"Remember the Rays that are unseen." (T-11.in.3:3)

"The closer you come to the foundation of the ego's thought system, the darker and more obscure becomes the way. Yet even the little spark in your mind is enough to lighten it. Bring this light fearlessly with you, and bravely hold it up to the foundation of the ego's thought system." (T-11.in.3:5-7)

"My brother, you are part of God and part of me." (T-11.in.4:1)

"I give you the lamp and I will go with you. You will not take this journey alone." (T-11.in.4:5-6)

In summary, Chapter 11 – Introduction is saying:

"The ego cannot be our father, for we invented it, and what we made, cannot turn around and claim to have made us. We come from One Source: God the Father of all Creation Whose Great Rays of Light shine within us. If this is true, and what God has created cannot change itself into something other than what He created it to be, then we cannot be an ego. One or the other must be true. Are we part of God or the ego? The answer appears quite obvious when looked upon with the light of true understanding.

CHAPTER 11—GOD OR THE EGO

I. The Gifts of Fatherhood

"You dwell in the Mind of God with your brother, for God Himself did not will to be alone." (T-11.I.1:6)

"To be alone is to be separated from infinity, but how can this be if infinity has no end?" (T-11.I.2:1)

"If you were not part of God, His Will would not be unified. Is this conceivable?" (T-11.I.3:1-2)

"The laws of the universe do not permit contradiction. What holds for God holds for you. If you believe you are absent from God, you will believe that He is absent from you." (T-11.I.5:1-3)

"God has given you a place in His Mind that is yours forever." (T-11.I.6:1)

"Could any part of God be without His Love, and could any part of His Love be contained? God is your heritage, because His one gift is Himself." (T-11.I.7:1-2)

"You are asked to trust the Holy Spirit only because He speaks for you. He is the Voice for God, but never forget that God did not will to be alone. He shares His Will with you; He does not thrust it upon you." (T-11.I.11:1-3)

"Blessed are you who learn that to hear the Will of your Father is to know your own." (T-11.I.11:6)

"That is why healing is the beginning of the recognition that your will is His." (T-11.I.11:9)

In summary, Chapter 11 – I. "The Gifts of Fatherhood" is saying:
The greatest gift from God, is that we exist, and will continue to exist as part of Him for all eternity. God specifically created each and every one of us and He makes no mistakes. We were brought into being *on purpose*, and therefore, we each must be very important, wanted, and desired by God. God's Will is that we come to realize this is true; that we come to truly *believe* we are treasured by God as His holy child. Our healing begins with the recognition of our true relationship with Him as our Creator-Father. The gift of His Fatherhood is our Union with Him.

II. The Invitation to Healing

"If sickness is separation, the decision to heal and to be healed is the first step toward recognizing what you truly want. Every attack is a step away from this, and every healing thought brings it closer." (T-11.II.1:1-2)

"Every healing thought that you accept, either from your brother or in your own mind, teaches you that you are God's Son. In every hurtful thought you hold, wherever you perceive it, lies the denial of God's Fatherhood and of your Sonship." (T-11.II.2:5-6)

"Healing is a sign that you want to make whole. And this willingness opens your ears to the Voice of the Holy Spirit, Whose healing message is wholeness." (T-11.II.4:1-2)

"The Holy Spirit cannot speak to an unwelcoming host, because He will not be heard. The Eternal Guest remains, but His Voice grows faint in alien company." (T-11.II.5:1-2)

"Think like Him ever so slightly, and the little spark becomes a blazing light that fills your mind so that He becomes your only Guest. Whenever you ask the ego to enter, you lessen His welcome." (T-11.II. 5:4-5)

"Would you be hostage to the ego or host to God? You will accept only whom you invite." (T-11.II.7:1-2)

"The Holy Spirit is there, although He cannot help you without your invitation. And the ego is nothing, whether you invite it in or not. Real freedom depends on welcoming reality, and of your guests only the Holy Spirit is real. Know, then, Who abides with you merely by recognizing what is there already, and do not be satisfied with imaginary comforters, for the Comforter of God is in you." (T-11.II.7:5-8)

In summary, Chapter 11 – II. "The Invitation to Healing" is saying:
The invitation to healing is simply any thought that is loving, peaceful and without judgment. It is a thought of unity with one another. Such thoughts are invitations, because healing does not come from us alone, but *through us from God*. God's Will is that we know our wholeness, but if our minds are preoccupied with thoughts of separation, which are thoughts opposite to love, peace and non-judgment, then our mind is closed to the Voice of the Holy Spirit. Move your mind ever so slightly in the direction of peace and you will

CHAPTER 11—GOD OR THE EGO

be released from the bondage of the ego's thinking. Though always present, the Holy Spirit will not barge into our minds uninvited. He must first be welcomed through our willingness and desire to be like Him. We express this desire through recognizing the spark of God within each other. The invitation to healing is any thought that promotes all-inclusive Love.

III. From Darkness to Light

"God is very quiet, for there is no conflict in Him. Conflict is the root of all evil, for being blind it does not see whom it attacks. Yet it always attacks the Son of God, and the Son of God is you." T-11.III.1:6-8)

"God's Son is indeed in need of comfort, for he knows not what he does, believing his will is not his own. The Kingdom is his, and yet he wanders homeless." (T-11.III. 2:1-2)

"O my child, if you knew what God wills for you, your joy would be complete!" (T-11.III. 3:1)

"The way is not hard, but it is very different. Yours is the way of pain, of which God knows nothing." (T-11.III. 4:1-2)

"Walk in light and do not see the dark companions, for they are not fit companions for the Son of God, who was created of light and in light. The Great Light always surrounds you and shines out from you." (T-11.III. 4:6-7)

"God hides nothing from His Son, even though His Son would hide himself." (T-11.III. 5:1)

"When you wander, you but undertake a journey that is not real. The dark companions, the dark way, are all illusions. Turn toward the light, for the little spark in you is part of a light so great that it can sweep you out of all darkness forever." (T-11.III. 5:4-6)

"Do not be deceived by the dark comforters, and never let them enter the mind of God's Son, for they have no place in His temple." (T-11.III. 6:2)

"Only God's Comforter can comfort you. In the quiet of His temple, He waits to give you the peace that is yours. Give His peace, that you may enter the temple and find it waiting for you." (T-11.III.7:1-3)

"In your mind you can accept the whole Sonship and bless it with the light your Father gave it. Then you will be worthy to dwell in the temple with Him, because it is your will not to be alone." (T-11.III. 8:1-2)

In summary, Chapter 11 – III. "From Darkness to Light" is saying:
Thoughts of conflict are "dark thoughts" and therefore blind us from God's Light within one another. Conflict is called the "root of all evil" because when we see each other as bodies, we are not seeing Who We Are as part of God's One Light. The body is a deception of the ego to keep our minds in the dark about our true Identity as part of God's Sonship. We are encouraged to not see these "dark companions" but know instead that God walks with us within each body we see. The Light of God is always surrounding us and within us. We can know this Light when we still our thoughts about the world and simply allow ourselves to rest in quiet, for God Himself is quiet; there is no conflict in His mind—He has no thoughts about bodies and their works. Here is the temple in which we desire to reside. Here we will know we are never alone, for in God's quiet we will witness to the truth of our Oneness with all creation. We move from darkness to light when we engage our minds with thoughts of our Unity instead of as separate bodies.

IV. The Inheritance of God's Son

"Never forget that the Sonship is your salvation, for the Sonship is your Self." (T-11.IV.1:1)

"You are not saved *from* anything, but you are saved *for* glory." (T-11.IV. 1:4)

"Yet if you hate part of your Self all your understanding is lost, because you are looking on what God created as yourself without love." (T-11. IV. 1:7)

"Can the Son deny the Father without believing that the Father has denied him?" (T-11.IV. 2:2)

"Therefore, look only to the power that God gave to save you, remembering that it is yours because it is His, and join with your brothers in His peace." (T-11.IV. 2:5)

"Your peace lies in its limitlessness. Limit the peace you share, and your Self must be unknown to you." (T-11.IV.3:1-2)

"*Only you can deprive yourself of anything*. Do not oppose this realization for it is truly the beginning of the dawn of light." {T-11.IV.4:1-2)

"This is a crucial step in the reawakening. The beginning phases of this reversal are often quite painful, for as blame is withdrawn from without, there is a strong tendency to harbor it within." (T-11.IV.4:4-6)

CHAPTER 11—GOD OR THE EGO

"If your brothers are part of you and you blame them for your deprivation, you are blaming yourself." (T-11.IV.5:1)

"That is why blame must be undone, not seen elsewhere. Lay it to yourself and you cannot know yourself, for only the ego blames at all. Self-blame is therefore ego identification, and as much an ego defense as blaming others. You cannot enter God's Presence if you attack His Son." (T-11.IV.5:3-6)

"Peace be unto you who rest in God, and in whom the whole Sonship rests." (T-11.IV.8:4)

In summary, Chapter 11 – IV. "The Inheritance of God's Son" is saying:

"Your inheritance from God is everything He created along with you. This includes all of the other souls in existence—they are part of you, and you are a part of them. To realize this, and accept it as something you want, is to have accepted your inheritance. Our ego wants to maintain our separation and thinks it preposterous that there be no one to blame for its unhappiness. It endlessly seeks ways to blame others or ourselves for what it perceives as unfair treatment. We are One Self, and to blame another is to blame an aspect of ourselves. There is no difference. Self-blame is the same as blaming another. How do we get out of this circle of blame? Blame no one and nothing. Only the ego places blame for its unhappiness, for it would never see anyone as guiltless (bodiless/unseparated from you). Rather, allow your mind to rest in the peace of the present moment. There you will find the whole Sonship waiting for you with love. Claim them as your inheritance as part of God's Son rather than rejecting them through blame and you will find your true treasure.

V. The "Dynamics" of the Ego

"The "dynamics" of the ego will be our lesson for a while, for we must look first at this to see beyond it, since you have made it real. We will undo this error quietly together, and then look beyond it to truth." (T-11.V.1:5-6)

"Let us begin this lesson in "ego dynamics" by understanding that the term itself does not mean anything." (T-11.V.3:1)

""Dynamics" implies the power to do something, and the whole separation fallacy lies in the belief that the ego has the power to do anything. The ego is fearful to you because you believe this. Yet the truth is very simple:

V. The "Dynamics" of the Ego

"All power is of God. What is not of Him has no power to do anything." (T-11.V.3:3-7)

"You can surely regard a delusional system without fear, for it cannot have any effects if its source is not real." (T-11.V.4:2)

"You must recognize that the last thing the ego wishes you to realize is that you are afraid of it." (T-11.V.8:1)

"Without this belief you would not listen to it at all." (T-11.V.8:4)

"Minimizing fear, but not its undoing, is the ego's constant effort, and is indeed a skill at which it is very ingenious. How can it preach separation without upholding it through fear, and would you listen to it if you recognized this is what it is doing?" (T-11.V.9:2-3)

"Your recognition that whatever seems to separate you from God is only fear, regardless of the form it takes and quite apart from how the ego wants you to experience it, is therefore the basic ego threat." (T-11.V.10:1)

"Only by learning what fear is can you finally learn to distinguish the possible from the impossible and the false from the true." (T-11.V.11:2)

"Recognize only that the ego's goal, which you have pursued so diligently, has merely brought you fear, and it becomes difficult to maintain that fear is happiness." (T-11.V.12:5)

"For only the insane would choose fear in place of love, and only the insane could believe that love can be gained by attack." (T-11.V.12:9)

"The ego analyzes; the Holy Spirit accepts. The appreciation of wholeness comes only through acceptance, for to analyze means to break down or to separate out." (T-11.V.13:1-2)

"Every brother you meet becomes a witness for Christ or for the ego, depending on what you perceive in him." (T-11.V.18:1)

"Every brother has the power to release you, if you choose to be free." (T-11.V.18:4)

"If he speaks not of Christ to you, you spoke not of Christ to him. You hear but your own voice, and if Christ speaks through you, you will hear Him." (T-11.V.18:6-7)

CHAPTER 11—GOD OR THE EGO

In summary, Chapter 11 – V. "The "Dynamics" of the Ego" is saying:
The ego's goal is always separation. It lives only because we think we are separate bodies. The ego knows that once we understand this, we will cease to fear it and its whole existence will be undone. Our fear of Unity and love holds the ego in place. One fear-tactic the ego uses to preserve itself, is to set our minds to analyzing the "whys" and the "what for" in every relationship we have. This seems to diminish our ego-fear, for we think we will find a logical explanation for our problems. This is not so. And once we give up such analyzations, we also give up interest in the ego's fear-based agenda. Every relationship we have, no matter how brief the contact, can become an open door through which we walk away from the ego. But this all depends on how we see them. If they seem hostile, or we have a long history of conflict with them, we have not given them our peace. Speak only of peace to them, and we will hear Christ speak of peace to us in return. And the "dynamics" of the ego are undone.

VI. Waking to Redemption

"It is impossible not to believe what you see, but it is equally impossible to see what you do not believe." (T-11.VI.1:1)

"It is not until beliefs are fixed that perceptions stabilize." (T-11.VI.1:3)

"This course is perfectly clear. If you do not see it clearly, it is because you are interpreting against it, and therefore do not believe it. And since belief determines perception, you do not perceive what it means and therefore do not accept it." (T-11.VI.3:1-3)

"I am leading you to a new kind of experience that you will become less and less willing to deny." (T-11.VI.3:6)

"You live in me because you live in God. And everyone lives in you, as you live in everyone. Can you, then, perceive unworthiness in a brother and not perceive it in yourself? And can you perceive it in yourself and not perceive it in God?" (T-11.VI.4:2-5)

"For we ascend unto the Father together, as it was in the beginning, is now and ever shall be, for such is the nature of God's Son as his Father created him." (T-11.VI.4:9)

"Resurrection must compel your allegiance gladly, because it is the symbol of joy. Its whole compelling power lies in the fact that it represents what you want to be. The freedom to leave behind everything that hurts you and humbles you and frightens you cannot be thrust

VII. The Condition of Reality

upon you, but it can be offered you through the grace of God." (T-11.VI.6:1-3)

"You have nailed yourself to a cross, and placed a crown of thorns upon your own head. Yet you cannot crucify God's Son, for the Will of God cannot die. His Son has been redeemed from his own crucifixion, and you cannot assign to death whom God has given eternal life. The dream of crucifixion still lies heavy on your eyes, but what you see in dreams is not reality. While you perceive the Son of God as crucified, you are asleep. And as long as you believe that you can crucify him, you are only having nightmares." (T-11.VI.8:1-6)

"God's Son is saved. Bring only this awareness to the Sonship and you will have a part in the redemption as valuable as mine." (T-11.VI.10:1-2)

"There is no order of difficulty in miracles because all of God's Sons are of equal value, and their equality is their oneness." (T-11.VI.10:5)

"To God all things are possible." (T-11.VI.10:8)

In summary, Chapter 11 – VI. "Waking to Redemption" is saying:
The ego says, "Seeing is believing." The Holy Spirit says, "Believing is seeing." Our beliefs are the seeds of our experience in this world. They spawn what we will see. Therefore, believing is seeing, not the other way around. However, what we see does not make a fundamental change until our beliefs become fixed. We will only see what we can accept as true, according to our beliefs. In truth, we live in God, and He in us. Are we ready to see this oneness? Are our beliefs such that, seeing this oneness would not cause us fear? And yet, God promises that one day we will indeed truly believe the words in this course. We are currently dreaming a dream we are trapped within these bodies, doomed to suffer, and die. Yet, this is not so, for what God has created immortal, eternal and everlasting in His joy remains as it ever was. We are not crucified and have not crucified. We are awake and redeemed from our nightmares, but have only to believe it, to see it—and as we gradually accept belief in our Oneness, we waken to our redemption.

VII. The Condition of Reality

"God created only the eternal, and everything you see is perishable. Therefore, there must be another world that you do not see." (T-11.VII.1:2-3)

CHAPTER 11—GOD OR THE EGO

"The real world can actually be perceived. All that is necessary is a willingness to perceive nothing else. For if you perceive both good and evil, you are accepting both the false and the true and making no distinction between them." (T-11.VII.2:6-8)

"The ego may see some good, but never only good." (T-11.VII.3:1)

"It does not reject goodness entirely, for that you could not accept." (T-11.VII.3:3)

"The perception of goodness is not knowledge, but the denial of the opposite of goodness enables you to recognize a condition in which opposites do not exist. And this is the condition of knowledge." (T-11.VII.4:1-2)

"To believe that you can perceive the real world is to believe that you can know yourself." (T-11.VII.4:7)

"The real world is all that the Holy Spirit has saved for you out of what you have made, and to perceive only this is salvation, because it is the recognition that reality is only what is true." (T-11.VII.4:9)

In summary, Chapter 11 – VII. "The Condition of Reality" is saying: "Only what is eternal is real. Yet, everything we see around us is degrading and disintegrating even as our eyes rest upon it. We are looking at an "un-real" world then and would indeed like to see the real one—the eternal one—God created for, and with us. Since beliefs create our experience, we must give up belief in this reality in order to see the true reality that lies beyond this one. This does not mean we walk around pretending we do not see what we are currently seeing; it is to see it, and simply know it is not the truth. It is to "Know Thyself;" to know beyond a doubt, you are not a body, but a being of Love and Light, unified with All That Is. Then you will have met the condition for seeing God's Reality.

VIII. The Problem and the Answer

"This is a very simple course. Perhaps you do not feel you need a course which, in the end, teaches that only reality is true. But do you believe it? When you perceive the real world, you will recognize that you did not believe it." (T-11.VIII.1:1-4)

"Do not make the mistake of believing that you understand what you perceive, for its meaning is lost to you." (T-11.VIII.2:3)

VIII. The Problem and the Answer

"You do not know the meaning of anything you perceive. Not one thought you hold is wholly true. The recognition of this is your firm beginning. You are not misguided; you have accepted no guide at all." (T-11.VIII.3:1-4)

"Perceptions are learned, and you are not without a Teacher. Yet your willingness to learn of Him depends on your willingness to question everything you learned of yourself, for you who learned amiss should not be your own teacher." (T-11.VIII.3:7-8)

"You made the problem God has answered. Ask yourself, therefore, but one simple question: *"Do I want the problem or do I want the answer?* (T-11.VIII.4:4-6)

"You may complain that this course is not sufficiently specific for you to understand and use. Yet perhaps you have not done what it specifically advocates. This is not a course in the play of ideas, but in their practical application. Nothing could be more specific than to be told that if you ask you will receive." (T-11.VIII.5:1-4)

"The Holy Spirit will give you only what is yours, and will take nothing in return. For what is yours is everything, and you share it with God." (T-11.VIII.6:1-2)

"Beautiful child of God, you are asking only for what I promised you." (T-11.VIII.8:1)

"Do not, then, be deceived in your brother, and see only his loving thoughts as his reality, for by denying that his mind is split you will heal yours." (T-11.VIII.9:2)

"In the real world there is no sickness, for there is no separation and no division. Only loving thoughts are recognized, and because no one is without your help, the Help of God goes with you everywhere." (T-11.VIII.10:1-2)

"Do not accept your brother's variable perception of himself for his split mind is yours, and you will not accept your healing without his." (T-11.VIII.11:1)

"Brother, we heal together as we live together and love together." (T-11.VIII.11:4)

"If you perceive offense in a brother pluck the offense from your mind, for you are offended by Christ and are deceived in Him." (T-11.VIII.12:1)

CHAPTER 11 — GOD OR THE EGO

"Would you not exchange your fears for truth, if the exchange is yours for the asking? For if God is not deceived in you, you can be deceived only in yourself." (T-11.VIII.15:1-2)

"When you perceive yourself without deceit, you will accept the real world in place of the false one you have made. And then your Father will lean down to you and take the last step for you, by raising you unto Himself." (T-11.VIII.15:4-5)

In summary, Chapter 11 – VIII. "The Problem and the Answer" is saying:

"Our only problem is the ego's perception of our separation from one another. The Answer to this problem, is the Holy Spirit, Who sees only our Unity. We need to make the conscious choice to see only through the eyes of the Holy Spirit and we allow our only problem to be corrected for us. When we feel our peace disturbed, we have only to remind ourselves we are seeing incorrectly and then allow our vision to be corrected through asking the simple question: "Do I want the problem, or do I want the answer?" Choosing the Answer is what will heal our minds and allow us to perceive one another without the veil of the ego covering our eyes. The bodies we see, and all our problems associated with them will become meaningless, as we choose God over the ego as our reality. He then will take the final step for us, by taking our outstretched hand and lifting us up unto Himself. The problem is separation, and the Answer is God's Unity. Always, we are choosing between only two things: God or the ego.

CHAPTER 12
THE HOLY SPIRIT'S CURRICULUM

I. The Judgment of the Holy Spirit

"You have been told not to make error real, and the way to do this is very simple." (T-12.I.1:1)

"If you decide that someone is really trying to attack you or desert you or enslave you, you will respond as if he had actually done so, having made his error real to you. To interpret error is to give it power, and having done this you will overlook truth." (T-12.I.1:7-8)

"The analysis of ego motivation is very complicated, very obscuring, and never without you own ego involvement." (T-12.I.2:1)

"There is but one interpretation of motivation that makes any sense." (T-12.I.3:1)

"Every loving thought is true. Everything else is an appeal for healing and help, regardless of the form it takes." (T-12.I.3:3-4)

"If you believe that an appeal for help is something else you will react to something else." (T-12.I.3:9)

"There is nothing to prevent you from recognizing all calls for help as exactly what they are except your own imagined need to attack." (T-12.I.4:1)

"Only appreciation is an appropriate response to your brother. Gratitude is due him for both his loving thoughts and his appeals for help, for both are capable of bringing love into your awareness if you perceive them truly. All your sense of strain comes from your attempts not to do just this. How simple, then, is God's plan for salvation." (T-12.I.6:1-4)

"By applying the Holy Spirit's interpretation of the reactions of others more and more consistently, you will gain an increasing awareness that His criteria are equally applicable to you." (T-12.I.8:1)

"If you would look upon love, which is the world's reality, how could you do better than to recognize, in every defense against it, the underlying appeal for it?" (T-12.I.10:1)

CHAPTER 12—THE HOLY SPIRIT'S CURRICULUM

"The Holy Spirit's interpretation of fear does dispel it, for the awareness of truth cannot be denied. Thus does the Holy Spirit replace fear with love and translate error into truth. And thus will you learn of Him how to replace your dream of separation with the fact of unity." (T-12.I.10:3-5)

In summary, Chapter 12 – I. "The Judgment of the Holy Spirit" is saying:

The judgment of the Holy Spirit is always in the positive. All things are seen as either love, or a *call* for love. Therefore, all forms of pain and suffering are merely a call for love. To see the world in any other way is to react to it from the mindset of the ego. And as we interpret the world more and more as the Holy Spirit does, we will learn it is how we must see ourselves as well. We must learn to see every call for love as an aspect of our own Mind in need of healing and help. We help by supplying the love that is called for. As stated above, we can do this through gratitude for our brethren's call for love—gratitude to them for bringing an unhealed portion of our Mind to our attention so that our own Self Love can be activated. You do not have to love what anyone is saying or doing out of their call for love, but you do have to see them as part of your One Self in need of love. That is all. This new interpretation of the world will literally dissolve the illusion we see now. This is the exact process through which this world is transformed into God's Kingdom. Through using the judgment of the Holy Spirit, we replace the separation the ego shows us with the unity of Heaven.

"II. The Way to Remember God

"Miracles are merely the translation of denial into truth. If to love oneself is to heal oneself, those who are sick do not love themselves. Therefore, they are asking for the love that would heal them, but which they are denying to themselves." (T-12.II.1:1-3)

"The task of the miracle worker thus becomes *to deny the denial of truth*." (T-12.II.1:5)

"The light in them shines as brightly regardless of the density of the fog that obscures it. If you give no power to the fog to obscure the light, it has none." (T-12.II.2:1-2)

"You can remember this for all the Sonship." (T-12.II.2:5)

"II. The Way to Remember God

"This is what you have forgotten. To perceive the healing of your brother as the healing of yourself is thus the way to remember God." (T-12.II.2:8-9)

"Perceive in sickness but another call for love, and offer your brother what he believes he cannot offer himself. Whatever the sickness, there is but one remedy." (T-12.II.3:1-2)

"Remember what was said about the frightening perceptions of little children, which terrify them because they do not understand them. If they ask for enlightenment and accept it, their fears vanish." (T-12.II.4:1-2)

"Let us not save nightmares, for they are not fitting offerings for Christ, and so they are not fit gifts for you. Take off the covers and look at what you are afraid of. Only the anticipation will frighten you, for the reality of nothingness cannot be frightening." (T-12.II.5:1-3)

"You still want what God wills, and no nightmare can defeat a child of God in his purpose." (T-12.II.6:1)

"There is no fear in perfect love." (T-12.II.8:1)

"You who have tried to banish love have not succeeded, but you who choose to banish fear must succeed. The Lord is with you, but you know it not." (T-12.II.9:1-2)

"When we have overcome fear—not by hiding it, not by minimizing it, and not by denying its full import in any way—this is what you will really see." (T-12.II.9:5)

"We are therefore embarking on an organized, well-structured and carefully planned program aimed at learning how to offer to the Holy Spirit everything you do not want." (T-12.II.10:1)

"Surely He will not fail to help you, since help is His only purpose." (T-12.II.10:6)

In summary, Chapter 12 – II. "The Way to Remember God" is saying:
The way to remember God is simply to see Him exactly where He is: Within yourself and your brothers in Christ. Yet as our eyes are led by the ego, we often only see sickness, separation and suffering instead. We must remember this is just a fog covering the truth of our true Being. Once this is completely

141

CHAPTER 12 — THE HOLY SPIRIT'S CURRICULUM

understood and accepted as the truth, the fog lifts, just as a nightmare vanishes from a child's mind upon waking and realizing the truth of their safety. Though the experience of fear in this world is very real indeed, we must learn to overcome it by looking directly at it for what it is—a cover over the truth of our safety in Oneness. Seeing the purpose of fear for what it is, is the way to remember God.

"III. The Investment in Reality"

"I once asked you to sell all you have and give to the poor and follow me. This is what I meant: If you have no investment in anything in this world, you can teach the poor where their treasure is." (T-12.III.1:1-2)

"For poverty is lack, and there is but one lack since there is but one need." (T-12.III.1:6)

"Remember that those who attack are poor." (T-12.III.3:3)

"You who could help them are surely acting destructively if you accept their poverty as yours." (T-12.III.3:5)

"Recognize what does not matter, and if your brothers ask you for something "outrageous," do it *because* it does not matter. Refuse, and your opposition establishes that it does matter to you." (T-12.III.4:1-2)

"He is asking for salvation, as you are." (T-12.III.4:6)

"Salvation is for the mind, and it is attained through peace." (T-12.III.5:1)

"Any response other than love arises from a confusion about the "what" and the "how" of salvation, and this is the only answer." (T-12.III.5:3)

"To identify with the ego is to attack yourself and make yourself poor. That is why everyone who identifies with the ego feels deprived." (T-12.III.6: 1-2)

"The world you perceive is a world of separation." (T-12.III.9:1)

"Do not believe it is outside of yourself, for only by recognizing where it is will you gain control over it. For you do have control over your mind, since the mind is the mechanism of decision." (T-12.III.9:9-10)

"If you will recognize that all the attack you perceive is in your own mind and nowhere else, you will at last have placed its source, and where it begins it must end. For in this same place also lies salvation." (T-12.III.10:1-2)

IV. Seeking and Finding

"Yet to find the place, you must relinquish your investment in the world as you project it, allowing the Holy Spirit to extend the real world to you from the altar of God." (T-12.III.10:9)

In summary, Chapter 12 – III. "The Investment in Reality" is saying: "We are deeply invested in this world; the evidence of it lies in how tightly we hold onto it. Our true treasure, God's Love, lies within us yet we are completely unaware of it. We are throwing away God's gift to us and don't even know it. The way to salvage this situation is to remember to react to one another only from a place of love. Make this mental shift in the opposite direction from attack, rejection and lovelessness and the world will shift accordingly, because the world is within our own mind. Let us relinquish investment in what holds no value; that which will one day perish and disappear. Let us instead make a sound investment in only our eternal Reality in God's Love. Then our minds will perceive our true treasure at last.

IV. Seeking and Finding

"The ego is certain that love is dangerous, and this is always its central teaching. It never puts it this way; on the contrary, everyone who believes that the ego is salvation seems to be intensely engaged in the search for love. Yet the ego, though encouraging the search for love very actively, makes one proviso; do not find it. Its dictates, then, can be summed up simply as: "Seek and do not find." This is the one promise the ego holds out to you, and the one promise it will keep." (T-12.IV.1:1-5)

"And since it also teaches that it is your identification, its guidance leads you to a journey which must end in perceived self-defeat. For the ego cannot love, and in its frantic search for love it is seeking what it is afraid to find." (T-12.IV.2:2-3)

"Yet it is also your mind that has the power to deny the ego's existence, and you will surely do so when you realize exactly what the journey is on which the ego set you." (T-12.IV.2:6)

"To seek and not to find is hardly joyous." (T-12.IV.4:2)

"The Holy Spirit offers you another promise, and one that will lead to joy. For His promise is always, "Seek and you will find," and under His guidance you cannot be defeated." (T-12.IV.4:4-5)

"You will undertake a journey because you are not at home in this

CHAPTER 12—THE HOLY SPIRIT'S CURRICULUM

world. And you will search for your home whether you realize where it is or not. If you believe it is outside you the search will be futile, for you will be seeking it where it is not." (T-12.IV.5:1-3)

"Behold the Guide your Father gave you, that you might learn you have eternal life. For death is not your Father's Will nor yours, and whatever is true is the Will of the Father." (T-12.IV.6:1-2)

"The Holy Spirit guides you into life eternal, but you must relinquish your investment in death, or you will not see life though it is all around you." (T-12.IV.7:6)

In summary, Chapter 12 – IV. "Seeking and Finding" is saying:
"The ego would send us on a wild goose chase, seeking for love outside of us, where we will never find it. Love dwells within us. In order to experience love in the world we see, we must extend the love within us, to it, and we will receive what we have given. This is an immutable universal law of giving and receiving and is always in operation. Therefore, let us cease to listen to the ego, who will only list our wants and needs. Let us instead follow the only True Guide Who knows our one true need: To understand we already *have* and *are* a being of eternal Love. We want for nothing and need nothing. Let us seek to understand this truth alone and we will find *everything*.

V. The Sane Curriculum

"Only love is strong because it is undivided. The strong do not attack because they see no need to do so." (T-12.V.1:1-2)

"That is why the recognition of your own invulnerability is so important to the restoration of your sanity. For if you accept your invulnerability, you are recognizing that attack has no effect." (T-12.V.2:1-2)

"You will never realize the utter uselessness of attack except by recognizing that your attack on yourself has no effects. For others do react to attack if they perceive it, and if you are trying to attack them you will be unable to avoid interpreting this as reinforcement." (T-12.V.3:1-2)

"The Holy Spirit's Love is your strength, for yours is divided and therefore not real." (T-12.V.4:1)

"You have learning handicaps in a very literal sense. There are areas in your learning skills that are so impaired that you can progress only under constant, clear-cut direction, provided by a Teacher Who can transcend your limited resources." (T-12.V.5:1-2)

"You do not know the meaning of love, and that is your handicap." (T-12.V.6:1)

"You who have tried to learn what you do not want should take heart, for although the curriculum you set yourself is depressing indeed, it is merely ridiculous if you look at it." (T-12.V.8:1)

"Resign now as you own teacher. This resignation will not lead to depression." (T-12.V.8:3-4)

"Your learning potential, properly understood, is limitless because it will lead you to God." (T-12.V.9:1)

"The curriculum is totally unambiguous, because the goal is not divided and the means and the end are in complete accord. You need offer only your undivided attention. Everything else will be given you. For you really want to learn aright, and nothing can oppose the decision of God's Son." (T-12.V.9:3-6)

In summary, Chapter 12 – V. "The Sane Curriculum" is saying:

"The only sane curriculum is the one Love teaches. And what does Love teach, but our Unity? It is undivided in its giving—all of God's Love is given to all—and if we have learned His Lessons in Love truly, then this is how we will give His Love also. We will have no exceptions, no one left outside our Love. To attack, is to demonstrate we do not know what Love is. Attack is what we have taught ourselves, through seeing through the ego's eyes and judging what is acted out with our bodily identities. The ego's teaching is our greatest learning handicap, in that it teaches nothing about Love, the only sane curriculum. Let us resign now, then, from following it, for we truly want to learn the truth! The Holy Spirit teaches only Unity, the truth of Who We Are. In order to learn this single goal of His curriculum, we must become single-minded in our efforts. Let nothing the ego teaches tempt us to replace the only sane curriculum.

VI. The Vision of Christ

"The ego is trying to teach you how to gain the whole world and lose your own soul. The Holy Spirit teaches that you cannot lose your soul and there is no gain in the world, for of itself it profits nothing." (T-12. VI.1:1-2)

CHAPTER 12—THE HOLY SPIRIT'S CURRICULUM

"Not only is there no profit in the investment, but the cost to you is enormous." (T-12.VI.1:4)

"You cannot sell your soul, but you can sell your awareness of it." (T-12.VI.1:6)

"You do not want the world. The only thing of value in it is whatever part of it you look upon with love." (T-12.VI.3:1-2)

"To open the eyes of the blind is the Holy Spirit's mission, for He knows that they have not lost their vision, but merely sleep." (T-12.VI.4:2)

"In His sight the Son of God is perfect, and He longs to share His vision with you." (T-12.VI.4:6)

"The awakening of His Son begins with his investment in the real world, and by this he will learn to re-invest in himself." (T-12.VI.4:9)

"Yet you must learn the cost of sleeping, and refuse to pay it." (T-12.VI.5:2)

"As you perceive more and more common elements in all situations, the transfer of training under the Holy Spirit's guidance increases and becomes generalized. Gradually you learn to apply it to everyone and everything, for its applicability is universal." (T-12.VI.6:5-6)

"What is one cannot be perceived as separate, and the denial of the separation is the reinstatement of knowledge." (T-12.VI.7:1)

"The world has no purpose as it blends into the purpose of God. For the real world has slipped quietly into Heaven, where everything eternal in it has always been." (T-12.VI.7:4-5)

"Heaven is your home, and being in God it must also be in you." (T-12.VI.7:7)

In summary, Chapter 12 – VI. "The Vision of Christ" is saying:
Christ sees us as the perfect Unified beings of Light we were created as. This is His Vision of us. We too, would see one another in this way, but have instead chosen to forsake our True Sight in exchange for the vision of the ego, who can only see a world of separation in the form of physical bodies. In this sense, it could indeed be said we have "sold" the sight of our soul in order to gain the world we see now. This is the "cost" we pay for what we think we want. But as we notice our union more and more over that which seems to make us separate, we are thus denying the separation and welcoming the truth. Watch

VII. Looking Within

"Miracles demonstrate that learning has occurred under the right guidance, for learning is invisible and what has been learned can be recognized only by its results." (T-12.VII.1:1)

"You will recognize that you have learned there is no order of difficulty in miracles when you apply them to all situations. There is no situation to which miracles do not apply, and by applying them to all situations you will gain the real world. For in this holy perception you will be made whole, and the Atonement will radiate from your acceptance of it for yourself to everyone the Holy Spirit sends you for your blessing." (T-12.VII.1:3-5)

"You cannot see the invisible. Yet if you see its effects you know it must be there." (T-12.VII.2:2-3)

"And by what it does, you learn what it is." (T-12.VII.2:5)

"The Holy Spirit is invisible, but you can see the results of His Presence, and through them you will learn that He is there." (T-12.VII.3:1)

"You see what you expect, and you expect what you invite." (T-12.VII.5:1)

"Whose manifestations would you see?" (T-12.VII.5:3)

"I am the manifestation of the Holy Spirit, and when you see me it will be because you have invited Him." (T-12.VII.6:1)

"When you want only love you will see nothing else." (T-12.VII.8:1)

"The power of decision is your one remaining freedom as a prisoner of this world. You can decide to see it right." (T-12.VII.9:1-2)

"When you look within and see me, it will be because you have decided to manifest truth. And as you manifest it you will see it both without and within. You will see it without because you saw it first within." (T-12.VII.12:1-2)

"When you are tempted to yield to the desire for death, *remember that I did not die.* You will realize that this is true when you look within and see me." (T-12.VII.15:1-2)

CHAPTER 12 — THE HOLY SPIRIT'S CURRICULUM

In summary, Chapter 12 – VII. "Looking Within" is saying:

"We cannot "see" the power behind miracles, the Holy Spirit, our own Inner Light, or our unity through the Atonement. All of these things belong to a realm beyond the ego's vision. Yet, we can know these things to be true by their effects. But before we can see such effects, we must first look within our own mind to manifest them. We do this through invitation only; we must invite the right Guide into our mind. This is our power of decision—we can decide how we want to see the world and thus manifest the truth. All we must do is notice when our thoughts are aligned with the ego, and then decide to look within and choose to let such thoughts go. When we look within and want only thoughts of Love, we will see nothing else, within and without.

VIII. The Attraction of Love for Love

"The Father has hidden His Son safely within Himself, and kept him far away from your destructive thoughts, but you know neither the Father nor the Son because of them. You attack the real world every day and every hour and every minute, and yet you are surprised that you cannot see it." (T-12.VIII.1:1-3)

"When you made visible what is not true, what is true became invisible to you." (T-12.VIII.3:1)

"For what you made invisible is the only truth, and what you have not heard is the only Answer." (T-12.VIII.4:4)

"For the memory of God can dawn only in a mind that chooses to remember, and that has relinquished the insane desire to control reality. You who cannot even control yourself should hardly aspire to control the universe." (T-12.VIII.5:3-4)

"The real world was given you by God in loving exchange for the world you made and the world you see." (T-12.VIII.8:1)

"Its reality will make everything else invisible, for beholding it is total perception. And as you look upon it you will remember that it was always so." (T-12.VIII.8:3-4)

"The Atonement is but the way back to what was never lost. Your Father could not cease to love His Son." (T-12.VIII.8:8-9)

VIII. The Attraction of Love for Love

In summary, Chapter 12 – VIII. "The Attraction of Love for Love" is saying:

The attraction of Love for Love is the attraction of our True Self for God, and it is this aspect of our Inner Being that seeks to return our minds to a state of Union. We yearn to know our Oneness once again. Even so, we know not that with every breath we take, we are resisting this union through the endless distractions of this world. Everything we see represents separation and is therefore a false reality, and we fall for it every time. This "fall" is literal. Our vibration literally "falls" away from our union in Love every time we accept the separation as true, and this blocks the knowing of our Total Union. It is an attack on our awareness of God's Reality. We have made our Union invisible to ourselves through our choice to see separation. We must give up the idea we can make a reality for ourselves that is not true. We cannot change or destroy what God has created eternal and whole. The only way back to remembering our eternal Reality, is through learning the Holy Spirit's curriculum: We are One. This is the message of the Atonement and you have only to follow your own attraction to Love to learn it.

CHAPTER 13
THE GUILTLESS WORLD

Introduction

[Handwritten note: Ohhh Good Stuff!]

"If you did not feel guilty you could not attack, for condemnation is the root of attack. It is the judgment of one mind by another as unworthy of love and deserving of punishment." (T-13.in.1:1-2)

"All this is but the delusional attempt of the mind to deny itself, and escape the penalty of denial." (T-13.in.1:5)

"The acceptance of guilt into the mind of God's Son was the beginning of the separation, as the acceptance of the Atonement is its end." (T-13.in.2:1)

"Love does not kill to save. If it did, attack would be salvation, and this is the ego's interpretation, not God's." (T-13.in.3:3)

"The world is a picture of the crucifixion of God's son. And until you realize that God's Son cannot be crucified, this is the world you will see. Yet you will not realize this until you accept the eternal fact that God's Son is not guilty. He deserves only love because he has given only love." (T-13.in.4:1-4)

[Handwritten note: Always been a weird story to me – even as a kid]

In summary, Chapter 13 – Introduction is saying:
The word guilt is interchangeable with the word "body." Therefore, guilt is embodied in this world through our bodies. And it is the words and actions committed through our bodies that we wish to condemn if we decide we are unhappy. Yet we are accusers of nothing and no one, for no one is truly their body or what they think they can do with it. No one can be killed, for we cannot die. Love knows this, for it knows you are eternal and cannot be crucified in any way. Love knows you are not guilty—you are not a body and being in a body cannot change Who You Are in truth. Until we realize this and extend only love to one another through overlooking the body and embracing the Light within ourselves, the real world, the guiltless (bodiless) world, will escape our vision.

[Handwritten note: There was a lot of Body stuff in that crucifixion/Resurrection]

I. Guiltlessness and Invulnerability

"Guilt hides Christ from your sight, for it is the denial of the blamelessness of God's Son." (T-13.I.1:5)

"For the blamelessness of Christ is the proof that the ego never was, and can never be. Without guilt the ego has no life, and God's Son is without guilt." (T-13.I.2:4-5)

"As you look upon yourself and judge what you do honestly, you may be tempted to wonder how you can be guiltless. Yet consider this: You are not guiltless in time, but in eternity." (T-13.I.3:1-2)

"For the Son of God is guiltless now, and the brightness of his purity shines untouched forever in God's Mind. God's Son will always be as he was created. Deny your world and judge him not, for his eternal guiltlessness is in the Mind of his Father, and protects him forever." (T-13.I.5:6-8)

"When you have accepted the Atonement for yourself, you will realize there is no guilt in God's Son. And only as you look upon him as guiltless can you understand his oneness." (T-13.I.6:1-2)

"As you perceive the holy companions who travel with you, you will realize that there is no journey, but only an awakening." (T-13.I.7:1)

"You are immortal because you are eternal, and "always" must be now. Guilt, then, is a way of holding past and future in your mind to ensure the ego's continuity." (T-13.I.8:5-6)

"The ego teaches you to attack yourself because you are guilty, and this must increase the guilt, for guilt is the result of attack. In the ego's teaching, then, there is no escape from guilt." (T-13.I.11:1-2)

"The Holy Spirit dispels it simply through the calm recognition that it has never been." (T-13.I.11:4)

In summary, Chapter 13 – I. "Guiltlessness and Invulnerability" is saying:

If we substitute the word "guilt" anywhere in *A Course In Miracles*, with the word "body," a clearer understanding comes forth. Take this sentence for example: "Without guilt (the body) the ego has no life, and God's Son is without guilt (a body)." (T-13.I.2:4-5). And this example: "As you look upon yourself and judge what you do honestly, you may be tempted to wonder how you can be

CHAPTER 13 — THE GUILTLESS WORLD

guiltless (bodiless). Yet consider this: You are not guiltless (bodiless) in time, but in eternity." (T-13.I.3:1-2). With this substitution things make a lot more sense, for we get confused with the world's definition of "guilt" as something deserving of punishment. Here it is redefined as merely our decision to be in physical form—the mistake of the decision to experience separation. This is certainly not something deserving of punishment. The Holy Spirit dispels all guilt (body identification) through the calm recognition that it has never been. We are still the invulnerable beings He created us as and we are still One. This recognition of our guiltlessness or "bodiless-ness" is the acceptance of our Oneness or the Atonement.

II. The Guiltless Son of God

"The ultimate purpose of projection is always to get rid of guilt." (T-13.II.1:1)

"Only by persuading you that it is you could the ego possibly induce you to project guilt, and thereby keep it in your mind." (T-13.II.1:4)

"Yet consider how strange a solution the ego's arrangement is. You project guilt to get rid of it, but you are actually merely concealing it. You do experience the guilt, but you have no idea why." (T-13.II.2:1-3)

"Yet you have no idea that you are failing the Son of God by seeing him as guilty. Believing you are no longer you, you do not realize that you are failing yourself." (T-13.II.2:5-6)

"The darkest of your hidden cornerstones holds your belief in guilt from your awareness." (T-13.II.3:1)

"It does not know who the Son of God is because it is blind." (T-13.II.3:4)

"To the ego, *the guiltless are guilty*. Those who do not attack are its "enemies" because, by not valuing its interpretation of salvation, they are in an excellent position to let it go. They have approached the darkest and deepest cornerstone in the ego's foundation, and while the ego can withstand your raising all else to question, it guards this one secret with its life, for its existence depends on keeping this secret." (T-13.II.4:1-4)

"In the calm light of truth, let us recognize that you believe you have crucified God's Son. You have not admitted to this "terrible" secret because you would still wish to crucify him if you could find him." (T-13.II.5:1-2)

We crucify Gods son every time we judge, jealous, angry, frustrated

III. The Fear of Redemption

"You have handled this wish to kill yourself by not knowing who you are, and identifying with something else." (T-13.II.5:4)

"I have said that the crucifixion is the symbol of the ego. When it was confronted with the real guiltlessness of God's Son it did attempt to kill him, and the reason was that guiltlessness is blasphemous to God. To the ego, the ego is God, and guiltlessness must be interpreted as the final guilt that fully justifies murder." (T-13.II.6:1-3)

"Atonement has always been interpreted as the release from guilt, and this is correct if it is understood." (T-13.II.8:1)

"In this understanding lies your remembering, for it is the recognition of love without fear. There will be great joy in Heaven on your homecoming, and the joy will be yours. For the redeemed son of man is the guiltless Son of God, and to recognize him is your redemption." (T-13.II.9:5-7)

In summary, Chapter 13 – II. The Guiltless Son of God" is saying:
Again, the word guilt is synonymous with the word body. When we decided to forget our "bodiless" life and come into physical form, we felt guilty for doing this. And so, the body became the symbol of our guilty choice. And just as we are not guilty in God's eyes, neither are we really bodies. This is the greatest secret the ego holds against us, the darkest cornerstone of our beliefs we are afraid to give up: *we are not bodies.* The instant we truly believe this, we are released from guilt. This is the Atonement: the knowing of our Unity in Love and the denial of our separation as bodies. Yet until then, we will believe we crucified God's Son, condemning Him to an experience of separated bodies. Let us cease to crucify God's Son; let us cease to see bodies as our true identity. The guiltless Son of God is the bodiless Son of God.

III. The Fear of Redemption

"You may wonder why it is so crucial that you look upon your hatred and realize its full extent. You may also think that it would be easy enough for the Holy Spirit to show it to you, and to dispel it without the need for you to raise it to awareness yourself." (T-13.III.1:1-2)

"We have said that no one will countenance fear if he recognizes it. Yet in your disordered state of mind you are not afraid of fear. You do not like it, but it is not your desire to attack that really frightens you. You are not seriously disturbed by your hostility." (T-13.III.1:4-7)

CHAPTER 13 — THE GUILTLESS WORLD

"Your real terror is of redemption." (T-13.III.1:11)

"Under the ego's dark foundation is the memory of God, and it is of this that you are really afraid. For this memory would instantly restore you to your proper place, and it is this place that you have sought to leave. Your fear of attack is nothing compared to your fear of love." (T-13.III.2:1-3)

"For this wish caused the separation, and you have protected it because you do not want the separation healed." (T-13.III.2:5)

"In honesty, is it not harder for you to say "I love" than "I hate"? You associate love with weakness and hatred with strength, and your own real power seems to you as your real weakness." (T-13.III.3:1-2)

"You are afraid it would sweep you away from yourself and make you little, because you believe that magnitude lies in defiance, and that attack is grandeur." (T-13.III.4:2)

"Therefore, you have used the world to cover your love, and the deeper you go into the blackness of the ego's foundation, the closer you come to the Love that is hidden there. And it is this that frightens you." (T-13.III.4:4-5)

"Beneath all the grandiosity you hold so dear is your real call for help." (T-13.III.8:1)

"In that place which you have hidden, you will only to unite with the Father, in loving remembrance of Him. You will find this place of truth as you see it in your brothers, for though they may deceive themselves, like you they long for the grandeur that is in them. And perceiving it you will welcome it, and it will be yours." (T-13.III.8:3-5)

"But seek this place and you will find it, for Love is in you and will lead you there." (T-13.III.12:10)

In summary, Chapter 13 – III. "The Fear of Redemption" is saying:
It seems unbelievable to hear that we are actually afraid of love. Isn't this what we have been seeking for with all of our hearts combined? Yet we have been led by the ego on this hunt, and it has led us only deeper into darkness, and this is exactly where we need to go in order to find the Love that we have hidden there. We cannot skim the surface of life, looking for love outside of us—this is exactly where the ego would have us endlessly waste our time. It would have us seek for it in relationships, things, and locations in the world. We need

go nowhere and seek for it in no one. We carry the sacred space where Love resides within us. And whence we see it in all those around us, we will have found it within ourselves. Let go of the fear of redemption—the fear of seeing only love instead of hate—and you will find what was never lost.

IV. The Function of Time

"And now the reason why you are afraid of this course should be apparent. For this is a course on love, because it is about you." (T-13.IV.1:1-2)

"For you believe that attack is your reality, and that your destruction is the final proof that you were right." (T-13.IV.2:5)

"Under the circumstances, would it not be more desirable to have been wrong, even apart from the fact that you were wrong?" (T-13.IV.3:1)

"And even though you know not Heaven, might it not be more desirable than death?" (T-13.IV.3:6)

"The ego invests heavily in the past, and in the end believes that the past is the only aspect of time that is meaningful. Remember that its emphasis on guilt enables it to ensure its continuity by making the future like the past, and thus avoiding the present." (T-13.IV.4:2-3)

"'Now' has no meaning to the ego. The present merely reminds it of past hurts, and it reacts to the present as if it *were* the past." (T-13.IV.5:1-2)

"It dictates your reactions to those you meet in the present from a past reference point, obscuring their present reality." (T-13.IV.5:4)

"The shadowy figures from the past are precisely what you must escape. They are not real, and have no hold over you unless you bring them with you." (T-13.IV.6:1-2)

"Unless you learn that past pain is an illusion, you are choosing a future of illusions and losing the many opportunities you could find for release in the present. The ego would preserve your nightmares, and prevent you from awakening and understanding they are past." (T-13.IV.6:5-6)

"It is evident that the Holy Spirit's perception of time is the exact opposite of the ego's." (T-13.IV.7:1)

"The Holy Spirit interprets time's purpose as rendering the need for time unnecessary." (T-13.IV.7:3)

CHAPTER 13 — THE GUILTLESS WORLD

"For only "now" is here, and only "now" presents the opportunities for the holy encounters in which salvation can be found." (T-13.IV.7:7)

"If you accept your function in the world of time as one of healing, you will emphasize only the aspect of time in which healing can occur." (T-13.IV.9:2)

"It must be accomplished in the present to release the future." (T-13.IV.9:4)

In summary, Chapter 13 – IV. "The Function of Time" is saying:
The ego would use time to perpetuate its own existence. It needs time in order to keep past memories of hurtful images in your mind, which keeps you focused on this reality. Without the focus on such thoughts of the past, the future would be open to a new reality; the only other reality that can be experienced: God's Reality of Love. So, we unknowingly allow the ego to poison our present with its hateful, painful thoughts of past events which only manifests a future that reflects such thinking. If we cut off such thoughts, we cut off the ego's seeming power to manifest more of what we say we do not want. We then use time in the way the Holy Spirit uses it: to see no past in anyone and render the effects of time undone. And when time is used in this way, *time itself* is undone. You will be living purely in the present moment, and it is only in the present moment you can be healed of the past. This is the only function of time: to be healed *now* through true forgiveness, which is the letting go of all we think or know about what we see in the here and *now*.

V. The Two Emotions

"I have said you have but two emotions, love and fear. One is changeless but continually exchanged, being offered by the eternal to the eternal." (T-13.V.1:1-2)

"The other has many forms, for the content of individual illusions differs greatly. Yet they have one thing in common; they are all insane." (T-13.V.1:4-5)

"They make up a private world that cannot be shared." (T-13.V.1:7)

"In this world their maker moves alone, for only he perceives them." (T-13.V.1:9)

"Each one peoples his world with figures from his individual past, and it is because of this that private worlds do differ. Yet the figures that he

V. The Two Emotions

sees were never real, for they are made up only of his reactions to his brothers, and do not include their reactions to him." (T-13.V.2:1-2)

"It is through these strange and shadowy figures that the insane relate to their insane world." (T-13.V.3:1)

"You have but two emotions, yet in your private world you react to each of them as though it were the other." (T-13.V.5:1)

"Everyone draws nigh unto what he loves, and recoils from what he fears. And you react with fear to love, and draw away from it. Yet fear attracts you, and believing it is love, you call it to yourself. Your private world is filled with figures of fear you have invited into it, and all the love your brothers offer you, you do not see." (T-13.V.5:4-7)

"As you look with open eyes upon your world, it must occur to you that you have withdrawn into insanity." (T-13.V.6:1)

"But let the darkness go and all you made you will no longer see, for sight of it depends upon denying vision." (T-13.V.8:5)

"Dreams disappear when light has come and you can see." (T-13.V.8:9)

"You have but two emotions, and one you made and one was given you. Each is a way of seeing, and different worlds arise from their different sights. See through the vision that is given you, for through Christ's vision He beholds Himself." (T-13.V.10:1-3)

"And all who would behold Him can see Him, for they have asked for light." (T-13.V.11:2)

"In the sanity of His vision they looked upon themselves with love, seeing themselves as the Holy Spirit sees them." (T-13.V.11:6)

In summary, Chapter 13 – V. "The Two Emotions" is saying:
We look upon the world and it never occurs to us that we are seeing only half the picture. The part we are missing, is everyone else's experience of us. We have no idea what anyone else is going through or what they are dealing with. And so, we walk this world with our one-sided egocentric perspective, completely ignorant of any other world but the small one we have inside our head. This narrow vision stems from fear, the ego. Yet, we have another choice in seeing. We can choose to see through the eyes of the Holy Spirit Who sees that we are one, and what we do to another we do to ourselves. We may not know the story someone else is carrying around inside their head, but do we

CHAPTER 13—THE GUILTLESS WORLD

need to? Is it not enough to know we share an eternal Love in our beingness with them? The only sane thing to do in this insane world of one-sided perception is to ask for the light; to see sanely. The light is our understanding of our unity, and it will shine away all dark thoughts of separate existences. The two emotions, love and fear, will then be reconciled as One Love.

VI. Finding the Present

"To perceive truly is to be aware of all reality through the awareness of your own." (T-13.VI.1:1)

"This means that you perceive a brother only as you see him now." (T-13.VI.1:3)

"If you remember the past as you look upon your brother, you will be unable to perceive the reality that is now." (T-13.VI.1:7)

"You consider it "natural" to use your past experience as the reference point from which to judge the present." (T-13.VI.2:1)

"When you have learned to look on everyone with no reference at all to the past, either his or yours as you perceived it, you will be able to learn from what you see now. For the past can cast no shadow to darken the present, unless you are afraid of light." (T-13.VI.2:3-4)

"The Christ as revealed to you now has no past, for He is changeless, and in His changelessness lies your release." (T-13.VI.3:2)

"To be born again is to let the past go, and look without condemnation upon the present." (T-13.VI.3:5)

"Time can release as well as imprison, depending on whose interpretation of it you use." (T-13.VI.4:1)

"You would anticipate the future on the basis of your past experience, and plan for it accordingly. Yet by doing so you are aligning past and future, and not allowing the miracle, which could intervene between them, to free you to be born again." (T-13.VI.4:7-8)

"The miracle enables you to see your brother without his past, and so perceive him as born again." (T-13.VI.5:1)

"Judgment and condemnation are behind you, and unless you bring them with you, you will see that you are free of them." (T-13.VI.6:1)

"The present offers you your brothers in the light that would unite you

VI. Finding the Present

with them, and free you from the past." (T-13.VI.7:1)

"In timeless union with them is your continuity, unbroken because it is wholly shared." (T-13.VI.8:3)

"Child of Light, you know not that the light is in you. Yet you will find it through its witnesses, for having given light to them they will return it." (T-13.VI.10:1-2)

"Love always leads to love." (T-13.VI.10:4)

"Awakening unto Christ is following the laws of love of your free will, and out of quiet recognition of the truth in them. The attraction of light must draw you willingly, and willingness is signified by giving." (T-13.VI.12:1-2)

"You dream of isolation because your eyes are closed. You do not see your brothers, and in the darkness you cannot look upon the light you gave to them." (T-13.VI.12:6-7)

"Even in sleep has Christ protected you, ensuring the real world for you when you awake." (T-13.VI.13:3)

In summary, Chapter 13 – VI. "Finding the Present" is saying:

If we are truly being present-minded, that is, living fully in the present moment, then no thoughts about another's past can intrude upon our mind. This seems like an impossible task. How can we simply just forget about the past we have had with people? Yet here we are only being asked to let go of the pain we remember and understand that the situation that caused it, is now done and over with. We need not hold onto such charged negative emotions. Here in the present, we remain as God created us: united, whole, and completely unharmed. There is no sense in hanging onto what is gone. To let go of the past, is to forgive. And to forgive is to allow the present moment to dawn into reality without the past imposing itself upon it. And now a miracle can happen because you have made space for it in the present moment by clearing away the past. The real world, as God created it out of His Love, is then free to come into your awareness. The real world can only come to us in the present. We find the present by letting go of the past.

CHAPTER 13 — THE GUILTLESS WORLD

VII. Attainment of the Real World

"Sit quietly and look upon the world you see, and tell yourself: 'The real world is not like this. It has no buildings and there are no streets where people walk alone and separate. There are no stores where people buy an endless list of things they do not need. It is not lit with artificial light, and night comes not upon it. There is no day that brightens and grows dim. There is no loss. Nothing is there but shines, and shines forever.'" (T-13.VII.1:1-7)

"You do not really want the world you see, for it has disappointed you since time began." (T-13.VII.3:1)

"Yet the real world has the power to touch you even here, because you love it. And what you call with love will come to you." (T-13.VII.4:1-2)

"No one in this distracted world but has seen some glimpse of the other world about him. Yet while he still lays value on his own, he will deny the vision of the other, maintaining that he loves what he loves not, and following not the road that love points out." (T-13.VII.6:1-2)

"You will first dream of peace, and then awaken to it. Your first exchange of what you made for what you want is the exchange of nightmares for the happy dreams of love." (T-13.VII.9:1-2)

"In your world you do need things." (T-13.VII.10:4)

"Everything the ego tells you that you need will hurt you. For although the ego urges you again and again to get, it leaves you nothing, for what you get it will demand of you." (T-13.VII.11:1-2)

"Only the Holy Spirit knows what you need. For He will give you all things that do not block the way to light." (T-13.VII.12:1-2)

"Leave, then, your needs to Him. He will supply them with no emphasis at all upon them." (T-13.VII.13:1-2)

"Whenever you are tempted to undertake a useless journey that would lead away from light, remember what you really want, and say:

The Holy Spirit leads me unto Christ, and where else would I go? What need have I but to awake in Him?" (T-13.VII.14:1-3)

"Then follow Him in joy, with faith that He will lead you safely through all dangers to your peace of mind this world may set before you." (T-13.VII.15:1)

"In me you have already overcome every temptation that would hold you back. We walk together on the way to quietness that is the gift of God. Hold me dear, for what except your brothers can you need?" (T-13.VII.16:1-3)

"We cannot sing redemption's hymn alone." (T-13.VII.17:1)

"Give thanks to every part of you that you have taught how to remember you." (T-13.VII.17:8)

In summary, Chapter 13 – VII. "Attainment of the Real World" is saying:

Throughout the Course, we are told over and over that this world is an illusion and there is another world just beyond this one that is our true reality. We can all agree that we would love a better reality, but most of us think we have to die in order to reach it. Yet here we are told that we can experience our true reality even before that. We can reach it through relinquishing the value we hold on this one. It is through the tight hold we have on it, that keeps it before our eyes. We hold onto it through our striving for the things within it. These "needs" supersede our one true need: to awaken to our oneness, which *is* our true reality. We can practice this now, here in a world that shows us anything *but* oneness and call the real world forth. We call it forth through appreciation of the oneness we know and believe is true, though we cannot yet see it. Through seeing one another in this way, the real world is attained.

VIII. From Perception to Knowledge

"All healing is release from the past." (T-13.VIII.1:1)

"For the mind that knows this unequivocally knows also it dwells in eternity, and utilizes no perception at all." (T-13.VIII.1:5)

"It knows that it is everywhere, just as it has everything, and forever." (T-13.VIII.1:7)

"You are an aspect of knowledge, being in the Mind of God, Who knows you. All knowledge must be yours, for in you is all knowledge. Perception, at its loftiest, is never complete. Even the perception of the Holy Spirit, as perfect as perception can be, is without meaning in Heaven." (T-13.VIII.2:3-6)

"Perfect perception, then, has many elements in common with knowledge, making transfer to it possible. Yet the last step must be taken by

God, because the last step in your redemption, which seems to be in the future, was accomplished by God in your creation. The separation has not interrupted it." (T-13.VIII.3:1-3)

"This is the miracle of creation; *that it is one forever.*" (T-13.VIII.5:1)

"Though every aspect is the whole, you cannot know this until you see that every aspect is the same, perceived in the same light and therefore one. Everyone seen without the past thus brings you nearer to the end of time by bringing healed and healing sight into the darkness, and enabling the world to see." (T-13.VIII.5:3-4)

"They are all the same; all beautiful and equal in their holiness." (T-13.VIII.6:1)

"Offer Christ's gift to everyone and everywhere, for miracles, offered the Son of God through the Holy Spirit, attune you to reality." (T-13.VIII.7:2)

"Knowledge is far beyond your individual concern. You who are part of it and all of it need only realize that it is of the Father, not of you. Your role in the redemption leads you to it be re-establishing its oneness in your mind." (T-13.VIII.7:4-6)

"God waits your witness to His Son and to Himself. The miracles you do on earth are lifted up to Heaven and to Him. They witness to what you do not know, and as they reach the gates of Heaven, God will open them." (T-13.VIII.10:4-6)

In summary, Chapter 13 – VIII. "From Perception to Knowledge" is saying:

We can only *perceive within our minds* the oneness that we share; we cannot yet "see it" any other way. We cannot *know it* until God takes us that last and final step into the *experience* of our unity. Until then, we must continually practice the mindset necessary to make the final leap; we can release everyone from their past through letting go of all the emotions we hold against them. We can learn to see all people as the same; all beautiful and equal in their unity with us. To offer this thought, is to offer a miracle, for such thoughts "attune" you to God's reality. Exactly what that reality is like, is none of our concern. Our only job is to hold the vibration of oneness in our mind. These miraculous thoughts will literally lift us up to the gates of Heaven itself. And when God takes the final step for us, we will have made the shift from perception to knowledge—from perceiving only the physical, to knowing the eternal.

IX. The Cloud of Guilt

"Guilt remains the only thing that hides the Father, for guilt is the attack upon His Son. The guilty always condemn, and having done so they will still condemn, linking the future to the past as is the ego's law." (T-13.IX.1:1-2)

"Therefore give no obedience to its laws, for they are laws of punishment. And those who follow them believe that they are guilty, and so they must condemn. Between the future and the past the laws of God must intervene, if you would free yourself." (T-13.IX.1:5-7)

"Release from guilt is the ego's whole undoing. *Make no one fearful*, for his guilt is yours, and by obeying the ego's harsh commandments you bring its condemnation on yourself, and you will not escape the punishment it offers those who obey it." (T-13.IX.2:1-2)

"You *will* accept your treasure, and if you place your faith in the past, the future will be like it. Whatever you hold dear you think is yours. The power of your valuing will make it so." (T-13.IX.3:3-5)

"Atonement brings a re-evaluation of everything you cherish, for it is the means by which the Holy Spirit can separate the false and the true, which you have accepted into your mind without distinction." (T-13.IX.4:1)

"The idea that the guiltless Son of God can attack himself and make himself guilty is insane. In any form, in anyone, *believe this not*." (T-13.IX.5:3-4)

"See no one, then, as guilty, and you will affirm the truth of guiltlessness unto yourself." (T-13.IX.6:1)

"If you would look within you would see only the Atonement, shining in quiet and in peace upon the altar to your Father." (T-13.IX.7:6)

"Do not be afraid to look within. The ego tells you all is black with guilt within you, and bids you not to look." (T-13.IX.8:1-2)

"Can you see guilt where God knows there is perfect innocence?" (T-13.IX.8:11)

"Look, then, upon the light He placed within you, and learn that what you feared was there has been replaced with love." (T-13.IX.8:13)

CHAPTER 13 — THE GUILTLESS WORLD

In summary, Chapter 13 – IX. "The Cloud of Guilt" is saying:
Let us remember that the term "guilt" is synonymous with the word "body," as the body is the ego's manifestation of our seeming separation from God and each other. The body represents the "guilty secret" we keep from our memory—it is the cloud behind which we hide from God and one another. We cannot see past this "cloud" because we see nothing but the body in whomever we look upon. The only way to see beyond it, is to understand it is false, which is to forgive it. Forgive our guilt (the body we see) in one another and we forgive it in ourselves. Forgive the bodies we see, and we forgive the existence of our own. To do this, we must re-evaluate everything we see. Believe in our innocence, our "bodiless-ness" and you will see past the "cloud of guilt" and look upon the light within instead.

X. Release from Guilt

"You are accustomed to the notion that the mind can see the source of pain where it is not." (T-13.X.1:1)

"Displacement always is maintained by the illusion that the source of guilt, from which attention is diverted, must be true; and must be fearful, or you would not have displaced the guilt onto what you believe to be less fearful." (T-13.X.1:3)

"In any union with a brother in which you seek to lay your guilt upon him, or share it with him or perceive his own, you will feel guilty. Nor will you find satisfaction and peace with him, because your union with him is not real." (T-13.X.3:1-2)

"When you maintain that you are guilty but the source of your guilt lies in the past, you are not looking inward." (T-13.X.4:1)

"Determine, then, to be not as you were. Use no relationship to hold you to the past, but with each one each day be born again. A minute, even less, will be enough to free you from the past, and give your mind in peace over to the Atonement. When everyone is welcome to you as you would have yourself be welcome to your Father, you will see no guilt in you." (T-13.X.5:1-4)

"Look through the cloud of guilt that dims your vision, and look past darkness to the holy place where you will see the light." (T-13.X.9:6)

"Release from guilt as you would be released." (T-13.X.10:1)

"You cannot enter into real relationships with any of God's Sons unless you love them all and equally. Love is not special. If you single out part of the Sonship for your love, you are imposing guilt on all your relationships and making them unreal. You can only love as God loves." (T-13.X.11:1-4)

"Behold the Son of God, and look upon his purity and be still. In quiet look upon his holiness and offer thanks unto his Father that no guilt has ever touched him." (T-13.X.11:10-11)

"I thank You, Father, for the purity of Your most holy Son, whom You have created guiltless forever." (T-13.X.12:6)

"Praise be to you who make the Father one with His Own Son. Alone we are all lowly, but together we shine with brightness so intense that none of us alone can even think of it." (T-13.X.14:1)

"United in this praise we stand before the gates of Heaven where we will surely enter in our sinlessness." (T-13.X.14:6)

In summary, Chapter 13 – X. "Release from Guilt" is saying:
Often, we displace our pain and suffering onto other people, believing they are the cause. And sometimes we lay blame on ourselves. Both viewpoints hold us equally in the cold hard grasp of guilt. Our release from this situation is simple: see no one as a body. If guilt is represented in this world as the body, then remembering it is not who we are, will release you from it. Then you must also release every word and action that came from the body, or else no one is truly released. Without this form of release, all relationships will eventually fall apart, because you are seeing yourselves as *being* apart. Our union is not through the physical. Our union is in Spirit. We have set up worldly institutions that allow us to lay claim to one another through marriage and other forms of familial bonds, which all have their place and function. However, we will not see that we are all equally part of One Love, while guilt (the body) remains the only thing we see. Let us be glad and give thanks it is not the truth of our existence, and thus we are all released from guilt, "the body."

XI. The Peace of Heaven

"Forgetfulness and sleep and even death become the ego's best advice for dealing with the perceived and harsh intrusion of guilt on peace." (T-13.XI.1:1)

CHAPTER 13—THE GUILTLESS WORLD

"When we are all united in Heaven, you will value nothing that you value here." (T-13.XI.3:1)

"In Heaven is everything God values, and nothing else." (T-13.XI.3:7)

"Everything is clear and bright, and calls forth one response." (T-13.XI.3:9)

"There is a sense of peace so deep that no dream in this world has ever brought even a dim imagining of what it is." (T-13.XI.3:13)

"Nothing in this world can give this peace, for nothing in this world is wholly shared." (T-13.XI.4:1)

"Whatever your reactions to the Holy Spirit's Voice may be, whatever voice you choose to listen to, whatever strange thoughts may occur to you, God's Will is done. You will find the peace in which He has established you, because He does not change His Mind." (T-13.XI.5:4-5)

"Fear not the Holy Spirit will fail in what your Father has given Him to do. The Will of God can fail in nothing." (T-13.XI.6:8-9)

"Have faith in only this one thing, and it will be sufficient: God wills you be in Heaven and nothing can keep you from it, or it from you." (T-13.XI.7:1)

"The Communication Link that God Himself placed within you, joining your mind with His, cannot be broken." (T-13.XI.8:1)

"Peace will be yours because His peace still flows to you from Him Whose Will is peace. You have it now. The Holy Spirit will teach you how to use it, and by extending it, to learn that it is in you." (T-13.XI.8:4-6)

"Learn that even the darkest nightmare that disturbs the mind of God's sleeping Son holds no power over him." (T-13.XI.9:5)

"You do not have to know that Heaven is yours to make it so. It *is* so. Yet to know it, the Will of God must be accepted as your will." (T-13.XI.10:5-7)

In summary, Chapter 13 – XI. "The Peace of Heaven" is saying:
There is such a sharp contrast between our life in Heaven and our life here in this world, that the only way the ego can convince us to stay is through deception. We have had to completely obliterate the memory of Heaven from our minds, in order to tolerate this world of separate forms. And though we find many things here that we think we want, all of it is nothing compared to what lies in wait for us in the real world. For in it, is a peace and joy that nothing in

this world can give. And so it is, that we will value nothing we leave behind. We are promised by God Himself that we will find our way back from whence we came. We have a Communication Link, the Holy Spirit, embedded within our very soul, linking us to God. Yet, in order to make our communication two-way—where we can hear God as well as He can hear us—we must match our thoughts to His. Our vibrations must be in accord with the Will of the Holy Spirit, the Voice for God. We do this through forgiveness. It is God's Will that we forgive this world of guilt, this world of bodies and separate forms. Forgiveness looks beyond what we see here and sees only our eternal unity. And so it is, that even here, we can live in a guiltless (bodiless) world.

CHAPTER 14
TEACHING FOR TRUTH

Introduction

"Yes, you are blessed indeed. Yet in this world you do not know it. But you have the means for learning it and seeing it quite clearly." (T-14.in.1:1-3)

"We have followed much of the ego's logic, and have seen its logical conclusions." (T-14.in.1:6)

"Let us now turn away from them, and follow the simple logic by which the Holy Spirit teaches the simple conclusions that speak for truth, and only truth." (T-14.in.1:8)

In summary, Chapter 14 – Introduction is saying:
The introduction is quite clear and needs little explanation. We are blessed beyond our current comprehension, but once we let go of the ego's teachings, we will learn *the truth of Who We Are*.

I. The Conditions of Learning

"If you are blessed and do not know it, you need to learn it must be so." (T-14.I.1:1)

"That is why miracles offer you the testimony that you are blessed." (T-14.I.1:6)

"If you decide to have and give and be nothing except a dream, you must direct your thoughts unto oblivion. And if you have and give and are everything, and all this has been denied, your thought system is closed off and wholly separated from the truth." (T-14.I.2:4-5)

"Seeing is always outward." (T-14.I.3:1)

"The thoughts the mind of God's Son projects or extends have all the power that he gives to them. The thoughts he shares with God are beyond his belief, but those he made are his beliefs." (T-14.I.3:3-4)

"They will not be taken from him. But they can be given up by him, for the Source of their undoing is in him." (T-14.I.3:6-7)

"Undoing is indirect, as doing is. You were created only to create, neither to see nor do." (T-14.I.4:3-4)

"The Holy Spirit, therefore, must begin His teaching by showing you what you can never learn. His message is not indirect, but He must introduce the simple truth into a thought system which has become so twisted and so complex you cannot see that it means nothing." (T-14.I.5:1-2)

"But you who cannot undo what you have made, nor escape the heavy burden of its dullness that lies upon your mind, cannot see through it." (T-14.I.5:4)

"Those who choose to be deceived will merely attack direct approaches, because they seem to encroach upon deception and strike at it." (T-14.I.5:6)

In summary, Chapter 14 – I. "The Conditions of Learning" is saying: We are so embedded in the thought system of the ego we cannot conceive of learning anything else. We have only known ourselves as separate bodies living in a world of separation since birth. We remember nothing else and so we can conceive of nothing else. Here then, is the Holy Spirit's task: To teach us we are the *opposite* of what we *think* we are. We are blessed in Union as one and do not know it. We cannot undo our false beliefs alone, and yet the Holy Spirit must tread carefully around our ego-beliefs, lest we simply reject the new beliefs outright, being too threatening to the ego's existence. The "conditions of learning" are merely how much willingness are we willing to give towards exchanging our old beliefs for the truth of Who We Are.

II. The Happy Learner

"The Holy Spirit needs a happy learner, in whom His mission can be happily accomplished. You who are steadfastly devoted to misery must first recognize that you are miserable and not happy. The Holy Spirit cannot teach without this contrast, for you believe that misery is happiness." (T-14.II.1:1-3)

"The Holy Spirit, seeing where you are but knowing you are elsewhere, begins His lesson in simplicity with the fundamental teaching that truth is true. This is the hardest lesson you will ever learn, and in the end the only one." (T-14.II.2:1-2)

"The simple and the obvious are not apparent to those who would make palaces and royal robes of nothing, believing they are kings with golden crowns because of them." (T-14.II.2:7)

CHAPTER 14—TEACHING FOR TRUTH

"All this the Holy Spirit sees, and teaches, simply, that all this is not true. To those unhappy learners who would teach themselves nothing, and delude themselves into believing that it is not nothing, the Holy Spirit says, with steadfast quietness:

The truth is true. Nothing else matters, nothing else is real, and everything beside it is not there. Let Me make the one distinction for you that you cannot make, but need to learn. Your faith in nothing is deceiving you. Offer your faith to Me, and I will place it gently in the holy place where it belongs. You will find no deception there, but only the simple truth. And you will love it because you will understand it." (T-14.II.3:1-9)

"They will be happy learners of the lesson this light brings to them, because it teaches them release from nothing and from all the works of nothing." (T-14.II.4:5)

"When you teach anyone that truth is true, you learn it with him." (T-14.II.5:1)

"Learn to be a happy learner. You will never learn how to make nothing everything." (T-14.II.5:3-4)

"If you would be a happy learner, you must give everything you have learned to the Holy Spirit, to be unlearned for you. And then begin to learn the joyous lessons that come quickly on the firm foundation that truth is true." (T-14.II.6:1-2)

"Behold your brothers in their freedom, and learn of them how to be free of darkness." (T-14.II.8:1)

"God is everywhere, and His Son is in Him with everything." (T-14.II.8:7)

In summary, Chapter 14 – II. "The Happy Learner" is saying:

A happy learner is one who is willing to accept the only truth that has ever been true: We are eternal beings, eternally united with each other and our Creator. The happy learner begins to accept this truth through relinquishing the idea that anything less could be real. Nothing we see with our physical eyes will last for all eternity. The truth states that only what is eternal is real, and so our current reality must be "nothing." This does not mean we should cease to care for this world, our bodies, and each other. On the contrary. We should care *more*. For only Love can teach us that we are love. And to learn we are Love we must learn to see it everywhere. The happy learner has learned they

III. The Decision for Guiltlessness

do not live in a world of darkness, separation and physical bodies, but rather, we live in God's Love, which is everywhere and in everything. Knowing this, makes learning a happy process and therefore you, a happy learner—happily exchanging the false for the true at every opportunity.

III. The Decision for Guiltlessness

"The happy learner cannot feel guilty about learning. This is so essential to learning that it should never be forgotten. The guiltless learner learns easily because his thoughts are free." (T-14.III.1:1-3)

"Whenever the pain of guilt seems to attract you, remember that if you yield to it, you are deciding against your happiness, and will not learn how to be happy. Say therefore, to yourself, gently, but with the conviction born of the Love of God and of His Son:

What I experience I will make manifest. If I am guiltless, I have nothing to fear. I choose to testify to my acceptance of the Atonement, not to its rejection. I would accept my guiltlessness by making it manifest and sharing it. Let me bring peace to God's Son from his Father." (T-14.III.3:3-9)

"Each day, each hour and minute, even each second, you are deciding between the crucifixion and the resurrection; between the ego and the Holy Spirit. The ego is the choice for guilt; the Holy Spirit the choice for guiltlessness." (T-14.III.4:1-2)

"The miracle teaches you that you have chosen guiltlessness, freedom and joy. It is not a cause, but an effect." (T-14.III.5:1-2)

"The way to teach this simple lesson is merely this: Guiltlessness is invulnerability." (T-14.III.7:1)

"Those who accept the Atonement *are* invulnerable." (T-14.III.10:1)

"Nothing can shake God's conviction of the perfect purity of everything that He created, for it *is* wholly pure. Do not decide against it, for being of Him it must be true." (T-14.III.12:2-3)

"The Holy Spirit knows that all salvation is escape from guilt." (T-14.III.13:4)

"Let Him, therefore, be the only Guide that you would follow to salvation." (T-14.III.14:1)

"Seek not to appraise the worth of God's Son whom He created holy,

CHAPTER 14 — TEACHING FOR TRUTH

for to do so is to evaluate his Father and judge against Him." (T-14.III.15:1)

"Say to the Holy Spirit only, "Decide for me," and it is done." (T-14.III.16:1)

"How gracious it is to decide all things through Him Whose equal Love is given equally to all alike!" (T-14.III.17:1)

"You have taught yourself the most unnatural habit of not communicating with your Creator." (T-14.III.18:1)

"Whenever you are in doubt what you should do, think of His Presence in you, and tell yourself this, and only this:

He leadeth me and knows the way, which I know not. Yet He will never keep from me what He would have me learn. And so I trust Him to communicate to me all that He knows for me.

Then let Him teach you quietly how to perceive your guiltlessness, which is already there." (T-14.III.19:1-5)

In summary, Chapter 14 – III "The Decision for Guiltlessness" is saying:

We established in chapter 13 that the word "guilt" can be equally substituted with the word "body" and so, our decision for "guiltlessness" is really the decision to see ourselves as "bodiless." This frees us from all pain and suffering because our thoughts are free of all "harm" caused by the body, knowing it is not who we are. It is a miracle to choose to see yourself as "guiltless" or "bodiless," because it is the decision to be free and therefore happy. This is salvation, the escape from all "guilt" or the escape from the pain and suffering of the body. We cannot perceive bodilessness with our bodily eyes, but the Holy Spirit *can*, and so we must ask for His assistance in seeing others through His eyes. This is the decision to see guiltlessness or everyone's true Identity—our bodilessness—as One eternal Love.

IV. Your Function in the Atonement

"When you accept a brother's guiltlessness you will see the Atonement in him." (T-14.IV.1:1)

"His guiltlessness is your Atonement." (T-14.IV.1:4)

"When you have let all that obscured the truth in your most holy mind be undone for you, and therefore stand in grace before your Father, He will give Himself to you as He has always done." (T-14.IV.3:1)

IV. Your Function in the Atonement

"Atonement becomes real and visible to those who use it. On earth this is your only function, and you must learn that it is all you want to learn." (T-14.IV.3:6-7)

"Decide that God is right and you are wrong about yourself." (T-14.IV.4:5)

"Fail not in your function of loving in a loveless place made out of darkness and deceit, for thus are darkness and deceit undone." (T-14.IV.4:10)

"Your function here is only to decide against deciding what you want, in recognition that you do not know." (T-14.IV.5:2)

"When you have learned to decide with God, all decisions become easy and as right as breathing. There is no effort, and you will be led as gently as if you were being carried down a quiet path in summer." (T-14.IV.6:1-2)

"You who are tired will find this is more restful than sleep." (T-14.IV.6:7)

"Unless you are guiltless you cannot know God, Whose Will is that you know Him." (T-14.IV.7:1)

"Yet if you do not accept the necessary conditions for knowing Him, you have denied Him and do not recognize Him, though He is all around you." (T-14.IV.7:3)

"The guiltless and the guilty are totally incapable of understanding one another." (T-14.IV.10:1)

"God can communicate only to the Holy Spirit in your mind, because only He shares the knowledge of what you are with God." (T-14.IV.10:3)

"Everything else that you have placed within your mind cannot exist, for what is not in communication with the Mind of God has never been." (T-14.IV.10:5)

In summary, Chapter 14 – IV. "Your Function in the Atonement" is saying:

Our function in the Atonement is to cease to define ourselves as we see fit. It is to realize that we do not know our own Identity, as God created us in His Love. It is our function to decide that God is right about us, and we have been wrong. Once we accept the guiltless or bodiless identity of our brethren, we will see our Oneness—the Atonement in them. So, let us decide *with* God, that His definition of us is true; let us cease to resist Him. And then all our effort and strain will cease as well. Life will become as gentle as a "quiet path in summer." Unless we decide to see everyone as "guiltless" or "bodiless" we will be blocking our communication with the Holy Spirit. We know bodies cannot truly join with Spirit, only the mind can. Therefore, only through our mind can we fulfill our function in the Atonement, the acceptance of our Unity.

V. The Circle of Atonement

"The only part of your mind that has reality is the part that links you still with God." (T-14.V.1:1)

"Everyone has a special part to play in the Atonement, but the message given to each one is always the same; *God's Son is guiltless.*" (T-14.V.2:1)

"Your only calling here is to devote yourself, with active willingness, to the denial of guilt in all its forms. To accuse is not to understand. The happy learners of the Atonement become the teachers of the innocence that is the right of all that God created." (T-14.V.3:5-7)

"The inheritance of the Kingdom is the right of God's Son, given him in his creation." (T-14.V.4:1)

"We are all joined in the Atonement here, and nothing else can unite us in this world. So will the world of separation slip away, and full communication be restored between the Father and the Son." (T-14.V.5:1-2)

"Teachers of innocence, each in his own way, have joined together, taking their part in the unified curriculum of the Atonement." (T-14.V.6:1)

"Each effort made on its behalf is offered for the single purpose of release from guilt, to the eternal glory of God and His creation." (T-14.V.6:4)

"There is no pain, no trial, no fear that teaching this can fail to overcome." (T-14.V.6:6)

"Join your own efforts to the power that cannot fail and must result in peace." (T-14.V.7:1)

"Peace, then, be unto everyone who becomes a teacher of peace." (T-14.V.8:1)

"Stand quietly within this circle, and attract all tortured minds to join with you in the safety of its peace and holiness." (T-14.V.8:6)

"Blessed are you who teach with me." (T-14.V.9:1)

"I stand within the circle, calling you to peace." (T-14.V.9:4)

"Stand not outside, but join with me within. Fail not the only purpose to which my teaching calls you. Restore to God His Son as He created him, by teaching him his innocence." (T-14.V.9:8-10)

"Each one you see you place within the holy circle of Atonement or leave outside, judging him fit for crucifixion or for redemption. If you bring him into the circle of purity, you will rest there with him. If you leave him without, you join him there." (T-14.V.11:1-3)

"Come, let us join him in the holy place of peace which is for all of us, united as one within the Cause of peace." (T-14.V.11:9)

In summary, Chapter 14 – V. "The Circle of Atonement" is saying:
The circle of Atonement is merely the place within your mind where you have decided whether we are "guilty bodies" or whether we are united in Spirit and bodies play no part in the truth of our being. If you decide we are bodies, then you choose to stand outside the circle of Atonement and suffering will be your experience. If you decide we are one in truth and overlook our seeming separation, you will have placed yourself and everyone you see within the circle of Atonement, where we will rest in quiet forgiveness of all that is not true. The circle of Atonement is the safe refuge from all that the world shows us. Seek to know our Unity there, and you join with God in His holy place of peace, the circle of atonement.

VI. The Light of Communication

"The journey that we undertake together is the exchange of dark for light, of ignorance for understanding." (T-14.VI.1:1)

"The quiet light in which the Holy Spirit dwells within you is merely perfect openness, in which nothing is hidden and therefore nothing is fearful. Attack will always yield to love if it is brought to love, not hidden from it. There is no darkness that the light of love will not dispel, unless it is concealed from love's beneficence." (T-14.VI.2:1-3)

"Death yields to life simply because destruction is not true." (T-14.VI.4:1)

"You have regarded the separation as a means for breaking your communication with your Father." (T-14.VI.5:1)

"You who speak in dark and devious symbols do not understand the language you have made. It has no meaning, for its purpose is not communication, but rather the disruption of communication." (T-14.VI.6:1-2)

"You know not what you say, and so you know not what is said to you. Yet your Interpreter perceives the meaning in your alien language." (T-14.VI.7:1-2)

"The Holy Spirit's function is entirely communication. He therefore must remove whatever interferes with communication in order to restore it." (T-14.VI.8:1-2)

"We must open all doors and let the light come streaming through."

"No one can fail to come where God has called him, if he close not the door himself upon his Father's welcome." (T-14.VI.8:8)

In summary, Chapter 14 – VI. "The Light of Communication" is saying:
The Holy Spirit is the Communication Link between us and God. This link can never be broken, but we can close our ears to His Voice. We have used the idea of separation as the means through which to do this. Bodies symbolize the idea of our separation; symbols of the dark voice of the ego proclaiming our bodies are all we have. It is the symbol of our attack on God, Who knows we are eternal. Yet the light of the Holy Spirit's communication says that death will always yield to life, simply because you cannot die for you are not separate from God, Who *is Life*. The only thing that interferes with our understanding of the Holy Spirit's communication is our steadfast belief in being bodies. We do not know we are proclaiming our independence from God through being a body. We think it natural to live in this way, in these bodies, and yet if we unlocked our belief in this identity, we would open wide the door to the light of understanding and the Holy Spirit's communication.

VII. Sharing Perception with the Holy Spirit

"What do you want? Light or darkness, knowledge or ignorance are yours, but not both." (T-14.VII.1:1-2)

"In union, everything that is not real must disappear, for truth is union. As darkness disappears in light, so ignorance fades away when knowledge dawns. Perception is the medium by which ignorance is brought to knowledge." (T-14.VII.1:5-7)

"The search for truth is but the honest searching out of everything that interferes with truth." (T-14.VII.2:1)

VII. Sharing Perception with the Holy Spirit

"It is not possible to convince the unknowing that they know." (T-14.VII.3:1)

"To God, unknowing is impossible. It is therefore not a point of view at all, but merely a belief in something that does not exist. It is only this belief that the unknowing have, and by it they are wrong about themselves. They have defined themselves as they were not created." (T-14.VII.3:5-8)

"Light cannot enter darkness when a mind believes in darkness, and will not let it go." (T-14.VII.5:1)

"Defenses, like everything you made, must be gently turned to your own good, translated by the Holy Spirit from means of self-destruction to means of preservation and release." (T-14.VII.5:8)

"Joining with Him in seeing is the way in which you learn to share with Him the interpretation of perception that leads to knowledge." (T-14.VII.7:1)

"It is the recognition that nothing you see means anything alone." (T-14.VII.7:4)

"God has one purpose which He shares with you. The single vision which the Holy Spirit offers you will bring this oneness to your mind with clarity and brightness so intense you could not wish, for all the world not to accept what God would have you have." (T-14.VII.7:6-7)

In summary, Chapter 14 – VII. "Sharing Perception with the Holy Spirit" is saying:

We cannot see through both the eyes of the ego and the vision of the Holy Spirit at the same time. It is easy to understand that this would be impossible. And so, we must decide: do we want to see darkness or light? Here we are being told that knowledge is light. What is it we must learn to know? That we remain as we were created; as God's eternal Son in union with Him and each other. "Light" is the acceptance of this knowledge, and darkness is the preservation of an identity that will self-destruct in time—the ego is literally "self-destructive." We live in a world seeing bodies all around us, and so we must learn to perceive differently in order to overcome the barriers to light the ego has erected. One way is to recognize that nothing we see means anything alone, without the shared perception of the Holy Spirit of our Unity in God's Love.

VIII. The Holy Meeting Place

"In the darkness you have obscured the glory God gave you, and the power He bestowed upon His guiltless Son." (T-14.VIII.1:1)

"Banish not power from your mind, but let all that would hide your glory be brought to the judgment of the Holy Spirit, and there undone." (T-14.VIII.1:5)

"He has promised the Father that through Him you would be released from littleness to glory." (T-14.VIII.1:7)

"Everything that promises otherwise, great or small, however much or little valued, He will replace with the one promise given unto Him to lay upon the altar to your Father and His Son." (T-14.VIII.2:2)

"Can you offer guilt to God? You cannot, then, offer it to His Son. For They are not apart, and Gifts to One are offered to the Other. You know not God because you know not this." (T-14.VIII.2:5-8)

"The holy meeting place of the unseparated Father and His Son lies in the Holy Spirit and in you." (T-14.VIII.2:13)

"Unbroken and uninterrupted love flows constantly between the Father and the Son, as Both would have it be. And so it is." (T-14.VIII.2:15-16)

"Let your mind wander not through darkened corridors, away from light's center. You and your brother may choose to lead yourselves astray, but you can be brought together only by the Guide appointed for you." (T-14.VIII.3:1-2)

"And truth will make this plain to you as you are brought into the place where you must meet with truth." (T-14.VIII.4:2)

"Where God is, there are you. Such is the truth." (T-14.VIII.4:4-5)

"The link with which the Father joins Himself to those He gives the power to create can never be dissolved." (T-14.VIII.5:1)

"And Heaven remains the Will of God for you. Lay no gifts other than this upon your altars, for nothing can coexist with it." (T-14.VIII.5:3-4)

"Your little gifts will vanish on the altar, where He has placed His Own." (T-14.VIII.5:7)

In summary, Chapter 14 – VIII. "The Holy Meeting Place" is saying: There is a holy meeting place within each and every one of us; a holy altar unto God, upon which we join our mind to His. It is the place within our mind where our thoughts are generated, initiated by our beliefs. What we think about reflects what we believe, and these thoughts are what populate our altars. How cluttered with nonsensical debris must our altars appear to God? So far, we have known not what we offer, but we do now. These "thought-offerings" are our conversation with God in which we "ask" for the reality of our choosing; this is our power to create. If we think about the world and all the bodily identities with which we find fault—including our own—then this is what we are placing upon our altar as our offering to God. This is what we are saying is valuable to us and what we want *more* of. Let us not offer such dark thoughts to God. Let us only accept what *He* offers *us*: the unbroken and uninterrupted love that flows constantly between us and our Creator within, in the holy meeting place where Father and Son are joined.

IX. The Reflection of Holiness

"The Atonement does not make holy. You were created holy. It merely brings unholiness to holiness; or what you made to what you are. Bringing illusion to truth, or the ego to God, is the Holy Spirit's only function." (T-14.IX.1:1-4)

"Bringing the ego to God is but to bring error to truth, where it stands corrected because it is the opposite of what it meets. It is undone because the contradiction can no longer stand." (T-14.IX.2:1-2)

"What disappears in light is not attacked. It merely vanishes because it is not true." (T-14.IX.2:4-5)

"The Atonement is so gentle you need but whisper to it, and all its power will rush to your assistance and support. You are not frail with God beside you." (T-14.IX.3:2-3)

"God has not left His altar, though His worshipers placed other gods upon it." (T-14.IX.3:8)

"In the temple, Holiness waits quietly for the return of them that love it." (T-14.IX.4:1)

"In this world you can become a spotless mirror, in which the Holiness of your Creator shines forth from you to all around you. You can reflect Heaven here. Yet no reflections of the images of other gods must dim the mirror that would hold God's reflection in it." (T-14.IX.5:1-3)

"Reflections are seen in light. In darkness they are obscure, and their meaning seems to lie only in shifting interpretations, rather than in themselves. The reflection of God needs no interpretation." (T-14.IX.6:1-3)

"Clean but the mirror, and the message that shines forth from what the mirror holds out for everyone to see, no one can fail to understand." (T-14.IX.6:5)

"Could you but realize for a single instant the power of healing that the reflection of God, shining in you, can bring to all the world, you could not wait to make the mirror of your mind clean to receive the image of the holiness that heals the world." (T-14.IX.7:1)

"Those who have learned to offer only healing, because of the reflection of holiness in them, are ready at last for Heaven." (T-14.IX.8:4)

"They do not merely reflect truth, for they are truth." (T-14.IX.8:7)

In summary, Chapter 14 – IX. "The Reflection of Holiness" is saying:
Our minds are capable of reflecting God's Thoughts; the purity of His love for us and ours for Him. Yet our minds are cluttered with thoughts quite the opposite of love in every way. Our thoughts are typically in a near constant state of worry, despair, depression, anger, self-depreciation, or self-aggrandizement. The mirror of our mind is at times, dark indeed. No reflection has ever been seen in a mirror placed in the dark. What is our motivation for bringing it out into the light? We are certainly afraid of what we will see, and yet God promises us that if for only a single instant we would allow ourselves to see His Thoughts reflected there, we would heal the world. We are God's Thoughts, so let us see Him in all whom we look upon in our mind. In this light, our mind becomes a clear reflection of His holiness and Heaven is brought to earth.

X. The Equality of Miracles

"The reflections you accept into the mirror of your mind in time but bring eternity nearer or farther." (T-14.X.1:2)

"Reflect the peace of Heaven here, and bring this world to Heaven." (T-14.X.1:6)

"In Heaven reality is shared and not reflected. By sharing its reflection

X. The Equality of Miracles

here, its truth becomes the only perception the Son of God accepts." (T-14.X.2:1)

"In this world, it is not true that anything without order of difficulty can occur." (T-14.X.2:5)

"The miracle is the one thing you can do that transcends order, being based not on difference but on equality." (T-14.X.2:7)

"Miracles are not in competition, and the number of them that you can do is limitless." (T-14.X.3:1)

"Perhaps you have been unaware of lack of competition among your thoughts, which even though they may conflict, can occur together and in great numbers." (T-14.X.4:1)

"For some are reflections of Heaven, while others are motivated by the ego, which but seems to think." (T-14.X.4:5)

"The result is a weaving, changing pattern that never rests and is never still. It shifts unceasingly across the mirror of your mind, and the reflections of Heaven last but a moment and grow dim, as darkness blots them out." (T-14.X.5:1-2)

"It will seem difficult for you to learn that you have no basis at all for ordering your thoughts. This lesson the Holy Spirit teaches by giving you the shining examples of miracles to show you that your way of ordering is wrong, but that a better way is offered you. The miracle offers exactly the same response to every call for help." (T-14.X.6:1-3)

"It does not consider which call is louder or greater or more important." (T-14.X.6:6)

"The power of God is limitless. And being always maximal, it offers everything to every call from anyone. There is no order of difficulty here." (T-14.X.6:12-14)

"The only judgment involved is the Holy Spirit's one division into two categories; one of love, and the other the call for love." (T-14.X.7:1)

"The ego is incapable of understanding content, and is totally unconcerned with it." (T-14.X.8:1)

"The study of the ego is not the study of the mind. In fact, the ego enjoys studying itself, and thoroughly approves the undertakings of students who would "analyze" it, thus approving its importance. Yet

CHAPTER 14—TEACHING FOR TRUTH

they but study form with meaningless content." (T-14.X.8:6-8)

"Every interpretation you would lay upon a brother is senseless. Let the Holy Spirit show him to you, and teach you both his love and his call for love. Neither his mind nor yours holds more than these two orders of thought." (T-14.X.11:4-5)

"The miracle is the recognition that this is true." (T-14.X.12:1)

"Earlier I said this course will teach you how to remember what you are, restoring to you your Identity. We have already learned that this Identity is shared. The miracle becomes the means of sharing It." (T-14.X.12:4-6)

"How, then, can there be any order of difficulty among them?" (T-14.X.12:10)

In summary, Chapter 14 – X. "The Equality of Miracles" is saying:
Our thoughts hold our power to create, and therefore, our thoughts also hold our miracle-working power. The importance of being consciously aware of the quality of our thoughts, cannot be emphasized enough. We give little attention to the direction of our thoughts. They range all over the emotional scale, shifting more quickly than clouds on a windy day. The ego is unconcerned with the content of our mind and is happy to let us go on living in a world of chaos, driven forward by minds in chaos. Do not waste any time analyzing your thoughts. If they are based on what you see and experience here in this world of form, all thoughts about such things are false interpretations, because it is a world stemming from ego-thoughts. You will be having false thoughts about a false world. Learn to re-direct your thinking once you catch yourself analyzing the world. You want to offer miraculous thoughts instead; thoughts that will restore this world to its proper vibration, which is Unity, peace, and Oneness. Believe this miraculous thought about everyone and everything and you will have learned the equality of miracles, by extending such thoughts to all.

XI. The Test of Truth

"Yet the essential thing is learning that you do not know." (T-14.XI.1:1)

"Everything you have taught yourself has made your power more and more obscure to you. You know not what it is, nor where." (T-14.XI.1:5-6)

"Be willing, then, for all of it to be undone, and be glad that you are not bound to it forever. For you have taught yourself how to imprison the Son of God, a lesson so unthinkable that only the insane, in deepest

XI. The Test of Truth

sleep, could even dream of it." (T-14.XI.2:1-2)

"What have you taught yourself that you can possibly prefer to keep, in place of what you have and what you *are*?" (T-14.XI.2:5)

"Atonement teaches you how to escape forever from everything that you have taught yourself in the past, by showing you only what you are *now*." (T-14.XI.3:1)

"Nothing you have ever learned can help you understand the present, or teach you how to undo the past. Your past is what you have taught yourself. *Let it all go.* Do not attempt to understand any event or anything or anyone in its "light," for the darkness in which you try to see can only obscure." (T-14.XI.3:5-8)

"You have one test, as sure as God, by which to recognize if what you learned is true. If you are wholly free of fear of any kind, and if all those who meet or even think of you share in your perfect peace, then you can be sure that you have learned God's lesson, and not your own. Unless all this is true, there are dark lessons in your mind that hurt and hinder you, and everyone around you." (T-14.XI.5:1-3)

"Do not be concerned about how you can learn a lesson so completely different from everything that you have taught yourself. How could you know? Your part is very simple. You need only recognize that everything you learned you do not want. Ask to be taught, and do not use your experiences to confirm what you have learned. When your peace is threatened or disturbed in any way, say to yourself:

> *I do not know what anything, including this, means. And so I do not know how to respond to it. And I will not use my own past learning as the light to guide me now."*

By this refusal to attempt to teach yourself what you do not know, the Guide Whom God has given you will speak to you. He will take His rightful place in your awareness the instant you abandon it, and offer it to Him." (T-14.XI.6:6-11)

"You have no problems that He cannot solve by offering you a miracle. Miracles are for you. And every fear or pain or trial you have has been undone." (T-14.XI.9:2-4)

"The lessons you would teach yourself He has corrected already. They do not exist in His Mind at all." (T-14.XI.9:7-8)

CHAPTER 14—TEACHING FOR TRUTH

"God's Son will always be indivisible. As we are held as one in God, so do we learn as one in Him." (T-14.XI.11:1)

"Listen in silence, and do not raise your voice against Him." (T-14.XI.11:4)

"Those who remember always that they know nothing, and who have become willing to learn everything, will learn it." (T-14.XI.12:1)

"It is impossible to deny the Source of effects so powerful they could not be of you. Leave room for Him, and you will find yourself so filled with power that nothing will prevail against your peace. And this will be the test by which you recognize that you have understood." (T-14.XI.15:4-6)

In summary, Chapter 14 – XI. "The Test of Truth" is saying:
The ego has taught us many un-truths; the most unthinkable being that we can depart from God's loving Unity; that we can come into bodies of separation and live life independently from Him and each other. Our minds are polluted with such un-truths. There seems no end and no escaping them. Yet, there is a single, clear-cut way: *admit you do not know what anything is, what it means or how to deal with it.* How could we possibly know when all we have learned is illusion? This admission will restore peace to your mind, simply by taking the responsibility for knowing the mysteries of the universe *off* your mind. The next step is to give full control of your mind over to the Holy Spirit, Who *does* know of such things. His mind does not contain your problems; only the solution: *Let it all go,* for this is not your real life. Then, silence your mind of all thoughts of the world, which resist the peace of God. Then your mind will expand to include the truth; there is nothing in all the world that can disturb your peace, for it is of God. The one sure test you have indeed learned the truth, is a mind that rests in peaceful thoughts of others, and they of you. Always, in every thought, we are either teaching for the truth of our Oneness or against it.

CHAPTER 15
THE HOLY INSTANT

I. The Two Uses of Time

"Can you imagine what it means to have no cares, no worries, no anxieties, but merely to be perfectly calm and quiet all the time? Yet that is what time is for; to learn just that and nothing more." (T-15.I.1:1-2)

"One source of perceived discouragement from which you may suffer is your belief that this takes time, and that the results of the Holy Spirit's teaching are far in the future. This is not so. For the Holy Spirit uses time in His Own way, and is not bound by it." (T-15.I.2:1-3)

"The ego, like the Holy Spirit, uses time to convince you of the inevitability of the goal and end of teaching. To the ego the goal is death, which is its end. But to the Holy Spirit the goal is life, which has no end." (T-15.I.2:7-9)

"No one who follows the ego's teaching is without the fear of death." (T-15.I.4:7)

"How bleak and despairing is the ego's use of time! And how terrifying!" (T-15.I.6:1-2)

"The only way in which the ego allows the fear of hell to be experienced is to bring hell here, but always as a foretaste of the future." (T-15.I.6:6)

"The Holy Spirit teaches thus: There is no hell. Hell is only what the ego has made of the present." (T-15.I.7:1-2)

"The Holy Spirit would undo all of this *now*. Fear is not of the present, but only of the past and future, which do not exist." (T-15.I.8:1-2)

"Each instant is a clean, untarnished birth, in which the Son of God emerges from the past into the present. And the present extends forever." (T-15.I.8:4-5)

"This lesson takes no time. For what is time without at past and future?" (T-15.I.9:1-2)

"Begin to practice the Holy Spirit's use of time as a teaching aid to happiness and peace. Take this very instant, now, and think of it as all there is of time. Nothing can reach you here out of the past, and it is here

CHAPTER 15—THE HOLY INSTANT

that you are completely absolved, completely free and wholly without condemnation." (T-15.I.9:4-6)

"If you are tempted to be dispirited by thinking how long it would take to change your mind so completely, ask yourself, "How long is an instant?" Could you not give so short a time to the Holy Spirit for your salvation?" (T-15.I.11:1-2)

"You will never give this holy instant to the Holy Spirit on behalf of your release while you are unwilling to give it to your brothers on behalf of theirs." (T-15.I.12:1)

"Remember, then, when you are tempted to attack a brother, that his instant of release is yours. Miracles are the instants of release you offer, and will receive. They attest to your willingness to be released, and to offer time to the Holy Spirit for His use of it." (T-15.I.12:3-5)

"How long is an instant? As long as it takes to re-establish perfect sanity, perfect peace and perfect love for everyone, for God and for yourself." (T-15.I.14:1-2)

"Offer the miracle of the holy instant through the Holy Spirit, and leave His giving it to you to Him." (T-15.I.15:11)

In summary, Chapter 15 – I. "The Two Uses of Time" is saying:
The ego uses time for stress and worry; it is the aspect of our mind concerned with the past and future, rarely pausing to rest in the present moment. The Holy Spirit uses time for *only* living in the present moment, which is actually eternity. It feels restful to be present, because you have stepped out of time, *and into eternity*, which feels like heaven. It takes but an instant to do this; the amount of time it takes to decide to release everyone from all the mistakes you perceive in them. It is a miracle to exchange attack for release. It is a miracle to release your past and future thoughts about all the things people are doing with their bodies that you are unhappy with. Release them as you would have yourself be released. Do this, and you offer time to the Holy Spirit Who will use it to bring you only happiness and peace in the present. There are but two uses of time: you can either spend it with ego-thoughts or with the peaceful Thoughts of God. One traps you in time and the other releases you from it.

II. The End of Doubt

"The Atonement is *in* time, but not for time." (T-15.II.1:1)

"In the blessed instant you will let go all your past learning, and the Holy Spirit will quickly offer you the whole lesson of peace." (T-15.II.1:7)

"Do not be concerned with time, and fear not the instant of holiness that will remove all fear. For the instant of peace is eternal because it is without fear." (T-15.II.2:1-2)

"How long can it take to be where God would have you? For you are where you have forever been and will forever be. All that you have, you have forever. The blessed instant reaches out to encompass time, as God extends Himself to encompass you. You who have spent days, hours and even years in chaining your brothers to your ego in an attempt to support it and uphold its weakness, do not perceive the Source of strength." (T-15.II.3:1-5)

"You do not realize how much you have misused your brothers by seeing them as sources of ego support. As a result, they witness to the ego in your perception, and seem to provide reasons for not letting it go." (T-15.II.4:1-2)

"And because of this, you have not given a single instant completely to the Holy Spirit." (T-15.II.4:10)

"You will doubt until you hear one witness whom you have wholly released through the Holy Spirit. And then you will doubt no more." (T-15.II.4:13-14)

"Start now to practice your little part in separating out the holy instant. You will receive very specific instructions as you go along." (T-15.II.T-15.II.6:1-2)

"Fear not that you will not be given help in this." (T-15.II.6:4)

"It is only your weakness that will depart from you in this practice, for it is the practice of the power of God in you. Use it but for one instant, and you will never deny it again. Who can deny the Presence of what the universe bows to, in appreciation and gladness? Before the recognition of the universe that witnesses to It, your doubts must disappear." (T-15.II.6:6-9)

CHAPTER 15 — THE HOLY INSTANT

In summary, Chapter 15 – II. "The End of Doubt" is saying:
Currently, we doubt the Atonement is real; we doubt that we are One. This is self-evident in how we treat one another. If we truly believed in our unity, we would love each other as we love ourselves. The "blessed instant" is the instant we let go of all past ideas we hold of one another and reach only for the truth of God's holy Light within us. This is the instant we cease to abuse our brothers by seeing them as evidence the ego is real. And because what we believe is what we see, they in turn will then show us the Light of God within them. It may sound impossible to achieve this level of vision but fear not! We are promised much help in this. God Himself supports our thoughts whenever we practice the holy instant and allow ourselves to let go of all doubt that we are not what He created us to be. The end of doubt is the moment we can manage to see beyond our doubts for even a single holy instant, and believe we are the Son God loves.

III. Littleness versus Magnitude

"Be not content with littleness. But be sure you understand what littleness is, and why you could never be content with it." (T-15.III.1:1)

"Everything in this world is little because it is a world made out of littleness, in the strange belief that littleness can content you. When you strive for anything in this world in the belief that it will bring you peace, you are belittling yourself and blinding yourself to glory." (T-15.III.1:5-6)

"Choose littleness and you will not have peace, for you will have judged yourself unworthy of it. And whatever you offer as a substitute is much too poor a gift to satisfy you. It is essential that you accept the fact, and accept it gladly, that there is no form of littleness that can ever content you. You are free to try as many as you wish, but all you will be doing is to delay your homecoming." (T-15.III.2:2-5)

"The lesson may seem hard at first, but you will learn to love it when you realize that it is true and is but a tribute to your power. You who have sought and found littleness, remember this: Every decision you make stems from what you think you are, and represents the value that you put upon yourself." (T-15.III.3:2-3)

"All your striving must be directed against littleness, for it does require vigilance to protect your magnitude in this world. To hold your mag-

III. Littleness versus Magnitude

nitude in perfect awareness in a world of littleness is a task the little cannot undertake." (T-15.III.4:4-5)

"Nor is it asked of you alone. The power of God will support every effort you make on behalf of His dear Son." (T-15.III.4:7-6)

"In this season (Christmas) which celebrates the birth of holiness into this world, join with me who decided for holiness for you. It is our task together to restore the awareness of magnitude to the host whom God appointed for Himself." (T-15.III.7:1-2)

"For God would give Himself through you." (T-15.III.7:4)

"Learn that you must be worthy of the Prince of Peace, born in you in honor of Him Whose host you are." (T-15.III.8:4)

"Holy child of God, when will you learn that only holiness can content you and give you peace?" (T-15.III.9:1)

"If you are wholly willing to leave salvation to the plan of God and unwilling to attempt to grasp for peace yourself, salvation will be given you." (T-15.III.11:1)

"Call forth in everyone only the remembrance of God, and of the Heaven that is in him. For where you would have your brother be, there will you think you are." (T-15.III.12:1-2)

In summary, Chapter 15 – III. "Littleness versus Magnitude" is saying:

"Littleness" is simply another word to describe your separate physical ego-self, which is not eternal. "Magnitude" describes your magnified, expanded eternal Self; the "You" God created and will therefore exist forever. Our bodies, and everything that exists in the world of form is considered "littleness." Our spirit, and all that exists eternally is considered "magnitude." Deep down, we have an inner knowing that we belong only in the world of magnitude. This awareness causes our ego to be forever dissatisfied with everything it attains in this world, knowing it can never become everlasting. Littleness will never satisfy us. Therefore, be vigilant against thoughts of littleness—thoughts about the ego's wanting for this world—and learn to see only the magnitude of our Unity in God in everyone and everything, and Heaven is where you will find yourself.

CHAPTER 15—THE HOLY INSTANT

IV. Practicing the Holy Instant

"This course is not beyond your immediate learning, unless you believe that what God wills takes time. And this means only that you would rather delay the recognition that His Will is so. The holy instant is this instant and every instant." (T-15.IV.1:1-3)

"Yet you cannot bring it into glad awareness while you do not want it, for it holds the whole release from littleness." (T-15.IV.1:9)

"Your practice must therefore rest upon your willingness to let all littleness go. The instant in which magnitude dawns upon you is but as far away as your desire for it." (T-15.IV.2:1-2)

"I call you to fulfill your holy part in the plan that He has given to the world for its release from littleness." (T-15.IV.3:4)

"You can claim the holy instant any time and anywhere you want it. In your practice, try to give over every plan you have accepted for finding magnitude in littleness. *It is not there.* Use the holy instant only to recognize that you alone cannot know where it is, and can only deceive yourself." (T-15.IV.4:4-7)

"I stand within the holy instant, as clear as you would have me. And the extent to which you learn to accept me is the measure of the time in which the holy instant will be yours." (T-15.IV.5:1-2)

"The reason this course is simple is that truth is simple." (T-15.IV.6:1)

"The simple reason, simply stated, is this: The holy instant is a time in which you receive and give perfect communication. This means, however, that it is a time in which your mind is open, both to receive and give. It is the recognition that all minds are in communication. It therefore seeks to change nothing, but merely to accept everything." (T-15.IV.6:5-8)

"The necessary condition for the holy instant does not require that you have no thoughts that are not pure. But it does require that you have none that you would keep." (T-15.IV.9:1-2)

"You will not be able to accept perfect communication as long as you would hide it from yourself." (T-15.IV.9:6)

"In your practice, then, try only to be vigilant against deception, and seek not to protect the thoughts you would keep to yourself. Let the

Holy Spirit's purity shine them away, and bring all your awareness to the readiness for purity He offers you. Thus will He make you ready to acknowledge that you are host to God, and hostage to no one and to nothing." (T-15.IV.9:8-10)

In summary, Chapter 15 – IV. "Practicing the Holy Instant" is saying:
The holy instant is something that we must practice, being a state of mind completely opposite to the ego's way of thinking. It is a state of mind in which you willingly extend yourself in total communication with all living things. "Communication" is another word for God's Love, Who is in a constant state of communication, or "communion" with us at all times—His Love is connected to us in an unceasing and unbreakable flow. The holy instant is the instant you accept that this love is real, and you recognize you share in it with all living things. And not only do you share in it, but you can extend it willingly from your mind to the minds of others. Practice the holy instant then, by watching your thoughts. Thoughts of separation are of the ego and must be given over to the Holy Spirit the instant you notice them, and thoughts of the holy instant are peaceful thoughts in alignment with our shared Unity in God's Love. Practicing the holy instant is nothing more than the practice of loving others as part of your One Self.

V. The Holy Instant and Special Relationships

"The holy instant is the Holy Spirit's most useful learning device for teaching you love's meaning. For its purpose is to suspend judgment entirely." (T-15.V.1:1-2)

"The past is the ego's chief learning device, for it is in the past that you learned to define your own needs and acquired methods for meeting them on your own terms." (T-15.V.2:1)

"To believe that special relationships, with special love, can offer you salvation is the belief that separation is salvation." (T-15.V.3:3)

"How can you decide that special aspects of the Sonship can give you more than others?" (T-15.V.3:5)

"Because of guilt, all special relationships have elements of fear in them. This is why they shift and change so frequently. They are not based on changeless love alone." (T-15.V.4:1-3)

CHAPTER 15—THE HOLY INSTANT

"In His function as Interpreter of what you made, the Holy Spirit uses special relationships, which you have chosen to support the ego, as learning experiences that point to truth. Under His teaching, every relationship becomes a lesson in love." (T-15.V.4:5-6)

"There is no substitute for love. If you would attempt to substitute one aspect of love for another, you have placed less value on one and more on the other. You have not only separated them, but you have also judged against both." (T-15.V.6:2-4)

"Everyone on earth has formed special relationships, and although this is not so in Heaven, the Holy Spirit knows how to bring a touch of Heaven to them here." (T-15.V.8:1)

"In the holy instant, you see in each relationship what it will be when you perceive only the present." (T-15.V.8:5)

"God knows you now." (T-15.V.9:1)

"The holy instant reflects His knowing by bringing all perception out of the past, thus removing the frame of reference you have built by which to judge your brothers. Once this is gone, the Holy Spirit substitutes His frame of reference for it. His frame of reference is simply God." (T-15.V.9:3-5)

"The meaning of love is the meaning God gave to it. Give to it any meaning apart from His, and it is impossible to understand it. God loves every brother as He loves you; neither less nor more." (T-15.V.10:3-4)

"Yet in the holy instant you unite directly with God, and all your brothers join in Christ. Those who are joined in Christ are in no way separate." (T-15.V.10:8-9)

"In the holy instant there is no conflict of needs, for there is only one." (T-15.V.11:4)

In summary, Chapter 15 – V. "The Holy Instant and Special Relationships" is saying;

The ego's love is fragmented into separate bodies it has given separate roles to, to love us in special ways. And if one of them should fail our ego, it will lash out in pain, for fear its "love" will be withdrawn by the other. In the holy instant, all this is undone, for in the holy instant, love is seen and experienced only as it is now, in the present moment. How angry, hurt or upset could you be with someone if you looked at them as though for the first time, before you had any past experiences with them? Remove this frame of reference, and you are left with nothing but peace. This is how God loves us—as though we have no past and we have done nothing wrong and deserve only His unconditional Love. The holy instant is the moment all "special" relationships dissolve, and we know only peaceful unity with God and one another.

VI. The Holy Instant and the Laws of God

"It is impossible to use one relationship at the expense of another and not to suffer guilt." (T-15.VI.1:1)

"And there will be guilt as long as you accept the possibility, and cherish it, that you can make a brother into what he is not, because you would have him so." (T-15.VI.1:6)

"You have so little faith in yourself because you are unwilling to accept the fact that perfect love is in you. And so you seek without for what you cannot find without." (T-15.VI.2:1-2)

"If you seek for satisfaction in gratifying your needs as you perceive them, you must believe that strength comes from another, and what you gain he loses." (T-15.VI.3:3)

"You do not find it difficult to believe that when another calls on God for love, your call remains as strong. Nor do you think that when God answers him, your hope of answer is diminished. On the contrary, you are more inclined to regard his success as witness to the possibility of yours." (T-15.VI.4:1-3)

"In the world of scarcity, love has no meaning and peace is impossible. For gain and loss are both accepted, and so no one is aware that perfect love is in him." (T-15.VI.5:1-2)

"The holy instant thus becomes a lesson in how to hold all of your brothers in your mind, experiencing not loss but completion." (T-15.VI.5:5)

"And this is love, for this alone is natural under the laws of God. In the holy instant the laws of God prevail, and only they have meaning." (T-15.VI.5:7-8)

"Fear not the holy instant will be denied you, for I denied it not." (T-15.VI.6:7)

CHAPTER 15—THE HOLY INSTANT

"It is through us that peace will come." (T-15.VI.7:1)

"In the holy instant God is remembered, and the language of communication with all your brothers is remembered with Him." (T-15.VI.8:1)

"There is no exclusion in the holy instant because the past is gone, and with it goes the whole basis for exclusion." (T-15.VI.8:3)

In summary, Chapter 15 – VI. "The Holy Instant and the Laws of God" is saying:
There are only two types of relationships: One of separation through the ego and one of union through God. We cannot experience both simultaneously within our awareness, though only one relationship exists in truth. When we try to make another into something they are not; when we seek relationships with others as separate bodies from us whom we hold responsible for giving us their special love, we sacrifice the experience of our true relationship of unity in God. We place undo expectations on another, whose body-relationship can never give us what God can. God's law is that there is no loss, and all love is given equally and to all. No exclusions, no exceptions. And in His Love is completion known by us, as we choose to extend our love to all, even as God does.

VII. The Needless Sacrifice

"Beyond the poor attraction of the special love relationship, and always obscured by it, is the powerful attraction of the Father for His Son. There is no other love that can satisfy you, because there is no other." (T-15.VII.1:1-2)

"Being complete, it asks nothing. Being wholly pure, everyone joined in it has everything." (T-15.VII.1:4-5)

"The ego establishes relationships only to get something. And it would keep the giver bound to itself through guilt." (T-15.VII.2:1-2)

"We said before that the ego attempts to maintain and increase guilt, but in such a way that you do not recognize what it would do to you." (T-15.VII.4:1)

"The ego wishes no one well." (T-15.VII.4:3)

"And thus it embarks on an endless, unrewarding chain of special relationships, forged out of anger and dedicated to but one insane belief; that the more anger you invest outside yourself, the safer you become." (T-15.VII.4:6)

VII. The Needless Sacrifice

"It is this chain that binds the Son of God to guilt, and it is this chain the Holy Spirit would remove from his holy mind." (T-15.VII.5:1)

"It is only by attack without forgiveness that the ego can ensure the guilt that holds all its relationships together." (T-15.VII.7:8)

"Yet they only seem to be together. For relationships, to the ego, mean only that bodies are together. It is always this that the ego demands, and it does not object where the mind goes or what it thinks, for this seems unimportant. As long as the body is there to receive its sacrifice, it is content." (T-15.VII.8:1-4)

"Ideas are basically of no concern, except as they bring the body of another closer or farther." (T-15.VII.8:6)

"Suffering and sacrifice are the gifts with which the ego would "bless" all unions." (T-15.VII.9:1)

"Whenever you are angry, you can be sure that you have formed a special relationship which the ego has "blessed," for anger is its blessing." (T-15.VII.10:1)

"All anger is nothing more than an attempt to make someone feel guilty, and this attempt is the only basis the ego accepts for special relationships." (T-15.VII.10:3)

"As long as you believe that to be with a body is companionship, you will be compelled to attempt to keep your brother in his body, held there by guilt." (T-15.VII.12:2)

"In the holy instant guilt holds no attraction, since communication has been restored." (T-15.VII.14:2)

"In the protection of your wholeness, all are invited and made welcome. And you understand that your completion is God's, Whose only need is to have you be complete." (T-15.VII.14:7-8)

In summary, Chapter 15 – VII. "The Needless Sacrifice" is saying:
We have a perfect relationship with our Father God, and through Him, we also have a perfect relationship with each other. It is a relationship that asks nothing because we need nothing, for Love makes no demands. Only the ego-based relationship needs anything from another. It is a relationship based upon the perception of a lack of love. This is the "sacrifice" the ego demands—that no one ever leave us in the physical—ever—or we will suffer a sense of loss of love. To keep others in our life, we often use anger, which seems counter

intuitive when looked at with clarity. Yet to the ego anger makes perfect sense; become angry and the other person must feel the risk of losing you. This works only for so long before we tire of this game and break off the relationship, only to begin a new one under the same ego-rules but a different form. To break this cycle and transform all your relationships into holy ones, simply see them as part of your One Self, from Whom you can never be parted. There is no needless sacrifice to be made, for we complete one another, and no "body" is needed for us to be complete.

VIII. The Only Real Relationship

"The holy instant does not replace the need for learning, for the Holy Spirit must not leave you as your Teacher until the holy instant has extended far beyond time. For a teaching assignment such as His, He must use everything in this world for your release." (T-15.VIII.1:1-2)

"Hear Him gladly, and learn of Him that you have need of no special relationships at all. You but seek in them what you have thrown away." (T-15.VIII.2:1-2)

"Let us join together in making the holy instant all that there is, by desiring that it be all that there is." (T-15.VIII.2:4)

"Relate only with what will never leave you, and what you can never leave." (T-15.VIII.3:1)

"Your relationships are with the universe. And this universe, being of God, is far beyond the petty sum of all the separate bodies you perceive." (T-15.VIII.4:4-5)

"Leave, then, what seems to you to be impossible, to Him Who knows it must be possible because it is the Will of God." (T-15.VIII.6:4)

"For God created the only relationship that has meaning, and that is His relationship with you." (T-15.VIII.6:6)

In summary, Chapter 15 – VIII. "The Only Real Relationship" is saying:
We do not remember how it feels to be in relationship with God. We have forgotten the peaceful security of His loving unity; the total contentment, sense of ease and joyful bliss that come from the restful knowing of our one Self. Yet deep down, this is the relationship we crave, and so, not knowing any other way, we allow our ego to seek for it through endless relationships with other

bodies. We do not realize that what we seek is spiritual. The holy instant is the instant we *do* realize this and consciously choose to seek *it* instead. We have a deep abiding relationship of total unconditional love with an entire universe of creation, and yet we know it not. We think it inconceivable to love on such a grand scale. And so, we are asked to leave the impossible to God, Who knows how to love all creation, and Who will teach us all things are possible in Him. Our relationship with God then is the only real relationship we must seek.

IX. The Holy Instant and the Attraction of God

"As the ego would limit your perception of your brothers to the body, so would the Holy Spirit release your vision and let you see the Great Rays shining from them, so unlimited that they reach to God. It is a shift to vision that is accomplished in the holy instant. Yet it is needful for you to learn just what this shift entails, so you will become willing to make it permanent." (T-15.IX.1:1-3)

"Once you have accepted it as the only perception you want, it is translated into knowledge by the part that God Himself plays in the Atonement, for it is the only step in it He understands." (T-15.IX.1:5)

"Our task is but to continue, as fast as possible, the necessary process of looking straight at all the interference and seeing it exactly as it is." (T-15.IX.2:1)

"The body is the symbol of the ego, as the ego is the symbol of the separation. And both are nothing more than attempts to limit communication, and thereby to make it impossible." (T-15.IX.2:3-4)

"In the holy instant, where the Great Rays replace the body in awareness, the recognition of relationships without limits is given you. But in order to see this, it is necessary to give up every use the ego has for the body, and to accept the fact that the ego has no purpose you would share with it." (T-15.IX.3:1-2)

"If you would but let the Holy Spirit tell you of the Love of God for you, and the need your creations have to be with you forever, you would experience the attraction of the eternal. No one can hear Him speak of this and long remain willing to linger here." (T-15.IX.5:1-2)

"You have no conception of the limits you have placed on your perception, and no idea of all the loveliness that you could see." (T-15.IX.6:1)

CHAPTER 15—THE HOLY INSTANT

"And your sight grows weak and dim and limited, for you have attempted to separate the Father from the Son, and limit Their communication. Seek not Atonement in further separation." (T-15.IX.6:5-6)

"When the body ceases to attract you, and when you place no value on it as a means of getting anything then there will be no interference in communication and your thoughts will be as free as God's. As you let the Holy Spirit teach you how to use the body only for purposes of communication, and renounce its use for separation and attack which the ego sees in it, you will learn you have no need of a body at all. In the holy instant there are no bodies, and you experience only the attraction of God. Accepting it as undivided you join Him wholly, in an instant, for you would place no limits on your union with Him." (T-15.IX.7:1-4)

In summary, Chapter 15 – IX. "The Holy Instant and the Attraction of God" is saying:
The holy instant is the moment we let go of all our false perceptions of one another and ourselves. It is the moment we no longer accept the body as our identification, and once this belief is undone, the vision of the body lifts; giving way to what Christ sees in us: The Great Rays shining in limitless relationship with all creation. It is a vision of total unity and oneness with all things eternal—all Life as God created It—not as we would hide it behind physical forms. The body limits our perception of our true Self. To see beyond it, we merely have to cease to believe it is our identity. The proof this belief has shifted, will be reflected in how we treat one another. Do we love each other as we love ourselves? Do you love your neighbor as Jesus loves you? Do unto others as you would have them do unto you, is truly the "Golden Rule." It is the gold standard by which we should all live in order to hasten the holy instant. In the holy instant, we will be attracted only to God, and we will see bodies no more.

X. The Time of Rebirth

"It is in your power, in time, to delay the perfect union of the Father and the Son." (T-15.X.1:1)

"This is the season when you would celebrate my birth into the world. Yet you know not how to do it. Let the Holy Spirit teach you, and let me celebrate your birth through Him." (T-15.X.1:5-7)

"The holy instant is truly the time of Christ. For in this liberating in-

X. The Time of Rebirth

stant no guilt is laid upon the Son of God, and his unlimited power is thus restored to him. What other gift can you offer me, when only this I choose to offer you? And to see me is to see me in everyone, and offer everyone the gift you offer me." (T-15.X.2:1-4)

"Learn now that sacrifice of any kind is nothing but a limitation imposed on giving. And by this limitation you have limited acceptance of the gift I offer you." (T-15.X.2:6-7)

"When you are willing to accept our relationship as real, guilt will hold no attraction for you. For in our union you will accept all of our brothers." (T-15.X.3:2-4)

"It is in your power to make this season holy, for it is in your power to make the time of Christ be now." (T-15.X.4:1)

"The idea is simply this: You believe it is possible to be host to the ego or hostage to God." (T-15.X.5:4)

"You see no other alternatives, for you cannot accept the fact that sacrifice gets nothing." (T-15.X.5:6)

"Your confusion of sacrifice and love is so profound that you cannot conceive of love without sacrifice. And it is this that you must look upon; sacrifice is attack, not love." (T-15.X.5:8-9)

"The ego will never let you perceive this, since this recognition would make it homeless." (T-15.X.6:5)

"Each form will be recognized as but a cover for the one idea that hides behind them all; that love demands sacrifice, and is therefore inseparable from attack and fear." (T-15.X.6:7)

"You will not succeed in being partial hostage to the ego, for it keeps no bargains and would leave you nothing. Nor can you be partial host to it. You must choose between total freedom and total bondage, for there are no alternatives but these." (T-15.X.9:1-3)

"And yet it is the recognition of the decision, just as it is, that makes the decision so easy. Salvation is simple, being of God, and therefore very easy to understand." (T-15.X.9:5-6)

"In you are both the question and the answer, the demand for sacrifice and the peace of God." (T-15.X.9:8)

CHAPTER 15—THE HOLY INSTANT

In summary, Chapter 15 – X. "The Time of Rebirth" is saying:
During the time of Christmas, we celebrate the birth of God into an ego-body. Let us make this season different. Let us give a gift to God every day in every holy instant, the gift of our rebirth into our true Identity—the birth of our Christ-body into God's Light and Love. We sacrifice the knowing of our Identity in God, through insisting we are ego-bodies instead. Yet this is our choice: To be hostage to the ego or host to God. To recognize that we have only and ever been host to God, is the egos' whole undoing. In this recognition, lies our salvation from all forms of sacrifice and suffering, for only the body can be made to sacrifice and suffer. We have it within our power of decision to be reborn into a new Christmas season—the time we choose to give up all attack upon God's Unity through separation *and give birth to seeing only the Light of Christ in all.*

XI. Christmas as the End of Sacrifice

"Fear not to recognize the whole idea of sacrifice as solely of your making." (T-15.XI.1:1)

"Your brothers and your Father have become very fearful to you. And you would bargain with them for a few special relationships, in which you think you see some scraps of safety." (T-15.XI.1:3-4)

"The sign of Christmas is a star, a light in darkness. See it not outside yourself, but shining in the Heaven within, and accept it as the sign the time of Christ has come." (T-15.XI.2:1-2)

"And you need but invite Him in Who is there already, by recognizing that His Host is One, and no thought alien to His Oneness can abide with Him there. Love must be total to give Him welcome, for the Presence of Holiness creates the holiness that surrounds it." (T-15.XI.2:7-8)

"This Christmas give the Holy Spirit everything that would hurt you. Let yourself be healed completely that you may join with Him in healing, and let us celebrate our release together by releasing everyone with us." (T-15.XI.3:1-2)

"All pain and sacrifice and littleness will disappear in our relationship, which is as innocent as our relationship with our Father, and as powerful." (T-15.XI.3:4)

"As long as you perceive the body as your reality, so long will you perceive yourself as lonely and deprived. And so long will you also perceive yourself as victim of sacrifice, justified in sacrificing others." (T-15.XI.5:1-2)

"In the holy instant the condition of love is met, for minds are joined without the body's interference, and where there is communication there is peace. The Prince of Peace was born to reestablish the condition of love by teaching that communication remains unbroken even if the body is destroyed, provided that you see not the body as the necessary means of communication. And if you understand this lesson, you will realize that to sacrifice the body is to sacrifice nothing, and communication, which must be of the mind, cannot be sacrificed." (T-15.XI.7:1-3)

"The lesson I was born to teach, and still would teach to all my brothers, is that sacrifice is nowhere and love is everywhere." (T-15.XI.7:5)

"Let no despair darken the joy of Christmas, for the time of Christ is meaningless apart from joy. Let us join in celebrating peace by demanding no sacrifice of anyone, for so you offer me the love I offer you. What can be more joyous than to perceive we are deprived of nothing? Such is the message of the time of Christ, which I give you that you may give it and return it to the Father, Who gave it to me. For in the time of Christ communication is restored, and He joins us in the celebration of His Son's creation." (T-15.XI.8:1-5)

"This is the time in which a new year will soon be born from the time of Christ. I have perfect faith in you to do all that you would accomplish. Nothing will be lacking, and you will make complete and not destroy. Say, then, to your brother:

I give you to the Holy Spirit as part of myself.
I know that you will be released, unless I want to use you to imprison myself.
In the name of my freedom I choose your release, because I recognize that we will be released together."

So will the year begin in joy and freedom." (T-15.XI.10:1-8)

"Accept the holy instant as this year is born, and take your place, so long left unfulfilled, in the Great Awakening. Make this year different by making it all the same. And let all your relationships be made holy for you. This is our will. Amen." (T-15.XI.10:10-14)

CHAPTER 15—THE HOLY INSTANT

In summary, Chapter 15 – XI. "Christmas as the End of Sacrifice" is saying:

You light your own inner Christmas star by recognizing the Light of Christ within everyone. Through this inner recognition, you release everyone from the bondages of the ego-body, including yourself. This is the greatest gift you can give—a Christmas gift that can be given through all time and for all time. It is a gift of total unconditional love. It is the gift of the holy instant. So, let us demand that no one be a body, an ego-identity which sacrifices the peace and unity of God. Give the ego-sight of all bodies over to the Holy Spirit, that He may release them for you. And so, let this time be Christmas for you, as it marks the end of sacrifice, and the beginning of a new era of your own joy and freedom. Join all creation in the Great Awakening as you recognize the holy instant everywhere, in all your relationships united in God's Love.

CHAPTER 16
THE FORGIVENESS OF ILLUSIONS

I. True Empathy

"To empathize does not mean to join in suffering, for that is what you must *refuse* to understand. That is the ego's interpretation of empathy, and is always used to form a special relationship in which the suffering is shared." (T-16.I.1:1-2)

"The clearest proof that empathy as the ego uses it is destructive lies in the fact that it is applied only to certain types of problems and in certain people." (T-16.I.2:1)

"Make no mistake about this maneuver; the ego always empathizes to weaken, and to weaken is always to attack. You do not know what empathizing means. Yet of this you may be sure; if you will merely sit quietly by and let the Holy Spirit relate through you, you will empathize with strength, and will gain in strength and not in weakness." (T-16.I.2:5-7)

"You do not know what healing is. All you have learned of empathy is from the past." (T-16.I.3:3-4)

"Do not use empathy to make the past real, and so perpetuate it. Step gently aside, and let healing be done for you. Keep but one thought in mind and do not lose sight of it, however tempted you may be to judge any situation, and to determine your response *by* judging it. Focus your mind only on this:

> *I am not alone, and I would not intrude the past upon my Guest.*
> *I have invited Him, and He is here.*
> *I need do nothing except not to interfere.*" (T-16.I.3:6-12)

"You cannot know how to respond to what you do not understand. Be tempted not in this, and yield not to the ego's triumphant use of empathy for its glory." (T-16.I.4:6-7)

"The meaning of love is lost in any relationship that looks to weakness, and hopes to find love there. The power of love, which is its meaning, lies in the strength of God that hovers over it and blesses it silently by enveloping it in healing wings. Let this be, and do not try to substitute your "miracle" for this. I have said that if a brother asks a foolish thing of you to do it. But be certain that this does not mean to do a foolish thing that would hurt either him or you, for what would hurt one will hurt the other. Foolish requests are foolish merely because they conflict, since they always contain some element of specialness." (T-16.I.6:1-6)

In summary, Chapter 16 – I. "True Empathy" is saying:
We are eternal beings, created by God as perfect. When we look upon a body, and see that it is sick, dying, or in some way suffering, our first response is an ego-based form of empathy. We want to relate to and share in their suffering, thus further diminishing the truth about the divine perfection that they are. We are thus reinforcing the ego and blocking true healing. In order to avoid this reaction, we must learn to step aside from what we see and allow the Holy Spirit to look through us. He will see not a suffering body, but rather, a healed and whole, perfect, and complete, courageous being of Love. Do not make any foolish requests to heal the body alone, for this interferes with His Vision. Merely allow all things to be healed through knowing we are Love's Perfection. True empathy is to look upon what another is going through, and refuse to believe they are anything less than Perfection.

II. The Power of Holiness

"You may still think that holiness is impossible to understand, because you cannot see how it can be extended to include everyone." (T-16.II.1:1)

"Why should you worry how the miracle extends to all the Sonship when you do not understand the miracle itself?" (T-16.II.1:6)

"If miracles are at all, their attributes would have to be miraculous, being part of them." (T-16.II.1:8)

"There is a tendency to fragment, and then to be concerned about the truth of just a little part of the whole. And this is but a way of avoiding, or looking away from the whole, to what you think you might be better able to understand." (T-16.II.2:1-2)

"To you the miracle cannot seem natural, because what you have done to hurt you mind has made it so unnatural that it does not remember what is natural to it. And when you are told what is natural, you cannot understand it." (T-16.II.3:1-2)

"You have done miracles, but it is quite apparent that you have not done them alone. You have succeeded whenever you have reached another mind and joined with it." (T-16.II.4:1-2)

"When you have made this joining as the Holy Spirit bids you, and have offered it to Him to use as He sees fit, His natural perception of your gift enables Him to understand it, and you to use His understanding on your behalf." (T-16.II.4:4)

"Miracles are natural to the One Who speaks for God." (T-16.II.5:4)

"This is a year of joy, in which your listening will increase and peace will grow with its increase. The power of holiness and the weakness of attack are both being brought into your awareness." (T-16.II.7:1-2)

"Do not interpret against God's Love, for you have many witnesses that speak of it so clearly that only the blind and deaf could fail to see and hear them. This year determine not to deny what has been given you by God. Awake and share it, for that is the only reason He has called to you." (T-16.II.8:1-3)

"For love asks only that you be happy, and will give you everything that makes for happiness." (T-16.II.8:8)

"This year invest in truth, and let it work in peace." (T-16.II.9:7)

In summary, Chapter 16 – II. "The Power of Holiness" is saying:
Our holiness is our *wholeness*, the unity we have as part of God's One Son; His One Love. His Son is One, and we each play our own part in His Total Sonship. When we extend this thought to everyone we look upon or think of, we are extending a miracle. It is a miracle to see beyond our separate bodies, to the Oneness we all share in truth. Do not interpret anyone otherwise, or you interpret against God's One Love. This year do not deny our unity. Awaken to it and share it through your loving thoughts towards others. You love them, because they complete you, despite whatever ill-begotten thoughts the ego may have towards them. This year invest in the truth of our peaceful existence as one in God's Love—invest in the power of our holiness—the power of our Wholeness.

III. The Reward of Teaching

"We have already learned that everyone teaches, and teaches all the time." (T-16.III.1:1)

"I said earlier, "By their fruits ye shall know them, and they shall know themselves." For it is certain that you judge yourself according to your teaching." (T-16.III.2:2-3)

CHAPTER 16—THE FORGIVENESS OF ILLUSIONS

"Does not the fact that you have not learned what you have taught show you that you do not perceive the Sonship as one? And does it not also show you that you do not regard yourself as one?" (T-16.III.3:1-2)

"This is a course in how to know yourself." (T-16.III.4:1)

"Illusions are but beliefs in what is not there. And the seeming conflict between truth and illusion can only be resolved by separating yourself from the illusion and not from truth. (T-16.III.4:9-10)

"You are not two selves in conflict." (T-16.III.6:1)

"This year you will begin to learn, and make learning commensurate with teaching. You have chosen this by your own willingness to teach. Though you seemed to suffer for it, the joy of teaching will yet by yours." (T-16.III.7:1-3)

"As you learn, your gratitude to your Self, Who teaches you what He is, will grow and help you honor Him. And you will learn His power and strength and purity, and love Him as His Father does. His Kingdom has no limits and no end, and there is nothing in Him that is not perfect and eternal. All this is you, and nothing outside of this is you." (T-16.III.7:5-8)

"Sooner or later must everyone bridge the gap he imagines exists between his selves." (T-16.III.8:2)

"Your bridge is builded stronger than you think, and your foot is planted firmly on it. Have no fear that the attraction of those who stand on the other side and wait for you will not draw you safely across. For you will come where you would be, and where your Self awaits you." (T-16.III.9:1-3)

In summary, Chapter 16 – III. "The Reward of Teaching" is saying:
What is it we are always teaching, whether we are aware of it or not? We are always teaching what we believe we are. And we will know if we are teaching the truth about who we believe we are, by the "fruits" we yield; the peace we extend to others, knowing everyone is part of our One Self in God. Our fruits will be self-evident by the response others give to us. Teach only love and peace, for that is what you are. Do not believe in the illusion of the body, for it is not your truth. Though we seem to suffer for being in a bodily experience now, the joy that comes from teaching we are otherwise, is a reward beyond measure. Sooner or later we each must cross over from the belief in bodies

IV. The Illusion and the Reality of Love

to the belief in our One Self. Yet have no doubt you will get there, for even now the attraction of our Oneness draws you across the bridge. The reward of teaching our Oneness is the experience of your true Self.

IV. The Illusion and the Reality of Love

"Be not afraid to look upon the special hate relationship, for freedom lies in looking at it. It would be impossible to know the meaning of love, except for this. For the special love relationship, in which the meaning of love is hidden, is undertaken solely to offset the hate, but not to let it go." (T-16.IV.1:1-3)

"You will go through this last undoing quite unharmed, and will at last emerge as yourself. This is the last step in the readiness for God. Be not unwilling now; you are too near, and you will cross the bridge in perfect safety, translated quietly from war to peace." (T-16.IV.2:3-5)

"The special love relationship is an attempt to limit the destructive effects of hate by finding a haven in the storm of guilt." (T-16.IV.3:1)

"The special love partner is acceptable only as long as he serves this purpose." (T-16.IV.3:5)

"Love is not an illusion. It is a fact. Where disillusionment is possible, there was not love but hate. For hate is an illusion, and what can change was never love." (T-16.IV.4:1-4)

"Your task is not to seek for love, but merely to seek and find all of the barriers within yourself that you have built against it." (T-16.IV.6:1)

"If you seek love outside yourself you can be certain that you perceive hatred within, and are afraid of it." (T-16.IV.6:5)

"Recognize this, for it is true, and truth must be recognized if it is to be distinguished from illusion: The special love relationship is an attempt to bring love into separation." (T-16.IV.7:1)

"In fundamental violation of love's one condition, the special love relationship would accomplish the impossible. How but in illusion could this be done?" (T-16.IV.7:3-4)

"The special love relationship is but a shabby substitute for what makes you whole in truth, not in illusion." (T-16.IV.8:4)

"Across the bridge is your completion, for you will be wholly in God, willing for nothing special, but only to be wholly like to Him, completing Him by your completion." (T-16.IV.9:1)

"Seek not for this in the bleak world of illusion, where nothing is certain and where everything fails to satisfy." (T-16.IV.9:4)

"In any relationship in which you are wholly willing to accept completion, and only this, there is God completed, and His Son with Him." (T-16.IV.9:6)

"Every illusion you accept into your mind by judging it to be attainable removes your own sense of completion, and thus denies the Wholeness of your Father. Every fantasy, be it of love or hate, deprives you of knowledge for fantasies are the veil behind which truth is hidden. To lift the veil that seems so dark and heavy, it is only needful to value truth beyond all fantasy, and to be entirely unwilling to settle for illusion in place of truth." (T-16.IV.10:2-4)

"If special relationships of any kind would hinder God's completion, can they have any value to you?" (T-16.IV.13:1)

"There is no veil the Love of God in us together cannot lift. The way to truth is open. Follow it with me." (T-16.IV.13:9-11)

In summary, Chapter 16 – IV. "The Illusion and the Reality of Love" is saying:
The special love relationship is the special hate relationship. Why are they the same? Because to select a specific person out for a specific form of what the ego calls "love" is actually an attempt to limit this person to an identity they are not. It is to ask them to serve your ego for a specific purpose, which it calls "love." If they fail to fulfill what you have tried to guilt them into being, then such relationships quickly fall apart and turn into special hate relationships. For the ego knows not how to love. So, does this mean we can never marry one another, form families or deep abiding friendships? No indeed, for such relationships are deeply needed, but such relationships are an illusion of separation until we transform them into what God intended them to be: a unified aspect of His One Love. So, how do we free all whom we love from the bodily identities our ego has assigned to them? Through one simple thought. In your mind, say to whomever you are tempted to hold in any special love or hate relationship:

You are beloved of God Himself, even as I am. He sees nothing but what is good, true, and beautiful in you, even as He does in me. You complete Him, and therefore you complete me. And for that I am grateful. All else is an illusion of love, and I would know only Love's Reality. Amen.

V. The Choice for Completion

"In looking at the special relationship, it is necessary first to realize that it involves a great amount of pain. Anxiety, despair, guilt and attack all enter into it, broken into by periods in which they seem to be gone." (T-16.V.1:1-2)

"Whatever form they take, they are always an attack on the self to make the other guilty." (T-16.V.1:4)

"Very simply, the attempt to make guilty is always directed against God." (T-16.V.2:1)

"The special love relationship is the ego's chief weapon for keeping you from Heaven. It does not appear to be a weapon, but if you consider how you value it and why, you will realize what it must be." (T-16.V.2:3-4)

"It is in the special relationship, born of the hidden wish for special love from God, that the ego's hatred triumphs." (T-16.V.4:1)

"For the ego would never have you see that separation could only be loss, being the one condition in which Heaven could not be." (T-16.V.4:4)

"To everyone Heaven is completion. There can be no disagreement on this, because both the ego and the Holy Spirit accept it. They are, however, in complete disagreement on what completion is, and how it is accomplished. The Holy Spirit knows that completion lies first in union, and then in the extension of union. To the ego completion lies in triumph, and in the extension of the "victory" even to the final triumph over God." (T-16.V.5:1-5)

"The special relationship is the triumph of this confusion. It is a kind of union from which union is excluded, and the basis for the attempt at union rests on exclusion." (T-16.V.6:3-4)

"The "better" self the ego seeks is always one that is more special. And whoever seems to possess a special self is "loved" for what can be taken from him. Where both partners see this special self in each other the ego sees "a union made in Heaven." For neither one will recognize that he has asked for hell, and so he will not interfere with the ego's illusion

CHAPTER 16 — THE FORGIVENESS OF ILLUSIONS

of Heaven, which it offered him to interfere with Heaven." (T-16.V.8:1-4)

"The conviction of littleness lies in every special relationship, for only the deprived could value specialness. The demand for specialness, and the perception of the giving of specialness as an act of love, would make love hateful." (T-16.V.9:2-3)

"If you perceived the special relationship as a triumph over God, would you want it?" (T-16.V.10:1)

"The special relationship is a ritual of form, aimed at raising the form to take the place of God at the expense of content. There is no meaning in the form, and there will never be." (T-16.V.12:2-3)

"See in the special relationship nothing more than a meaningless attempt to raise other gods before Him, and by worshiping them to obscure their tininess and His greatness. In the name of your completion you do not want this." (T-16.V.13:1-2)

"Salvation lies in the simple fact that illusions are not fearful because they are not true." (T-16.V.14:1)

"The core of the separation illusion lies simply in the fantasy of destruction of love's meaning." (T-16.V.15:1)

"Separation is only the decision not to know yourself. This whole thought system is a carefully contrived learning experience, designed to lead away from truth and into fantasy." (T-16.V.15:3-4)

"The decision whether or not to listen to this course and follow it is but the choice between truth and illusion." (T-16.V.16:1)

"How simple does this choice become when it is perceived as only what it is." (T-16.V.16:3)

"This year is thus the time to make the easiest decision that ever confronted you, and also the only one. You will cross the bridge into reality simply because you will recognize that God is on the other side, and nothing at all is here. It is impossible not to make the natural decision as this is realized." (T-16.V.17:1-3)

In summary, Chapter 16 – V. "The Choice for Completion" is say-

ing:

The ego is deceptive in its seeking for love. It would have us seek out others for what the ego thinks they can give us—the unity we so desperately desire. Those we find who share this goal with us then bind us equally to their own desire for false unity. Then, we enter a "special relationship" with them; one in which it is understood that the other will pledge their special love only to us and ours to them. It is a pledge of one body to another. The ego desires to destroy the unity of love by claiming it can be separated into many and varied body-relationships. This is a meaningless attempt to use our ego-body relationships to deny our one true relationship in Union with God's Love. And so, while we still find ourselves here within our ego-bodies, it is our task to heal all our special relationships through choosing to see beyond the body, understanding that each relationship is actually a love relationship completing God Himself. And so it is, we make the choice for completion.

VI. The Bridge to the Real World

"The search for the special relationship is the sign that you equate yourself with the ego and not with God." (T-16.VI.1:1)

"Love is freedom. To look for it by placing yourself in bondage is to separate yourself from it." (T-16.VI.2:1-2)

"As you release, so will you be released." (T-16.VI.2:4)

"The special relationship is totally meaningless without a body." (T-16.VI.4:1)

"The special relationship is a device for limiting your self to a body, and for limiting your perception of others to theirs. The Great Rays would establish the total lack of value of the special relationship, if they were seen. For in seeing them the body would disappear, because its value would be lost." (T-16.VI.4:4-6)

"You see the world you value. On this side of the bridge you see the world of separate bodies, seeking to join each other in separate unions and to become one by losing." (T-16.VI.5:1-2)

"Across the bridge it is so different! For a time the body is still seen, but not exclusively, as it is seen here. The little spark that holds the Great Rays within it is also visible, and this spark cannot be limited long to littleness." (T-16.VI.6:1-3)

CHAPTER 16—THE FORGIVENESS OF ILLUSIONS

"The bridge itself is nothing more than a transition in the perspective of reality." (T-16.VI.7:1)

"Fear not that you will be abruptly lifted up and hurled into reality. Time is kind, and if you use it on behalf of reality, it will keep gentle pace with you in your transition." (T-16.VI.8:1-2)

"The period of disorientation, which precedes the actual transition, is far shorter than the time it took to fix your mind so firmly on illusions. Delay will hurt you now more than before, only because you realize it is delay, and that escape from pain is really possible." (T-16.VI.8:5-6)

"Be glad you have escaped the mockery of salvation the ego offered you, and look not back with longing on the travesty it made of your relationships." (T-16.VI.10:1)

"And be you thankful that there is a place where truth and beauty wait for you." (T-16.VI.10:6)

"The Holy Spirit asks only this little help of you: Whenever your thoughts wander to a special relationship which still attracts you, enter with Him into a holy instant, and there let Him release you. He needs only your willingness to share His perspective to give it to you completely." (T-16.VI.12:1-2)

In summary, Chapter 16 – VI. "The Bridge to the Real World" is saying:

The bridge to the real world is merely a shift in your perspective; a change in how you see your worldly relationships. In order to make this transition, you must learn to see your relationships as the Holy Spirit sees them: Through the eyes of God's way of loving us. Therefore, make no demands of anyone, for love makes no demands. It simply is, and this is freedom. It neither needs nor takes. Do not let the ego fool you into thinking that by demanding special love from anyone that you will find satisfaction. You will only find suffering. Let all those you love and care for deeply be released from all demands and you will free yourself with them—for a heart not bound by the need for someone else to fulfill it, is a heart that is free to love as God does—*without condition.* Know this: The goal of any relationship is peace. Peace can be found whether bodies are together or not. In some instances, you may feel called to leave a bodily relationship in order to relate peacefully with them, and in other situations, letting go of your ego demands will be enough to set you both on the path to peace. It is only through finding peace in our relationships with one another that we can cross the bridge to the real world and our relationship with God. There we will no longer see bodies, but the Great Rays of love and light shining as the truth of Who We Are. Our peaceful, loving relationships are the bridge to the real world.

VII. The End of Illusions

"It is impossible to let the past go without relinquishing the special relationship." (T-16.VII.1:1)

"Imagined slights, remembered pain, past disappointments, perceived injustices and deprivations all enter into the special relationship, which becomes a way in which you seek to restore your wounded self-esteem." (T-16.VII.1:3)

"The special relationship takes vengeance on the past. By seeking to remove suffering in the past, it overlooks the present in its preoccupation with the past and its total commitment to it. No special relationship is experienced in the present." (T-16.VII.2:1-3)

"The past is nothing. Do not seek to lay the blame for deprivation on it, for the past is gone. You cannot really not let go what has already gone. It must be, therefore, that you are maintaining the illusion that it has not gone because you think it serves some purpose that you want fulfilled." (T-16.VII.2:8-11)

"Do not underestimate the intensity of the ego's drive for vengeance on the past. It is completely savage and completely insane. For the ego remembers everything you have done that has offended it, and seeks retribution of you. The fantasies it brings to its chosen relationships in which to act out its hate are fantasies of your destruction." (T-16.VII.3:1-4)

"In the special relationship you are allowing your destruction to be." (T-16.VII.3:7)

"In the special relationship it does not seem to be an acting out of vengeance that you seek. And even when the hatred and the savagery break briefly through, the illusion of love is not profoundly shaken. Yet the one thing the ego never allows to reach awareness is that the special relationship is the acting out of vengeance on yourself." (T-16.VII.5:1-3)

"Against the ego's insane notion of salvation the Holy Spirit gently lays the holy instant." (T-16.VII.6:1)

CHAPTER 16—THE FORGIVENESS OF ILLUSIONS

"In the holy instant it is understood that the past is gone, and with its passing the drive for vengeance has been uprooted and has disappeared. The stillness and the peace of now enfold you in perfect gentleness. Everything is gone except the truth." (T-16.VII.6:4-6)

"What God has given you is truly given, and will be truly received." (T-16.VII.8:1)

"When He willed that His Son be free, His Son was free. In the holy instant is His reminder that His Son will always be exactly as he was created." (T-16.VII.8:6-7)

"All that must be forgiven are the illusions you have held against your brothers." (T-16.VII.9:2)

"God holds nothing against anyone, for He is incapable of illusions of any kind. Release your brothers from the slavery of their illusions by forgiving them for the illusions you perceive in them." (T-16.VII.9:4-5)

"Forgive us our illusions, Father, and help us to accept our true relationship with You, in which there are no illusions, and where none can ever enter. Our holiness is Yours. What can there be in us that needs forgiveness when Yours is perfect? The sleep of forgetfulness is only the unwillingness to remember Your forgiveness and Your Love. Let us not wander into temptation, for the temptation of the Son of God is not Your Will. And let us receive only what You have given, and accept but this into the minds which You created and which You love. Amen." (T-16.VII.12:1-7)

In summary, Chapter 16 – VII. "The End of Illusions" is saying:
The special relationship revolves around our bodies and what we are doing and saying with them. The conflict that inevitably erupts from such interactions, is in truth, representative of the conflict within your own mind. It is a mind that perceives itself as separate from all other minds. Therefore, all conflict stems from your own mind. This is what the ego would never have you know, for once understood, we would strive to make peace our only goal. The body is the ego's chief illusion it holds against the memory of the truth of Who We Are. In the holy instant, we forgive this illusion, knowing without seeing that it is not the truth—and this is true forgiveness. For in the holy instant is everything associated with the body—every word and deed—let go of. Nothing is held against anyone, for it is seen and known as merely nothing, for it originated from the illusion of our bodily identity, which

is nothing. In the holy instant, we become still, for we are at last living truly in the present moment of the truth of our Identity as One Love. In this instant, truly, all illusions have been forgiven. Forgiveness is the catalyst for the end of all illusions.

CHAPTER 17
FORGIVENESS AND THE HOLY RELATIONSHIP

I. Bringing Fantasy to Truth

"The betrayal of the Son of God lies only in illusions, and all his "sins" are but his own imagining." (T-17.I.1:1)

"He need not be forgiven but awakened. In his dreams he has betrayed himself, his brothers and his God. Yet what is done in dreams has not been really done." (T-17.I.1:3-5)

"Only in waking is the full release from them, for only then does it become perfectly apparent that they had no effect upon reality at all, and did not change it." (T-17.I.1:7)

"It is, then, only your wish to change reality that is fearful, because by your wish you think you have accomplished what you wish." (T-17.I.2:1)

"What you use in fantasy you deny to truth." (T-17.I.2:5)

"When you maintain that there must be an order of difficulty in miracles, all you mean is that there are some things you would withhold from truth." (T-17.I.3:1)

"Very simply, your lack of faith in the power that heals all pain arises from your wish to retain some aspects of reality for fantasy." (T-17.I.3:3)

"As long as you would have it so, so long will the illusion of an order of difficulty in miracles remain with you." (T-17.I.4:1)

"Think you that you can bring truth to fantasy, and learn what truth means from the perspective of illusions?" (T-17.I.5:1)

"When you try to bring truth to illusions, you are trying to make illusions real, and keep them by justifying your belief in them." (T-17.I.5:4)

"Be willing, then, to give all you have held outside the truth to Him Who knows the truth, and in Whom all is brought to truth. Salvation from separation would be complete, or will not be at all. Be not concerned with anything except your willingness to have this be accomplished." (T-17.I.6:1-3)

"But forget not this: When you become disturbed and lose your peace of mind because another is attempting to solve his problems through fantasy, you are refusing to forgive yourself for just this same attempt." (T-17.I.6:5)

"As you forgive him, you restore to truth what was denied by both of you." (T-17.I.6:7)

In summary, Chapter 17 – I. "Bringing Fantasy to Truth" is saying:
The fantasy we have all contrived through the ego, is that we could become something other than the beings of perfection, love and light that God created us as. We have had a collective fantasy that we could be bodies. This "sin" is a mere imagining, for what God created cannot be changed. He creates only what is eternal, good, and true. Therefore, our only task then, is to awaken from the dream that we have done this. We must be willing to bring our fantasies to the truth to be transformed, for we cannot make illusions true. And everything in this world is a fantasy; it must *all* be given over to the Holy Spirit—which is to forgive—for correction, or none of it will be transformed. If you believe that your problems can be solved through using the means of this world, you are using an illusion to fix an illusion. Forgive yourself and others for attempting this. By doing so, you are both released, as you willingly bring fantasy to truth for healing which is the result of forgiveness.

II. The Forgiven World

"Can you imagine how beautiful those you forgive will look to you? In no fantasy have you ever seen anything so lovely." (T-17.II.1:1-2)

"For you will see the Son of God. You will behold the beauty the Holy Spirit loves to look upon, and which He thanks the Father for." (T-17.II.1:6-7)

"This loveliness is not a fantasy. It is the real world, bright and clean and new, with everything sparkling under the open sun." (T-17.II.2:1-2)

"The bridge between that world and this is so little and so easy to cross, that you could not believe it is the meeting place of worlds so different." (T-17.II.2:4)

"This little step, so small it has escaped your notice, is a stride through time into eternity, beyond all ugliness into beauty that will enchant you, and will never cease to cause you wonderment at its perfection." (T-17.II.2:6)

"This step, the smallest ever taken, is still the greatest accomplishment

CHAPTER 17—FORGIVENESS AND THE HOLY RELATIONSHIP

of all in God's plan of Atonement." (T-17.II.3:1)

"Fantasies are all undone, and no one and nothing remain still bound by them, and by your own forgiveness you are free to see." (T-17.II.3:5)

"The real world is attained simply by the complete forgiveness of the old, the world you see without forgiveness. The great Transformer of perception will undertake with you the careful searching of the mind that made this world, and uncover to you the seeming reasons for your making it. In the light of the real reason that He brings, as you follow Him, He will show you that there is no reason here at all." (T-17.II.5:1-3)

"For forgiveness literally transforms vision, and lets you see the real world reaching quietly and gently across chaos, removing all illusions that had twisted your perception and fixed it on the past. The smallest leaf becomes a thing of wonder, and a blade of grass a sign of God's perfection." (T-17.II.6:2-3)

"How much do you want salvation? It will give you the real world, trembling with readiness to be given you. The eagerness of the Holy Spirit to give you this is so intense He would not wait, although He waits in patience. Meet His patience with your impatience at delay in meeting Him." (T-17.II.8:1-4)

In summary, Chapter 17 – II. "The Forgiven World" is saying:
The forgiven world is the reality we will see whence we have let go of all that our ego shows us now. Letting go, is simply to change our beliefs—to believe in the opposite of what the ego shows us. It is to look upon bodies, physicality, and everything we see outside of us now and know it is not the truth. The truth is, nothing is separated by anything. We are one with all things. And this truth is gloriously beautiful beyond all comprehension. The bridge between our world and God's Reality is small, but it is a giant stride from what disappears in time, to what lasts for all eternity. Forgiveness of this world, speeds us across the bridge, into the real world.

III. Shadows of the Past

"To forgive is merely to remember only the loving thoughts you gave in the past, and those that were given you. All the rest must be forgotten." (T-17.III.1:1-2)

"For the shadow figures you would make immortal are "enemies" of

III. Shadows of the Past

reality. Be willing to forgive the Son of God for what he did not do." (T-17.III.1:4-5)

"It is these shadow figures that would make the ego holy in your sight, and teach you what you do to keep it safe is really love. The shadow figures always speak for vengeance, and all relationships into which they enter are totally insane." (T-17.III.2:1-2)

"That bodies are central to all unholy relationships is evident. Your own experience has taught you this." (T-17.III.2:7)

"Time is indeed unkind to the unholy relationship." (T-17.III.4:1)

"The attraction of the unholy relationship begins to fade and to be questioned almost at once. Once it is formed, doubt must enter in, because its purpose is impossible. The "ideal" of the unholy relationship thus becomes one in which the reality of the other does not enter at all to "spoil" the dream." (T-17.III.4:3-5)

"How can the Holy Spirit bring His interpretation of the body as a means of communication into relationships whose only purpose is separation from reality? What forgiveness is enables Him to do so. If all but loving thoughts have been forgotten, what remains is eternal." (T-17.III.5:1-3)

"No longer does the past conflict with now." (T-17.III.5:5)

"In these loving thoughts is the spark of beauty hidden in the ugliness of the unholy relationship where hatred is remembered; yet there to come alive as the relationship is given to Him Who gives it life and beauty." (T-17.III.5:7)

"Let Him uncover the hidden spark of beauty in your relationships, and show it to you." (T-17.III.6:7)

"For you will want it more and more, and become increasingly unwilling to let it be hidden from you." (T-17.III.6:10)

"God's Son is one. Whom God has joined as one, the ego cannot put asunder." (T-17.III.7:2-3)

"It is still up to you to choose to join with truth or with illusion. But remember that to choose one is to let the other go." (T-17.III.9:1-2)

"My holy brother, I would enter into all your relationships, and step between you and your fantasies. Let my relationship to you be real to

CHAPTER 17—FORGIVENESS AND THE HOLY RELATIONSHIP

you, and let me bring reality to your perception of your brothers." (T-17.III.10:1-2)

In summary, Chapter 17 – II. "Shadows of the Past" is saying:
Our shadows of the past are merely our unloving thoughts. Our unloving thoughts stem only from all things associated with the body. For what else could cause us to feel unloving? To forgive and thus heal these shadowy thoughts, is to think only on loving thoughts. Think how your brothers and sisters have come into these bodies, even as you have, to learn how not to struggle against them. Have empathy, for we each face the same struggle. These shadow figures, our bodies, are what we form our unholy relationships around. And yet, if for a moment, we can forget about the bodies we see, the peace that follows will heal our mind and heart of all pain. Do not give in to illusions. God's Son is One and can never be otherwise. Join with truth and let Christ's relationship be real to you. Let go of the shadow-thoughts of the past and remember our present Oneness.

IV. The Two Pictures

"God established His relationship with you to make you happy, and nothing you do that does not share His purpose can be real." (T-17.IV.1:1)

"Because of His reason for creating His relationship with you, the function of relationships became forever "to make happy." *And nothing else.*" (T-17.IV.1:3-4)

"For nothing God created is apart from happiness, and nothing God created but would extend happiness as its Creator did. Whatever does not fulfill this function cannot be real." (T-17.IV.1:6-7)

"I have said repeatedly that the Holy Spirit would not deprive you of your special relationships, but would transform them. And all that is meant by that is that He will restore to them the function given them by God. The function you have given them is clearly not to make happy." (T-17.IV.2:3-5)

"In a sense, the special relationship was the ego's answer to the creation of the Holy Spirit, Who was God's Answer to the separation." (T-17.IV.4:1)

"You have but little difficulty now in realizing that the thought system

IV. The Two Pictures

the special relationship protects is but a system of delusions. You recognize, at least in general terms, that the ego is insane." (T-17.IV.6:1-2)

"Every defense operates by giving gifts, and the gift is always a miniature of the thought system the defense protects, set in a golden frame. The frame is very elaborate, all set with jewels, and deeply carved and polished. Its purpose is to be of value in itself, and to divert your attention from what it encloses. But the frame without the picture you cannot have. Defenses operate to make you think you can." (T-17.IV.7:4-8)

"The special relationship has the most imposing and deceptive frame of all the defenses the ego uses." (T-17.IV.8:1)

"Look at the *picture*. Do not let the frame distract you." (T-17.IV.9:1-2)

"You cannot have the frame without the picture. What you value is the frame, for there you see no conflict. Yet the frame is only the wrapping for the gift of conflict." (T-17.IV.9:4-6)

"The holy instant is a miniature of Heaven, sent you from Heaven. It is a picture, too, set in a frame. Yet if you accept this gift you will not see the frame at all, because the gift can only be accepted through your willingness to focus all your attention on the picture. The holy instant is a miniature of eternity." (T-17.IV.11:1-4)

"Two gifts are offered you. Each is complete, and cannot be partially accepted." (T-17.IV.12:1-2)

"You who have tried so hard, and are still trying, to fit the better picture into the wrong frame and so combine what cannot be combined, accept this and be glad: These pictures are each framed perfectly for what they represent." (T-17.IV.13:1)

"The dark picture, brought to light, is not perceived as fearful, but the fact that it is just a picture is brought home at last. And what you see there you will recognize as what it is; a picture of what you thought was real, and nothing more." (T-17.IV.14:6-7)

"The picture of light, in clear-cut and unmistakable contrast, is transformed into what lies beyond the picture. As you look on this, you realize that it is not a picture, but a reality." (T-17.IV.15:1-2)

"The frame fades gently and God rises to your remembrance, offering you the whole of creation in exchange for your little picture, wholly without value and entirely deprived of meaning." (T-17.IV.15:5)

"As God ascends into His rightful place and you to yours, you will experience again the meaning of relationship and know it to be true." (T-17.IV.16:1)

"The whole reality of your relationship with Him lies in our relationship to one another." (T-17.IV.16:7)

"For here is God, and where He is only the perfect and complete can be." (T-17.IV.16:10)

In summary, Chapter 17 – V. "The Two Pictures" is saying:
"The two pictures" are a metaphor representing the two types of relationships we can have: A special one of the ego, or a holy one of God. The picture of the special relationship is framed by a body, and only the body is seen and valued. The light within, which is the true gift and the only picture that will last for all eternity, is completely overlooked. Such a relationship is set in an ornate frame of turmoil, conflict, and stress; distractions blinding you to the picture of light and goodness within. The holy relationship is framed in peace. A frame so delicate that it disappears into the background, allowing only the picture of light to be seen. When we look upon one another as though we do not see the bodily frame the ego has set us in, we transform what we see into a holy relationship. And in that relationship a new picture, a new reality, is born.

V. The Healed Relationship

"The holy relationship is the expression of the holy instant in living in this world." (T-17.V.1:1)

"The holy relationship, a major step toward the perception of the real world, is learned." (T-17.V.2:1)

"The holy relationship is a phenomenal teaching accomplishment." (T-17.V.2:3)

"Be comforted in this; the only difficult phase is the beginning. For here, the goal of the relationship is abruptly shifted to the exact opposite of what it was." (T-17.V.2:5-6)

"This is accomplished very rapidly, but it makes the relationship seem disturbed, disjunctive and even quite distressing." (T-17.V.3:3)

"Now it seems to make no sense. Many relationships have been broken off at this point, and the pursuit of the old goal re-established in another

V. The Healed Relationship

relationship. For once the unholy relationship has accepted the goal of holiness, it can never again be what it was." (T-17.V.3:7-9)

"It would not be kinder to shift the goal more slowly, for the contrast would be obscured, and the ego given time to reinterpret each slow step according to its liking. Only a radical shift in purpose could induce a complete change of mind about what the whole relationship is for. As this change develops and is finally accomplished, it grows increasingly beneficent and joyous." (T-17.V.5:1-3)

"This is the time for *faith*. You let this goal be set for you." (T-17.V.6:1-2)

"Have faith in your brother in what but seems to be a trying time. The goal is set. And your relationship has sanity as its purpose." (T-17.V.6:6-8)

"Now the ego counsels thus; substitute for this another relationship to which your former goal was quite appropriate. You can escape your distress only by getting rid of your brother." (T-17.V.7:1-2)

"*Hear this not now*! Have faith in Him Who answered you." (T-17.V.7:5-6)

"This relationship has been reborn as holy." (T-17.V.7:14)

"You will find many opportunities to blame your brother for the "failure" of your relationship, for it will seem at times to have no purpose." (T-17.V.8:2)

"For your relationship has not been disrupted. It has been saved." (T-17.V.8:5-6)

"In your newness, remember that you and your brother have started again, *together*." (T-17.V.9:3)

"You undertook, together, to invite the Holy Spirit into your relationship." (T-17.V.11:1)

"Have you consistently appreciated the good efforts, and overlooked mistakes? Or has your appreciation flickered and grown dim in what seemed to be the light of the mistakes? Perhaps you are now entering upon a campaign to blame him for the discomfort of the situation in which you find yourself. And by this lack of thanks and gratitude you make yourself unable to express the holy instant, and thus lose sight of it." (T-17.V.11:7-10)

"You have received the holy instant, but you may have established a condition in which you cannot use it." (T-17.V.13:1)

CHAPTER 17—FORGIVENESS AND THE HOLY RELATIONSHIP

"You and your brother stand together in the holy presence of truth itself." (T-17.V.14:1)

"You are joined in purpose, but remain still separate and divided on the means. Yet the goal is fixed, firm and unalterable, and the means will surely fall in place because the goal is sure. And you will share the gladness of the Sonship that it is so." (T-17.V.14:7-9)

In summary, Chapter 17 – V. "The Healed Relationship" is saying:
A healed relationship is a holy relationship. A holy relationship is one that is focused on peace, which is a relationship in which the ego does not impose its will on the other. The moment either participant decides peace is their goal, the relationship is turned over to the Holy Spirit for healing. This may initially appear to make the conflict worse. This happens because the goal of peace is out of accord with the ego's goal of conflict and often, disharmony and blame are the result. Rejoice at this phase and do not lose faith that the goal of peace will be achieved! For what you have asked the Holy Spirit to heal, will *be healed.* Your only task is not to interfere. You only interfere when you attempt to determine the outcome yourself. Do not specify in your mind, what the relationship will look like after it is healed. Accept that you do not know and trust it will be the best possible outcome. The whole Sonship will share in the joy of your healed relationship because the Sonship is healed with you.

VI. Setting the Goal

"The practical application of the Holy Spirit's purpose is extremely simple, but it is unequivocal. In fact, in order to be simple it must be unequivocal." (T-17.VI.1:1-2)

"The setting of the Holy Spirit's goal is general. Now He will work with you to make it specific, for application is specific." (T-17.VI.1:4-5)

"In any situation in which you are uncertain, the first thing to consider, very simply, is "What do I want to come of this? What is it *for*?" The clarification of the goal belongs at the beginning, for it is this which will determine the outcome." (T-17.VI.2:1-3)

"The ego does not know what it wants to come of the situation. It is aware of what it does not want, but only that. It has no positive goal at all." (T-17.VI.2:7-9)

"Without a clear-cut, positive goal, set at the outset, the situation

VII. The Call for Faith

just seems to happen, and makes no sense until it has already happened." (T-17.VI.3:1)

"The value of deciding in advance what you want to happen is simply that you will perceive the situation as a means to make it happen. You will therefore make every effort to overlook what interferes with the accomplishment of your objective, and concentrate on everything that helps you meet it." (T-17.VI.4:1-2)

"If the situation is used for truth and sanity, its outcome must be peace." (T-17.VI.5:2)

"If you experience peace, it is because the truth has come to you and you will see the outcome truly, for deception cannot prevail against you. You will recognize the outcome because you are at peace." (T-17.VI.5:6-7)

"No one will fail in anything. This seems to ask for faith beyond you, and beyond what you can give. Yet this is so only from the viewpoint of the ego, for the ego believes in "solving" conflict through fragmentation, and does not perceive the situation as a whole." (T-17.VI.6:7-9)

"And it will seem to be successful, except that this attempt conflicts with unity, and must obscure the goal of truth." (T-17.VI.7:2)

In summary, Chapter 17 – VI. "Setting the Goal" is saying:
At the outset of our day, or any situation we are about to enter, it is important to align your mind with Christ-mindedness. That is, to set the goal for the situation. There is only and ever one goal of the Christ-minded and that is peace. The ego has many goals, and they vary greatly in type and difficulty of achievement. The goals of the ego can also change on a whim, whereas the goal of the Holy Spirit is always constant and unchanging peace. Only what brings peace is true and what brings conflict is false. Do not fail to see this as another way of saying that the body is false, because it conflicts with our Eternal Identity given us by God. This is the truth that brings peace to our mind in this insane world. We heal our separated ego state of mind, through setting peace as our only goal.

VII. The Call for Faith

"The substitutes for aspects of the situation are the witnesses to your lack of faith." (T-17.VII.1:1)

"The problem was the lack of faith, and it is this you demonstrate when

CHAPTER 17—FORGIVENESS AND THE HOLY RELATIONSHIP

you remove it from its source and place it elsewhere. As a result, you do not see the problem." (T-17.VII.1:3-4)

"There is no problem in any situation that faith will not solve." (T-17.VII.2:1)

"A situation is a relationship, being the joining of thoughts. If problems are perceived, it is because the thoughts are judged to be in conflict. But if the goal is truth, this is impossible. Some idea of bodies must have entered, for minds cannot attack. The thought of bodies is the sign of faithlessness, for bodies cannot solve anything." (T-17.VII.3:1-5)

"But remember this; the goal of holiness was set for your relationship, and not by you." (T-17.VII.4:2)

"Every situation in which you find yourself is but a means to meet the purpose set for your relationship. See it as something else and you are faithless." (T-17.VII.5:1-2)

"The goal of illusion is as closely tied to faithlessness as faith to truth." (T-17.VII.6:1)

"Yet think on this, and learn the cause of faithlessness: You think you hold against your brother what he has done to you. But what you really blame him for is what you did to him." (T-17.VII.8:1-2)

"You call for faith because of Him Who walks with you in every situation." (T-17.VII.10:1)

"You whose relationship shares the Holy Spirit's goal are set apart from loneliness because the truth has come." (T-17.VII.10:4)

In summary, Chapter 17 – VII. "The Call for Faith" is saying:
Faith here is defined as truth, and what is the truth but that we are not bodies? Faith*less*ness is to believe in what you are not, and so you perceive yourself as *less*. Faith*ful*ness is to remember the *fullness* of Who You Are in unity with all creation. Faith is to believe in the truth. There is no problem faith cannot solve. All problems are solved through having faith in our Oneness and overlooking the illusion of our separation. Oneness is our true relationship and to know it is to be at peace with all you see here in this world. Your call for faith is to overlook all situations—relationships—and see them for what they are in truth. We are called to have faith in our Oneness, despite seeing our bodily separation.

VIII. The Conditions of Peace

"The holy instant is nothing more than a special case, or an extreme example, of what every situation is meant to be." (T-17.VIII.1:1)

"The holy instant is the shining example, the clear and unequivocal demonstration of the meaning of every relationship and every situation, seen as a whole. Faith has accepted every aspect of the situation, and faithlessness has not forced any exclusion on it. It is a situation of perfect peace, simply because you have let it be what it is." (T-17.VIII.1:4-6)

"This simple courtesy is all the Holy Spirit asks of you. Let truth be what it is. Do not intrude upon it, do not attack it, do not interrupt its coming. Let it encompass every situation and bring you peace." (T-17.VIII.2:1-4)

"When you accepted truth as the goal for your relationship, you became a giver of peace as surely as your Father gave peace to you." (T-17.VIII.6:1)

"Your release is certain. Give as you have received. And demonstrate that you have risen far beyond any situation that could hold you back, and keep you separate from Him Whose Call you answered." (T-17.VIII.6:5-7)

In summary, Chapter 17 – VIII. "The Conditions of Peace" is saying: The conditions for peace are but one thing: To love without exclusion, understanding your unity with all creation. To love without conditions is to love as God loves us. All aspects are accepted; nothing and no one is excluded. It is a situation (relationship) of perfect peace, simply because you have let this truth be exactly what it is. This level of loving is the goal of every relationship (situation). Give peace to others as God has given His peace to you, for He sees you as One in Him. See your oneness with everyone, and you will have met the conditions for peace. See your oneness with everyone, and you will understand the correlation between forgiveness and the holy relationship.

CHAPTER 18
THE PASSING OF THE DREAM

I. The Substitute Reality

"To substitute is to accept instead. If you would but consider exactly what this entails, you would perceive at once how much at variance this is with the goal the Holy Spirit has given you, and would accomplish for you. To substitute is to choose between, renouncing one aspect of the Sonship in favor of the other." (T-18.I.1:1-3)

"Where the ego perceives one person as a replacement for another, the Holy Spirit sees them joined and indivisible. He does not judge between them, knowing they are one." (T-18.I.2:1-2)

"Substitution is clearly a process in which they are perceived as different. One would unite; the other separate." (T-18.I.2:5-6)

"The one emotion in which substitution is impossible is love. Fear involves substitution by definition, for it is love's replacement. Fear is both a fragmented and fragmenting emotion." (T-18.I.3:1-3)

"No one is seen complete. The body is emphasized, with special emphasis on certain parts, and used as the standard for comparison of acceptance or rejection for acting out a special form of fear." (T-18.I.3:6-7)

"You who believe that God is fear made but one substitution. It has taken many forms, because it was the substitution of illusion for truth; of fragmentation for wholeness." (T-18.I.4:1-2)

"You may be surprised to hear how very different is reality from what you see. You do not realize the magnitude of that one error. It was so vast and so completely incredible that from it a world of total unreality *had* to emerge. What else could come of it?" (T-18.I.5:1-4)

"That was the first projection of error outward. The world arose to hide it, and became the screen on which it was projected and drawn between you and the truth." (T-18.I.6:1-2)

"Call it not sin but madness, for such it was and so it still remains. Invest it not with guilt, for guilt implies it was accomplished in reality. And above all, *be not afraid of it.*" (T-18.I.6:7-9)

I. The Substitute Reality

"When you seem to see some twisted form of the original error rising to frighten you, say only, "God is not fear, but Love," and it will disappear. The truth will save you." (T-18.I.7:1-2)

"Inward is sanity; insanity is outside you." (T-18.I.7:4)

"And turn you to the stately calm within, where in holy stillness dwells the living God you never left, and Who never left you." (T-18.I.8:2)

"Within yourself you love your brother with a perfect love. Here is holy ground, in which no substitution can enter, and where only the truth in your brother can abide. Here you are joined in God, as much together as you are with Him." (T-18.I.9:3-5)

"In you there is no separation, and no substitute can keep you from your brother." (T-18.I.10:1)

"Heaven is restored to all the Sonship through your relationship, for in it lies the Sonship, whole and beautiful, safe in your love." (T-18.I.11:1)

"And God Himself is glad that your relationship is as it was created. The universe within you stands with you, together with your brother. And Heaven looks with love on what is joined in it, along with its Creator." (T-18.I.11:6-8)

"You have been called, together with your brother, to the most holy function this world contains." (T-18.I.13:1)

In summary, Chapter 18 – I. "The Substitute Reality" is saying:
We have made but one single substitution: Our identity as Oneself united in God for that of an ego; a separated, desperate parody of the holiness and light that we are in truth. One identity is based in Love and the other fear. We have substituted a body for Spirit. When you feel any form of fear, be sure you are identifying with the body and therefore the ego. When these times come, simply remind yourself of the truth and say to yourself, "God is not fear, but Love," and the fear will disappear. This truth will always save you. Remembering this truth is your most holy function. It is to remember your oneness with those whom God created in holy relationship with you and there is no other substitute for His Reality.

CHAPTER 18—THE PASSING OF THE DREAM

II. The Basis of the Dream

"Does not a world that seems quite real arise in dreams?" (T-18.II.1:1)

"Dreams are chaotic because they are governed by your conflicting wishes, and therefore they have no concern with what is true. They are the best example you could have of how perception can be utilized to substitute illusions for truth." (T-18.II.2:1-2)

"You do not find the differences between what you see in sleep and on awaking disturbing. You recognize that what you see on waking is blotted out in dreams. Yet on awakening, you do not expect it to be gone." (T-18.II.3:1-3)

"No limits on substitution are laid upon you. For a time it seems as if a world were given you, to make it what you wish." (T-18.II.3:6-7)

"Dreams are perceptual temper tantrums, in which you literally scream, 'I want it thus!' And thus it seems to be." (T-18.II.4:1-2)

"Dreams show you that you have the power to make a world as you would have it be, and that because you want it you see it. And while you see it you do not doubt that it is real. Yet here is a world, clearly within your mind, that seems to be outside. You do not respond to it as though you made it, nor do you realize that the emotions the dream produces must come from you."

"You seem to waken, and the dream is gone. Yet what you fail to recognize is that what caused the dream has not gone with it. Your wish to make another world that is not real remains with you. And what you seem to waken to is but another form of this same world you see in dreams. All your time is spent in dreaming. Your sleeping and your waking dreams have different forms, and that is all." (T-18.II.5:8-13)

"They are your protest against reality, and your fixed and insane idea that you can change it." (T-18.II.5:15)

"The special relationship is your determination to keep your hold on unreality, and to prevent yourself from waking. And while you see more value in sleeping than in waking, you will not let go of it." (T-18.II.5:19-20)

"I said before that the first change, before dreams disappear, is that your dreams of fear are changed to happy dreams." (T-18.II.6:3)

"Your special relationship will be a means for undoing guilt in every-

III. Light in the Dream

one blessed through your holy relationship. It will be a happy dream, and one which you will share with all who come within your sight." (T-18.II.7:1-2)

"You are so used to choosing among dreams you do not see that you have made, at last, the choice between truth and all illusions." (T-18.II.8:6)

"Yet Heaven is sure. This is no dream. Its coming means that you have chosen truth, and it has come because you have been willing to let your special relationship meet it conditions. In your relationship the Holy Spirit has gently laid the real world; the world of happy dreams, from which awaking is so easy and so natural." (T-18.II.9:1-4)

In summary, Chapter 18 – II. "The Basis of the Dream" is saying:
It may seem a bit disconcerting to learn that whether we are sleeping or awake, we never leave a world of dreams. Here we are told that since our birth into a body, we have never seen true reality. We have only been living one continuous dream. And yet, it is well within our power to awaken from it once we understand that we have total power and control over whether we choose to remain asleep or awaken. To awaken, we must choose to shift our perception of others to the truth of the light in them. Our special relationships are all whom we associate with a body. Such special relationships are the cause of our unhappiness because what we are seeing in others is false—a "dream identity." Forgive all this and every relationship you ever had in the past, present, and future will be healed for all eternity. You will be happy whence you have let go of all things associated with the body. For it is through letting go of the drama of our bodily or "special relationships" that the whole basis of the dream is let go of.

III. Light in the Dream

"Each dream has led to other dreams, and every fantasy that seemed to bring a light into the darkness but made the darkness deeper." (T-18.III.1:3)

"As the light comes nearer you will rush to darkness, shrinking from the truth, sometimes retreating to the lesser forms of fear, and sometimes to stark terror. But you will advance, because your goal is the advance from fear to truth." (T-18.III.2:1-2)

"If you knew Who walks beside you on the way that you have chosen, fear would be impossible. You do not know because the journey into

CHAPTER 18—THE PASSING OF THE DREAM

darkness has been long and cruel, and you have gone deep into it." (T-18.III.3:2-3)

"You go toward love still hating it, and terribly afraid of its judgment upon you. And you do not realize that you are not afraid of love, but only of what you have made of it." (T-18.III.3:5-6)

"You who hold your brother's hand also hold mine, for when you joined each other you were not alone. Do you believe that I would leave you in the darkness that you agreed to leave with me? In your relationship is this world's light." (T-18.III.4:1-3)

"The holiness of your relationship is established in Heaven." (T-18.III.4:10)

"In your relationship you have joined with me in bringing Heaven to the Son of God, who hid in darkness." (T-18.III.6:1)

"You who are now the bringer of salvation have the function of bringing light to darkness." (T-18.III.7:1)

"We are made whole in our desire to make whole." (T-18.III.7:4)

"You have gone past fear, for no two minds can join in the desire for love without love's joining them." (T-18.III.7:7)

"Heaven is joined with you in your advance to Heaven. When such great lights have joined with you to give the little spark of your desire the power of God Himself, can you remain in darkness? You and your brother are coming home together, after a long and meaningless journey that you undertook apart, and that led nowhere. You have found your brother, and you will light each other's way. And from this light will the Great Rays extend back into darkness and forward unto God, to shine away the past and so make room for His eternal Presence, in which everything is radiant in the light." (T-18.III.8:3-7)

In summary, Chapter 18 – III. "Light in the Dream" is saying:
The word "light" is synonymous with "knowledge" in *A Course In Miracles*. To know or understand and accept the truth of our reality, is to therefore bring *light* to it. As we come closer and closer to understanding the light of truth, our ego will at times retreat into the dark and drag us with it. We will refuse to believe what is being taught. Let us cease to make such retreats now. Let us accept the truth and bring light into this dream, thus dispelling the dark as one does when turning on a lightbulb. We have all journeyed into the forgetfulness

of our Unity together, but we also brought Christ with us. So, let us return together, through seeing ourselves as One once again; let us see only our unity with Christ and thus bring light into this dream.

IV. The Little Willingness

"The holy instant is the result of your determination to be holy. It is the answer. The desire and the willingness to let it come precede its coming. You prepare your mind for it only to the extent of recognizing that you want it above all else. It is not necessary that you do more; indeed, it is necessary that you realize that you cannot do more." (T-18.IV.1:1-5)

"It is your realization that you need do so little that enables Him to give so much." (T-18.IV.1:10)

"But trust implicitly your willingness, whatever else may enter. Concentrate only on this, and be not disturbed that shadows surround it. That is why you came. If you could come without them you would not need the holy instant." (T-18.IV.2:3-6)

"Humility will never ask that you remain content with littleness. But it does require that you be not content with less than greatness that comes not of you. Your difficulty with the holy instant arises from your fixed conviction that you are not worthy of it." (T-18.IV.3:1-3)

"The holy instant does not come from your little willingness alone. It is always the result of your small willingness combined with the unlimited power of God's Will." (T-18.IV.4:1-2)

"Rather than seek to prepare yourself for Him, try to think thus:

I who am host to God am worthy of Him. He Who established His dwelling place in me created it as He would have it be. It is not needful that I make it ready for Him, but only that I do not interfere with His plan to restore to me my own awareness of my readiness, which is eternal. I need add nothing to His plan. But to receive it, I must be willing not to substitute my own in place of it." (T-18.IV.5:8-13)

"Remember that you made guilt, and that your plan for the escape from guilt has been to bring Atonement to it, and make salvation fearful. And it is only fear that you will add, if you prepare yourself for love." (T-18.IV.6:3-4)

"Release yourself to Him Whose function is release." (T-18.IV.6:6)

CHAPTER 18—THE PASSING OF THE DREAM

"It is this that makes the holy instant so easy and so natural. You make it difficult, because you insist there must be more that you need do." (T-18.IV.7:1-2)

"Forget not that it has been your decision to make everything that is natural and easy for you impossible." (T-18.IV.8:1)

"Everything God wills is not only possible, but has already happened." (T-18.IV.8:4)

In summary, Chapter 18 – IV. "The Little Willingness" is saying:
Our willingness to allow ourselves to be as God created us, rather than the bodies our ego perceives us to be now, triggers the holy instant. Our desire merely precedes it but does not add anything to it. The rest is of God and God alone. Our role is simply to step out of God's way by remembering Who We Are. We are host to God. We are worthy to be such a host. We need do nothing to be deserving of such companionship except to do nothing that interferes with our awareness of Him within us and everyone else. It may seem impossible to see those who cause you the most struggle as one whom carries God Himself within. Yet do not forget, it is unnatural for them to be anything less than the holy vessel they are. You need but this small willingness to see your brethren as such and God's Will is done; the holy instant will follow soon behind such powerful, willing thoughts.

V. The Happy Dream

"Prepare you now for the undoing of what never was. If you already understood the difference between truth and illusion, the Atonement would have no meaning. The holy instant, the holy relationship, the Holy Spirit's teaching, and all the means by which salvation is accomplished, would have no purpose. For they are all but aspects of the plan to change your dreams of fear to happy dreams, from which you waken easily to knowledge. Put yourself not in charge of this, for you cannot distinguish between advance and retreat. Some of your greatest advances you have judged as failures, and some of your deepest retreats you have evaluated as success." (T-18.V.1:1-6)

"Through your holy relationship, reborn and blessed in every holy instant you do not arrange, thousands will rise to Heaven with you." (T-18.V.3:1)

V. The Happy Dream

"A purpose such as this, without the means, is inconceivable. He will provide the means to anyone who shares His purpose." (T-18.V.3:8-9)

"Happy dreams come true, not because they are dreams, but only because they are happy. And so they must be loving. Their message is, "Thy Will be done," and not, "I want it otherwise."" (T-18.V.4:1-3)

"It is no dream to love your brother as yourself. Nor is your holy relationship a dream." (T-18.V.5:1-2)

"It will become the happy dream through which He can spread joy to thousands on thousands who believe that love is fear, not happiness." (T-18.V.5:5)

"When you feel the holiness of your relationship is threatened by anything, stop instantly and offer the Holy Spirit your willingness, in spite of fear, to let Him exchange this instant for the holy one that you would rather have. He will never fail in this." (T-18.V.6:1-2)

"Whoever is saner at the time the threat is perceived should remember how deep is his indebtedness to the other and how much gratitude is due him, and be glad that he can pay his debt by bringing happiness to both. Let him remember this, and say:

> *I desire this holy instant for myself, that I may share it with my brother, whom I love.*
> *It is not possible that I can have it without him, or he without me.*
> *Yet it is wholly possible for us to share it now.*
> *And so I choose this instant as the one to offer to the Holy Spirit, that His blessing may descend on us, and keep us both in peace."* (T-18.V.7:1-6)

In summary, Chapter 18 – V. "The Happy Dream" is saying:

A "happy dream" is merely an experience of living without fear of anything in this dream. It is to have no fear of any illusion you may encounter, regardless of the form it takes. The form most difficult for us to let go of our fear of, surrounds our relationships—our bodily experiences with other bodies. It is difficult to feel loving towards those whom we also feel our greatest conflict. And yet, if we allow ourselves the willingness to let this illusion of them go and place them into the hands of the Holy Spirit, He will transform our relationship for us. All it takes is for one of us to remember to do this and He will carry our holy relationship into a happier dream, a happy dream of peace.

VI. Beyond the Body

"There is nothing outside you. That is what you must ultimately learn, for it is the realization that the Kingdom of Heaven is restored to you." (T-18.VI.1:1-2)

"Heaven is not a place nor a condition. It is merely an awareness of perfect Oneness, and the knowledge that there is nothing else; nothing outside this Oneness, and nothing else within." (T-18.VI.1:5-6)

"The belief that you could give and get something else, something outside yourself, has cost you the awareness of Heaven and of your Identity." (T-18.VI.2:3)

"Minds are joined; bodies are not. Only by assigning to the mind the properties of the body does separation seem to be possible." (T-18.VI.3:1-2)

"Mind cannot attack, but it can make fantasies and direct the body to act them out." (T-18.VI.3:5)

"In this, the mind is clearly delusional. It cannot attack, but it maintains it can, and uses what it does to hurt the body to prove it can." (T-18.VI.4:1-2)

"Would you not have the instruments of separation reinterpreted as means for salvation, and used for purposes of love?" (T-18.VI.5:1)

"It is insane to use the body as the scapegoat for guilt, directing its attack and blaming it for what you wished it to do." (T-18.VI.6:1)

"This is the host of God that you have made. And neither God nor His most holy Son can enter an abode that harbors hate, and where you have sown the seeds of vengeance, violence and death." (T-18.VI.7:1-2)

"The body is outside you, and but seems to surround you, shutting you off from others and keeping you apart from them, and them from you. It is not there. There is no barrier between God and His Son, nor can His Son be separated from Himself except in illusions." (T-18.VI.9:1-3)

"Everyone has experienced what he would call a sense of being transported beyond himself. This feeling of liberation far exceeds the dream of freedom sometimes hoped for in special relationships. It is a sense of actual escape from limitations." (T-18.VI.11:1-3)

"There is no violence at all in this escape. The body is not attacked, but simply properly perceived. It does not limit you, merely because you would not have it so. You are not really "lifted out" of it; it cannot contain you." (T-18.VI.13:1-4)

"The sudden expansion of awareness that takes place with your desire for it is the irresistible appeal the holy instant holds. It calls you to be yourself, within its safe embrace." (T-18.VI.14:2-3)

"Not through destruction, not through a breaking out, but merely by a quiet melting in. For peace will join you there, simply because you have been willing to let go the limits you have placed upon love, and joined it where it is and where it led you, in answer to its gentle call to be at peace." (T-18.VI.14:6-7)

In summary, Chapter 18 – VI. "Beyond the Body" is saying:
To move "beyond the body" we must undergo an inner journey, for we do not actually move away from anything outside of us. The body seems to surround us in a prison of flesh and pain, but really, it is not there. This may sound difficult to believe, given how profound the feelings of the body can be. Yet, such feelings actually first originate in the mind, then pass through the body secondly. The body is merely a device with which we use to interpret what our mind perceives. Change what we think, and we can change what we experience. The body can only be escaped through expansion of our beliefs of what we think we are. Desire peace and the body itself, as well as its relationships to other bodies, will be brought into a state of peace. The holy instant comes when you let go of all things, all limits, you have placed upon yourself through the idea of being a body. Then you will join with love and move beyond the body.

VII. I Need Do Nothing

"You still have too much faith in the body as a source of strength. What plans do you make that do not involve its comfort or protection or enjoyment in some way?" (T-18.VII.1:1-2)

"There is one thing that you have never done; you have not utterly forgotten the body. It has perhaps faded at times from your sight, but it has not yet completely disappeared. You are not asked to let this happen for more than an instant, yet it is in this instant that the miracle of Atonement happens. Afterwards you will see the body again, but never quite the same. And every instant that you spend without awareness of it gives you a different view of it when you return." (T-18.VII.2:1-5)

CHAPTER 18—THE PASSING OF THE DREAM

"At no single instant does the body exist at all. It is always remembered or anticipated, but never experienced just *now*. Only its past and future make it seem real." (T-18.VII.3:1-3)

"It is impossible to accept the holy instant without reservation unless, just for an instant, you are willing to see no past or future." (T-18.VII.4:1)

"Enormous effort is expended in the attempt to make holy what is hated and despised. Nor is a lifetime of contemplation and long periods of meditation aimed at detachment from the body necessary." (T-18.VII.4:8-9)

"Your way will be different, not in purpose but in means. A holy relationship is a means of saving time. One instant spent together with your brother restores the universe to both of you." (T-18.VII.5:1-3)

"Now you need but to remember you need do nothing." (T-18.VII.5:5)

"Here is the ultimate release which everyone will one day find in his own way, at his own time." (T-18.VII.6:1)

"Save time for me by only this one preparation, and practice doing nothing else. "I need do nothing" is a statement of allegiance, a truly undivided loyalty. Believe it for just one instant, and you will accomplish what is given to a century of contemplation, or of struggle against temptation." (T-18.VII.6:6-8)

"To do anything involves the body. And if you recognize you need do nothing, you have withdrawn the body's value from your mind. Here is the quick and open door through which you slip past centuries of effort, and escape from time." (T-18.VII.7:1-3)

"To do nothing is to rest, and make a place within you where the activity of the body ceases to demand attention." (T-18.VII.7:7)

"This quiet center, in which you do nothing, will remain with you, giving you rest in the midst of every busy doing on which you are sent." (T-18.VII.8:3)

"It is this center, from which the body is absent, that will keep it so in your awareness of it." (T-18.VII.8:5)

In summary, Chapter 18 – VII. "I Need Do Nothing" is saying:

Our minds are always engaged, busy "doing something" regarding our bodies. Our minds are never at rest where the body is concerned. How often have we simply allowed ourselves "to rest in peace?" Not often or never for most. And yet we are told here that it is exactly this uncomplicated practice that we must do—or rather not do—in order to accomplish our whole release from suffering. Give your relationships a rest. Do not think about them. Give your body a rest. Do not think about it. And in this quiet center, in which you think nothing and therefore do nothing, you will transcend the body entirely. Do not struggle to empty your mind, but rather fill it with light. Light is understanding, therefore, fill your mind with the understanding that ultimately nothing associated with the body matters. It is not real. And in the light of this understanding, you will go about your busy tasks in the world and will do nothing to interfere with the holy instant from dawning upon your mind.

VIII. The Little Garden

"It is only the awareness of the body that makes love seem limited. For the body is a limit on love. The belief in limited love was its origin, and it was made to limit the unlimited." (T-18.VIII.1:1-2)

"You cannot even think of God without a body, or in some form you think you recognize." (T-18.VIII.1:7)

"The body cannot know. And while you limit your awareness to its tiny senses, you will not see the grandeur that surrounds you." (T-18.VIII.2:1-2)

"The body is a tiny fence around a little part of a glorious and complete idea. It draws a circle, infinitely small, around a very little segment of Heaven, splintered from the whole, proclaiming that within it is your kingdom, where God can enter not." (T-18.VIII.2:5-6)

"Within this kingdom the ego rules, and cruelly." (T-18.VIII.3:1)

"This fragment of your mind is such a tiny part of it that, could you but appreciate the whole, you would see instantly that it is like the smallest sunbeam to the sun, or like the faintest ripple on the surface of the ocean." (T-18.VIII.3:3)

"Yet neither the sun nor ocean is even aware of all this strange and meaningless activity. They merely continue, unaware that they are feared and hated by a tiny segment of themselves." (T-18.VIII.4:1-2)

CHAPTER 18—THE PASSING OF THE DREAM

"Such is the strange position in which those in a world inhabited by bodies seem to be." (T-18.VIII.5:1)

"Like to the sun and ocean your Self continues, unmindful that this tiny part regards itself as you." (T-18.VIII.6:1)

"Do not accept this little, fenced-off aspect as yourself. The sun and ocean are as nothing beside what you are." (T-18.VIII.7:1-2)

"Love knows no bodies, and reaches to everything created like itself." (T-18.VIII.8:1)

"The Thought of God surrounds your little kingdom, waiting at the barrier you built to come inside and shine upon the barren ground." (T-18.VIII.9:1)

"And everyone you welcome will bring love with him from Heaven for you." (T-18.VIII.9:5)

"The love they brought with them will stay with them, as it will stay with you. And under its beneficence your little garden will expand, and reach out to everyone who thirsts for living water, but has grown too weary to go on alone." (T-18.VIII.9:7-8)

"The holy instant is your invitation to love to enter into your bleak and joyless kingdom, and to transform it into a garden of peace and welcome." (T-18.VIII.11:1)

"Asking for everything, you will receive it." (T-18.VIII.11:5)

"Be sure of this; love has entered your special relationship, and entered fully at your weak request. You do not recognize that love has come, because you have not yet let go of all the barriers you hold against your brother." (T-18.VIII.12:1-2)

"You have reached the end of an ancient journey, not realizing yet that it is over." (T-18.VIII.13:1)

"Yet He Whom you welcomed has come to you, and would welcome you. He has waited long to give you this. Receive it now of Him, for He would have you know Him." (T-18.VIII.13:3-5)

"And walk into the garden love has prepared for both you." (T-18.VIII.13:8)

IX. The Two Worlds

In summary, Chapter 18 – VIII. "The Little Garden" is saying:
Our body is the "little garden" we made for ourselves and us alone. It is the idea we are separate and isolated patches of life, disconnected from All That Is, Which surrounds us in everlasting love. We are in dire need of expanding our garden. We do this through expanding our love for others, the ones we seem to have mistakenly excluded. And with their inclusion, we also include God once again within our garden; within our full awareness. Let all our relationships become holy through our perspective of the all-inclusive love God holds for us. Let our little garden expand to join the Heavenly garden God has prepared for us.

IX. The Two Worlds

"You have been told to bring the darkness to the light, and guilt to holiness. And you have been also been told that error must be corrected at its source. Therefore, it is the tiny part of yourself, the little thought that seems split off and separated, the Holy Spirit needs." (T-18.IX.1:1-3)

"Let the Holy Spirit remove it from the withered kingdom in which you set it off, surrounded by darkness, guarded by attack and reinforced by hate." (T-18.IX.1:9)

"How is this done? It is extremely simple, being based on what this little kingdom really is." (T-18.IX.2:2-3)

"From the world of bodies, made by insanity, insane messages seem to be returned to the mind that made it. And these messages bear witness to this world, pronouncing it as true." (T-18.IX.3:1-2)

"The circle of fear lies just below the level the body sees, and seems to be the whole foundation on which the world is based. Here are all the illusions, all the twisted thoughts, all the insane attacks, the fury, the vengeance and betrayal that were made to keep the guilt in place, so that the world could rise from it and keep it hidden." (T-18.IX.4:1-2)

"The body will remain guilt's messenger, and will act as it directs as long as you believe that guilt is real. For the reality of guilt is the illusion that seems to make it heavy and opaque, impenetrable, and a real foundation for the ego's thought system." (T-18.IX.5:1-2)

"This heavy-seeming barrier, the artificial floor that looks like rock, is a like a bank of low dark clouds that seem to be a solid wall before the sun. Its impenetrable appearance is wholly an illusion." (T-18.IX.6:1-2)

CHAPTER 18—THE PASSING OF THE DREAM

"Yet in this cloud bank it is easy to see a whole world rising." (T-18.IX.7:1)

"Figures stand out and move about, actions seem real, and forms appear and shift from loveliness to the grotesque. And back and forth they go, as long as you would play the game of children's make-believe. Yet however long you play, and regardless of how much imagination you bring to it, you do not confuse it with the world below, nor seek to make it real." (T-18.IX.7:3-5)

"So should it be with the dark clouds of guilt, no more impenetrable and no more substantial." (T-18.IX.8:1)

"Let your Guide teach you their unsubstantial nature as He leads you past them, for beneath them is a world of light whereon they cast no shadows." (T-18.IX.8:3)

"This world of light, this circle of brightness is the real world, where guilt meets with forgiveness." (T-18.IX.9:1)

"Here are you forgiven, for here you have forgiven everyone. Here is the new perception, where everything is bright and shining with innocence, washed in the waters of forgiveness, and cleansed of every evil thought you laid upon it." (T-18.IX.9:3-4)

"Yet even forgiveness is not the end." (T-18.IX.10:1)

"It is the source of healing, but it is the messenger of love and not its Source." (T-18.IX.10:3)

"A step beyond this holy place of forgiveness, a step still further inward but the one you cannot take, transports you to something completely different. Here is the Source of light; nothing perceived, forgiven nor transformed. But merely known." (T-18.IX.10:5-6)

"This course will lead to knowledge, but knowledge itself is still beyond the scope of our curriculum." (T-18.IX.11:1)

"Love is not learned. Its meaning lies within itself. And learning ends when you have recognized all it is not." (T-18.IX.12:1-3)

"Your relationship with your brother has been uprooted from the world of shadows, and its unholy purpose has been safely brought through the barriers of guilt, washed with forgiveness, and set shining and firmly rooted in the world of light." (T-18.IX.13:1)

"The holy instant in which you and your brother were united is but the messenger of love, sent from beyond forgiveness to remind you of all that lies beyond it." (T-18.IX.13:3)

"And when the memory of God has come to you in the holy place of forgiveness you will remember nothing else, and memory will be as useless as learning, for your only purpose will be creating." (T-18.IX.14:1)

"Forgiveness removes only the untrue, lifting the shadows from the world and carrying it, safe and sure within its gentleness, to the bright world of new and clean perception. There is your purpose now. And it is there that peace awaits you." (T-18.IX.14:3-5)

In summary, Chapter 18 – IX. "The Two Worlds" is saying:

There are two worlds we can choose from to experience: A world of fear, based on the ego's insane thoughts or a world of love, based on the loving Thought of God. The world of fear is nothing but a child's make-believe game; a world where we are free to be what we are not. To be what is "not love," is the only other option because in truth, there is only love. And so, a world of fear arose in response to our desire for an experience of what is "not love." We can leave this world at any time. It is surrounded by nothing but thin clouds of guilt in our minds. Guilt is synonymous with the word "body" and therefore we need only to forgive or look beyond the body to see past the clouds of illusion surrounding our true state of love. The holy instant is when we have at last forgiven or let go of, the idea we are anything less than united with each other in God's loving Mind, as one of His Thoughts. Let this be the only message carried through our eyes into our mind when we look upon the world we made out of fear, and we will safely witness the passing of this dream at last.

CHAPTER 19
THE ATTAINMENT OF PEACE

I. Healing and Faith

"We said before that when a situation has been dedicated wholly to truth peace is inevitable." (T-19.I.T-19.I.1:1)

"Every situation, properly perceived, becomes an opportunity to heal the Son of God. And he is healed *because* you offered faith to him, giving him to the Holy Spirit and releasing him from every demand your ego would make of him. Thus do you see him free, and in this vision does the Holy Spirit share." (T-19.I.2:1-3)

"It is obvious that a segment of the mind can see itself as separated from the Universal Purpose. When this occurs the body becomes its weapon, used against this Purpose, to demonstrate the "fact" that separation has occurred." (T-19.I.3:4-5)

"Do not overlook our earlier statement that faithlessness leads straight to illusions. For faithlessness is the perception of a brother as a body, and the body cannot be used for purposes of union." (T-19.I.4:1-2)

"Your faithlessness has thus opposed the Holy Spirit's purpose, and brought illusions, centered on the body, to stand between you. And the body will seem to be sick, for you have made of it an "enemy" of healing and the opposite of truth." (T-19.I.4:5-6)

"Truth is the absence of illusion; illusion the absence of truth. Both cannot be together, nor perceived in the same place." (T-19.I.5:8-9)

"The inevitable compromise is the belief that the body must be healed, and not the mind." (T-19.I.6:1)

"Truth and illusion have no connection." (T-19.I.7:1)

"The idea of separation produced the body and remains connected to it, making it sick because of the mind's identification with it. You think you are protecting the body by hiding this connection, for this concealment seems to keep your identification safe from the "attack" of truth." (T-19.I.7:7-8)

"Faith is the acknowledgment of union. It is the gracious acknowledgment of everyone as a Son of your most loving Father, loved by Him like you, and therefore loved by you as yourself. It is His Love that joins you and your brother, and for His Love you would keep no one separate from yours." (T-19.I.10:2-3)

"Grace is not given to a body, but to a mind. And the mind that receives it looks instantly beyond the body, and sees the holy place where it was healed. There is the altar where the grace was given, in which it stands." (T-19.I.13:1-3)

"And be you healed by grace together, that you may heal through faith." (T-19.I.13:5)

"In the holy instant, you and your brother stand before the altar God has raised unto Himself and both of you. Lay faithlessness aside, and come to it together. There you will see the miracle of your relationship as it was made again through faith." (T-19.I.14:1-3)

"For faith brings peace, and so it calls on truth to enter and make lovely what has already been prepared for loveliness." (T-19.I.15:2)

"Let, then, your dedication be to the eternal, and learn how not to interfere with it and make it slave to time. For what you think you do to the eternal you do to *you*." (T-19.I.16:1-2)

In summary, Chapter 19 – I. "Healing and Faith" is saying:
Truth is peaceful because the truth is, we are not in conflict with one another, we are One. We are called here to have faith in this truth, despite the separated bodies our eyes perceive. It is through faith in our union that our bodies are healed; it is the idea of separation that produced the body and so our healing lies in the idea that is the opposite to this illusion; the idea we are not separate bodies but joined in God's peace—God's grace. Grace is the feeling of our union in God. To realize this with our full faith, is grace. Grace, being an idea, can only occur to a mind, not a body. So, healing must first be of the mind, and the body will follow. Let us then be dedicated with full faithfulness only to what is eternal within everyone. Each time you remember that you do not need anyone to be a body for you, is a holy instant. In this remembrance, your faith will heal you both for healing and faith go hand in hand.

CHAPTER 19 — THE ATTAINMENT OF PEACE

II. Sin versus Error

"It is essential that error be not confused with sin, and it is this distinction that makes salvation possible. For error can be corrected, and the wrong made right. But sin, were it possible, would be irreversible." (T-19.II.1:1-3)

"To sin would be to violate reality, and to succeed. Sin is the proclamation that attack is real and guilt is justified." (T-19.II.2:2-3)

"The Son of God can be mistaken; he can deceive himself; he can even turn the power of his mind against himself. But he cannot sin. There is nothing he can do that would really change his reality in any way, nor make him really guilty." (T-19.II.3:1-3)

"A major tenet in the ego's insane religion is that sin is not error but truth, and it is innocence that would deceive." (T-19.II.4:1)

"It can indeed be said the ego made its world on sin. Only in such a world could everything be upside down." (T-19.II.6:1-2)

"For sin has changed creation from an idea of God to an ideal the ego wants; a world it rules, made up of bodies, mindless and capable of complete corruption and decay. If this is a mistake, it can be undone easily by truth. But if the mistake is given the status of truth, to what can it be brought?" (T-19.II.6:5-8)

"There is no stone in all the ego's embattled citadel that is more heavily defended than the idea that sin is real; the natural expression of what the Son of God has made himself to be, and what he is." (T-19.II.7:1)

"Would you not rather that all this be nothing more than a mistake, entirely correctable, and so easily escaped from that its whole correction is like walking through a mist into the sun? For that is all it is." (T-19.II.8:1-2)

"Yet think you carefully before you allow yourself to make this choice. Approach it not lightly, for it is the choice of hell or Heaven." (T-19.II.8:4-5)

In summary, Chapter 19 – II. "Sin versus Error" is saying:
Here the Course makes it very clear: We have never sinned, for sin is defined as an uncorrectable wrong act. We have made an *error*, and errors can be corrected. What is the irreversible sin we are afraid we have committed? We

think we have made this world of separation a real place, where the wrongs we commit in time carry over into the realm of eternity. This is not so! This world is merely a place where ego ideals are allowed to play out in full, but never are they made *real*, for to be real, such acts would have to be *eternal*. Nothing in this world of form is eternal—no act and no effect of such acts can affect our eternal Self, which is indestructible forever. Bodies can hurt, be abandoned and all will one day die. Spirit cannot. Mind cannot. Therefore, there is no sin we can commit against what cannot be harmed. Be glad then, that our "sins" are not real and that all we have done is made an error in believing we are bodies.

III. The Unreality of Sin

"The attraction of guilt is found in sin, not error." (T-19.III.1:1)

"But while the guilt remains attractive the mind will suffer and not let go of the idea of sin." (T-19.III.1:4)

"The ego does not think it possible that love, not fear, is really called upon by sin, *and always answers*. For the ego brings sin to fear, demanding punishment." (T-19.III.2:1-2)

"An error, on the other hand, is not attractive. What you see clearly as a mistake you want corrected." (T-19.III.3:1-2)

"Now you will not repeat it; you will merely stop and let it go, unless the guilt remains." (T-19.III.3:5)

"Every mistake must be a call for love. What, then, is sin? What could it be but a mistake you would keep hidden; a call for help that you would keep unheard and thus unanswered?" (T-19.III.4:7-9)

"And when correction is completed, time is eternity. The Holy Spirit can teach you how to look on time differently and see beyond it, but not while you believe in sin. In error, yes, for this can be corrected by the mind. But sin is the belief that your perception is unchangeable, and that the mind must accept as true what it is told through it." (T-19.III.5:4-7)

"When you are tempted to believe that sin is real, remember this: If sin is real, both God and you are not." (T-19.III.6:1)

"While you believe that your reality or your brother's is bounded by a body, you will believe in sin." (T-19.III.7:1)

CHAPTER 19 — THE ATTAINMENT OF PEACE

"Your holy relationship has, as its purpose now, the goal of proving this is impossible." (T-19.III.8:4)

"In the holy instant, you will see the smile of Heaven shining on both you and your brother." (T-19.III.10:1)

"The barriers to Heaven will disappear before your holy sight, for you who were sightless have been given vision, and you can see." (T-19.III.10:6)

"Your relationship is now a temple of healing; a place where all the weary ones can come and rest. Here is the rest that waits for all, after the journey. And it is brought nearer to all by your relationship." (T-19.III.11:3-5)

In summary, Chapter 19 – III. "The Unreality of Sin" is saying:

Why is feeling guilt (seeing the body) so attractive to us? If it were not, we would instantly give up this debilitating emotion that ultimately chains us to this world. This is in fact, the very reason we refuse to give it up; the ego knows it binds us to this world, and to cease to feel guilty (believe we are bodies) would mean we would not only give up our attachment to this world, but the ego as well. And so, through listening to the voice of the ego, we hear nothing but that we have "sinned"—or committed unforgivable wrongs that cannot be corrected. The Voice for truth; the Holy Spirit would tell us that we have merely been mistaken in who we think we are. We believe we are bodies that can commit heinous crimes against one another, but in truth, nothing at all has happened to our Light bodies—our Christ Identity. Sin, therefore, is unreal. To make sin real, would mean our mistakes would become eternal, but only Love is eternal, and we are Love—we are not our mistakes. To correct our mistakes, we must move our thinking from time to eternity, since Eternal Light is our true Identity. We do this, through ceasing to believe in sin (separation)—it is to cease to need another to be a body for our ego's satisfaction. It is to transform your relationship into a holy one, thus bringing about the holy instant. In this instant, you lift all barriers between yourself and God, Who lives within the one you cease to see as a body. And thus, the unreality of sin will be understood.

IV. The Obstacles to Peace

"As peace extends from deep inside yourself to embrace all the Sonship and give it rest, it will encounter many obstacles. Some of them you will try to impose. Others will seem to arise from elsewhere; from your brothers, and from various aspects of the world outside. Yet peace will gently cover them, extending past completely unencumbered." (T-19.IV.1:1-4)

"And you will carry its message of love and safety and freedom to everyone who draws nigh unto your temple, where healing waits for him." (T-19.IV.1:7)

"All this will you do. Yet the peace that already lies deeply within must first expand, and flow across the obstacles you placed before it." (T-19.IV.2:1-2)

"You can indeed be sure of nothing you see outside you, but of this you can be sure: The Holy Spirit asks that you offer Him a resting place where you will rest in Him." (T-19.IV.2:4)

"And when you look with gentle graciousness upon your brother, you are beholding Him." (T-19.IV.3:2)

"When the peace in you has been extended to encompass everyone, the Holy Spirit's function here will be accomplished." (T-19.IV.3:6)

In summary, Chapter 19 – IV. "The Obstacles to Peace" is saying:
Peace is the natural state of being for each and every one of us. Peace is what happens to our mind when it rests in the truth. The truth is, we are One Love and what is One cannot be anything but at peace with Itself. If there is conflict, oneness becomes divided in two; between the ego and our One Mindedness in God. In order to know the peace of our One Mindedness in God, we must lift the barriers we have placed in front of our awareness of It. We do this, through looking with gentleness and love upon our brothers and beholding their inner light instead. And so, we learn to look past the obstacles to our peace; there are but four, under which all forms of conflict fall.

A. The First Obstacle:
The Desire to Get Rid of It

"The first obstacle that peace must flow across is your desire to get rid of it. For it cannot extend unless you keep it." (T-19.IV.A.1:1-2)

"If it would spread across the whole creation, it must begin with you, and from you reach to everyone who calls, and bring him rest by joining you." (T-19.IV.A.1:6)

"The Holy Spirit's purpose rests in peace within you. Yet you are still

CHAPTER 19—THE ATTAINMENT OF PEACE

unwilling to let it join you wholly." (T-19.IV.A.3:1)

"Would you thrust salvation away from the giver of salvation?" (T-19.IV.A.4:1)

"Peace could no more depart from you than from God. Fear not this little obstacle. It cannot contain the Will of God." (T-19.IV.A.4:3-5)

"The little wall will fall away so quietly beneath the wings of peace." (T-19.IV.A.4:11)

"To overcome the world is no more difficult than to surmount your little wall. For in your holy relationship, without this barrier, is every miracle contained. There is no order of difficulty in miracles, for they are all the same. Each is a gentle winning over from the appeal of guilt to the appeal of love." (T-19.IV.A.5:1-4)

"Look not upon the little wall of shadows. The sun has risen over it. How can a shadow keep you from the sun? No more can you be kept by shadows from the light in which illusions end." (T-19.IV.A.6:4-7)

"This feather of a wish, this tiny illusion, this microscopic remnant of the belief in sin, is all that remains of what once seemed to be the world." (T-19.IV.A.8:1)

"How mighty can a little feather be before the great wings of truth?" (T-19.IV.A.9:1)

"The attraction of guilt produces fear of love, for love would never look on guilt at all. It is the nature of love to look upon only the truth, for there it sees itself, with which it would unite in holy union and completion." (T-19.IV.A.10:1-3)

"Love is attracted only to love." (T-19.IV.A.10:5)

"Fear is attracted to what love sees not, and each believes that what the other looks upon does not exist." (T-19.IV.A.10:8)

"And each has messengers which it sends forth, and which return to it with messages written in the language in which their going forth was asked." (T-19.IV.A.10:10)

"Love's messengers are gently sent, and return with messages of love and gentleness." (T-19.IV.A.11:1)

"What love would look upon is meaningless to fear, and quite invisible." (T-19.IV.A.11:7)

"Relationships in this world are the result of how the world is seen. And this depends on which emotion was called on to send its messengers to look upon it, and return with word of what they saw." (T-19.IV.A.12:1-2)

"The Holy Spirit has given you love's messengers to send instead of those you trained through fear." (T-19.IV.A.14:1)

"If you send them forth, they will see only the blameless and the beautiful, the gentle and the kind." (T-19.IV.A.14:3)

"They offer you salvation. Theirs are the messages of safety, for they see the world as kind." (T-19.IV.A.14:7-8)

"I am made welcome in the state of grace, which means you have at last forgiven me. For I became the symbol of your sin, and so I had to die instead of you. To the ego sin means death, and so atonement is achieved through murder." (T-19.IV.A.17:1-3)

"No one can die for anyone, and death does not atone for sin. But you can live to show it is not real. The body does appear to be the symbol of sin while you believe that it can get you what you want." (T-19.IV.A.17:8-10)

"To think you could be satisfied and happy with so little is to hurt yourself, and to limit the happiness that you would have calls upon pain to fill your meager store and make your life complete. This is completion as the ego sees it." (T-19.IV.A.17:12-13)

"Communion is another kind of completion which goes beyond guilt, because it goes beyond the body." (T-19.IV.A.17:15)

In summary, Chapter 19 – IV.A. "The First Obstacle: The Desire to Get Rid of It" is saying:
Let us remember that the word "guilt" is synonymous with the word "body." These two words can be equally substituted for the other in the Course teachings, and when done, understanding becomes quite clear. While we still desire conflict with others, we are desiring to get rid of our peace. While guilt (the body) is still attractive, or rather, while believing we are bodies is still attractive, guilt (the body) will remain a barrier to our peace. We will desire to get rid of the peace of seeing our union in exchange for the conflict of our relationships as bodies. Love sees none of this. Love cannot see our guilt, our bodies. Love sees only our union. Because we see only our bodies, we think

CHAPTER 19—THE ATTAINMENT OF PEACE

that dying will solve our problem. We thought that the death of Christ would absolve us of our sin; that if *His* body died, we would no longer have to suffer being in a body either. This cannot be true if the body is not Who We Are in truth. But we can live in a body and choose to not see each other as bodies; we can choose peace instead of conflict. We can see beyond sin (separation) to oneness we all share. This is to desire communion, rather than to desire to get rid of our peace through imagined separation.

B. The Second Obstacle:
The Belief the Body is Valuable for What It Offers

"We said that peace must first surmount the obstacle of your desire to get rid of it. Where the attraction of guilt holds sway, peace is not wanted. The second obstacle that peace must flow across, and closely related to the first, is the belief that the body is valuable for what it offers. For here is the attraction of guilt made manifest in the body, and seen in it." (T-19.IV.B.1:1-4)

"This is the value that you think peace would rob you of. This is what you believe that it would dispossess, and leave you homeless." (T-19.IV.B.2:1-2)

"What has the body really given you that justifies your strange belief that in it lies salvation? Do you not see that this is the belief in death? Here is the focus of the perception of Atonement as murder. Here is the source of the idea that love is fear." (T-19.IV.B.2:6-9)

"Is it a sacrifice to be removed from what can suffer? The Holy Spirit does not demand you sacrifice the hope of the body's pleasure; it has no hope of pleasure." (T-19.IV.B.3:4-5)

"Pain is the only "sacrifice" the Holy Spirit asks, and this He would remove." (T-19.IV.B.3:7)

"The second obstacle is no more solid than the first.. For you want neither to get rid of peace nor limit it." (T-19.IV.B.4:3-4)

"You want communion, not the feast of fear. You want salvation, not the pain of guilt. And you want your Father, not a little mound of clay, to be your home. In your holy relationship is your Father's Son." (T-19.IV.B.4:6-9)

"The end of guilt is in your hands to give. Would you stop now to look for guilt in your brother?" (T-19.IV.B.5:7-8)

IV. The Obstacles to Peace

"Let me be to you the symbol of the end of guilt, and look upon your brother as you would look on me." (T-19.IV.B.6:1)

"From your holy relationship truth proclaims the truth, and love looks on itself." (T-19.IV.B.7:1)

"And we are there together, in the quiet communion in which the Father and Son are joined." (T-19.IV.B.7:3)

"Forgive me your illusions, and release me from punishment for what I have not done. So will you learn the freedom that I taught by teaching freedom to your brother, and so releasing me. I am within your holy relationship, yet you would imprison me behind the obstacles you raise to freedom, and bar my way to you." (T-19.IV.B.8:2-3)

"Your little part is but to give the Holy Spirit the whole idea of sacrifice." (T-19.IV.B.9:1)

"Would you invest your hope of peace and happiness in what must fail?" (T-19.IV.B.9:8)

"It is impossible to seek for pleasure through the body and not find pain. It is essential that this relationship be understood, for it is one the ego sees as proof of sin." (T-19.IV.B.12:1-2)

"Why should the body be anything to you? Certainly what it is made of is not precious. And just as certainly it has no feeling. It transmits to you the feelings that you want." (T-19.IV.B.14:1-4)

"Who would send messages of hatred and attack if he but understood he sends them to himself?" (T-19.IV.B.14:11)

"Hear not its madness, and believe not the impossible is true." (T-19.IV.B.16:1)

"Not one but must regard the body as himself, without which he would die, and yet within which is his death equally inevitable." (T-19.IV.B.16:5)

"So does the ego find the death it seeks, returning it to you." (T-19.IV.B.17:6)

In summary, Chapter 19 – IV.B. "The Second Obstacle: The Belief the Body is Valuable for What It Offers" is saying:
We have only one thing to do and peace is ours: Release our desire to see ourselves as bodies. The body is a block to our peace because it represents the idea of separation—it is the direct manifestation of the ego's desire to

CHAPTER 19—THE ATTAINMENT OF PEACE

exist separate from God. It represents our desire for what is opposite of what God Wills for us—our union. Therefore, the body itself represents our opposition to peace. Can you forgive the illusion of your body in exchange for peace? The body is the symbol of guilt. To use the body as nothing more than a "getting mechanism" is to engage it in relationships where the body is your central focus. This is the attempt to make guilt, or the body, real. Forgive this illusion, for you are not a body, but the eternal Christ within. Let Christ be the symbol of the end of guilt—the end of the desire to identify with a bodily illusion. You do not need Christ to be a body, and neither should you need anyone else to be one either. The body has no value because it cannot offer you eternity. Let this obstacle go, through letting go your belief the body is valuable for what it offers. It can offer nothing, but the Christ within offers you everything forever.

C. The Third Obstacle: The Attraction of Death

"To you and your brother, in whose special relationship the Holy Spirit entered, it is given to release and be released from the dedication to death." (T-19.IV.C.1:1)

"Yet you must learn still more about this strange devotion, for it contains the third obstacle that peace must flow across." (T-19.IV.C.1:3)

"What seems to be the fear of death is really its attraction." (T-19.IV.C.1:5)

"And death is the result of the thought we call the ego, as surely as life is the result of the Thought of God." (T-19.IV.C.2:15)

"From the ego came sin and guilt and death, in opposition to life and innocence, and to the Will of God Himself. Where can such opposition lie but in the sick minds of the insane, dedicated to madness and set against the peace of Heaven? One thing is sure; God, Who created neither sin nor death, wills not that you be bound by them." (T-19.IV.C.3:1-3)

"But you who would release him are but honoring the Will of his Creator. The arrogance of sin, the pride of guilt, the sepulcher of separation, all are part of your unrecognized dedication to death." (T-19.IV.C.4:4-5)

"For what the ego loves, it kills for its obedience." (T-19.IV.C.4:7)

IV. The Obstacles to Peace

"You have another dedication that would keep the body incorruptible and perfect as long as it is useful for your holy purpose." (T-19.IV.C.5:1)

"You who are dedicated to the incorruptible have been given through your acceptance, the power to release from corruption. What better way to teach the first and fundamental principle in a course on miracles than by showing you the one that seems to be the hardest can be accomplished first?" (T-19.IV.C.6:1-2)

"The body can but serve your purpose. As you look on it, so will it seem to be. Death, were it true, would be the final and complete disruption of communication, which is the ego's goal." (T-19.IV.C.6:3-5)

"Yet the retreat to death is not the end of conflict. Only God's Answer is its end." (T-19.IV.C.7:3-4)

"Under the dusty edge of its distorted world the ego would lay the Son of God, slain by its orders, proof in his decay that God Himself is powerless before the ego's might, unable to protect the life that He created against the ego's savage wish to kill. My brother, child of our Father, this is a dream of death." (T-19.IV.C.8:1-2)

"The fear of death will go as its appeal is yielded to love's real attraction. The end of sin, which nestles quietly in the safety of your relationship, protected by your union with your brother, and ready to grow into a mighty force for God is very near." (T-19.IV.C.9:1-2)

"When anything seems to you to be a source of fear, when any situation strikes you with terror and makes your body tremble and the cold sweat of fear comes over it, remember it is always for one reason; the ego has perceived it as a symbol of fear, a sign of sin and death." (T-19.IV.C.11:1)

"Remember the holy Presence of the One given to you to be the Source of judgment. Give it to Him to judge for you, and say:

> *Take this from me and look upon it, judging it for me. Let me not see it as a sign of sin and death, nor use it for destruction. Teach me how not to make of it an obstacle to peace, but let You use it for me, to facilitate its coming.*" (T-19.IV.C.11:6-10)

CHAPTER 19—THE ATTAINMENT OF PEACE

In summary, Chapter 19 – IV.C. "The Third Obstacle: The Attraction of Death" is saying:

Through our attraction to being bodies and all things associated with bodies, we are also attracted to death. This association cannot be escaped because the body always dies. Anything involving it is equally given to death. Yet, death is false. It does not exist because you are eternal and cannot die. Only the body dies, and it is not you. Yet we can be dedicated to something else—the part of us that is real—the Eternal Life within us. Our attraction to death—the body—will go as we yield to the attraction to love. Then will the body serve a new purpose. We will use it to see only the truth within all bodies, and with this new association, the body will live on until we decide to set it aside. Awaken from this dream that you can die and fear nothing in this ego-built world. Learn to look only upon the eternal within all living things and there will be nothing left to fear, for you will know nothing that lives can ever die. Then will you no longer be attracted to death and this obstacle to your peace will be lifted from your mind.

D. The Fourth Obstacle:
The Fear of God

"What would you see without the fear of death? What would you feel and think if death held no attraction for you? Very simply, you would remember your Father." (T-19.IV.D.1:1-3)

"And as this memory rises in your mind, peace must still surmount a final obstacle, after which is salvation completed, and the Son of God entirely restored to sanity. For here your world does end." (T-19.IV.D.1:5-6)

"The dedication to death and to its sovereignty is but the solemn vow, the promise made in secret to the ego never to lift this veil, not to approach it, nor even to suspect that it is there. This is the secret bargain made with the ego to keep what lies beyond the veil forever blotted out and unremembered. Here is your promise never to allow union to call you out of separation; the great amnesia in which the memory of God seems quite forgotten; the cleavage of your Self from you; - the fear of God, the final step in your dissociation." (T-19.IV.D.3:2-4)

"Every obstacle that peace must flow across is surmounted in just the same way; the fear that raised it yields to the love beyond, and so the fear is gone. And so it is with this. The desire to get rid of peace and

IV. The Obstacles to Peace

drive the Holy Spirit from you fades in the presence of the quiet recognition that you love Him. The exaltation of the body is given up in favor of the spirit, which you love as you could never love the body." (T-19.IV.D.5:1-4)

"It seems to you the world will utterly abandon you if you but raise your eyes. Yet all that will occur is you will leave the world forever." (T-19.IV.D.7:1-2)

"Look upon it, open-eyed, and you will nevermore believe that you are at the mercy of things beyond you, forces you cannot control, and thoughts that come to you against your will." (T-19.IV.D.7:4)

"Forget not that you came this far together, you and your brother." (T-19.IV.D.8:1)

"But first, lift up your eyes and look on your brother in innocence born of complete forgiveness of his illusions, and through the eyes of faith that sees them not." (T-19.IV.D.8:7)

"No one can look upon the fear of God unterrified, unless he has accepted the Atonement and learned illusions are not real." (T-19.IV.D.9:1)

"This is the place to which everyone must come when he is ready. Once he has found his brother he is ready." (T-19.IV.D.10:2-3)

"To look upon the fear of God does need some preparation. Only the sane can look on stark insanity and raving madness with pity and compassion, but not with fear." (T-19.IV.D.11:1-2)

"This brother who stands beside you still seems to be a stranger. You do not know him, and your interpretation of him is very fearful." (T-19.IV.D.12:1-2)

"Beside you is one who offers you the chalice of Atonement, for the Holy Spirit is in him. Would you hold his sins against him, or accept his gift to you? Is this giver of salvation your friend or enemy? Choose which he is, remembering that you will receive of him according to your choice." (T-19.IV.D.13:1-4)

"Behold your Friend, the Christ Who stands beside you." (T-19.IV.D.14:1)

"This is your brother, crucified by sin and waiting for release from pain. Would you not offer him forgiveness, when only he can offer it to you?" (T-19.IV.D.15:1-2)

"Here is the holy place of resurrection, to which we come again; to

CHAPTER 19 — THE ATTAINMENT OF PEACE

which we will return until redemption is accomplished and received. Think who your brother is, before you would condemn him." (T-19.IV.D.16:1-2)

"Join him in gladness, and remove all trace of guilt from his disturbed and tortured mind." (T-19.IV.D.16:4)

"Let us give redemption to each other and share in it, that we may rise as one in resurrection, not separate in death." (T-19.IV.D.17:5)

"Free your brother here, as I freed you." (T-19.IV.D.18:1)

"Together we will disappear into the Presence beyond the veil, not to be lost but found; not to be seen but known." (T-19.IV.D.19:1)

"Think carefully how you would look upon the giver of this gift, for as you look on him so will the gift appear to be. As he is seen as either the giver of guilt or of salvation, so will his offering be seen and so received. The crucified give pain because they are in pain. But the redeemed give joy because they have been healed of pain." (T-19.IV.D.20:1-4)

"You came this far because the journey was your choice. And no one undertakes to do what he believes is meaningless." (T-19.IV.D.21:1-2)

"You and your brother stand together, still without conviction they have a purpose. Yet it is given you to see this purpose in your holy Friend, and recognize it as your own." (T-19.IV.D.21:6-7)

In summary, Chapter 19 – IV.D. "The Fourth Obstacle: The Fear of God" is saying:

No one likes to think that they fear God. Most of us tell ourselves we love Him, and yet for many, there is an underlying fear of our Oneness just beneath the surface. What if God does not really love us unconditionally? What if, upon death, we are punished? Or perhaps we are being punished now? The description of "Oneness" also implies we will lose our personal identities and become absorbed into a wholeness that does not allow for our individual perception or freedom. We may also fear what some call "The Rapture," in which God will suddenly swoop us off to Heaven, leaving nothing but our empty clothes and our loved ones behind. *We fear to lose what little we seem to have and to be even more alone than we are now.* Cease to listen to the fears of the ego! The Holy Spirit asks, would a loving Father cause us more fear and suffering than we now know? Only the ego would have us believe it possible. Know this, in our resurrection, we are One. This means that when each of us translates into our eternal reality, when we resurrect, *everyone goes with us together*. No one is lost or loses their personal identity. Together, we are not lost but found. Our only job is to believe in the Christ within all who walk this world with us, as One Love. This unity is what carries us forward *together*. The fear of God, our final obstacle, is overcome through faith in our Union and promised joy that lies beyond this world. Have faith only in this and you will achieve the attainment of peace.

CHAPTER 20
THE VISION OF HOLINESS

I. Holy Week

"This is Palm Sunday, the celebration of victory and the acceptance of the truth. Let us not spend this holy week brooding on the crucifixion of God's Son, but happily in the celebration of his release. For Easter is the sign of peace, not pain." (T-20.I.1:1-3)

"Let no dark sign of crucifixion intervene between the journey and its purpose; between the acceptance of the truth and its expression. This week we celebrate life, not death." (T-20.I.2:2-3)

"You stand beside your brother, thorns in one hand and lilies in the other, uncertain which to give. Join now with me and throw away the thorns, offering the lilies to replace them. This Easter I would have the gift of your forgiveness offered by you to me, and returned by me to you." (T-20.I.2:6-8)

"A week is short, and yet this holy week is the symbol of the whole journey the Son of God has undertaken." (T-20.I.3:1)

"Easter is not the celebration of the cost of sin, but of its end." (T-20.I.4:1)

"I was a stranger and you took me in, not knowing who I was." (T-20.I.4:3)

"In your forgiveness of this stranger, alien to you and yet your ancient Friend, lies his release and your redemption with him." (T-20.I.4:5)

"For Easter is the time of your salvation, along with mine." (T-20.I.4:8)

In summary, Chapter 20 – I: "Holy Week" is saying:
Here we are being called by Christ to make *every* week a "holy week." We are asked not to look upon His death as a time of accusation, fear and hatred towards anything that happened to Him during His time of crucifixion. It is our tendency to lay blame when faced with atrocities and we take sides against one another. Let us not see the dark side of what has been done to our Lord and God. Rather, let us remember it is our only task to forgive everything we see or remember in this world, knowing it is not our true reality and neither is it Christ's. Let us remember that regardless of what we do to one another here in this illusion, we will go in God's glory, as powerful and complete as we were

created. Nothing can stop our resurrection. Make every week a holy week through seeing only the Light of Christ in your fellow people, knowing they are not strangers, but your dear Friend whom you have temporarily forgotten and thought you could crucify. In this remembrance lies your salvation along with Christ's each week you make holy.

II. The Gift of Lilies

"Look upon all the trinkets made to hang upon the body, or to cover it or for its use. See all the useless things made for its eyes to see." (T-20.II.1:1-2)

"Gifts are not made through bodies, if they be truly given and received." (T-20.II.2:1)

"Only the mind can value, and only the mind decides on what it would receive and give. And every gift it offers depends on what it wants." (T-20.II.2:3-4)

"Each gift is an evaluation of the receiver and the giver. No one but sees his chosen home as an altar to himself." (T-20.II.3:1-2)

"Here is the value that you lay upon your brother and on yourself. Here is your gift to both; your judgment on the Son of God for what he is." (T-20.II.3:5-6)

"Offer him thorns and you are crucified. Offer him lilies and it is yourself you free." (T-20.II.3:8-9)

"I have a great need for lilies, for the Son of God has not forgiven me." (T-20.II.4:1)

"You look still with the body's eyes, and they can see but thorns. Yet you have asked for and received another sight. Those who accept the Holy Spirit's purpose as their own share also His vision." (T-20.II.5:1-3)

"This Easter, look with different eyes upon your brother. You have forgiven me." (T-20.II.6:1-2)

"The Holy Spirit's vision is no idle gift, no plaything to be tossed about a while and laid aside." (T-20.II.6:5)

"You have the vision now to look past all illusions." (T-20.II.7:1)

"Who is afraid to look upon illusions, knowing his savior stands beside him? With him, your vision has become the greatest power for the un-

CHAPTER 20 — THE VISION OF HOLINESS

doing of illusion that God Himself could give." (T-20.II.7:4-5)

"Your chosen home is on the other side, beyond the veil." (T-20.II.8:1)

"You will not see it with the body's eyes." (T-20.II.8:3)

"Would you not have your holy brother lead you there?" (T-20.II.9:1)

"Let him be to you the savior from illusions, and look on him with the new vision that looks upon the lilies and brings you joy." (T-20.II.9:3)

"This is the way to Heaven and to the peace of Easter, in which we join in glad awareness that the Son of God is risen from the past, and has awakened to the present." (T-20.II.10:1)

"Here is your savior and your friend, released from crucifixion through your vision, and free to lead you now where he would be." (T-20.II.11:1)

"The lamp is lit in you for your brother. And by the hands that gave it to him shall you be led past fear to love." (T-20.II.11:6-7)

In summary, Chapter 20 – II: "The Gift of Lilies" is saying:
Lilies here, represent the correct vision of our brothers—the pureness of sight that sees past the body and all its adornments—those things we dress it up with to please ourself and seek approval from others. The Holy Spirit sees none of this. He sees only our Oneness and our Light. And thus, He sees only through the eyes of forgiveness. Let us then, see each other only this way, and when we do, we are seeing only the Christ in one another. This vision is the way beyond the veil, to Heaven and the peace of Easter. The peace of Easter is our resurrection as we join Christ in His way of seeing us. The lamp in one another is lit, and as we see only this light, we will be led by it from fear to love. The gift of lilies, the vision of Christ, is the only gift we need to give to see as the Holy Spirit sees.

III. Sin as an Adjustment

"The belief in sin is an adjustment. And an adjustment is a change; a shift in perception, or a belief that what was so before has been made different." (T-20.III.1:1-2)

"Adjustments of any kind are of the ego." (T-20.III.2:1)

"The holy do not interfere with truth. They are not afraid of it, for it is within the truth they recognize their holiness, and rejoice at what they see. They look on it directly, without attempting to adjust themselves

III. Sin as an Adjustment

to it, or it to them." (T-20.III.3:1-3)

"A simple question yet remains, and needs an answer. Do you like what you have made?—a world of murder and attack, through which you thread your timid way through constant dangers, alone and frightened, hoping at most that death will wait a little longer before it overtakes you and you disappear. *You made this up.*" (T-20.III.4:1-3)

"All these are but fearful thoughts of those who would adjust themselves to a world made fearful by their adjustments." (T-20.III.4:6)

"Have you not wondered what the world is really like; how it would look through happy eyes? The world you see is but a judgment on yourself. It is not there at all. Yet judgment lays a sentence on it, justifies it and makes it real." (T-20.III.5:1-4)

"And to this world must you adjust as long as you believe this picture is outside, and has you at its mercy." (T-20.III.5:7)

"Seek not to make the Son of God adjust to his insanity." (T-20.III.7:1)

"And of the one blind thing in all the seeing universe of truth you ask, "How shall I look upon the Son of God?"" (T-20.III.7:10)

"Does one ask judgment of what is totally bereft of judgment?" (T-20.III.8:1)

"You asked this puff of madness for the meaning of your unholy relationship, and adjusted it according to its insane answer. How happy did it make you?" (T-20.III.8:4-5)

"Did you see the holiness that shone in both you and your brother, to bless the other? That is the purpose of your holy relationship." (T-20.III.8:8-9)

"Such is my will for you and your brother, and for each of you for one another and for himself." (T-20.III.10:1)

"For what is Heaven but union, direct and perfect, and without the veil of fear upon it? Here are we one, looking with perfect gentleness upon each other and on ourselves." (T-20.III.10:3-4)

"You and your brother now will lead the other to the Father as surely as God created His Son holy, and kept him so. In your brother is the light of God's eternal promise of your immortality. See him as sinless, and there can be no fear in you." (T-20.III.11:7-9)

CHAPTER 20 — THE VISION OF HOLINESS

In summary, Chapter 20 – III: "Sin as an Adjustment" is saying:

To see "sin" is to see separation. When we accepted the ego's view of ourselves as separate bodies, we made an "adjustment" to our seeing. We changed our self-perception from the truth of our eternal Oneness, to something we are not. Such false seeing was then labeled as a "sin" or wrong viewpoint—an error in judgment. And now we must ask ourselves, "Do we like what we see?" Adjustments of any kind are of the ego. Because of this, we are now blind, and do not see our reality as it is in truth. We cannot ask the ego to look upon the world and each other, for we will only see sin, the error of our separation. We must refuse to accept this ego-viewpoint and look with our inner eyes to behold the truth: The light of Christ within one another, uniting us in God. When we "readjust" our mind to see only this, the adjustments we made through the ego will disappear. The world and everyone one in it will be transformed into the truth. The sin, or ego-adjustment of seeing ourselves as separate, will be healed.

IV. Entering the Ark

"Nothing can hurt you unless you give it the power to do so." (T-20.IV.1:1)

"Power is of God, given by Him and reawakened by the Holy Spirit, Who knows that as you give you gain. He gives no power to sin, and therefore it has none; nor to its results as this world sees them, - sickness and death and misery and pain. These things have not occurred because the Holy Spirit sees them not, and gives no power to their seeming source." (T-20.IV.1:4-6)

"Sin has no place in Heaven, where its results are alien and can no more enter than can their source. And therein lies your need to see your brother sinless. In him is Heaven." (T-20.IV.2:1-3)

"But see him as he is, and what is yours shines from him to you." (T-20.IV.2:5)

"Salvation is a lesson in giving, as the Holy Spirit interprets it." (T-20.IV.2:9)

"Those who choose freedom will experience only its results. Their power is of God, and they will give it only to what God has given, to share with them." (T-20.IV.4:1-2)

"The sinless give as they received. See, then, the power of sinlessness

IV. Entering the Ark

within your brother, and share with him the power of the release from sin you offered him." (T-20.IV.5:1-2)

"And each one finds his savior when he is ready to look upon the face of Christ, and see Him sinless." (T-20.IV.5:6)

"The plan is not of you, nor need you be concerned with anything except the part that has been given you to learn." (T-20.IV.6:1)

"The ark of peace is entered two by two, yet the beginning of another world goes with them. Each holy relationship must enter here, to learn its special function in the Holy Spirit's plan, now that it shares His purpose." (T-20.IV.6:5-6)

"This is the purpose given you. Think not that your forgiveness of your brother serves but you two alone. For the whole new world rests in the hands of every two who enter here to rest." (T-20.IV.7:1-3)

"You may wonder how you can be at peace when, while you are in time, there is so much that must be done before the way to peace is open. Perhaps this seems impossible to you. But ask yourself if it is possible that God would have a plan for your salvation that does not work. Once you accept His plan as the one function that you would fulfill, there will be nothing else the Holy Spirit will not arrange for you without your effort. He will go before you making straight your path, and leaving in your way no stones to trip on, and no obstacles to bar your way. Nothing you need will be denied you. Not one seeming difficulty but will melt away before you reach it. You need take thought for nothing, careless of everything except the only purpose that you would fulfill." (T-20.IV.8:1-8)

In summary, Chapter 20 – IV: "Entering the Ark" is saying:

Here the process of "entering the ark" is a metaphor for entering the state of mind that brings us God's peace. To do this, we must first recognize our God-given power. We have the power to overcome all forms of suffering, because all suffering is experienced in our minds only. Have we not each experienced the truth of this? Have we not gone through seeming tribulations and yet survived them unscathed? And at other times, small upsets seem to bring more upheaval than they should. All this variation is due to our inner perception of what is happening to us—the power we give to what is nothing. Here we are told that the Ark of Peace is entered through establishing peace in our unholy relationships. We enter two by two as we establish peace with each one. We need but see each person as they are in truth—to look upon the face of Christ within them and see Him sinless, not as a body, but as God's loving Light. To do this, is to forgive. And when we make seeing this way our only purpose, there is nothing God will deny us in order to fulfill our holy purpose here—we *will* enter the ark of peace.

V. Heralds of Eternity

"In this world, God's Son comes closest to himself in a holy relationship." (T-20.V.1:1)

"Each miracle of joining is a mighty herald of eternity." (T-20.V.1:6)

"No one who shares his purpose with him can not be one with him." (T-20.V.1:8)

"Each herald of eternity sings of the end of sin and fear. Each speaks in time of what is far beyond it." (T-20.V.2:1-2)

"Peace to your holy relationship, which has the power to hold the unity of the Son of God together." (T-20.V.2:5)

"Do you recognize the fear that rises from the meaningless attempt to judge what lies so far beyond your judgment you cannot even see it? Judge not what is invisible to you or you will never see it, but wait in patience for its coming. It will be given you to see your brother's worth when all you want for him is peace." (T-20.V.3:4-6)

"Your brother's body is as little use to you as it is to him." (T-20.V.5:1)

"For minds need not the body to communicate." (T-20.V.5:3)

"Here is the perfect faith that you will one day offer to your brother already offered you; and here the limitless forgiveness you will give him already given, the face of Christ you yet will look upon already seen." (T-20.V.6:7)

"And through His vision will you see it, and through His understanding recognize it and love it as your own." (T-20.V.7:10)

"Be comforted, and feel the Holy Spirit watching over you in love and perfect confidence in what He sees." (T-20.V.8:1)

VI. The Temple of the Holy Spirit

In summary, Chapter 20 – V: "Heralds of Eternity" is saying:
It is a miracle to see beyond the body and look upon one another through our inner eyes, seeing only the Light of Christ within. The choice to see in this way, is a miraculous herald of the eternal truth within us. It means we have chosen a holy relationship with them. To be in a holy relationship, is to see yourself and another as One in God's Love. To see in this way, is the end of fear, for who could fear oneself? To see in this way is to bring peace to your relationship, for who could be in conflict with oneself? We recognize that the mind does not need a body to know Itself. To see beyond the body may seem impossible at times, and yet, be comforted in knowing this: The Holy Spirit will be with us, supporting us, and thus ensuring our success each time we make the choice to extend a miracle; a mighty herald proclaiming our eternal truth within.

VI. The Temple of the Holy Spirit

"The meaning of the Son of God lies solely in his relationship with his Creator." (T-20.VI.1:1)

"And this is wholly loving and forever. Yet the Son of God invented an unholy relationship between him and his Father. His real relationship is one of perfect union and unbroken continuity." (T-20.VI.1:3-5)

"Nothing can show the contrast better than the experience of both a holy and an unholy relationship. The first is based on love, and rests on it serene and undisturbed. The body does not intrude upon it. Any relationship in which the body enters is based not on love, but on idolatry." (T-20.VI.2:1-4)

"The Holy Spirit's temple is not a body, but a relationship." (T-20.VI.5:1)

"You cannot make the body the Holy Spirit's temple, and it will never be the seat of love." (T-20.VI.6:1)

"This is the temple dedicated to no relationships and no return. Here is the "mystery" of separation perceived in awe and held in reverence." (T-20.VI.6:5-6)

"Idolaters will always be afraid of love, for nothing so severely threatens them as love's approach. Let love draw near them and overlook the body, as it will surely do, and they retreat in fear, feeling the seeming firm foundation of their temple begin to shake and loosen." (T-20.VI.7:1-2)

"An unholy relationship is no relationship. It is a state of isolation, which seems to be what it is not. Not more than that." (T-20.VI.8:3-5)

"The holy relationship reflects the true relationship the Son of God has with his Father in reality. The Holy Spirit rests within it in the certainty it will endure forever." (T-20.VI.10:1-2)

"The body is the ego's idol; the belief in sin made flesh and then projected outward. This produces what seems to be a wall of flesh around the mind, keeping it prisoner in a tiny spot of space and time, beholden unto death, and given but an instant in which to sigh and grieve and die in honor of its master. And this unholy instant seems to be life; an instant of despair, a tiny island of dry sand, bereft of water and set uncertainly upon oblivion." (T-20.VI.11:1-3)

"This is no time for sadness." (T-20.VI.12:3)

"You have a real relationship, and it has meaning." (T-20.VI.12:5)

"Idolatry is past and meaningless." (T-20.VI.12:7)

"Yet what is that to those who have been given one true relationship beyond the body? Can they be long held back from looking on the face of Christ?" (T-20.VI.12:9-10)

In summary, Chapter 20 – VI "The Temple of the Holy Spirit" is saying:
The body can never be a worthy temple unto that which is our eternal Self. The body is a false manifestation of our idea to be separate from God, and so it lessens our experience of Oneness with Him. A temple is a place that enhances what it holds; not impeding it but magnifying it. The body impedes our glory; it dims the light within us by covering our holiness in pain and suffering. The only true temple worthy of the Holy Spirit lies in our holy relationships with one another—the only place God's Love can be magnified. Our holy relationships rest not on what the body can give us, but rather on what the light within us can share. Therefore, let love draw near to your heart in every encounter you have and overlook the bodies you see. Then watch the ego disappear as you enter the temple of the Holy Spirit through your holy relationship with them.

VII. The Consistency of Means and End

"We have said much about discrepancies of means and end, and how these must be brought in line before your holy relationship can bring you only joy." (T-20.VII.1:1)

"The period of discomfort that follows the sudden change in a relationship from sin to holiness may now be almost over. To the extent you still experience it, you are refusing to leave the means to Him Who changed the purpose. You recognize you want the goal. Are you not also willing to accept the means?" (T-20.VII.2:1-4)

"How can one be sincere and say, "I want this above all else, and yet I do not want the means to get it?""

"To obtain the goal, the Holy Spirit indeed asks little." (T-20.VII.3:1)

"It is impossible to see your brother as sinless and yet to look upon him as a body. Is this not perfectly consistent with the goal of holiness? For holiness is merely the result of letting the effects of sin be lifted, so what was always true is recognized." (T-20.VII.4:1-3)

"The body is the means by which the ego tries to make the unholy relationship seem real." (T-20.VII.5:1)

"Who sees a brother's body has laid a judgment on him, and sees him not." (T-20.VII.6:1)

"And here, in darkness, is your brother's reality imagined as a body, in unholy relationship with other bodies, serving the cause of sin an instant before he dies." (T-20.VII.6:7)

"The body cannot be looked upon except through judgment. To see the body is the sign that you lack vision, and have denied the means the Holy Spirit offers you to serve His purpose." (T-20.VII.8:1-2)

"Your question should not be, "How can I see my brother without a body?" Ask only, "Do I really wish to see him sinless?" And as you ask, forget not that his sinlessness is your escape from fear. Salvation is the Holy Spirit's goal. The means is vision." (T-20.VII.9:1-5)

In summary, Chapter 20 – VII: "The Consistency of Means and End" is saying:

We want to be healed of all pain and suffering, and yet, are we willing to do what it takes to experience this? All that is being asked here, is that we do not believe the body is our true identity. We may agree with this wholeheartedly, and yet the fact we continue to suffer from bodily effects is evidence we do not. Do not forget that to see someone as "sinless" is to see them as "bodiless." How badly do we want the inner peace and endless joy of Heaven, now, here on earth while we still walk it within these bodies? For this indeed is possible. Not only possible, but inevitable once we learn to look upon all as eternal expressions of God's Holy Love—and sincerely treat them thus, through the fullness of our hearts. When we see through the eyes of all-inclusive Love consistently, it becomes the means that will bring us salvation, our end goal.

VIII. The Vision of Sinlessness

"Vision will come to you at first in glimpses, but they will be enough to show you what is given you who see your brother sinless. Truth is restored to you through your desire, as it was lost to you through your desire for something else." (T-20.VIII.1:1-2)

"Desire now its whole undoing, and it is done for you." (T-20.VIII.1:6)

"Do you not want to know your own Identity?" (T-20.VIII.2:1)

"Would you not willingly be free of misery, and learn again of joy? Your holy relationship offers all this to you." (T-20.VIII.2:3-4)

"All this is given you who would but see your brother sinless." (T-20.VIII.2:8)

"Your brother's sinlessness is given you in shining light, to look on with the Holy Spirit's vision and to rejoice in along with Him." (T-20.VIII.3:1)

"Be willing, then, to see your brother sinless, that Christ may rise before your vision and give you joy. And place no value on your brother's body, which holds him to illusions of what he is." (T-20.VIII.3:3-4)

"You have the vision that enables you to see the body not." (T-20.VIII.4:3)

"There is no problem, no event or situation, no perplexity that vision will not solve. All is redeemed when looked upon with vision. For this is not your sight, and brings with it the laws beloved of Him Whose sight it is." (T-20.VIII.5:7-9)

"Everything looked upon with vision falls gently into place, according to the laws brought to it by His calm and certain sight." (T-20.VIII.6:1)

"Hallucinations disappear when they are recognized for what they are. This is the healing and the remedy. Believe them not and they are gone. And all you need to do is recognize that you did this. Once you accept this simple fact and take unto yourself the power you gave them you are released from them." (T-20.VIII.8:1-5)

"Vision is the means by which the Holy Spirit translates your nightmares into happy dreams; your wild hallucinations that show you all the fearful outcomes of imagined sin into the calm and reassuring sights

VIII. The Vision of Sinlessness

with which He would replace them." (T-20.VIII.10:4)

"When you have looked on what seemed terrifying, and seen it change to sights of loveliness and peace; when you have looked on scenes of violence and death, and watched them change to quiet views of gardens under open skies, with clear, life-giving water running happily beside them in dancing brooks that never waste away; who need persuade you to accept the gift of vision?" (T-20.VIII.11:1)

"Think but an instant just on this; you can behold the holiness God gave His Son. And never need you think that there is something else for you to see." (T-20.VIII.11:3-4)

In summary, Chapter 20 – VIII: "The Vision of Sinlessness" is saying:
It may seem confusing to our mind to look at a body and not "see" it. What should we "see" instead? How do we "see" someone without the body's eyes? And yet, we are promised this is something we can do; in fact, we must do it for our salvation depends on learning how to use our gift of vision. Therefore, place no value on what someone says or does with their body. This identity is not who they are in truth. It is not who *you* are in truth. Let this hallucination disappear from your mind, even if only during meditation and you will engage in vision with your holy sight. You need not try to imagine *how* you should see them without their body, for that, as yet you cannot conceive of. Simply allow your mind to rest with the knowledge that all you see now is not true. And do not forget; to see with the vision of sinlessness, you must see all as bodiless—as part of God's all-inclusive Love. This then, *is* the vision of holiness.

CHAPTER 21
REASON AND PERCEPTION

Introduction

"Projection makes perception. The world you see is what you gave it, nothing more than that." (T-21.in.1:1-2)

"Therefore, to you it is important. It is the witness to your state of mind, the outside picture of an inward condition." (T-21.in.1:4-5)

"Perception is a result and not a cause. And that is why order of difficulty in miracles is meaningless. Everything looked upon with vision is healed and holy." (T-21.in.1:8-10)

"The world you see but shows you how much joy you have allowed yourself to see in you, and to accept as yours. And, if this is its meaning, then the power to give it joy must lie within you." (T-21.in.2:7-8)

In summary, Chapter 21 – Introduction is saying:
We are responsible for what we see and how we respond emotionally to it. Our world bears witness to our inner state of mind and therefore we have the power to change the world through changing our minds. Let us see it forgiven and make peace with all our relationships and it will change accordingly. We can do this with all things and anything. There is no order of difficulty in miracles.

I. The Forgotten Song

"Never forget the world the sightless "see" must be imagined, for what it really looks like is unknown to them." (T-21.I.1:1)

"And so it is with you. You do not see. Your cues for inference are wrong, and so you stumble and fall down upon the stones you did not recognize, but fail to be aware you can go through the doors you thought were closed, but which stand open before unseeing eyes, waiting to welcome you." (T-21.I.1:3-5)

"How foolish is it to attempt to judge what could be seen instead. It is not necessary to imagine what the world must look like. It must be seen before you recognize it for what it is." (T-21.I.2:1-3)

"There is no need to learn through pain. And gentle lessons are acquired joyously, and are remembered gladly." (T-21.I.3:1-2)

I. The Forgotten Song

"You are not a happy learner yet because you still remain uncertain that vision gives you more than judgment does, and you have learned that both you cannot have." (T-21.I.3:7)

"The blind become accustomed to their world by their adjustments to it." (T-21.I.4:1)

"They learned it, not through joyous lessons, but through the stern necessity of limits they believed they could not overcome." (T-21.I.4:3)

"Thus they define their life and where they live, adjusting to it as they think they must, afraid to lose the little that they have. And so it is with all who see the body as all they have and all their brothers have." (T-21.I.5:1-2)

"Listen, - perhaps you can catch a hint of an ancient state not quite forgotten; dim, perhaps, and yet not altogether unfamiliar, like a song whose name is long forgotten, and the circumstances in which you heard completely unremembered. Not the whole song has stayed with you, but just a little wisp of melody, attached not to a person or a place or anything particular. But you remember, from just this little part, how lovely was the song, how wonderful the setting where you heard it, and how you loved those who were there and listened with you." (T-21.I.6:1-3)

"Listen, and see if you remember an ancient song you knew so long ago and held more dear than any melody you taught yourself to cherish since." (T-21.I.7:5)

"Beyond the body, beyond the sun and stars, past everything you see and yet somehow familiar, is an arc of golden light that stretches as you look into a great and shining circle. And all the circle fills with light before your eyes." (T-21.I.8:1-2)

"The light expands and covers everything, extending to infinity forever shining and with no break or limit anywhere. Within it everything is joined in perfect continuity. Nor is it possible to imagine that anything could be outside, for there is nowhere that this light is not." (T-21.I.8:4-6)

"This is the vision of the Son of God, whom you know well." (T-21.I.9:1)

"Accept the vision that can show you this, and not the body." (T-21.I.9:4)

"And now the blind can see, for that same song they sing in honor of

CHAPTER 21—REASON AND PERCEPTION

their Creator gives praise to them as well. The blindness that they made will not withstand the memory of this song. And they will look upon the vision of the Son of God, remembering who he is they sing of. What is a miracle but this remembering?" (T-21.I.10:1-3)

"The light in one awakens it in all. And when you see it in your brother, you are remembering for everyone." (T-21.I.10:6-7)

In summary, Chapter 21 – I: "The Forgotten Song" is saying:
The "forgotten song" is the forgotten world we once could see with our spirit eyes. We have forgotten what the world looks like without the ego's impression upon our mind, clouding our vision. We look out on the world and each other and think what we are seeing is the truth of our reality, but in fact we are blind to the light within all. So, we adjust to what we *think* we see, and live according to what we understand to be the truth, though nothing could be further from it. We have forgotten the song of truth, but not entirely. The fact we are searching for truth at all, is a clear sign we remember a small refrain from this forgotten song. We know it is there; we search for the light within all living things. Let our minds accept this light and imagine it expanding, replacing the world we see through our ego's eyes. This light is our truth, not the body. This is the Vision of the Son of God, through which all are included in the symphony of the long-forgotten song of our Unity in God's Love and the miracle of remembering.

II. The Responsibility for Sight

"We have repeated how little is asked of you to learn this course. It is the same small willingness you need to have your whole relationship transformed to joy; the little gift you offer to the Holy Spirit for which He gives you everything; the very little on which salvation rests; the tiny change of mind by which the crucifixion is changed to resurrection." (T-21.II.1:1-2)

"This is the only thing that you need do for vision, happiness, release from pain and the complete escape from sin, all to be given you. Say only this, but mean it with no reservations, for here the power of salvation lies:

*I **am** responsible for what I see. I choose the feelings I experience, and I decide upon the goal I would achieve. And everything that seems to happen to me I ask for, and receive as I have asked*

Deceive yourself no longer that you are helpless in the face of what is done to you. Acknowledge but that you have been mistaken, and all effects of your mistakes will disappear." (T-21.II.2:1-7)

"No accident nor chance is possible within the universe as God created it, outside of which is nothing. Suffer, and you decided sin was your goal. Be happy, and you gave the power of decision to Him Who must decide for God for you. This is the little gift you offer to the Holy Spirit, and even this He gives to you to give yourself. For by this gift is given you the power to release your savior, that he may give salvation unto you." (T-21.II.3:4-8)

"Begrudge not then this little offering. Withhold it, and you keep the world as now you see it. Give it away, and everything you see goes with it." (T-21.II.4:1-3)

"Perhaps you do not see the need for you to give this little offering. Look closer, then, at what it is. And, very simply, see in it the whole exchange of separation for salvation." (T-21.II.6:1-3)

"The Holy Spirit can give you faith in holiness and vision to see it easily enough." (T-21.II.7:1)

"All you are asked to do is let it in; only to stop your interference with what will happen of itself; simply to recognize again the presence of what you thought you gave away." (T-21.II.7:8)

"Be willing, for an instant, to leave your altars free of what you placed upon them, and what is really there you cannot fail to see." (T-21.II.8:1)

"What you desire, you will see. And if its reality is false, you will uphold it by not realizing all the adjustments you have introduced to make it so." (T-21.II.9:5-6)

"It is as needful that you recognize you made the world you see, as that you recognize that you did not create yourself. *They are the same mistake*." (T-21.II.11:1-2)

"Yet the truth is you and your brother were both created by a loving Father, Who created you together and as one. See what "proves" otherwise, and you deny your whole reality." (T-21.II.13:1-2)

"This is the same mistake as thinking you are independent of the Source by which you were created, and have never left." (T-21.II.13:6)

In summary, Chapter 21 – II: "The Responsibility for Sight" is saying:

We are responsible for our how we see—we must choose between the ego and the Holy Spirit's vision. This is our one responsibility, because our whole reality depends on what we choose. We cannot see two realities at once. How much willingness does it take to decide to see beyond the body, knowing it is not who we are? Just a small willingness; simply the inner recognition of our oneness, is enough. If we can learn to recognize our mistake in seeing separation, our ego is undone, and a new world will be revealed to us. Clear your inner altar through the desire to see beyond that which is now presented to you by your ego and you will have taken responsibility for your sight.

III. Faith, Belief and Vision

"All special relationships have sin as their goal. For they are bargains with reality, toward which the seeming union is adjusted." (T-21.III.1:1-2)

"And that is why the Holy Spirit must change its purpose to make it useful to Him and harmless to you." (T-21.III.1:6)

"If you accept this change, you have accepted the idea of making room for truth. The source of sin is gone. You may imagine that you still experience its effects, but it is not your purpose and you no longer want it." (T-21.III.2:1-3)

"The power of faith is never recognized if it is placed in sin. But it is always recognized if it is placed in love." (T-21.III.2:6-7)

"Why is it strange to you that faith can move mountains? This is indeed a little feat for such a power." (T-21.III.3:1-2)

"Faith and belief and vision are the means by which the goal of holiness is reached. Through them the Holy Spirit leads you to the real world, and away from all illusions where your faith was laid." (T-21.III.4:1-2)

"His faith and His belief and vision are all for you. And when you have accepted them completely instead of yours, you will have need of them no longer. For faith and vision and belief are meaningful only before the state of certainty is reached. In Heaven they are unknown. Yet Heaven is reached through them." (T-21.III.4:5-9)

"The Holy Spirit has a use for all the means for sin by which you sought to find it. But as He uses them they lead away from sin, because His purpose lies in the opposite direction." (T-21.III.6:1-2)

III. Faith, Belief and Vision

"You made perception that you might choose among your brothers, and seek for sin with them. The Holy Spirit sees perception as a means to teach you that the vision of a holy relationship is all you want to see. Then will you give your faith to holiness, desiring and believing in it because of your desire." (T-21.III.6:5-7)

"Faith and belief become attached to vision, as all the means that once served sin are redirected now toward holiness." (T-21.III.7:1)

"Those who would free their brothers from the body can have no fear. They have renounced the means for sin by choosing to let all limitations be removed. As they desire to look upon their brothers in holiness, the power of their belief and faith sees far beyond the body, supporting vision, not obstructing it." (T-21.III.8:1-3)

"For all who choose to look away from sin are given vision, and are led to holiness." (T-21.III.8:6)

"Join your awareness to what has already been joined." (T-21.III.9:7)

"The body was made to be a sacrifice to sin, and in the darkness so it still is seen. Yet in the light of vision it is looked upon quite differently. You can have faith in it to serve the Holy Spirit's goal, and give it power to serve as means to help the blind to see. But in their seeing they look past it, as do you." (T-21.III.12:1-4)

"You gave perception and belief and faith from mind to body. Let them now be given back to what produced them, and use them still to save itself from what it made." (T-21.III.12: 6-7)

In summary, Chapter 21 – III: "Faith, Belief and Vision" is saying:
All special relationships, though they seem to be the joining of two people, are actually relationships based upon separation. This is because all special relationships are based upon the body; what it looks like and the impressive things the occupant of "said body" can achieve with it. Such bodily attractions are the whole attraction of sin—or separation. It is not wrong to love certain points about another, but it is a mistake in thinking it is solely who they truly are. We bargain with the reality of our union when we see them as anything other than One with All That Is. We must have faith in this truth and believe in what lies beyond the body. For faith and belief lead to true vision of the truth of our holy unified relationship with everyone around us. Faith, belief and vision will ultimately save us from the separation we think we live in now.

IV. The Fear to Look Within

"The Holy Spirit will never teach you that you are sinful. Errors He will correct, but this makes no one fearful. You are indeed afraid to look within and see the sin you think is there." (T-21.IV.1:1-3)

"Loudly the ego tells you not to look inward, for if you do your eyes will light on sin, and God will strike you blind. This you believe, and so you do not look." (T-21.IV.2:3-4)

"What if you looked within and saw no sin? This "fearful" question is one the ego never asks. And you who ask it now are threatening the ego's whole defensive system too seriously for it to bother to pretend it is your friend." (T-21.IV.3:1-3)

"Not wholly mad, you have been willing to look on much of your insanity and recognize its madness. Your faith is moving inward, past insanity and on to reason." (T-21.IV.4:2-3)

"The Holy Spirit's purpose was accepted by the part of your mind the ego knows not of." (T-21.IV.4:5)

"This part has seen your brother, and recognized him perfectly since time began. And it desired nothing but to join with him and to be free again, as once it was." (T-21.IV.5:1-2)

"And now the ego is afraid. Yet what it hears in terror, the other part hears as the sweetest music; the song it longed to hear since first the ego came into your mind. The ego's weakness is its strength." (T-21.IV.7:1-3)

"Look gently on your brother, and remember the ego's weakness is revealed in both your sight. What it would keep apart has met and joined, and looks upon the ego unafraid." (T-21.IV.8:1-2)

"The quiet way is open. Follow it happily, and question not what must be so." (T-21.IV.8:8-9)

In summary, Chapter 21 – IV: "The Fear to Look Within" is saying:
The ego's weakness is seeing separation while our strength lies in the truth of our union in God. Where the ego crumbles in pain over losses in this world, the Holy Spirit within us remains strong in knowing we can never lose any living thing, for all remain part of the Whole for eternity. The ego believes that if we look within, all we will see is emptiness and loss. Yet what if all we saw was wholeness, peace, and contentment? We are now not so insane that we

cannot look. There is a part of our mind that still remembers the truth and desires nothing more than to rejoin with That Which is Whole. To want to see only our Oneness, is nothing but the sweetest music to our One Self. Do not fear to look within and see this Light, for what the ego would have you believe is separate has been joined since the beginning of time and does not fear anything the ego believes.

V. The Function of Reason

"Perception selects, and makes the world you see. It literally picks it out as the mind directs." (T-21.V.1:1-2)

"For what you would look for you are far more likely to discover than what you would prefer to overlook." (T-21.V.1:5)

"Perception is a choice and not a fact. But on this choice depends far more than you may realize as yet. For on the voice you choose to hear, and on the sights you choose to see, depends entirely your whole belief in what you are." (T-21.V.1:7-9)

"Reality needs no cooperation from you to be itself. But your awareness of it needs your help, because it is your choice. Listen to what the ego says, and see what it directs you see, and it is sure that you will see yourself as tiny, vulnerable and afraid." (T-21.V.2:1-3)

"You will believe that you are helpless prey to forces far beyond your own control, and far more powerful than you." (T-21.V.2:5)

"There is another vision and another Voice in which your freedom lies, awaiting but your choice. And if you place your faith in Them, you will perceive another self in you. This other self sees miracles as natural." (T-21.V.3:1-3)

"You do not realize the whole extent to which the idea of separation has interfered with reason. Reason lies in the other self you have cut off from your awareness. And nothing you have allowed to stay in your awareness is capable of reason." (T-21.V.4:1-3)

"God's plan for your salvation could not have been established without your will and your consent." (T-21.V.5:1)

"Therefore, what joined the Will of God must be in you now, being eternal. You must have set aside a place in which the Holy Spirit can abide, and where He is." (T-21.V.5:4-5)

CHAPTER 21 — REASON AND PERCEPTION

"Such would your reason tell you, if you listened. Yet such is clearly not the ego's reasoning." (T-21.V.5:7-8)

"It is not meaningful to ask if what must be is so. But it is meaningful to ask why you are unaware of what is so, for this must have an answer if the plan of God for your salvation is complete." (T-21.V.6:4-5)

"Where would the answer be but in the Source? And where are you but there, where this same answer is?" (T-21.V.7:1-2)

"O yes, you know this, and more than this alone." (T-21.V.7:4)

"Faith and perception and belief can be misplaced, and serve the great deceiver's needs as well as truth. But reason has no place at all in madness, nor can it be adjusted to fit its end." (T-21.V.8:1-2)

"For the perception would fall away at once, if reason were applied." (T-21.V.8:5)

"The part of your mind where reason lies was dedicated, by your will in union with your Father's, to the undoing of insanity." (T-21.V.9:1)

"Faith and belief have shifted, and you have asked the question the ego will never ask." (T-21.V.10:2)

"Faith and belief, upheld by reason, cannot fail to lead to changed perception. And in this change is room made way for vision." (T-21.V.10:4-5)

In summary, Chapter 21 – V: "The Function of Reason" is saying:
Reason tells us that we cannot be the bodies we see, simply because we know we existed in some way or form before we entered them. We do in fact know, on some level, that we must be *something else*. Therefore, what was once joined with God, must *still be there*, within us, somewhere. It is not meaningful to ask whether or not this is true. It is only meaningful to ask, *why* can we not *see it*? It is because we have chosen another perception—one through the body's eyes—over that of our holy vision, which can see what the body cannot. We now ask the question the ego will never ask: How can we each appear separate from All Creation, when reason dictates, we must each still be a part of It in holy Unity? This is the function of God's Reason then, to strengthen our faith and belief in the truth of our Wholeness, which will lead to our changed perception, which begets a new vision of reality.

VI. Reason versus Madness

"Reason cannot see sin but can see errors, and leads to their correction." (T-21.VI.1:1)

"Reason will also tell you that when you think you sin, you call for help. Yet if you will not accept the help you call for, you will not believe that it is yours to give." (T-21.VI.1:3-4)

"For reason would not make way for correction in you alone." (T-21.VI.1:10)

"Correction cannot be accepted or refused by you without your brother." (T-21.VI.2:1)

"Sin would maintain you and your brother must be separate. But reason tells you that this must be wrong." (T-21.VI.2:6-7)

"For only bodies can be separate, and therefore unreal. The home of madness cannot be the home of reason. Yet it is easy to leave the home of madness if you see reason." (T-21.VI.3:4-6)

"The body does not separate you from your brother, and if you think it does you are insane." (T-21.VI.5:1)

"To see the body as a barrier between what reason tells you must be joined must be insane. Nor could you see it, if you heard the voice of reason." (T-21.VI.5:3-4)

"That you are joined to him is but a fact, not an interpretation." (T-21.VI.6:6)

"Reason will tell you that this fact is your release." (T-21.VI.6:8)

"The power to heal the son of God is given you because he must be one with you." (T-21.VI.7:4)

"And reason tells you it is given you to change his whole mind, which is one with you, in just an instant." (T-21.VI.7:6)

"That you and your brother are joined is your salvation; the gift of Heaven, not the gift of fear." (T-21.VI.8:1)

"Spend but an instant in the glad acceptance of what is given you to give your brother, and learn with him what has been given both of you." (T-21.VI.9:7)

"The Son of God is always blessed as one. And as his gratitude goes out

CHAPTER 21—REASON AND PERCEPTION

to you who blessed him, reason will tell you that it cannot be you stand apart from blessing." (T-21.VI.10:1-2)

"But where he chooses to condemn instead, there is he held a prisoner, waiting in chains his pardon on himself to set him free." (T-21.VI.11:10)

In summary, Chapter 21 – VI: "Reason versus Madness" is saying:
Reason tells us that when we think we see sin—when we believe we are bodies and act in hurtful ways with them—it is actually a call for help. The one caveat for receiving such help then is, we must *accept* it. And such help is always not only just for us, but for *everyone*, for they are also one with us. When we are healed, we are never healed alone. To see that we are joined, is in fact, our healing; it is the answer to our call for help. Reason will tell us this is our release, given the truth of our Oneness. To see this, have faith in it, and *believe it*, is our salvation from the madness of separation. It is the gift of Heaven to see the Oneness that is true in Heaven, here on earth. And where we choose not to see this is to condemn our brethren, and likewise ourselves, to the bondage of the ego. Do not react to the body through your ego. Let reason guide your mind to see only Oneness where there appears to be many and the madness of separation is healed.

VII. The Last Unanswered Question

"Do you not see that all your misery comes from the strange belief that you are powerless? Being helpless is the cost of sin." (T-21.VII.1:1-2)

"No one believes the Son of God is powerless. And those who see themselves as helpless must believe that they are not the Son of God. What can they be except his enemy?" (T-21.VII.2:1-3)

"Because they do not know that they are one with him, they know not whom they hate." (T-21.VII.2:7)

"Frantic and loud and strong the dark ones seem to be. Yet they know not their "enemy," except they hate." (T-21.VII.3:1-2)

"And love is turned to hate as easily." (T-21.VII.3:12)

"How treacherous does this enemy appear, who changes so it is impossible even to recognize him." (T-21.VII.4:7)

"Yet hate must have a target." (T-21.VII.5:1)

"Who that believes in sin would dare believe he has no enemy? Could

VII. The Last Unanswered Question

he admit that no one made him powerless? Reason would surely bid him seek no longer what is not there to find." (T-21.VII.5:3-5)

"But let him only ask himself these questions, which he must decide, to have it done for him:

Do I desire a world I rule instead of one that rules me?
Do I desire a world where I am powerful instead of helpless?
Do I desire a world in which I have no enemies and cannot sin?
And do I want to see what I denied because it is the truth?
(T-21.VII.5:10-14)

"You may already have answered the first three questions, but not yet the last. For this one still seems fearful, and unlike the others. Yet reason would assure they are all the same." (T-21.VII.6:1-3)

"Consider carefully your answer to the last question you have left unanswered still." (T-21.VII.8:1)

"And then it will be clear to you that, as you look on the effects of sin in any form, all you need do is simply ask yourself:
Is this what I would see? Do I want this? (T-21.VII.8:3-4)

"This is your one decision; this the condition for what occurs. It is irrelevant to how it happens, but not to why. You have control of this. And if you choose to see a world without an enemy, in which you are not helpless, the means to see it will be given you." (T-21.VII.9:1-4)

"Why is the final question so important? Reason will tell you why. It is the same as are the other three, except in time. The others are decisions that can be made, and then unmade and made again. But truth is constant, and implies a state where vacillations are impossible." (T-21.VII.10:1-5)

"Yet the last question adds the wish for constancy in your desire to see the real world, so the desire becomes the only one you have. By answering the final question "yes," you add sincerity to the decisions you have already made to all the rest. For only then have you renounced the option to change your mind again." (T-21.VII.11:4-6)

"No one decides against his happiness, but he may do so if he does not see he does it." (T-21.VII.12:5)

"Elusive happiness, or happiness in changing form that shifts with time

CHAPTER 21 — REASON AND PERCEPTION

and place, is an illusion that has no meaning. Happiness must be constant, because it is attained by giving up the wish for the inconstant." (T-21.VII.13:1-2)

"Desire what you want, and you will look on it and think it real. No thought but has the power to release or kill. And none can leave the thinker's mind, or leave him unaffected." (T-21.VII.13:6-8)

In summary, Chapter 21 – VII: "The Last Unanswered Question" is saying:
As human bodies, we feel powerless against the whims of the world around us. This is the cost of belief in sin—the belief in our bodily identity, for the body is indeed weak and on the path to death from the moment of its birth. What we do not realize, is that if we withdrew this belief and allowed the truth to replace our idea of who we are, we would activate our eternal power to change what we experience. To do this, we have only to answer one question. However, there is just one caveat; we have to *believe* the answer is true. What is the question? It is but this: Do we desire to see a world *not* made by the ego? A world we denied because we chose to become a body—an identity we are not? And are we then willing to give up this false identity and allow the truth to replace it? Can we see ourselves as eternal beings of love and light instead? Do we really *want* to see each other in this way? To make this change of mind takes vigilance. In all things you see, you must remember to ask yourself: Is this the world I want to see? Answer this last unanswered question, and your world will shift according to what you truly want.

VIII. The Inner Shift

"Are thoughts, then, dangerous? To bodies, yes! The thoughts that seem to kill are those that teach the thinker that he *can* be killed. And so he "dies" because of what he learned." (T-21.VIII.1:1-4)

"The constancy of joy is a condition quite alien to your understanding. Yet if you could even imagine what it must be, you would desire it although you understand it not." (T-21.VIII.2:1-2)

"It comes as surely unto those who see the final question is necessary to the rest, as peace must come to those who choose to heal and not to judge." (T-21.VIII.2:8)

"Reason will tell you that you cannot ask for happiness inconstantly.

VIII. The Inner Shift

For if what you desire you receive, and happiness is constant, then you need ask for it but once to have it always. And if you do not have it always, being what it is, you did not ask for it." (T-21.VIII.3:1-3)

"You who complete God's Will and are His happiness, whose will is powerful as His, a power that is not lost in your illusions, think carefully why you have not yet decided how you would answer the final question." (T-21.VIII.4:1)

"And yet it is the final one that really asks if you are willing to be wholly sane." (T-21.VIII.4:3)

"What is the holy instant but God's appeal to you to recognize what He has given you?" (T-21.VIII.5:1)

"Here is the constant peace you could experience forever." (T-21.VIII.5:3)

"For here the final question is already answered, and what you ask for given." (T-21.VIII.5:5)

"For you have asked that nothing stand between the holiness of your relationship and your awareness of its holiness." (T-21.VIII.5:7)

In summary, Chapter 21 – VIII: "The Inner Shift" is saying:
In order to shift your outer world, you must first make an inner shift. This is simply a change of mind about who people are to you in truth. What is your true relationship with them? Are they mother, father, brother, sister, child, partner, stranger, or enemy? All these categories are of the ego, for it loves to analyze, compartmentalize, and decide who is worthy of love and when. Once you make the inner shift to seeing all people as one with you—once you recognize the Light that joins us all—your heart will shift, and peace will come to all your relationships. The inner shift is merely an acknowledgement of this oneness, and it is this that makes every relationship you have, holy. All that is being asked of you, is that your only desire is to see no gap between yourself and all others. The inner shift is your desire to become aware of the holiness of God within all; He Who holds us all as One in His Love. Then will God's reason guide your mind at last, and your perception will make an inner shift into a new world.

CHAPTER 22
SALVATION AND THE HOLY RELATIONSHIP

Introduction

"Take pity on yourself, so long enslaved. Rejoice whom God hath joined have come together and need no longer look on sin apart." (T-22.in.1:1-2)

"Sin is a strictly individual perception, seen in the other yet believed by each to be within himself. And each one seems to make a different error, and one the other cannot understand. Brother, it is the same, made by the same, and forgiven for its maker in the same way. The holiness of your relationship forgives you and your brother, undoing the effects of what you both believed and saw. And with their going is the need for sin gone with them." (T-22.in.1:4-8)

"For an unholy relationship is based on differences, where each one thinks the other has what he has not." (T-22.in.2:5)

"And so they wander through a world of strangers, unlike themselves, living with their bodies perhaps under a common roof that shelters neither; in the same room and yet a world apart." (T-22.in.2:8)

"A holy relationship starts from a different premise. Each one has looked within and seen no lack. Accepting completion, he would extend it by joining with another, whole as himself. He sees no difference between these selves, for differences are only of the body." (T-22.in.3:1-4)

"Think what a holy relationship can teach! Here is belief in differences undone." (T-22.in.4:1-2)

"Reason now can lead you and your brother to the logical conclusion of your union." (T-22.in.4:5)

"Here is the golden circle where you recognize the Son of God." (T-22.in.4:9)

In summary, Chapter 22 – "Introduction" is saying:
We find our salvation through our holy relationships. And yet, what *is* a holy relationship? It is a relationship where you see no difference between yourself and another. And what does this mean? It means that we believe in a power

beneath or within our form that is greater than anything we can see with our bodily eyes. A power that supersedes what the ego is showing us. The ego is showing us separate bodies, but the power within those bodies is completely the opposite of separation. It is union *through* God and *with* God. Salvation then, is achieved through our relationships we make holy by recognizing this power, and only this power. It is the golden circle where we recognize everyone is equally contained within our One Self, in a holy relationship.

I. The Message of the Holy Relationship

"Let reason take another step. If you attack whom God would heal and hate the one He loves, then you and your Creator have a different will." (T-22.I.1:1-2)

"It is as though you wandered in without a plan of any kind except to wander off, for only that seems certain." (T-22.I.1:7)

"Reason would tell you that the world you see through eyes that are not yours must make no sense to you." (T-22.I.2:3)

"If this is not your vision, what can it show to you?" (T-22.I.2:6)

"You have received no messages at all you understand. For you have listened to what can never communicate at all." (T-22.I.3:2-3)

"Yet it must be the "something else" that sees, and as not you, explains its sight to you." (T-22.I.3:6)

"Your sight was given you, along with everything that you can understand. You will perceive no difficulty in understanding what this vision tells you, for everyone sees only what he thinks he is." (T-22.I.5:1-2)

"Only your vision can convey to you what you can see. It reaches you directly, without a need to be interpreted by you." (T-22.I.5:4-5)

"So in each holy relationship is the ability to communicate instead of separate reborn." (T-22.I.7:1)

"Where Christ has entered no one is alone, for never could He find a home in separate ones. Yet must He be reborn into His ancient home, so seeming new and yet as old as He, a tiny newcomer, dependent on the holiness of your relationship to let Him live." (T-22.I.8:6-7)

"Be certain God did not entrust His Son to the unworthy. Nothing but what is part of Him is worthy of being joined." (T-22.I.9:1-2)

"Here is the first direct perception that you can make." (T-22.I.10:1)

CHAPTER 22 — SALVATION AND THE HOLY RELATIONSHIP

"It is denial of illusions that calls on truth, for to deny illusions is to recognize that fear is meaningless. Into the holy home where fear is powerless love enters thankfully, grateful that it is one with you who joined to let it enter." (T-22.I.10:6-7)

"Christ comes to what is like Himself; the same, not different." (T-22.I.11:1)

"What is as like Him as a holy relationship?" (T-22.I.11:3)

"You are indeed correct in looking on your brother as His chosen home, for here you will with Him and with His Father. This is your Father's Will for you, and yours with His. And who is drawn to Christ is drawn to God as surely as Both are drawn to every holy relationship, the home prepared for Them as earth is turned to Heaven." (T-22.I.11:7-9)

In summary, Chapter 22 – I: "The Message of the Holy Relationship" is saying:

Here we are called to see the Christ in one another as replacement for the bodies our ego shows us. This vision is what makes our relationships holy. Seeing in this way may be understood in theory, but more difficult to do in practice. What does it mean to see the Christ in one another? What we see through the eyes of our ego, must first be interpreted by our minds—this means we must first judge what we see and the ego judges that we see a body. However, when we use Christ's Vision, no interpretation is necessary. This must mean that Christ's vision is not "seeing" as we understand it at all. Rather, it is an *experience*, or *feeling*, which conveys knowing directly, without any need for visual interpretation. We do not need our bodily eyes to *feel* something. And so, once we are able to *feel* God within all living things, we will understand the message of the holy relationship, our relationship of Union with All That Is.

II. Your Brother's Sinlessness

"The opposite of illusions is not disillusionment but truth." (T-22.II.1:1)

"Every illusion carries pain and suffering in the dark folds of the heavy garments in which it hides its nothingness." (T-22.II.1:5)

"Truth is the opposite of illusions because it offers joy." (T-22.II.2:1)

"To change illusions is to make no change." (T-22.II.2:4)

"All that is possible in the dark world of misery is to select some aspects out of it, see them as different, and define the difference as joy." (T-22.II.2:6)

II. Your Brother's Sinlessness

"Illusions carry only guilt and suffering, sickness and death, to their believers. The form in which they are accepted is irrelevant. No form of misery in reason's eyes can be confused with joy. Joy is eternal. You can be sure indeed that any seeming happiness that does not last is really fear. Joy does not turn to sorrow, for the eternal cannot change." (T-22.II.3:1-6)

"Reason will tell you that the only way to escape from misery is to recognize it *and go the other way*." (T-22.II.4:1)

"Both reason and the ego will tell you this, but what they make of it is not the same. The ego will assure you now that it is impossible for you to see no guilt in anyone." (T-22.II.5:1-2)

"Yet reason looks on this another way, for reason sees the source of an idea as what will make it either true or false. This must be so, if the idea is like its source." (T-22.II.5:4-5)

"This is a crucial period in this course, for here the separation of you and the ego must be made complete." (T-22.II.6:1)

"You know what your Creator wills is possible, but what you made believes it is not so. Now you must choose between yourself and an illusion of yourself." (T-22.II.6:5-6)

"Forsake not now your brother. For you who are the same will not decide alone nor differently. Either you give each other life or death; either you are each other's savior or his judge, offering him sanctuary or condemnation. This course will be believed entirely or not at all." (T-22.II.7:1-4)

"Behold the great projection, but look on it with the decision that it must be healed, and not with fear." (T-22.II.10:1)

"Are you not glad to learn it is not true? Is it not welcome news to hear not one of the illusions that you made replaced the truth?" (T-22.II.10:6-7)

"What God has given to your holy relationship is there." (T-22.II.11:5)

"Beyond the body that you interposed between you and your brother, and shining in the golden light that reaches it from the bright, endless circle that extends forever, is your holy relationship, beloved of God Himself. How still it rests, in time and yet beyond, immortal yet on earth." (T-22.II.12:1-2)

CHAPTER 22 – SALVATION AND THE HOLY RELATIONSHIP

"All you need do to dwell in quiet here with Christ is share His vision. Quickly and gladly is His vision given anyone who is but willing to see his brother sinless." (T-22.II.13:1-2)

"Heaven is the home of perfect purity, and God created it for you. Look on your holy brother, sinless as yourself, and let him lead you there." (T-22.II.13:6-7)

In summary, Chapter 22 – II: "Your Brother's Sinlessness" is saying: Remember that the word "sin" is interchangeable with the word "body." Therefore, our "sinless" brother is our "bodiless" brother. Reason tells us that when we feel suffering, we must learn to go the other way. The ego tells us to look upon the body and all its mistakes and continue towards it; continue to think about it, and do not let it go, thus projecting more of the same into our reality. Reason tells us to cease to look at the body; it only causes us suffering and see instead the Love of God within. The ego has interposed a bodily projection between what is the truth of Who We Are and what our eyes can see. Our holy relationship rests in the Light of God. How do we see this? Through stillness of thought—stillness of our ego-minded thinking—stop thinking about the body and all its works. And there we will rest our weary mind in eternity, though we may remain a body in time. Simply allow your thoughts to be quiet and you will welcome the Christ within both yourself and all others. This is how you see your brother's sinlessness (bodilessness).

III. Reason and the Forms of Error

"The introduction of reason into the ego's thought system is the beginning of its undoing, for reason and the ego are contradictory." (T-22.III.1:1)

"For reason's goal is to make plain, and therefore obvious. You can see reason. This is not a play on words, for here is the beginning of a vision that has meaning. Vision is sense, quite literally." (T-22.III.1:3-6)

"The ego's whole continuance depends on its belief you cannot learn this course. Share this belief, and reason will be unable to see your errors and make way for their correction. For reason sees through errors, telling you what you thought was real is not." (T-22.III.2:1-3)

"Reason is not salvation in itself, but it makes way for peace and brings you to a state of mind in which salvation can be given you. Sin is a block, set like a heavy gate, locked and without a key, across the road to peace." (T-22.III.3:1-2)

"Yet reason sees through it easily, because it is an error. The form it takes cannot conceal its emptiness from reason's eyes." (T-22.III.3:5-6)

"Only the form of error attracts the ego." (T-22.III.4:1)

"Everything the body's eyes can see is a mistake, an error in perception, a distorted fragment of the whole without the meaning that the whole would give." (T-22.III.4:3)

"Reason will tell you that the form of error is not what makes it a mistake." (T-22.III.5:1)

"The body's eyes see only form. They cannot see beyond what they were made to see. And they were made to look on error and not see past it." (T-22.III.5:3-5)

"Only mistakes have different forms, and so they can deceive." (T-22.III.7:1)

"Let not the form of his mistakes keep you from him whose holiness is yours. Let not the vision of his holiness, the sight of which would show you your forgiveness, be kept from you by what the body's eyes can see. Let your awareness of your brother not be blocked by your perception of his sins and of his body." (T-22.III.8:1-3)

"Yet reason sees a holy relationship as what it is; a common state of mind, where both give errors gladly to correction, that both may happily be healed as one." (T-22.III.9:7)

In summary, Chapter 22 – III: "Reason and the Forms of Error" is saying:

Reason can also be defined as truth. And truth can be defined as what has and always will be true: we are as God created us. Despite what our bodily eyes can see, we remain one with God, all creation, and each other. Only the ego will see otherwise, and the ego can only look through our bodily eyes, because the body is the physical expression of the ego. Therefore, guilt can be defined as the body, and sin can be defined as separation. Reason, being the truth, can be applied through seeing only through the eyes of forgiveness. Forgiveness is not a sight used by the eyes, but rather, it is an inner experience. It is the awareness of our shared Inner Stillness; the stillness of all ego thoughts, which are all thoughts of the world and bodies. A holy relationship comes forward when forgiveness, or stillness is applied to all those whom

CHAPTER 22—SALVATION AND THE HOLY RELATIONSHIP

your ego-vision mistakes for bodies. See them instead as forgiven, through a mind that is still. Still all your thoughts about the world of form and reason will tell you nothing but your Oneness is true. Reason (knowing our Unity) will then correct all forms of error (separation).

IV. The Branching of the Road

"When you come to the place where the branch in the road is quite apparent, you cannot go ahead. You must go either one way or the other." (T-22.IV.1:1-2)

"The way you came no longer matters. It can no longer serve. No one who reaches this far can make the wrong decision, although he can delay." (T-22.IV.1:5-7)

"It is but the first few steps along the right way that seem hard, for you have chosen, although you still may think you can go back and make the other choice. This is not so. A choice made with the power of Heaven to uphold it cannot be undone." (T-22.IV.2:1-3)

"And so you and your brother stand, here in this holy place, before the veil of sin that hangs between you and the face of Christ. Let it be lifted!" (T-22.IV.3:1-2)

"Yet it is almost over in your awareness, and peace has reached you even here, before the veil. Think what will happen after." (T-22.IV.3:5-6)

"Think of the loveliness that you will see, who walk with Him! And think how beautiful will you and your brother look to the other! How happy you will be together, after such a long and lonely journey where you walked alone." (T-22.IV.4:1-3)

"For in his sight your loveliness is his salvation, which he would protect from harm." (T-22.IV.5:2)

"So shall you walk the world with me, whose message has not yet been given everyone. For you are here to let it be received." (T-22.IV.5:4-5)

"To all who share the Love of God the grace is given to the givers of what they have received." (T-22.IV.6:1)

"Those who would let illusions be lifted from their minds are this world's saviors, walking the world with their Redeemer, and carrying His message of hope and freedom and release from suffering to everyone who needs a miracle to save him." (T-22.IV.6:5)

"Such is the function of a holy relationship; to receive together and give as you received. Standing before the veil, it still seems difficult." (T-22.IV.7:1-2)

"It is no solid wall. And only an illusion stands between you and your brother, and the holy Self you share together." (T-22.IV.7:7-8)

In summary, Chapter 22–IV: "The Branching of the Road" is saying: We come to the branching of the road once we become aware that we have an ego and that we have a choice in whether or not we can listen to it, or the Holy Spirit. The branching of the road is but this choice. It is the choice between love and fear. It is the choice between Reality and illusion. We are assured we cannot choose wrong, though we can delay ourselves at this crossroad. And we cannot go back, because once we learn we have a choice, it cannot be removed from our mind. How then, do we choose only love, so that we can move on from this branching in the road? Choose to see your brothers and sisters differently. That is all. Desire that the veil, the body that appears to stand between us, be lifted. It stands in front our awareness of the truth. We need not cease to see bodies, but merely choose to let our awareness of the truth be brought forth. Become aware of our Collective Stillness, instead of the body. This may seem difficult, for the body does indeed appear solid, but it is merely an illusion hiding the truth of our holy relationship. Your relationship becomes holy once you recognize that you share in the power of the Stillness within your brother. Now you would both be as you were created. God created you still; without ego-thoughts; thoughts of form, the world, and bodies. He created you as part of His Stillness. And now, at the branching of the road, choose only Love as your Guide in seeing.

V. Weakness and Defensiveness

"How does one overcome illusions? Surely not by force or anger, nor by opposing them in any way. Merely by letting reason tell you that they contradict reality. They go against what must be true." (T-22.V.1:1-4)

"You are the strong one in this seeming conflict. And you need no defense." (T-22.V.1:10-11)

"Consider what the ego wants defenses for. Always to justify what goes against the truth, flies in the face of reason and makes no sense. Can this *be* justified?" (T-22.V.2:1-3)

"In truth you and your brother stand together, with nothing in between." (T-22.V.3:4)

CHAPTER 22—SALVATION AND THE HOLY RELATIONSHIP

"God rests with you in quiet, undefended and wholly undefending, for in this quiet state alone is strength and power. Here can no weakness enter, for here is no attack and therefore no illusions. Love rests in certainty." (T-22.V.3:8-10)

"If you but recognized how little stands between you and your awareness of your union with your brother! Be not deceived by the illusions it presents of size and thickness, weight, solidity and firmness of foundation. Yes, to the body's eyes it looks like an enormous solid body, immovable as is a mountain. Yet within you is a Force that no illusions can resist." (T-22.V.5:1-4)

"Forget not, when you feel the need arise to be defensive about anything, you have identified yourself with an illusion." (T-22.V.6:1)

"Not one but rests on the belief that you are separate." (T-22.V.6:4)

"And not one that truth cannot pass over lightly, and so easily that you must be convinced, in spite of what you thought it was, that it is nothing. If you forgive your brother, this *must* happen. For it is your unwillingness to overlook what seems to stand between you and your brother that makes it look impenetrable, and defends the illusion of its immovability." (T-22.V.6:6-8)

In summary, Chapter 22 – V: "Weakness and Defensiveness" is saying:
Only what is weak needs defense. Only what is weak, is false, for truth is strong. Only the ego is weak because it is attempting to contradict the truth. The truth is, we stand together as One, with nothing separating us, though the ego shows us bodies all around. Yet God rests with us in the quiet of our mind, the place where no thoughts about bodies or the world reside. There are no thoughts of illusions here, and here it is we are strong and untouchable by anything that is not Love. See how little stands between us? The strength of our Oneness is just a mere shift in thought and focus on perception away. Focus on the body, and you defend your weakness; you defend illusions. Focus your attention on the Collective Stillness within the body, and you join with the strength of what is true, the strength of our Union. There is no illusion you cannot overcome by focusing on this truth. When you focus only on our joined, still, Oneness you will know there is no weakness or defensiveness within you.

VI. The Light of the Holy Relationship

"Do you want freedom of the body or of the mind? For both you cannot have. Which do you value?" (T-22.VI.1:1-3)

"Where freedom of the body has been chosen, the mind is used as means whose value lies in its ability to contrive ways to achieve the body's freedom. Yet freedom of the body has no meaning, and so the mind is dedicated to serve illusions." (T-22.VI.2:1-2)

"Yet even in this confusion, so profound it cannot be described, the Holy Spirit waits in gentle patience, as certain of the outcome as He is sure of His Creator's Love." (T-22.VI.2:4)

"Be not disturbed at all to think how He can change the role of means and end so easily in what God loves, and would have free forever. But be you grateful that you can be the means to serve His end. This is the only service that leads to freedom. To serve this end the body must be perceived as sinless, because the goal is sinlessness." (T-22.VI.3:1-4)

"And it will be impossible for you to hate what serves whom you would heal." (T-22.VI.3:7)

"This holy relationship, lovely in its innocence, mighty in strength, and blazing with a light far brighter than the sun that lights the sky you see, is chosen of your Father as a means for His Own plan." (T-22.VI.4:1)

"This holy relationship has the power to heal all pain, regardless of its form." (T-22.VI.4:4)

"For here your healing is, and here will you accept Atonement." (T-22.VI.4:7)

"Before a holy relationship there is no sin. The form of error is no longer seen, and reason, joined with love, looks quietly on all confusion, observing merely, "This was a mistake." And then the same Atonement you accepted in your relationship corrects the error, and lays a part of Heaven in its place." (T-22.VI.5:1-3)

"Child of peace, the light has come to you. The light you bring you do not recognize, and yet you will remember." (T-22.VI.6:1-2)

"When you have looked upon your brother with complete forgiveness, from which no error is excluded and nothing kept hidden, what mistake can there be anywhere you cannot overlook?" (T-22.VI.7:1)

CHAPTER 22—SALVATION AND THE HOLY RELATIONSHIP

"What can it be but universal blessing to look on what your Father loves with charity? Extension of forgiveness is the Holy Spirit's function. Leave this to Him. Let your concern be only that you give to Him that which can be extended." (T-22.VI.9:1-4)

"On your learning depends the welfare of the world. And it is only arrogance that would deny the power of your will. Think you the Will of God is powerless?" (T-22.VI.10:1-3)

"Let us look straight at how this error came about, for here lies buried the heavy anchor that seems to keep the fear of God in place, immovable and solid as a rock." (T-22.VI.10:7)

"You do not see that every sin and every condemnation that you perceive and justify is an attack upon your Father." (T-22.VI.11:3)

"If you were one with God and recognized this oneness, you would know His power is yours. But you will not remember this while you believe attack of any kind means anything." (T-22.VI.12:1-2)

"Only the different can attack. So you conclude because you can attack, you and your brother must be different. Yet does the Holy Spirit explain this differently. Because you and your brother are not different, you cannot attack." (T-22.VI.13:1-4)

"The only question to be answered in order to decide which must be true is whether you and your brother are different." (T-22.VI.13:7)

"From loving minds there is no separation." (T-22.VI.14:6)

"The light that joins you and your brother shines throughout the universe, and because it joins you and him, so it makes you and him one with your Creator." (T-22.VI.15:1)

"What teaches you that you cannot separate denies the ego. Let truth decide if you and your brother be different or the same, and teach you which is true." (T-22.VI.15:6-7)

In summary, Chapter 22 – VI: "The Light of the Holy Relationship" is saying:
Holiness is wholeness or the oneness of creation. To be holy, is merely to understand your unique place within the Whole of God. To be unholy, is impossible, but the word can be used to describe a state of mind in which you are unaware of your holiness. Wholeness can only be known by the mind and

VI. The Light of the Holy Relationship

experienced as the feeling of wholeness or total Union. It cannot be seen with bodily eyes, for bodies cannot truly join as the mind can. Therefore, an unholy relationship is one in which you see only the body and are ignorant of your deeper union through the mind. You must allow God's Light to come into your mind and illuminate your joint holiness or Wholeness with all whom He created as One with you. You do this, through deciding to look beyond the sin or separation that appears as the body and reach for the stillness within it; the stillness of thought that excludes the body and the outer world. There you will feel the truth; you will experience your oneness with all whom you thought were separate from you and you will love them as part of yourself. Attack will become impossible. Attack is merely to see another as a body. To give up attack is to give up the belief we are different bodies. We are not separate. Let the Light of our holy relationships teach us that salvation, or the experience of our Oneness, comes to us through one another.

CHAPTER 23
THE WAR AGAINST YOURSELF

Introduction

"Do you not see the opposite of frailty and weakness is sinlessness?" (T-23.in.1:1)

"The sinless cannot fear, for sin of any kind is weakness." (T-23.in.1:3)

"No one is strong who has an enemy, and no one can attack unless he thinks he has." (T-23.in.1:5)

"How strange indeed becomes this war against yourself! You will believe that everything you use for sin can hurt you and become your enemy." (T-23.in.2:1-2)

"It is certain you will fear what you attack as it is sure that you will love what you perceive as sinless. He walks in peace who travels sinlessly along the way love shows him." (T-23.in.2:4-5)

"Walk you in glory, with your head held high, and fear no evil. The innocent are safe because they share their innocence. Nothing they see is harmful, for their awareness of the truth releases everything from the illusion of harmfulness." (T-23.in.3:1-3)

"And every error disappeared because they saw it not." (T-23.in.3:6)

"Let not the little interferers pull you to littleness." (T-23.in.4:1)

"Think what a happy world you walk, with truth beside you! Do not give up this world of freedom for a little sigh of seeming sin, nor for a tiny stirring of guilt's attraction. Would you, for all these meaningless distractions, lay Heaven aside?" (T-23.in.4:3-5)

"Let us not let littleness lead God's Son into temptation." (T-23.in.5:1)

"Nothing around you but is part of you. Look on it lovingly, and see the light of Heaven in it." (T-23.in.6:1-2)

"In kind forgiveness will the world sparkle and shine, and everything you once thought sinful now will be reinterpreted as part of Heaven." (T-23.in.6:4)

"For here is your salvation and your freedom." (T-23.in.6:7)

I. The Irreconcilable Beliefs

In summary, Chapter 23 – Introduction is saying:
What we do not realize, during our day-to-day life as we walk this world, is that all living things are part of us. All human beings are part of our One Self. And what we do to *them*, we are essentially doing to *ourselves*. To see ourselves as separate from everything else, is to see ourselves as a body. And to see ourselves as a body, is also referred to as "sin" or "separation" in *A Course In Miracles*. Therefore, to see sin is to see *only* the body—and be completely oblivious to the Light we all share within ourselves. Here, the word "sin" is interchangeable with the word "body" or "separation." And so, we learn that to see someone sinless is to actually *see* them as bodiless.

Let us re-read several quotes from above:

"Do you not see the opposite of frailty and weakness is sinlessness (bodilessness)?" (T-23.in.1:1)

"The sinless (bodiless) cannot fear, for sin (a body or separation) of any kind is weakness." (T-23.in.1:3)

"It is certain you will fear what you attack as it is sure that you will love what you perceive as sinless (bodiless). He walks in peace who travels sinlessly (bodilessly) along the way love shows him." (T-23.in.2:4-5)

It is true forgiveness to see one another as sinless, or bodiless, for we have looked beyond form and overcome the temptation to believe in the bodies we see with our eyes. We have chosen instead to *feel* the truth of our Oneness. Herein lies our salvation. Herein lies our freedom and the end of the war against our Self.

I. The Irreconcilable Beliefs

"The memory of God comes to the quiet mind. It cannot come where there is conflict, for a mind at war against itself remembers not eternal gentleness." (T-23.I.1:1-2)

"Conflict within you must imply that you believe the ego has the power to be victorious." (T-23.I.1:5)

"Do you not realize a war against yourself would be a war on God? Is victory conceivable? And if it were, is this a victory that you would want?" (T-23.I.2:1-3)

"This is no war; only the mad belief the Will of God can be attacked and overthrown." (T-23.I.2:8)

CHAPTER 23—THE WAR AGAINST YOURSELF

"Brother, the war against yourself is almost over. The journey's end is at the place of peace." (T-23.I.4:1-2)

"The war against yourself was undertaken to teach the Son of God that he is not himself, and *not* his Father's Son. For this, the memory of his Father must be forgotten. It is forgotten in the body's life, and if you think you are a body, you will believe you have forgotten it. Yet truth can never be forgotten by itself, and you have not forgotten what you are. Only a strange illusion of yourself, a wish to triumph over what you are, remembers not." (T-23.I.5:1-5)

"What you remember is a part of you. For you must be as God created you." (T-23.I.7:1-2)

"See how the conflict of illusions disappears when it is brought to truth!" (T-23.I.9:1)

"You who are beloved of Him are no illusion, being as true and holy as Himself. The stillness of your certainty of Him and of yourself is home to Both of You, Who dwell as one and not apart." (T-23.I.10:1-2)

"You dwell in peace as limitless as its Creator, and everything is given those who would remember Him." (T-23.I.10:7)

"The meeting of illusions leads to war." (T-23.I.12:2)

"Peace is the state where love abides, and seeks to share itself. Conflict and peace are opposites. Where one abides the other cannot be; where either goes the other disappears. So is the memory of God obscured in minds that have become illusions' battleground. Yet far beyond this senseless war it shines, ready to be remembered when you side with peace." (T-23.I.12:5-9)

In summary, Chapter 23 – I: "The Irreconcilable Beliefs" is saying:
"We cannot be both a body and a bodiless creation of Love and Light. Both identities cannot be true, and therefore, these two beliefs are irreconcilable with each other, for one belief is a false illusionary self-perception. The conflict between these two self-perceptions, is the war within us. Yet if only the truth about us is true, then how can there be two opposing sides, if one is false? We are therefore, at war with nothing; an idea that only *seems* to be true. An idea we can let go of at any time and rest in peace. Let the stillness of the certainty of our Oneness in God triumph over all contrary beliefs. We dwell in peace as limitless as our Creator. Only the illusion of bodies can war with one an-

other. Peace comes to the mind that sees there is no war, for to see yourself as One, banishes the idea of separation from your mind. With this change in belief, are all irreconcilable beliefs thus reconciled into one belief in Oneness.

II. The Laws of Chaos

"The "laws" of chaos can be brought to light, though never understood. Chaotic laws are hardly meaningful, and therefore out of reason's sphere. Yet they appear to be an obstacle to reason and to truth. Let us, then, look upon them calmly, that we may look beyond them, understanding what they are, and not what they would maintain. It is essential it be understood what they are for, because it is their purpose to make meaningless, and to attack the truth. Here are the laws that rule the world you made." (T-23.II.1:1-6)

"The first chaotic law is that the truth is different for everyone. Like all these principles, this one maintains that each is separate and has a different set of thoughts that set him off from others." (T-23.II.2:1-2)

"Each one establishes this for himself, and makes it true by his attack on what another values. And this is justified because the values differ, and those who hold them seem to be unlike, and therefore enemies." (T-23.II.2:4-5)

"Think how this seems to interfere with the first principle of miracles. ("There is no order of difficulty in miracles." Principle 1.). For this establishes degrees of truth among illusions, making it seem that some of them are harder to overcome than others." (T-23.II.3:1-2)

"Errors of any kind can be corrected *because* they are untrue." (T-23.II.3:4)

"The second law of chaos, dear indeed to every worshiper of sin, is that each one must sin, and therefore deserves attack and death." (T-23.II.4:1)

"Think what this seems to do to the relationship between the Father and the Son. Now it appears that They can never be One again." (T-23.II.5:1-2)

"And fear of God and of each other now appears as sensible, made real by what the Son of God has done both to himself and his Creator." (T-23.II.5:7)

"The arrogance on which the laws of chaos stand could not be more

CHAPTER 23—THE WAR AGAINST YOURSELF

apparent than emerges here. Here is a principle that would define what the Creator of reality must be; what He must think and what He must believe; and how He must respond, believing it. (T-23.II.6:1-2)

"This leads directly to the *third* preposterous belief that seems to make chaos eternal. For if God cannot be mistaken, He must accept His Son's belief in what he is, and hate him for it." (T-23.II.6:5-6)

"See how the fear of God is reinforced by this third principle. Now it becomes impossible to turn to Him for help in misery." (T-23.II.7:1-2)

"The ego values only what it takes. This leads to the fourth law of chaos, which, if the others are accepted, must be true. This seeming law is the belief you have what you have taken. By this, another's loss becomes your gain, and thus it fails to recognize that you can never take away save from yourself." (T-23.II.9:1-4)

"And now there is a vague unanswered question, not yet "explained." What is this precious thing, this priceless pearl, this hidden secret treasure, to be wrested in righteous wrath from this most treacherous and cunning enemy? It must be what you want but never found." (T-23.II.11:1-3)

"For it was taken from you by this enemy, and hidden where you would not think to look. He hid it in his body, making it the cover for his guilt, the hiding place for what belongs to you. Now must his body be destroyed and sacrificed, that you may have that which belongs to you." (T-23.II.11:5-7)

"This is the reason why you must attack. Here is what makes your vengeance justified. Behold, unveiled, the ego's secret gift, torn from your brother's body, hidden there in malice and in hatred for the one to whom the gift belongs." (T-23.II.12:6-8)

"And all of your relationships have but the purpose of seizing it and making it your own." (T-23.II.12:12)

"Never is your possession made complete." (T-23.II.13:1)

"No one wants madness, nor does anyone cling to his madness if he sees that this is what it is. What protects madness is the belief that it is true." (T-23.II.14:1-2)

"These do not seem to be the goals of chaos, for by the great reversal they appear to be the laws of order." (T-23.II.15:1)

II. The Laws of Chaos

"And yet, how can it be that laws like these can be believed?" (T-23.II.16:1)

"Some forms it takes seem to have meaning, and that is all." (T-23.II.16:7)

"You would maintain, and think it true, that you do not believe these senseless laws, nor act upon them." (T-23.II.18:1)

"Brother, you *do* believe them. For how else could you perceive the form they take, with content such as this?" (T-23.II.18:3-4)

"There is no life outside of Heaven." (T-23.II.19:1)

"In any state apart from Heaven life is illusion. At best it seems like life; at worst, like death." (T-23.II.19:3-4)

"Life not in Heaven is impossible, and what is not in Heaven is not anywhere. Outside of Heaven, only the conflict of illusion stands; senseless, impossible and beyond all reason, and yet perceived as an eternal barrier to Heaven. Illusions are but forms. Their content is never true." (T-23.II.19:6-9)

"The laws of chaos govern all illusions. Their forms conflict, making it seem quite possible to value some above the others." (T-23.II.20:1-2)

"From the belief in sin, the faith in chaos must follow. It is because it follows that it seems to be a logical conclusion; a valid step in ordered thought. The steps to chaos do follow neatly from their starting point." (T-23.II.21:1-3)

"The whole descent from Heaven lies in each one." (T-23.II.21:6)

"Brother, take not one step in the descent to hell. For having taken one, you will not recognize the rest for what they are. And they will follow. Attack in any form has placed your foot upon the twisted stairway that leads from Heaven. Yet any instant it is possible to have all this undone. How can you know whether you chose the stairs to Heaven or the way to hell? Quite easily. How do you feel? Is peace in your awareness?" (T-23.II.22:1-9)

"If not, you walk alone. Ask, then, your Friend to join with you, and give you certainty of where you go." (T-23.II.22:12-13)

In summary, Chapter 23 – II: "The Laws of Chaos" is saying:
There are four laws of chaos, the "laws" or beliefs that lead us away from the bliss of Heaven, down into the depths of suffering in the ego's world.

CHAPTER 23—THE WAR AGAINST YOURSELF

One: The belief we are separate and can have separate desires, wishes and demands that will be what completes our perceived idea of happiness. Some of these separate things and people are more desirable than others in this world; in other words, some forms of illusion are more preferable than others. This idea of separation is also called "sin."

Two: The belief that each one of us must sin or must be separate. The ego believes this idea is irreversible and permanent. The ego also believes that the death of the body is proof this is true. Only what is separate can die alone, on its own. Now it seems that our Oneness with God and each other cannot be true.

Three: The belief that God also believes our mistaken idea we are separate; that He accepts this definition of ourselves and will punish us for our mistakes in this world. If we believe God will punish us, how can we possibly turn to Him for help?

Four: The belief that we must demand others behave in ways we feel will make us happy. For indeed, most unhappiness stems from someone else not behaving in the way our ego would prefer. If they do not do as we desire, we become upset, we attack and make demands in a variety of ways; sometimes claiming to act out of self-defense and at other times claiming to be unfairly treated. And by increasing another's guilt, does our ego attempt to control their actions.

And what is it we seek from others, even to the point of murder? What could the attempt to cause another to feel pain and guilt possibly give us? We are demanding from them what we think we do not have: Love. It is this the ego seeks, yet will never find, for it looks outside of you. All the ego knows is that somehow, Love is associated with our bodies. And it thinks it can pull It from our corpse through murder at worst or perhaps at least, through guilting others into behaving as we would deem loving. And we think such attack and control is justified, yet all we become is another's jailer.

Never can we truly possess another body, for that is not who we are. The body is nothing. What we truly seek, is the sense of loving completion and contentment that can only be given through the awareness of our Oneness with God, Who Unites All Things. This feeling, this experience, is Heaven. And there is no life outside of this. All perceived separate forms are but representations of our belief in sin, separation. If the belief in separation is accepted, the descent into hell is swift for it leads but downward into chaos. Your peace will be lost once you believe you are alone and separated from God's Great Love and seek for it where you will not find it. You will then feel the laws of chaos come into action through the myriad forms of your loss of peace. During these times, gently remind yourself you do not walk alone. God goes with you wherever you go, for what God has created as One, can never be separated, nor ruled by the laws of chaos.

III. Salvation Without Compromise

"Is it not true you do not recognize some of the forms attack can take? If it is true attack in any form will hurt you, and will do so just as much as in another form that you do recognize, then it must follow that you do not always recognize the source of pain." (T-23.III.1:1-2)

"The wrapping does not make the gift you give. An empty box, however beautiful and gently given, still contains nothing." (T-23.III.2:2-3)

"Withhold forgiveness from your brother and you attack him. You give him nothing, and receive of him but what you gave." (T-23.III.2:5-6)

"Salvation is no compromise of any kind. To compromise is to accept but part of what you want; to take a little and give up the rest. Salvation gives up nothing. It is complete for everyone." (T-23.III.3:1-4)

"This course is easy just because it makes no compromise. Yet it seems difficult to those who still believe that compromise is possible." (T-23.III.4:1-2)

"Forgiveness cannot be withheld a little. Nor is it possible to attack for this and love for that and understand forgiveness." (T-23.III.4:5-6)

"Those who believe that peace can be defended, and that attack is justified on its behalf, cannot perceive it lies within them." (T-23.III.5:1)

"To be released from conflict means that it is over. The door is open; you have left the battleground." (T-23.III.6:2-3)

"You can look down on it in safety from above and not be touched. But from within it you can find no safety." (T-23.III.6:6-7)

"Can guilt be absent from a battlefield?" (T-23.III.6:12)

In summary, Chapter 23 – III: "Salvation Without Compromise" is saying:

What is salvation? It is but the inner recognition of our Oneness; the full realization we are not separate but joined as One in God. To realize this, to truly feel it and believe it, is salvation from all else your eyes currently perceive

CHAPTER 23—THE WAR AGAINST YOURSELF

as reality. For in this knowing, you are released from the world, just as you have released the world from what you thought it was. You have left the battlefield and ascended to the vantage point above it—observing the world around you, but no longer engaging in battle with it. This shift in perception is forgiveness. To continue to engage with others as though they are separate from you is to continue to engage in attack, for such behavior attacks your perception of Oneness through seeing each other as separate. Herein lies your whole conflict with the world. Peace is an uncompromising stance. You cannot see some separation here and none there. Either you are One or you are not. Either you believe this is true, or you do not. Do not try to justify some forms of separation—usually with those you do not like—while accepting union with other forms—usually with whom you claim to love. You believe in Oneness with all or none. Salvation, our Oneness, is either true or false. There is no compromise.

IV. Above the Battleground

"Do not remain in conflict, for there is no war without attack. The fear of God is fear of life, and not of death. Yet He remains the only place of safety." (T-23.IV.1:1-3)

"Every illusion is an assault on truth, and every one does violence to the idea of love because it seems to be of equal truth." (T-23.IV.1:12)

"Murder and love are incompatible. Yet if they both are true, then must they be the same, and indistinguishable from one another. So will they be to those who see God's Son a body." (T-23.IV.2:2-4)

"God does not share His function with a body." (T-23.IV.3:1)

"It is not sinful to believe the function of the Son is murder, but it is insanity." (T-23.IV.3:3)

"Each form of murder and attack that still attracts you and that you do not recognize for what it is, limits the healing and the miracles you have the power to extend to all." (T-23.IV.4:3)

"This is your part; to realize that murder in any form is not your will. The overlooking of the battleground is now your purpose." (T-23.IV.4:6-7)

"Be lifted up, and from a higher place look down upon it. From there will your perspective be quite different. Here in the midst of it, it does seem real." (T-23.IV.5:1-3)

"Yet from above, the choice is miracles instead of murder. And the perspective coming from this choice shows you the battle is not real, and easily escaped." (T-23.IV.5:6-7)

"When the temptation to attack rises to make your mind darkened and murderous, remember you can see the battle from above. Even in forms you do not recognize, the signs you know. There is a stab of pain, a twinge of guilt, and above all, a loss of peace." (T-23.IV.6:1-3)

"When they occur leave not your place on high, but quickly choose a miracle instead of murder. And God Himself and all the lights of Heaven will gently lean to you, and hold you up. For you have chosen to remain where He would have you, and no illusion can attack the peace of God together with His Son." (T-23.IV.6:5-7)

"Perhaps you think the battleground can offer something you can win. Can it be anything that offers you a perfect calmness, and a sense of love so deep and quiet that no touch of doubt can ever mar your certainty? And that will last forever?" (T-23.IV.8:7-9)

"Those with the strength of God in their awareness could never think of battle." (T-23.IV.9:1)

"For everything fought for on the battleground is of the body; something it seems to offer or to own." (T-23.IV.9:3)

"The senselessness of conquest is quite apparent from the quiet sphere above the battleground." (T-23.IV.9:5)

"Who with the Love of God upholding him could find the choice of miracles or murder hard to make?" (T-23.IV.9:8)

In summary, Chapter 23 – IV: "Above the Battleground" is saying:
The world of separate forms we currently see, is the battleground on which the conflict between our separation and Unity is fought. Except there is no actual battle, for the world of separate forms merely covers the truth beneath a blanket of illusions. We are not separate. Yet every illusion of separation we see is an assault on the truth of our Union. It is a form of murder; the desire to separate from God and thus end the existence of our Unified Holy Self. When we believe our separated selves are the truth above all else, we are attempting violence against the idea of our eternal Union. However, we are not wholly conscious of these thoughts. We do not believe we are seceding from God at all but are desperately trying to come Home to Him. Yet now that it is understood exactly what we are doing when we think lovelessly about another,

we can end the battle altogether. We can rise above it by rising above the idea we are bodies. The choice to do this, is a miracle, for it takes great willingness and a mind ready to awaken, to decide to perceive others as they are in truth, as part of God's Great Stillness and not a body. If you can see that everything fought for on the battleground is of the body; something it seems to offer or to own, you will then rise above the battleground, no longer affected by the body and its needs. This choice effectively ends the war against your Self.

CHAPTER 24
THE GOAL OF SPECIALNESS

Introduction

"Forget not that the motivation for this course is the attainment and the keeping of the state of peace. Given this state the mind is quiet, and the condition in which God is remembered is attained." (T-24.in.1:1-2)

"God does not wait upon illusions to let Him be Himself. No more His Son. They *are*." (T-24.in.1:9-11)

"To learn this course requires willingness to question every value that you hold." (T-24.in.2:1)

"No belief is neutral." (T-24.in.2:3)

"For a decision is a conclusion based on everything that you believe." (T-24.in.2:5)

"There is no substitute for peace." (T-24.in.2:7)

"And your decisions come from your beliefs as certainly as all creation rose in His Mind because of what He knows." (T-24.in.2:10)

In summary, Chapter 24 – "Introduction" is saying:
The entire goal of this seemingly complex, lengthy course in miracles, is p*eace*. What is so difficult about attaining and keeping peace that it requires a book over a thousand pages long to teach it? It all comes down to our *beliefs*. Our peace is based upon what we *think*. Change what we believe and we either enter or leave a state of peace. The entirety of *A Course In Miracles* then, is a book that teaches us new beliefs; ones based upon the truth. Ones that lead to the attainment and the keeping of peace, for at the bottom of everything, a feeling of quiet, loving peace is the only thing we have ever wanted.

I. Specialness as a Substitute for Love

"Love is extension. To withhold the smallest gift is not to know love's purpose. Love offers everything forever. Hold back but one belief, one offering, and love is gone, because you asked a substitute to take its place." (T-24.I.1:1-4)

"The secret enemies of peace, your least decision to choose attack in-

CHAPTER 24 — THE GOAL OF SPECIALNESS

stead of love, unrecognized and swift to challenge you to combat and to violence far more inclusive than you think, are there by your election." (T-24.I.2:6)

"All that is ever cherished as a hidden belief, to be defended though unrecognized, is faith in specialness. This takes many forms, but always clashes with the reality of God's creation and with the grandeur that He gave His Son." (T-24.I.3:1-2)

"Only the special could have enemies, for they are different and not the same. And difference of any kind imposes orders of reality, and a need to judge that cannot be escaped." (T-24.I.3:5-6)

"For specialness not only sets apart, but serves as grounds from which attack on those who seem "beneath" the special one is "natural" and "just."" (T-24.I.4:4)

"Specialness is the great dictator of the wrong decisions. Here is the grand illusion of what you are and what your brother is. And here is what must make the body dear and worth preserving. Specialness must be defended." (T-24.I.5:1-3)

"Would it be possible for you to hate your brother if you were like him? Could you attack him if you realized you journey with him, to a goal that is the same?" (T-24.I.6:1-2)

"You are his enemy in specialness; his friend in a shared purpose." (T-24.I.6:4)

"Your brother is your friend because his Father created him like you. There is no difference. You have been given to your brother that love might be extended, not cut off from him." (T-24.I.7:1-3)

"The fear of God and of your brother comes from each unrecognized belief in specialness." (T-24.I.8:1)

"You would oppose this course because it teaches you you and your brother are alike." (T-24.I.8:6)

"Those who are special must defend illusions against the truth. For what is specialness but an attack upon the Will of God?" (T-24.I.9:1-2)

"Here must he be your enemy and not your friend. Never can there be peace among the different. He is your friend because you are the same." (T-24.I.9:6-7)

II. The Treachery of Specialness

In summary, Chapter 24 – I: "Specialness as a Substitute for Love" is saying:

Here the word "special" is interchangeable with the word "separate" or "body." And the word "love" of course means "union." When understood this way, specialness is the choice to believe we are separate bodies and not One in Love. When we believe in our separation, by default, we also believe it is possible to compete with one another, for only what is different can be in opposition to each other. What is the same, merely rests in peace, for by its very definition, what is the same, cannot be in conflict, for only *differences* conflict. Our beliefs must shift in order to see our shared goal of peace with all human beings. God created each of us with the same equality in His Love, not different. Only the ego sees bodies, separate, unequal, and different, but the Holy Spirit sees our Union as part of God's peace. Peace is *felt*, not *seen*. Therefore, it is possible then, to see separate, special bodies, but *feel* loving union with them, knowing the truth of our Oneness, despite what we may see. This is the way to undo the substitution of specialness for love.

II. The Treachery of Specialness

"Comparison must be an ego device, for love makes none. Specialness always makes comparisons." (T-24.II.1:1-2)

"And always whom it thus diminishes would be your savior, had you not chosen to make of him a tiny measure of your specialness instead." (T-24.II.1:5)

"Pursuit of specialness is always at the cost of peace. Who can attack his savior and cut him down, yet recognize his strong support?" (T-24.II.2:1-2)

"And who can use him as the gauge of littleness, and be released from limits?" (T-24.II.2:4)

"Specialness is the idea of sin made real." (T-24.II.3:1)

"You are not special. If you think you are, and would defend your specialness against the truth of what you really are, how can you know the truth?" (T-24.II.4:1-2)

"The special messages the special hear convince them they are different and apart; each in his special sins and "safe" from love, which does not see his specialness at all. Christ's vision is their "enemy," for it sees not what they would look upon, and it would show them that the special-

CHAPTER 24 — THE GOAL OF SPECIALNESS

ness they think they see is an illusion." (T-24.II.5:5-6)

"What would they see instead? The shining radiance of the Son of God, so like his Father that the memory of Him springs instantly to mind." (T-24.II.6:1-2)

"This is the only "cost" of truth: You will no longer see what never was, nor hear what makes no sound. Is it a sacrifice to give up nothing, and to receive the Love of God forever?" (T-24.II.6:5-6)

"You have come far along the way of truth; too far to falter now. Just one step more, and every vestige of the fear of God will melt away in love. Your brother's specialness and yours are enemies, and bound in hate to kill each other and deny they are the same." (T-24.II.9:1-3)

"Here is your savior from your specialness. He is in need of your acceptance of himself as part of you, as you for his." (T-24.II.10:1-2)

"Not special, but possessed of everything, including you." (T-24.II.10:6)

"Specialness is the seal of treachery upon the gift of love." (T-24.II.12:1)

"The hope of specialness makes it seem possible God made the body as the prison house that keeps His Son from Him. For it demands a special place God cannot enter, and a hiding place where none is welcome but your tiny self." (T-24.II.13:1-2)

"The death of specialness is not your death, but your awaking into life eternal. You but emerge from an illusion of what you are to the acceptance of yourself as God created you." (T-24.II.14:4-5)

In summary, Chapter 24 – II: "The Treachery of Specialness" is saying:

Specialness is the desire to be a separate body, seemingly unique and apart from everyone else. The treachery in this desire, is that it also creates conflict where there is none in truth. In truth, it is impossible that anyone exist outside the Union of God's Love, for it is His Love alone that sustains us. We are playing an imaginary game, creating an illusion of being something we are not, and it has us all tricked into thinking we are bodies. We are not special; meaning, we are not bodies. Would we hold onto what the body shows us as the truth, or exchange this illusion for reality, and know our shining radiance as part of the Son of God instead? "This is the only "cost" of truth: You will no longer see what never was, nor hear what makes no sound. Is it a sacrifice to give up nothing, and to receive the Love of God forever?" (T-24.II.6:5-6). Let go of the idea of being special, of being a body, and do not fall into the treachery of fallen thinking. No one here is special, for no one here is a body. You have come too far along the path of truth to believe in the treachery of specialness. For you have no enemies within God's Love.

III. The Forgiveness of Specialness

"Forgiveness is the end of specialness. Only illusions can be forgiven, and then they disappear." (T-24.III.1:1-2)

"No one who clings to one illusion can see himself as sinless, for he holds one error to himself as lovely still." (T-24.III.1:4)

"Whatever form of specialness you cherish, you have made sin." (T-24.III.2:1)

"So does it seem to split you off from God, and make you separate from Him as its defender." (T-24.III.2:4)

"It is not you who are so vulnerable and open to attack that just a word, a little whisper that you do not like, a circumstance that suits you not, or an event that you did not anticipate upsets your world, and hurls it into chaos. Truth is not frail. Illusions leave it perfectly unmoved and undisturbed. But specialness is not the truth in you. It can be thrown off balance by anything." (T-24.III.3:1-5)

"God asks for your forgiveness. He would have no separation, like an alien will, rise between what He wills for you and what you will." (T-24.III.5:1-2)

"Forgive the great Creator of the universe, the Source of life, of love and holiness, the perfect Father of a perfect Son, for your illusions of your specialness." (T-24.III.6:1)

"The special ones are all asleep, surrounded by a world of loveliness they do not see." (T-24.III.7:1)

"They are lost in dreams of specialness." (T-24.III.7:4)

"The slaves of specialness will yet be free. Such is the Will of God and of His Son." (T-24.III.8:1-2)

"God calls to you from him to join His Will to save you both from hell." (T-24.III.8:5)

"They ask of you but that your will be done. They seek your love that

CHAPTER 24—THE GOAL OF SPECIALNESS

you may love yourself. Love not your specialness instead of Them. The print of nails is on your hands as well. Forgive your Father it was not His Will that you be crucified." (T-24.III.8:10-13)

In summary, Chapter 24 – III: "The Forgiveness of Specialness" is saying:
Forgiveness ends specialness, because remember that forgiveness is the end of ego thoughts. Ego thoughts are all thoughts that surround the body, or specialness. Forgiveness is stillness of thought; inner stillness of a mind that rests in peace, merely observing the chaos of the world surrounding it, but not engaging with it as a body.
"No one who clings to one illusion (of being a body) can see himself as sinless (bodiless), for he holds one error to himself as lovely still." (T-24.III.1:4)
"Whatever form of specialness (being a body) you cherish, you have made sin (a way of being separate from God)." (T-24.III.2:1)
"So does it seem to split you off from God, and make you separate from Him as its defender." (T-24.III.2:4)
Forgive your Father (see yourself a part of His Stillness of ego thought) it was not His Will that you be crucified (separated from Him and the experience of His Love)." (T-24.III.8:10-13)
To still your ego-thoughts then, is to still those thoughts about bodies and the world we live in. This is the forgiveness of all forms of specialness.

IV. Specialness versus Sinlessness

"Specialness is a lack of truth in anyone except yourself. Faith is invested in yourself alone." (T-24.IV.1:1-2)

"What could the purpose of the body be but specialness?" (T-24.IV.2:1)

"It was conceived to make you frail and helpless. The goal of separation is its curse." (T-24.IV.2:3-4)

"Of itself the body can do nothing. See it as means to hurt, and it is hurt. See it as means to heal, and it is healed." (T-24.IV.2:10-12)

"You can but hurt yourself. This has been oft repeated, but is difficult to grasp as yet. To minds intent on specialness it is impossible." (T-24.IV.3:1-3)

"Nothing could make less sense to specialness. Nothing could make more sense to miracles. For miracles are merely change of purpose from hurt to healing." (T-24.IV.3:7-9)

"Earlier I said consider not the means by which salvation is attained, nor how to reach it. But do consider, and consider well, whether it is your wish that you might see your brother sinless." (T-24.IV.4:1-2)

"All that is real proclaims his sinlessness. All that is false proclaims his sins as real." (T-24.IV.4:6-7)

"Do not defend this senseless dream, in which God is bereft of what He loves, and you remain beyond salvation. Only this is certain in this shifting world that has no meaning in reality: When peace is not with you entirely, and when you suffer pain of any kind, you have beheld some sin within your brother, and have rejoiced at what you thought was there." (T-24.IV.5:1-2)

"And so is specialness his "enemy," and yours as well." (T-24.IV.5:6)

In summary, Chapter 24 – IV: "Specialness versus Sinlessness" is saying:
If the word specialness is equated with the idea of being a body, then sinlessness can be equated to bodilessness, or perfection in Spirit as God created us. We all have the human desire to be "special" somehow—we each strive for that feeling of being set apart, better or "more" than others. At the root of this feeling is the belief we are each a body—unique individuals each striving to be perfect through an identity we are really not. This is therefore a futile attempt at what can never be achieved, and it causes us much pain and suffering. The body does not make us special, but it does make us insane for our belief in it. Do we want to see our brothers and sisters as special bodies or as the sinless (bodiless) Light within the Body of Christ? What we choose to see, determines our path towards joy or away from it. Whether we choose to see specialness versus sinlessness, determines our path towards salvation or away from it.

V. The Christ in You

"The Christ in you is very still. He looks on what He loves, and knows it as Himself." (T-24.V.1:1-2)

"Specialness, too, takes joy in what it sees, although it is not true." (T-24.V.1:4)

"There is no dream of specialness, however hidden or disguised the form, however lovely it may seem to be, however much it delicately offers the hope of peace and the escape from pain, in which you suffer

CHAPTER 24 — THE GOAL OF SPECIALNESS

not your condemnation." (T-24.V.2:1)

"Where could your peace arise but from forgiveness? The Christ in you looks only on the truth, and sees no condemnation that could need forgiveness. He is at peace *because* He sees no sin." (T-24.V.3:1-3)

"Yet let your specialness direct his way, and you will follow." (T-24.V.4:1)

"Rejoice you have no eyes with which to see; no ears to listen, and no hands to hold nor feet to guide. Be glad that only Christ can lend you His, while you have need of them." (T-24.V.5:1-2)

"The Christ in you is very still. He knows where you are going, and He leads you there in gentleness and blessing all the way." (T-24.V.6:1-2)

"And so He sought for you completion in each living thing that He beholds and loves." (T-24.V.6:8)

"Yet is He quiet, for He knows that love is in you now, and safely held in you by that same hand that holds your brother's in your own." (T-24.V.7:1)

"The sight of Christ is all there is to see. The song of Christ is all there is to hear. The hand of Christ is all there is to hold. There is no journey but to walk with Him." (T-24.V.7:7-10)

"You who would be content with specialness, and seek salvation in a war with love, consider this: The holy Lord of Heaven has Himself come down to you, to offer you your own completion." (T-24.V.8:1)

"He is within you, yet He walks beside you and before, leading the way that He must go to find Himself complete. His quietness becomes your certainty. And where is doubt when certainty has come?" (T-24.V.9:5-7)

In summary, Chapter 24 – V: "The Christ in You" is saying:
The Christ in you is very still. Why is He so still? Because a mind that knows its Oneness in God has no conflict; such a mind is still, in its peace. A mind that is still, carries no thoughts about the world, the doings of bodies or fears of what may come. The Christ in us is still, because He knows there is nothing to fear, for our fears are unfounded, being founded in a world that is not our home, played out by bodies that are not who we are. *To be still, is to have forgiven.* For a mind that is still, is not busy wishing things were somehow different—that the circumstances the ego finds itself in, would bend to its meager will. Such is the meaning of forgiveness and the relinquishment of specialness. Do not be

content with specialness; with the goals of the body. Focus instead on the One Who knows the way to peace, who teaches through the stillness of thought; the Christ in you.

VI. Salvation from Fear

"Before your brother's holiness the world is still, and peace descends on it in gentleness and blessing so complete that not one trace of conflict still remains to haunt you in the darkness of the night." (T-24.VI.1:1)

"Without you there would be a lack in God, a Heaven incomplete, a Son without a Father." (T-24.VI.2:1)

"For what God wills is whole, and part of Him because His Will is One." (T-24.VI.2:3)

"Your brother's holiness shows you that God is one with him and you; that what he has is yours because you are not separate from him nor from his Father." (T-24.VI.2:5)

"And no thought within His Mind is absent from your own. It is His Will you share His Love for you, and look upon yourself as lovingly as He conceived of you before the world began, and as He knows you still." (T-24.VI.3:3-4)

"Your brother *is* as He created him." (T-24.VI.3:6)

"Forget not that the healing of God's Son is all the world is for." (T-24.VI.4:1)

"Until you see the healing of the Son as all you wish to be accomplished by the world, by time and all appearances, you will not know the Father nor yourself." (T-24.VI.4:3)

"Look on your brother, and behold in him the whole reversal of the laws that seem to rule this world." (T-24.VI.5:1)

"It is His sinlessness that eyes that see can look upon. It is His loveliness they see in everything. And it is He they look for everywhere, and find no sight nor place nor time where He is not." (T-24.VI.6:1-3)

"Let not your eyes be blinded by the veil of specialness that hides the face of Christ from him, and you as well." (T-24.VI.6:5)

"Choose, then, his body or his holiness as what you want to see, and which you choose is yours to look upon. Yet will you choose in countless situations, and through time that seems to have no end, until the

CHAPTER 24 — THE GOAL OF SPECIALNESS

truth be your decision." (T-24.VI.7:1-2)

"See him as what he is, that your deliverance may not be long." (T-24.VI.9:1)

"And both shall see God's glory in His Son, whom you mistook as flesh, and bound to laws that have no power over him at all." (T-24.VI.9:5)

"Would you not gladly realize these laws are not for you? Then see him not as prisoner to them." (T-24.VI.10:1-2)

"And never doubt but that your specialness will disappear before the Will of God, Who loves each part of Him with equal love and care. The Christ in you can see your brother truly." (T-24.VI.10:6-7)

"You who believe it easier to see your brother's body than his holiness, be sure you understand what made this judgment. Here is the voice of specialness heard clearly, judging against the Christ and setting forth for you the purpose that you can attain, and what you cannot do." (T-24.VI.13:1-2)

"For what you do through Christ it does not know. To Him this judgment makes no sense at all, for only what His Father wills is possible, and there is no alternative for Him to see. Out of His lack of conflict comes your peace. And from His purpose comes the means for effortless accomplishment and rest." (T-24.VI.13:4-7)

In summary, Chapter 24 – VI: "Salvation from Fear" is saying:
What is the one fear from which all other fears spring? What is the fear we need salvation from? It is the fear of everything associated with the body. Without the body, we have nothing to fear, for we then know ourselves as eternal in God. But until we reach such a place, we must practice fearlessness here, now in this world. We do this by perceiving each other's holiness, our bodilessness. This shift in perception is our salvation; our salvation from all the fear the body brings us. The Christ in us can see truly, for He looks upon the world through the stillness of thought about it. This stillness is a way of "seeing" through "feeling." Christ's vision is the feeling of stillness and peace within your heart that comes from ceasing to agree with what your eyes behold. You find your salvation from fear, through shifting from outer perception to inner recognition. Salvation from fear comes through the inner recognition of your still, quiet Oneness with all things in God.

VII. The Meeting Place

"How bitterly does everyone tied to this world defend the specialness he wants to be the truth!" (T-24.VII.1:1)

"No effort is too great, no cost too much, no price too dear to save his specialness from the least slight, the tiniest attack, the whispered doubt, the hint of threat, or anything but deepest reverence." (T-24.VII.1:6)

"What is this son that you have made to be your strength? What is this child of earth on whom such love is lavished? What is this parody of God's creation that takes the place of yours?" (T-24.VII.1:9-12)

"How can you know your worth while specialness claims you instead?" (T-24.VII.3:1)

"Seek not to make your specialness the truth, for if it were you would be lost indeed. Be thankful, rather, it is given you to see his holiness because it is the truth. And what is true in him must be as true in you." (T-24.VII.3:3-5)

"The Father keeps what He created safe. You cannot touch it with the false ideas you made, because it was created not by you." (T-24.VII.5:1-2)

"What is immortal cannot be attacked; what is but temporal has no effect." (T-24.VII.5:4)

"The test of everything on earth is simply this; "What is it for?" The answer makes it what it is for you." (T-24.VII.6:1)

"This course makes no attempt to teach what cannot easily be learned." (T-24.VII.8:1)

"It is essential it be kept in mind that all perception still is upside down until its purpose has been understood." (T-24.VII.8:5)

"Perception seems to teach you what you see. Yet it but witnesses to what you taught. It is the outward picture of a wish; an image that you wanted to be true." (T-24.VII.8:8-10)

"Look at yourself, and you will see a body. Look at this body in a different light and it looks different. And without a light it seems that it is gone. Yet you are reassured that it is there because you still can feel it with your hands and hear it move." (T-24.VII.9:1-4)

"It proves its own reality to you." (T-24.VII.9:8)

CHAPTER 24—THE GOAL OF SPECIALNESS

"Thus is the body made a theory of yourself, with no provisions made for evidence beyond itself, and no escape within its sight." (T-24.VII.10:1-2)

"And you cannot conceive of you apart from it." (T-24.VII.10:4)

"And thus are two sons made, and both appear to walk this earth without a meeting place and no encounter. One do you perceive outside yourself, your own beloved son. The other rests within, his Father's Son, within your brother as he is in you." (T-24.VII.11:1-3)

"Yet can perception serve another goal. It is not bound to specialness but by your choice. And it is given you to make a different choice, and use perception for a different purpose. And what you see will serve that purpose well, and prove its own reality to you." (T-24.VII.11:10-13)

In summary, Chapter 24 – VII: "The Meeting Place" is saying:
There is no meeting place between our bodily identity and our true Identity in Spirit, as One in God. We can experience only one or the other and only one identity can be true. How long will we continue to attempt to make the body real to us? How long will we strive to defend it against even the slightest misspoken word? But take heart; our false idea about who we are, cannot touch what God created us to be. Though we struggle to perceive ourselves apart from the bodies we think we are now, Who We Are in Truth will not be damaged by such misconceptions. Let us change our self-perception now, today. It is given us to make a new choice, one we never knew we had. We can choose to be as God created us. Choose to see only the light of Christ in one another through feeling your Oneness with them, and you choose to go to the meeting place of yourself and God. And you thus relinquish your goal of specialness; the goal of being a body; in exchange for a new goal; the healing of God's Son, with Whom you are One. The goal of specialness is relinquished at last, in this holy meeting place within you.

CHAPTER 25
THE JUSTICE OF GOD

Introduction

"The Christ in you inhabits not a body." (T-25.in.1:1)

"And thus it must be that you are not within a body." (T-25.in.1:3)

"Christ is within a frame of Holiness whose only purpose is that He may be made manifest to those who know Him not, that He may call to them to come to Him and see Him where they thought their bodies were." (T-25.in.1:8)

"No one who carries Christ in him can fail to recognize Him everywhere. Except in bodies." (T-25.in.2:1-2)

"And so he carries Him unknowingly, and does not make Him manifest." (T-25.in.2:4)

"The body needs no healing. But the mind that thinks it is a body is sick indeed! And it is here that Christ sets forth the remedy." (T-25.in.3:1-3)

"Such is the mission that your brother has for you. And such it must be that your mission is for him." (T-25.in.3:7-8)

In summary, Chapter 25 – "Introduction" is saying:
We each carry Christ within us, but cannot see Him while we believe we are bodies. Shift our belief, and we will shift what we see. In this way, our minds are healed. This is the mission given each of us; to see one another as Christ sees us—as part of His One Self. You will know when you have achieved this by the level of loving peace that you feel towards all those you see or think of.

I. The Link to Truth

"It cannot be that it is hard to do the task that Christ appointed you to do, since it is He Who does it." (T-25.I.1:1)

"His holiness directs the body through the mind at one with Him." (T-25.I.1:5)

"How can you manifest the Christ in you except to look on holiness and see Him there?" (T-25.I.2:1)

"Behold the body, and you will believe that you are there." (T-25.I.2:3)

CHAPTER 25 — THE JUSTICE OF GOD

"Perception is a choice of what you want yourself to be; the world you want to live in, and the state in which you think your mind will be content and satisfied." (T-25.I.3:1)

"And thus you learn what seems to have a life apart has none." (T-25.I.3:6)

"You are the means for God; not separate, nor with a life apart from His. His life is manifest in you who are His Son." (T-25.I.4:1-2)

"You and your brother stand before Him now, to let Him draw aside the veil that seems to keep you separate and apart." (T-25.I.4:6)

"Since you believe that you are separate, Heaven presents itself to you as separate, too. Not that it is in truth, but that the link that has been given you to join the truth may reach to you through what you understand." (T-25.I.5:1-2)

"The Holy Spirit serves Christ's purpose in your mind, so that the aim of specialness can be corrected where the error lies." (T-25.I.6:1)

"It is the Holy Spirit's function to teach you how this oneness is experienced, what you must do that it can be experienced, and where you should go to do it." (T-25.I.6:4)

"And It must use all learning to transfer illusions to the truth, taking all false ideas of what you are, and leading you beyond them to the truth that is beyond them. All this can very simply be reduced to this:

What is the same can not be different, and what is one can not have separate parts." (T-25.I.7:5-7)

In summary, Chapter 25 – I: "The Link to Truth" is saying:
The Holy Spirit within us is our link to Truth. His is the Voice that will teach us Who We Are in Truth if we will simply open our heart and listen. We open our inner ears by shifting our inner perception from separate bodies to oneness in Christ. This is the only task Christ has appointed to us to do in this world; to see each other differently than the ego perceives us. When we shift away from believing we are separate bodies, we correct the greatest error we have ever made in thinking. Through correcting this single thought, the Holy Spirit teaches us the experience of oneness. What must we do to have this experience? Cease to focus your mind on the many ways we are separate. Where should we go to do this? Go within where you can peacefully focus your mind on our Unity through the Holy Spirit, our Link to Truth.

II. The Savior from the Dark

"Is it not evident that what the body's eyes perceive fills you with fear?" (T-25.II.1:1)

"Despite your hopes and fancies, always does despair result." (T-25.II.1:5)

"The only value that the past can hold is that you learn it gave you no rewards which you would want to keep." (T-25.II.1:7)

"Is it not strange that you should cherish still some hope of satisfaction from the world you see? In no respect, at any time or place, has anything but fear and guilt been your reward." (T-25.II.2:1-2)

"Yet is this hopelessness your choice, while you would seek for hope where none is ever found." (T-25.II.2:6)

"Is it not also true that you have found some hope apart from this; some glimmering, - inconsistent, wavering, yet dimly seen, - that hopefulness is warranted on grounds that are not in this world?" (T-25.II.3:1)

"Take not the form for content, for the form is but a means for content." (T-25.II.4:3)

"Who hangs an empty frame upon a wall and stands before it, deep in reverence, as if a masterpiece were there to see? Yet if you see your brother as a body, it is but this you do." (T-25.II.5:1-2)

"The Holy Spirit is the frame God set around the part of Him that you would see as separate. Yet its frame is joined to its Creator, one with Him and with His masterpiece. This is its purpose, and you do not make the frame into the picture when you choose to see it in its place." (T-25.II.6:1-3)

"Accept God's frame instead of yours, and you will see the masterpiece." (T-25.II.7:1)

"Within the darkness see the savior from the dark, and understand your brother as his Father's Mind shows him to you. He will step forth from the darkness as you look on him, and you will see the dark no more." (T-25.II.8:1-2)

"How could the Lord of Heaven not be glad if you appreciate His masterpiece?" (T-25.II.9:1)

"This brother is His perfect gift to you." (T-25.II.9:6)

CHAPTER 25 — THE JUSTICE OF GOD

"Not one ray of darkness can be seen by those who will to make their Father's happiness complete, and theirs along with His." (T-25.II.9:10)

"Forgive your brother, and you cannot separate yourself from him nor from his Father." (T-25.II.10:1)

"You and your brother are the same, as God Himself is One and not divided in His Will." (T-25.II.11:1)

"To you and your brother is given the power of salvation, that escape from darkness into light be yours to share; that you may see as one what never has been separate, nor apart from all God's Love as given equally." (T-25.II.11:5)

In summary, Chapter 25 – II: "The Savior from the Dark" is saying: We are each other's savior from the dark. "Darkness" is ignorance if "light" is knowledge. To be in the dark then, is to not know our oneness. Separation is the state of a darkened mind. Forgiveness is the light that shines away such dark thoughts; to forgive is to see beyond the body. Forgiveness is how we save one another from the darkness; the idea of being separate. When I say, "I forgive you," I am saying, "I see you. I see our oneness and sameness in God's Love. I do not see my thoughts about your separate body or what you are doing with it. You are God's gift to me. For by your coming into a body, you allow me to see you as you are not. And I am given the opportunity to see you differently; to see you as One with me. And when I succeed in seeing only this truth in you, you become my savior from the dark."

III. Perception and Choice

"To the extent to which you value guilt, to that extent will you perceive a world in which attack is justified." (T-25.III.1:1)

"God's laws do not obtain directly to a world perception rules, for such a world could not have been created by the Mind to which perception has no meaning." (T-25.III.2:1)

"Only because His Son believes it is, and from His Son's belief He could not let Himself be separate entirely. He could not enter His Son's insanity with him, but He could be sure His sanity went there with him, so he could not be lost forever in the madness of his wish." (T-25.III.2:4-5)

"Perception rests on choosing; knowledge does not." (T-25.III.3:1)

"There is another purpose in the world that error made, because it has

III. Perception and Choice

another Maker Who can reconcile its goal with His Creator's purpose. In His perception of the world, nothing is seen but justifies forgiveness and the sight of perfect sinlessness. Nothing arises but is met with instant and complete forgiveness." (T-25.III.5:1-3)

"Everyone here has entered darkness, yet no one has entered it alone. Nor need he stay more than an instant. For he has come with Heaven's Help within him, ready to lead him out of darkness into light at any time." (T-25.III.6:1-3)

"And when he chooses to avail himself of what is given him, then will he see each situation that he thought before was means to justify his anger turned to an event which justifies his love." (T-25.III.6:5)

"How can a misperception be a sin? Let all your brother's errors be to you nothing except a chance for you to see the workings of the Helper given you to see the world He made instead of yours." (T-25.III.7:1-2)

"For it is seeing them as one that brings release from the belief there are two ways to see. This world has much to offer to your peace, and many chances to extend your own forgiveness. Such its purpose is, to those who want to see peace and forgiveness descend on them, and offer them the light." (T-25.III.7:7-9)

"Sin is the fixed belief perception cannot change." (T-25.III.8:4)

"The Holy Spirit, too, sees what He sees as far beyond the chance of change." (T-25.III.8:8)

"The Son of God could never sin, but he can wish for what would hurt him." (T-25.III.9:1)

"What could this be except a misperception of himself?" (T-25.III.9:3)

"Does he need help or condemnation?" (T-25.III.9:5)

"Make, then, your choice. But recognize that in this choice the purpose of the world you see is chosen, and will be justified." (T-25.III.9:9-10)

In summary, Chapter 25 – III: "Perception and Choice" is saying:
We have a choice in what we see in this world. We can see separate bodies, attacking and at war with one another, ranging from mere differing opinions to murder. Or we can see another world entirely. We can see the many parts of the Son of God, inhabiting bodies who are participating in an illusion of being in conflict. Is it wrong to participate? No, but such suffering is a needless misperception. We can choose to see differently. We can choose not to

CHAPTER 25 – THE JUSTICE OF GOD

misperceive. Do not miss your chances to forgive—to make the choice to see only God's Stillness within all whom you perceive through the ego's eyes. Making the peaceful choice in perception is your purpose here in this world.

IV. The Light You Bring

"Minds that are joined and recognize they are, can feel no guilt. For they cannot attack, and they rejoice that this is so, seeing their safety in this happy fact." (T-25.IV.1:1-2)

"Perception's basic law could thus be said, "You will rejoice at what you see because you see it to rejoice." And while you think that suffering and sin will bring you joy, so long will they be there for you to see." (T-25.IV.2:1-2)

"You maker of a world that is not so, take rest and comfort in another world where peace abides. This world you bring with you to all the wary eyes and tired hearts that look on sin and beat its sad refrain. From you can come their rest." (T-25.IV.3:1-3)

"In you there is a vision that extends to all of them, and covers them in gentleness and light." (T-25.IV.3:5)

"Would you not do this for the Love of God? And for yourself?" (T-25.IV.4:1-2)

"Those who offer peace to everyone have found a home in Heaven the world cannot destroy. For it is large enough to hold the world within its peace." (T-25.IV.4:9-10)

"In you is all of Heaven." (T-25.IV.5:1)

"How better could your own mistakes be brought to truth than by your willingness to bring the light of Heaven with you, as you walk beyond the world of darkness into light?" (T-25.IV.5:12)

In summary, Chapter 25 – IV: "The Light You Bring" is saying:
We bring light to this world every time we choose to shift our thoughts to peace instead of attack. True peace is to feel our Oneness, our sameness in God's Love. Peace is unity. A mind at peace recognizes itself as being beyond the body; beyond all guilt. While we believe that sin or separation is what we prefer to see, we will suffer from our choice. And so, as bringers of the light, we can offer a new world to all those we see. We can choose to see them differently and thus bring them into our world of peace. Heaven is within us. And how do we "see" Heaven with-

in ourselves? There is only one thing within us that we can sense, and that is what we *feel*. Let us be willing then, to overlook what we see with our outer, bodily eyes, and extend what is within us to the world. Let us then offer the world the light we feel; the light we bring through knowing we are One.

V. The State of Sinlessness

"The state of sinlessness is merely this: The whole desire to attack is gone, and so there is no reason to perceive the Son of God as other than he is." (T-25.V.1:1)

"Attack and sin are bound as one illusion, each the cause and aim and justifier of the other." (T-25.V.1:3)

"Attack makes Christ your enemy, and God along with Him." (T-25.V.2:1)

"For who could see the Son of God as innocent and wish him dead? Christ stands before you, each time you look upon your brother. He has not gone because your eyes are closed." (T-25.V.2:8-10)

"Forgiven by you, your savior offers you salvation. Condemned by you, he offers death to you. In everyone you see but the reflection of what you choose to have him be to you." (T-25.V.4:5-7)

"It is no sacrifice that he be saved, for by his freedom will you gain your own." (T-25.V.5:1)

"And so you walk toward Heaven or toward hell, but not alone. How beautiful his sinlessness will be when you perceive it! And how great your joy, when he is free to offer you the gift of sight God gave to him for you!" (T-25.V.5:3-5)

"Look once again upon your brother, not without the understanding that he is the way to Heaven or to hell, as you perceive him. But forget not this; the role you give to him is given you, and you will walk the way you pointed out to him because it is your judgment on yourself." (T-25.V.6:5-6)

In summary, Chapter 25 – V: "The State of Sinlessness" is saying:
The state of sinlessness is merely a state of mind where you look beyond all bodies. It is truly a state of forgiveness. You may still look upon bodies, seeing what they do and say, but react to them as they are in truth; as part of your One Self and God. You react to them lovingly, with patience and kindness, knowing they do not know who they are to you, and who you are to them in the Unity of

CHAPTER 25—THE JUSTICE OF GOD

Spirit. All bodies we see, offer us the opportunity to see this way. Some are more challenging than others, but it does not mean they are any less precious to God, and therefore to us. Herein lies the path away from hell and directly to Heaven; the role we would give everyone we see. See them all as resting in a state of forgiveness; God's stillness; in an eternal state of sinlessness or bodilessness.

VI. The Special Function

"The grace of God rests gently on forgiving eyes, and everything they look on speaks of Him to the beholder. He can see no evil; nothing in the world to fear, and no one who is different from himself." (T-25.VI.1:1-2)

"He would no more condemn himself for his mistakes than damn another." (T-25.VI.1:4)

"The kindness of his sight rests on himself with all the tenderness it offers others. For he would only heal and only bless. And being in accord with what God wills, he has the power to heal and bless all those he looks on with the grace of God upon his sight." (T-25.VI.1:6-8)

"The wish to see calls down the grace of God upon your eyes, and brings the gift of light that makes sight possible. Would you behold your brother? God is glad to have you look on him." (T-25.VI.3:1-3)

"Such is the Holy Spirit's kind perception of specialness; His use of what you made, to heal instead of harm. To each He gives a special function in salvation he alone can fill; a part for only him." (T-25.VI.4:1-2)

"Here, where the laws of God do not prevail in perfect form, can he yet do one perfect thing and make one perfect choice." (T-25.VI.5:1)

"Forgiveness is the only function meaningful in time. It is the means the Holy Spirit uses to translate specialness from sin into salvation. Forgiveness is for all. But when it rests on all it is complete, and every function of this world completed with it." (T-25.VI.5:3-6)

"Salvation is no more than a reminder this world is not your home." (T-25.VI.6:1)

"The Holy Spirit needs your special function, that His may be fulfilled." (T-25.VI.7:1)

"In light, you see it as your special function in the plan to save the Son of God from all attack, and let him understand that he is safe, as he has always been, and will remain in time and in eternity alike. This is the function given you for your brother." (T-25.VI.7:7-8)

"Do this one thing, that everything be given you." (T-25.VI.7:10)

In summary, Chapter 25 – VI: "The Special Function" is saying:
Our special function is forgiveness. And what is forgiveness but simply the stillness of thought; the quiet surrender of all thoughts that attack the peace of God's Son, of Whom we are all a part? It is the surrender of all thoughts about bodies and what others are doing or saying with them. It is to cease to judge such thoughts as "good" or "bad," but merely not true. When thoughts about bodies are released from our mind, "The grace of God rests gently on forgiving eyes, and everything they look on speaks of Him to the beholder. He can see no evil; nothing in the world to fear, and no one who is different from himself." (T-25.VI.1:2). And so it is, we can forgive, returning our mind to God's peace. This is salvation, the remembrance that this world and all it contains is not our home. Do not react to it as though it has the power to hurt you. Forgive it instead. See it as in need of the stillness of your thoughts about it, that it may rest in peace. Do this one thing, your special function of forgiveness, and the world will be given you—transformed into Heaven.

VII. The Rock of Salvation

"Yet if the Holy Spirit can commute each sentence that you laid upon yourself into a blessing, then it cannot be a sin." (T-25.VII.1:1)

"The magic of the world can seem to hide the pain of sin from sinners, and deceive with glitter and with guile. Yet each one knows the cost of sin is death." (T-25.VII.1:5-6)

"For sin is a request for death, a wish to make this world's foundation sure as love, dependable as Heaven, and as strong as God Himself." (T-25.VII.1:8)

"It cannot be the "sinner's" wish for death is just as strong as is God's Will for life." (T-25.VII.2:1)

"If you could realize nothing is changeless but the Will of God, this course would not be difficult for you. For it is this that you do not believe." (T-25.VII.2:8-9)

"Let us go back to what we said before, and think of it more carefully. It must be so that either God is mad, or is this world a place of madness." (T-25.VII.3:1-2)

CHAPTER 25—THE JUSTICE OF GOD

"If one belief so deeply valued here were true, then every Thought God ever had is an illusion. And if but one Thought of His is true, then all beliefs the world gives any meaning to are false, and make no sense at all. This is the choice you make." (T-25.VII.3:7-9)

"The rest is up to God, and not to you." (T-25.VII.3:12)

"To justify one value that the world upholds is to deny your Father's sanity and yours. For God and His beloved Son do not think differently." (T-25.VII.4:1-2)

"Sin is not real because the Father and Son are not insane." (T-25.VII.4:8)

"The Holy Spirit has the power to change the whole foundation of the world you see to something else; a basis not insane, on which a sane perception can be based, another world perceived." (T-25.VII.5:1)

"For here is everything perceived as one, and no one loses that each one may gain." (T-25.VII.5:4)

"Test everything that you believe against this one requirement, and understand that everything that meets this one demand is worthy of your faith." (T-25.VII.6:1)

"Love is the basis for a world perceived as wholly mad to sinners, who believe theirs is the way to sanity. But sin is equally insane within the sight of love, whose gentle eyes would look beyond the madness and rest peacefully on truth." (T-25.VII.6:4-5)

"Because He is not mad has God appointed One as sane as He to raise a saner world to meet the sight of everyone who chose insanity as his salvation." (T-25.VII.8:2)

"This One but points to an alternative, another way of looking at what he has seen before, and recognizes as the world in which he lives, and thought he understood before." (T-25.VII.8:4)

"What is dependable except God's Love? And where does sanity abide except in Him? The One who speaks for Him can show you this, in the alternative He chose especially for you. It is God's Will that you remember this, and so emerge from deepest mourning into perfect joy." (T-25.VII.10:1-4)

"Salvation is rebirth of the idea no one can lose for anyone to gain." (T-25.VII.12:1)

"Here is sanity restored. And on this single rock of truth can faith in God's eternal saneness rest in perfect confidence and perfect peace." (T-25.VII.12:3-4)

"This is the rock on which salvation rests, the vantage point from which the Holy Spirit gives meaning and direction to the plan in which your special function has a part." (T-25.VII.12:7)

"Salvation is His Will because you share it. Not for you alone, but for the Self that is the Son of God." (T-25.VII.13:4-5)

"And this is sane because it is the truth." (T-25.VII.13:7)

In summary, Chapter 25 – VII: "The Rock of Salvation" is saying:
Salvation is built upon one idea; that we are One in God and in each other. This is the rock upon which salvation rests. All other Thoughts of God spring forth from this premise, and all other ideas of the world must be tested against it for truth. We must ask ourselves with each thought, "Does this idea foster our unity or separation?" If it does not align with our unity and peace, then it is a false thought; a thought based on the ego and it must be seen as insane and disregarded. This is how we return our minds to sanity. A sane mind sees only Love, the binding force of all things in creation. Not the exterior of things, but the inner world that holds the power of God. To see separation is to see sin. These two words are interchangeable. To see Unity is to see salvation. These two words are interchangeable. Let our Oneness then, be the rock of salvation upon which all our thinking is based, and we will have sanity restored to us.

VIII. Justice Returned to Love

"The Holy Spirit can use all that you give to Him for your salvation. But He cannot use what you withhold, for He cannot take it from you without your willingness." (T-25.VIII.1:1-2)

"You need not give it to him wholly willingly, for if you could you had no need of Him. But this He needs; that you prefer He take it than that you keep it for yourself alone, and recognize that what brings loss to no one you would not know." (T-25.VIII.1:5-6)

"Here is the only principle salvation needs." (T-25.VIII.2:1)

"But remember salvation is not needed by the saved. You are not called upon to do what one divided still against himself would find impossible." (T-25.VIII.2:4

CHAPTER 25—THE JUSTICE OF GOD

"But be you thankful that only little faith is asked of you." (T-25.VIII.2:7)

"There is a kind of justice in salvation of which the world knows nothing. To the world, justice and vengeance are the same, for sinners see justice only as their punishment, perhaps sustained by someone else, but not escaped." (T-25.VIII.3:1-2)

"You who know not of justice still can ask, and learn the answer. Justice looks on all in the same way." (T-25.VIII.4:1-2)

"For He is wholly fair to everyone. Vengeance is alien to God's Mind because He knows of justice. To be just is to be fair, and not be vengeful." (T-25.VIII.5:4-6)

"It is impossible for you to share the Holy Spirit's justice with a mind that can conceive of specialness at all." (T-25.VIII.5:8)

"It is extremely hard for those who still believe sin meaningful to understand the Holy Spirit's justice." (T-25.VIII.6:1)

"And so they fear the Holy Spirit, and perceive the "wrath" of God in Him." (T-25.VIII.6:3)

"They do believe that Heaven is hell, and are afraid of love." (T-25.VIII.6:5)

"Yet justice cannot punish those who ask for punishment, but have a Judge Who knows that they are wholly innocent in truth." (T-25.VIII.8:1)

"And God rejoices as His Son receives what loving justice knows to be his due. For love and justice are not different. Because they are the same does mercy stand at God's right Hand, and gives the Son of God the power to forgive himself of sin." (T-25.VIII.9:9-11)

"As specialness cares not who pays the cost of sin, so it be paid, the holy Spirit heeds not who looks on innocence at last, provided it is seen and recognized." (T-25.VIII.11:1)

"You can be perfect witness to the power of love and justice, if you understand it is impossible the Son of God could merit vengeance." (T-25.VIII.12:1)

"Judge not because you cannot, not because you are a miserable sinner too. How can the special really understand that justice is the same for everyone?" (T-25.VIII.13:3-4)

"Their Father gave the same inheritance to both." (T-25.VIII.13:6)

"You have the right to all the universe; to perfect peace, complete deliverance from all effects of sin, and to the life eternal, joyous and complete in every way, as God appointed for His holy Son. This is the only justice Heaven knows, and all the Holy Spirit brings to earth." (T-25.VIII.14:1-2)

"Let love decide, and never fear that you, in your unfairness, will deprive yourself of what God's justice has allotted you." (T-25.VIII.14:7)

In summary, Chapter 25 – VIII: "Justice Returned to Love" is saying: We have a skewed and incorrect view of what justice truly is. We think justice is some form of payment of debt for wrongdoing. It is "just" when people are punished for what they have done "wrong." However, to God, justice is fair and impartial. He punishes no one. He only loves, for that is how we are seen through His eyes; incapable of harm because we are incapable of being separate bodies. Bodies can harm one another, but Spirit cannot. This does not mean we have to agree with the atrocities of the world; we merely are being asked to see things in a new way. We are being asked to see the world through the eyes of love. Love sees only Unity and the need for healing if such Unity is not perceived by any part of its One Self. And so, we who cannot see our own Unity, must give all judgment over to the Holy Spirit, Who can look upon the world correctly.

"Justice looks on all in the same way." (T-25.VIII.4:2)

"For Love and justice are not different. Because they are the same does mercy stand at God's right Hand, and gives the Son of God the power to forgive (or overlook) himself of sin (all forms of separation)." (T-25.VIII.9:10-11)

Justice, correctly perceived, is returned to being but another form of love.

IX. The Justice of Heaven

"What can it be but arrogance to think your little errors cannot be undone by Heaven's justice?" (T-25.IX.1:1)

"Are you willing to be released from all effects of sin? You cannot answer this until you see all that the answer must entail. For if you answer "yes" it means you will forego all values of this world in favor of the peace of Heaven. Not one sin would you retain." (T-25.IX.1:3-6)

"Be certain any answer to a problem the Holy Spirit solves will always be one in which no one loses." (T-25.IX.3:1)

"And every error is a perception in which one, at least, is seen unfairly." (T-25.IX.3:6)

CHAPTER 25—THE JUSTICE OF GOD

"When anyone is seen as losing, he has been condemned. And punishment becomes his due instead of justice." (T-25.IX.3:7-9)

"The sight of innocence makes punishment impossible, and justice sure." (T-25.IX.4:1)

"The Holy Spirit's problem solving is the way in which the problem ends. It has been solved because it has been met with justice. Until it has it will recur, because it has not yet been solved." (T-25.IX.5:1-3)

"Healing must be for everyone, because he does not merit an attack of any kind." (T-25.IX.6:3)

"If miracles, the Holy Spirit's gift, were given specially to an elect and special group, and kept apart from others as less deserving, then is He ally to specialness." (T-25.IX.7:2)

"Unless you think that all your brothers have an equal right to miracles with you, you will not claim your right to them because you were unjust to one with equal rights." (T-25.IX.8:1)

"Only forgiveness offers miracles." (T-25.IX.8:5)

"The unforgiven have no mercy to bestow upon another. That is why your sole responsibility must be to take forgiveness for yourself." (T-25.IX.9:5-6)

"Each miracle is an example of what justice can accomplish when it is offered to everyone alike." (T-25.IX.10:4)

"It is awareness that giving and receiving are the same. Because it does not make the same unlike, it sees no differences where none exists. And thus it is the same for everyone, because it sees no differences in them. Its offering is universal, and it teaches but one message: *What is God's belongs to everyone, and is his due.*" (T-25.IX.10:6-10)

In summary, Chapter 25 – IX: "The Justice of Heaven" is saying:
Are we willing to be released from all effects of sin, or separation? Answering "yes" to this question means that we are willing to let go of every grievance we ever had, allowing our thoughts about all situations to rest in peace; to rest in the knowing that what we thought was done to us, was never done, because we are not who we think we are to one another. To say "yes" is to agree to be released from all effects of separation, which means we have agreed to forgive the world. To forgive the world, is to overlook it entirely, knowing it is a false

IX. The Justice of Heaven

reality of separation. To forgive is to offer a miracle. And a miracle is an example of God's justice; an example of loving That Which Unites us within instead of attacking what we perceive as outside of us. God's miracle of justice is offered to everyone alike because the giver understands we are all alike. We are One Love and what love we give, is also then received by us, the love of our One Self. And what love belongs to us, must then belong to everyone. No one is excluded from God's love. This is the justice of Heaven—the justice of God.

CHAPTER 26
THE TRANSITION

I. The "Sacrifice" of Oneness

"In the "dynamics" of attack is sacrifice a key idea." (T-26.I.1:1)

"It is the symbol of the central theme that somebody must lose." (T-26.I.1:3)

"The body is itself a sacrifice; a giving up of power in the name of saving just a little for yourself. To see a brother in another body, separate from yours, is the expression of a wish to see a little part of him and sacrifice the rest." (T-26.I.1:5-6)

"The world you see is based on "sacrifice" of oneness." (T-26.I.2:1)

"The little that the body fences off becomes the self, preserved through sacrifice of all the rest." (T-26.I.3:1)

"The body is a loss, and can be made to sacrifice. And while you see your brother as a body, apart from you and separate in his cell, you are demanding sacrifice of him and you." (T-26.I.4:1-2)

"Those who would see the witness to truth instead of to illusion merely ask that they might see a purpose in the world that gives it sense and makes it meaningful." (T-26.I.5:1)

"No instant passes here in which your brother's holiness cannot be seen, to add a limitless supply to every meager scrap and tiny crumb of happiness that you allot yourself." (T-26.I.5:4)

"You can lose sight of oneness, but can not make sacrifice of its reality." (T-26.I.6:1)

"You who would make a sacrifice of life, and make your eyes and ears bear witness to the death of God and of His holy Son, think not that you have power to make of Them what God willed not They be. In Heaven, God's Son is not imprisoned in a body, nor is sacrificed in solitude to sin. And as he is in Heaven, so must he be eternally and everywhere." (T-26.I.7:3-5)

"God's justice rests in gentleness upon His Son, and keeps him safe from all injustice the world would lay upon him." (T-26.I.8:1)

"What is the Holy Spirit's special function but to release the holy Son of God from the imprisonment he made to keep himself from justice? Could your function be a task apart and separate from His Own?" (T-26.I.8:5-6)

In summary, Chapter 26 – I: "The "Sacrifice" of Oneness" is saying:
Many fear their return to Oneness, not always consciously and in many ways. The fear stems from the basic belief that we will be swallowed whole by the majestic All That Is, destined to disappear into a greater Self, "sacrificing" our individual personality in exchange for Oneness.

To all who fear this, I can only respectfully say; what part of God's Word, that we are created as eternal beings, is so difficult to accept and trust? By God's own definition, we will never cease to exist. We will be added to, but not diminished or erased. If a puzzle piece is fit into the larger whole, does it cease to exist as a distinguishable piece? No. It has merely become one with the total picture, while simultaneously remaining as itself. We too, are like puzzle pieces, designed to fit together within a Oneness our ego cannot conceive. Nothing can change the state of our oneness though we can be deceived and dream we are bodies. But with such a dream, you will "sacrifice" the knowing of our Oneness.

II. Many Forms; One Correction

"It is not so difficult to understand the reasons why you do not ask the Holy Spirit to solve all problems for you. He has not greater difficulty in resolving some than others. Every problem is the same to Him, because each one is solved in just the same respect and through the same approach." (T-26.II.1:1-3)

"It serves no purpose to attempt to solve it in a special form. It will recur and then recur again and yet again, until it has been answered for all time and will not rise again in any form. And only then are you released from it." (T-26.II.1:6-8)

"The Holy Spirit offers you release from every problem that you think you have. They are the same to Him because each one, regardless of the form it seems to take, is a demand that someone suffer loss and make a sacrifice that you might gain. And when the situation is worked out so no one loses is the problem gone, because it was an error in perception that now has been corrected." (T-26.II.2:1-3)

CHAPTER 26 — THE TRANSITION

"This one mistake, in any form, has one correction." (T-26.II.3:1)

"You have no problems, though you think you have." (T-26.II.3:3)

"The miracle of justice can correct all errors. Every problem is an error." (T-26.II.4:1-2)

"You who believe it safe to give but some mistakes to be corrected while you keep the others to yourself, remember this: Justice is total. There is no such thing as partial justice. If the Son of God is guilty then is he condemned, and he deserves no mercy from the God of justice. But ask not God to punish him because you find him guilty and would have him die." (T-26.II.5:1-4)

"If God is just, then can there be no problems that justice cannot solve." (T-26.II.6:1)

"Consider once again your special function. One is given you to see in him his perfect sinlessness." (T-26.II.6:5-6)

"The miracle of justice you call forth will rest on you as surely as on him." (T-26.II.6:8)

"Think, then, how great your own release will be when you are willing to receive correction for all your problems." (T-26.II.7:1)

"Sacrifice is gone. And in its place the Love of God can be remembered, and will shine away all memory of sacrifice and loss." (T-26.II.7:6-7)

"Your special function opens wide the door beyond which is the memory of His Love kept perfectly intact and undefiled." (T-26.II.8:4)

"For it is not your Father's Will that you should offer or receive less than He gave, when He created you in perfect love." (T-26.II.8:6)

In summary, Chapter 26 – II: "Many Forms; One Correction" is saying:

All of our problems stem from thinking we are separate bodies. Think of one problem that you have, that does not involve either the needs of your own body, or that of someone else's. When we are not at peace, it is always due to something we wish was different in our *bodily* life. Our problems take many forms, but there is only one problem, and therefore, one correction: See no one as a body. Of *yourself*, you cannot look on anyone and see beyond the body, but the Holy Spirit *can*. You allow Him to do this, through your one function: Forgiveness. Allow Him to look on all as sinless or "bodiless." In this, is all sacrifice (the seeing of suffering bodies) gone. In the open space created in your mind through forgiveness, the memory of God's Love will return. Forgive the many forms of bodies and their problems through knowing this is not our true identity. Forgive the many forms of problems you see with this one Correction.

III. The Borderland

"Complexity is not of God. How could it be, when all He knows is one?" (T-26.III.1:1-2)

"Nothing conflicts with oneness." (T-26.III.1:4)

"There is a borderland of thought that stands between this world and Heaven." (T-26.III.2:1)

"Here is the meeting place where thoughts are brought together; where conflicting values meet and all illusions are laid down beside the truth, where they are judged to be untrue. This borderland is just beyond the gate of Heaven." (T-26.III.2:3-4)

"This is the journey's end. We have referred to it as the real world." (T-26.III.3:1-2)

"Nothing the Son of God believes can be destroyed. But what is truth to him must be brought to the last comparison that he will ever make; the last evaluation that will be possible, the final judgment upon this world. It is the judgment of the truth upon illusion, of knowledge on perception: "It has no meaning, and does not exist."'" (T-26.III.4:1-3)

"Salvation stops just short of Heaven, for only perception needs salvation." (T-26.III.5:1)

"Yet who can make a choice between the wish for Heaven and the wish for hell unless he recognizes they are not the same? This difference is the learning goal this course has set." (T-26.III.5:3-4)

"There is no basis for a choice in this complex and overcomplicated world. For no one understands what is the same, and seems to choose where no choice really is." (T-26.III.6:1-2)

"Is not this like your special function, where the separation is undone by change of purpose in what once was specialness, and now is union? All illusions are but one. And in the recognition this is so lies the ability to give up all attempts to choose between them, and to make them different." (T-26.III.7:1-3)

CHAPTER 26—THE TRANSITION

"No sacrifice is possible in the relinquishment of an illusion recognized as such. Where all reality has been withdrawn from what was never true, can it be hard to give it up, and choose what *must* be true?" (T-26.III.7:6-7)

In summary, Chapter 26 – III: "The Borderland" is saying:
The borderland is the state of mind we enter, just before our full realization of our Oneness in God. It is a place of deep acceptance of the truth: this world is not real. None of it. And we are no longer trying to hold onto any single part of it to the point of pain and suffering. We have let go of our relationships; the need to control them is gone. We have let go of our money and possessions; the need to control wealth and property is gone. We have let go of our health; the need to control our body is gone. We rest in peace knowing that only good can come to us, and we act within this world only if it comes from a place of love. All illusions have been laid down; all complexity is seen as part of the same dream. We are awake. We see this world and all it contains and understand it is not the truth. Being in the borderland is to have truly forgiven all forms you see. It is the relinquishment of illusion for truth. We have ceased trying to control the dream through wishing it was different, and instead, we recognize it for the nothingness it is. The borderland is where dreams have been laid aside at last, and Heaven is just ahead.

IV. Wherez Sin Has Left

"Forgiveness is this world's equivalent of Heaven's justice. It translates the world of sin into a simple world, where justice can be reflected from beyond the gate behind which total lack of limits lies." (T-26.IV.1:1-2)

"Forgiveness always rests upon the one who offers it, until he sees himself as needing it no more." (T-26.IV.1:7)

"Forgiveness turns the world of sin into a world of glory, wonderful to see." (T-26.IV.2:1)

"There is no sadness and there is no parting here, for everything is totally forgiven. And what has been forgiven must join, for nothing stands between to keep them separate and apart." (T-26.IV.2:3-4)

"The holy place on which you stand is but the space that sin has left. And here you see the face of Christ, arising in its place." (T-26.IV.T-26.IV.3:1-2)

"Here the Son of God Himself comes to receive each gift that brings him nearer to his home. Not one is lost, and none is cherished more than any other." (T-26.IV.T-26.IV.4:2-3)

"Where sin once was perceived will rise a world that will become an altar to the truth, and you will join the lights of Heaven there, and sing their song of gratitude and praise." (T-26.IV.5:1-2)

"How little is the hindrance that withholds the wealth of Heaven from you. And how great will be the joy in Heaven when you join the mighty chorus to the Love of God!" (T-26.IV.6:2-3)

In summary, Chapter 26 – IV: "Where Sin Has Left" is saying:
Remember that the word "sin" is interchangeable with the word "separation." When the idea of separation has left us, there can be only an experience of union. These are the only two states we can perceive: separation or union. And only one is true. The words "forgiveness" and "justice" are also interchangeable because they both stand for overlooking what is separate and seeing only union in its place. It is truly "just" to give God's love equally and to all. All are deserving because to deny God's love to any part, is to deny love to a part of your One Self. And so, forgiveness (or justice), is to see union and turns the world of sin (separation) into a "world of glory, wonderful to see." There is no sadness, and there is no parting in this new world, because even in death, we are still one. Where once we perceived sin (separation), there will rise a world that will reflect only the truth of our Oneness. How little separates us! Just a mere change in thought and we are free of sin (separation). Where sin (separation) has left our mind, we will experience the total joy of our Union.

V. The Little Hindrance

"A little hindrance can seem large indeed to those who do not understand that miracles are all the same. Yet teaching that is what this course is for. This is its only purpose, for only that is all there is to learn." (T-26.V.1:1-3)

"All learning is a help or hindrance to the gate of Heaven." (T-26.V.1:5)

"There are but two teachers only, who point in different ways." (T-26.V.1:7)

"You but choose whether to go toward Heaven, or away to nowhere. There is nothing else to choose. (T-26.V.1:11-12)

"Nothing is ever lost but time, which in the end is meaningless. For it is but a little hindrance to eternity, quite meaningless to the real

CHAPTER 26—THE TRANSITION

Teacher of the world." (T-26.V.2:1-2)

"God gave His Teacher to replace the one you made, not to conflict with it. And what He would replace has been replaced. Time lasted but an instant in your mind, with no effect upon eternity." (T-26.V.3:1-3)

"The tiny tick of time in which the first mistake was made, and all of them within that one mistake, held also the Correction for that one, and all of them that came within the first." (T-26.V.3:5)

"To you who still believe you live in time and know not it is gone, the Holy Spirit still guides you through the infinitely small and senseless maze you still perceive in time, though it has long since gone." (T-26.V.4:1)

"The tiny instant you would keep and make eternal, passed away in Heaven too soon for anything to notice it had come." (T-26.V.5:1)

"Yet in each unforgiving act or thought, in every judgment and in all belief in sin, is that one instant still called back, as if it could be made again in time. You keep an ancient memory before your eyes. And he who lives in memories alone is unaware of where he is." (T-26.V.5:5-7)

"Forgiveness is the great release from time. It is the key to learning that the past is over." (T-26.V.6:1-2)

"For what has been undone no longer is." (T-26.V.6:5)

"Is this a hindrance to the place whereon he stands?" (T-26.V.7:1)

"And how much can his own illusions about time and place effect a change in where he really is?" (T-26.V.7:3)

"And do you want that fearful instant kept, when Heaven seemed to disappear and God was feared and made a symbol of your hate?" (T-26.V.8:4)

"Forget the time of terror that has been so long ago corrected and undone." (T-26.V.9:1)

"You cannot lose your way because there is no way but His, and nowhere can you go except to Him." (T-26.V.9:8)

"Would God allow His Son to lose his way along a road long since a memory of time gone by? This course will teach you only what is now." (T-26.V.10:1-2)

"The Son whom God created is as free as God created him." (T-26.V.11:1)

"Each day, and every minute in each day, and every instant that each minute holds, you but relive the single instant when the time of terror took the place of love." (T-26.V.13:1)

"Forgive the past and let it go, for it is gone." (T-26.V.14:1)

"There is no hindrance to the Will of God, nor any need that you repeat again a journey that was over long ago. Look gently on your brother, and behold the world in which perception of your hate has been transformed into a world of love." (T-26.V.14:4-5)

In summary, Chapter 26 – V: "The Little Hindrance" is saying:
We made but one mistake in thinking; that we could ever be separate from God and one another. And there is but one hindrance to correcting this mistake; that we believe the world we made through our mistaken thought is real. Forgive the first mistake and you have forgiven the world. When clearly stated, the process to returning to Heaven seems simple; merely a "little hindrance." Yet when faced with a world of seeming pain and suffering at every turn, such "a little hindrance can seem large indeed." Yet we are provided the answer and have the freedom to choose to apply it to the world. We can choose forgiveness. Forgiveness is the great release from time and therefore our mistake. To forgive is to release all ego-thoughts. To forgive is to free your mind from the world of form and time and allow it to rest in God's eternal peace. Do you want to keep reliving that fearful instant where you thought yourself separated from God and All That Is? Then let go of the past. For when our minds dwell on what has been done, we keep the past alive, here in the present. We have the power to choose to let all things go. Therefore, look with love on all whom you see or think of, and know there is no hindrance to your perception of Oneness.

VI. The Appointed Friend

"Anything in this world that you believe is good and valuable and worth striving for can hurt you, and will do so. Not because it has the power to hurt, but just because you have denied it is but an illusion, and made it real." (T-26.VI.1:1-2)

"All belief in sin, in power of attack, in hurt and harm, in sacrifice and death, has come to you. For no one can make one illusion real, and still escape the rest." (T-26.VI.1:6-7)

CHAPTER 26—THE TRANSITION

"Lead not your little life in solitude, with one illusion as your only friend." (T-26.VI.2:1)

"Yet God has given him a better Friend, in Whom all power in earth and Heaven rests." (T-26.VI.2:3)

"Make no illusion friend, for if you do, it can but take the place of Him Whom God has called your Friend. And it is He Who is your only Friend in truth. He brings you gifts that are not of this world, and only He to Whom they have been given can make sure that you receive them. He will place them on your throne, when you make room for Him on His." (T-26.VI.3:3-6)

In summary, Chapter 26 – VI: "The Appointed Friend" is saying:
Do not "make friends" with the ego and its desires; beware its false promises. The world you see holds nothing that you want, though it may tempt you to believe it can provide the peace and happiness you seek. This does not mean we cannot enjoy the world! In fact, we are told that we will enjoy the world with immense love once we have forgiven it. But in order to get there, we have to follow only our one true appointed Friend, the Voice of the Holy Spirit within us. To allow Him to guide us, we must clear our inner altar of all feelings of striving, want, and need of anything we think the world of form can provide us. This allows our spiritual gifts to be placed on the inner altar of our mind, the healing gifts of love and peace from the Holy Spirit, our appointed Friend.

VII. The Laws of Healing

"This is a course in miracles. As such, the laws of healing must be understood before the purpose of the course can be accomplished. Let us review the principles that we have covered, and arrange them in a way that summarizes all that must occur for healing to be possible." (T-26.VII.1:1-3)

"All sickness comes from separation. When the separation is denied, it goes. For it is gone as soon as the idea that thought it has been healed, and been replaced by sanity." (T-26.VII.2:1-3)

"Guilt asks for punishment, and its request is granted. Not in truth, but in the world of shadows and illusions built on sin." (T-26.VII.3:1-2)

"Yet is truth unchanged. It cannot be perceived but only known." (T-26.VII.3:5-6)

VII. The Laws of Healing

"Yet has God given answer to the world of sickness, which applies to all its forms." (T-26.VII.4:2)

"It is in this world, but not a part of it." (T-26.VII.4:4)

"God's answer lies where the belief in sin must be, for only there can its effects be utterly undone and without cause. Perception's laws must be reversed, because they are reversals of the laws of truth." (T-26.VII.5:1-2)

"It is impossible that one illusion be less amenable to truth than are the rest. But it is possible that some are given greater value, and less willingly offered to truth for healing and for help." (T-26.VII.6:1-2)

"And truth needs no defense to make it true." (T-26.VII.8:2)

"Forgiveness is the only function here, and serves to bring the joy this world denies to every aspect of God's Son where sin was thought to rule." (T-26.VII.8:5)

"Forgiveness takes away what stands between your brother and yourself. It is the wish that you be joined with him, and not apart." (T-26.VII.9:1-2)

"Yet is this wish in line with Heaven's state, and not in opposition to God's Will." (T-26.VII.9:4)

"Salvation, perfect and complete, asks but a little wish that what is true be true; a little willingness to overlook what is not there; a little sigh that speaks for Heaven as a preference to this world that death and desolation seem to rule. In joyous answer will creation rise within you, to replace the world you see with Heaven, wholly perfect and complete. What is forgiveness but a willingness that truth be true?" (T-26.VII.10:1-3)

"What is the Will of God? He wills His Son have everything." (T-26.VII.11:1-2)

"Let us consider what the error is, so it can be corrected, not protected." (T-26.VII.12:1)

"God wills you learn what always has been true: that He created you as part of Him, and this must still be true because ideas leave not their source." (T-26.VII.13:2)

"In every miracle all healing lies, for God gave answer to them all as one. And what is one to Him must be the same." (T-26.VII.15:4-5)

CHAPTER 26—THE TRANSITION

"His Kingdom is united; thus it was created, and thus will it ever be." (T-26.VII.15:8)

"The miracle but calls your ancient Name, which you will recognize because the truth is in your memory." (T-26.VII.16:1)

"Forgiveness is the answer to attack of any kind." (T-26.VII.17:2)

"To use the power God has given you as He would have it used is natural." (T-26.VII.18:1)

"But it is arrogant to lay aside the power that He gave, and choose a little senseless wish instead of what He wills." (T-26.VII.18:3)

"Abide in peace, where God would have you be." (T-26.VII.19:1)

"There is no difference among the Sons of God. The unity that specialness denies will save them all, for what is one can have no specialness." (T-26.VII.19:5-6)

"No wishes lie between a brother and his own." (T-26.VII.19:8)

"A miracle can make no change at all. But it can make what always has been true be recognized by those who know it not; and by this little gift of truth but let to be itself, the Son of God allowed to be himself, and all creation freed to call upon the Name of God as one." (T-26.VII.20:4-5)

In summary, Chapter 26 – VII: "The Laws of Healing" is saying:
There are laws, or rules to be followed when being healed. One law being, that healing begins in the mind, for it is our *thoughts* that govern what we experience. You know this is true; some experiences give people a wonderful thrill, while others are terrified by the exact same experience. The only difference between them, is what the mind perceived the experience to be. Therefore, it can be understood that all sickness comes from the *idea* of separation. If we were not separated bodies, but still knew our Oneness in God, sickness (or separation) would be impossible. The answer to our healing then, must be in our mind, where the idea of separation (or sickness) originated. The idea of forgiveness is the remedy to sickness. The thought of forgiveness (or Oneness) heals or corrects the idea of sickness because it is the opposite of separation. Forgiveness is the answer to our attack on the truth of our unity in God, for forgiveness is to wish for the experience of our oneness instead of separation. Such is the law of healing; first we must heal our own mind, then the world will follow.

VIII. The Immediacy of Salvation

"The one remaining problem that you have is that you see an interval between the time when you forgive, and will receive the benefits of trusting in your brother." (T-26.VIII.1:1)

"If it has been projected beyond your mind you think of it as time. The nearer it is brought to where it is, the more you think of it in terms of space." (T-26.VIII.1:4-5)

"There is a distance you would keep apart from your brother, and this space you perceive as time because you still believe you are external to him." (T-26.VIII.2:1)

"From this perception you cannot conceive of gaining what forgiveness offers now." (T-26.VIII.2:5)

"Salvation is immediate." (T-26.VIII.3:1)

"Salvation would wipe out the space you see between you still, and let you instantly become as one." (T-26.VIII.3:4)

"If you would keep a little space between you and your brother still, you then would want a little time in which forgiveness is withheld a little while." (T-26.VIII.3:8)

"Yet space between you and your brother is apparent only in the present, now, and cannot be perceived in future time." (T-26.VIII.4:1)

"A future cause as yet has no effects." (T-26.VIII.4:6)

"The plans you make for safety all are laid within the future, where you cannot plan. No purpose has been given it as yet, and what will happen has as yet no cause." (T-26.VIII.5:1-2)

"And in overlooking this, is it protected and kept separate from healing. For a miracle is now. It stands already here, in present grace, within the only interval of time that sin and fear have overlooked, but which is all there is to time." (T-26.VIII.5:7-9)

"The working out of all correction takes no time at all. Yet the acceptance of the working out can seem to take forever." (T-26.VIII.6:1-2)

"And you seek to be content with sighing, and with "reasoning" you do not understand it now, but will some day." (T-26.VIII.7:6)

"This is not reason, for it is unjust, and clearly hints at punishment until the time of liberation is at hand." (T-26.VIII.7:8)

CHAPTER 26 — THE TRANSITION

"This is the sacrifice of now, which could not be the cost the Holy Spirit asks for what He gave without a cost at all." (T-26.VIII.7:10)

"Be not content with future happiness." (T-26.VIII.9:1)

"Delay is senseless, and the "reasoning" that would maintain effects of present cause must be delayed until a future time, is merely a denial of the fact that consequence and cause must come as one." (T-26.VIII.9:6)

"The Holy Spirit's purpose now is yours. Should not His happiness be yours as well?" (T-26.VIII.9:9-10)

In summary, Chapter 26 – VIII: "The Immediacy of Salvation" is saying:

All thoughts that have to do with future events, are considered to exist only in *time*. Once the anticipated event arrives, it is considered to be happening in *physical space*—happening in the here and now. This is the delay we see between what we think and what we experience. Yet, the Holy Spirit tells us there is no need for such a delay when it comes to our salvation—our experience of Oneness. All miracles happen only *now*. And therefore, our happiness, being tied to miracles, can only be experienced *now* also. The miracle forgiveness brings is not a future event, though we can delay it for as long as we choose to. The Holy Spirit's purpose is to bring our thoughts into the present, rather than continue to project them into the future. He does this through forgiveness; seeing us as we are in truth, *now*. Right now, in this present moment, we exist as God created us. We are One Self. We rest in the peace of God's Love. We should not trouble our minds with the thoughts of the ego, that continuously revolve around its wishes and plans for the future. All such thoughts are ego "delay tactics" that keep us from our peace *now*. All such thoughts are an attempt to keep the immediacy of our salvation hidden from our awareness.

IX. For They Have Come

"Think but how holy you must be from whom the Voice for God calls lovingly unto your brother, that you may awake in him the Voice that answers to your call! And think how holy he must be when in him sleeps your own salvation, with his freedom joined! However much you wish he be condemned, God is in him. And never will you know He is in you as well while you attack His chosen home, and battle with His host. Regard him gently. Look with loving eyes on him who car-

IX. For They Have Come

ries Christ within him, that you may behold his glory and rejoice that Heaven is not separate from you." (T-26.IX.1:1-6)

"Forget not that a shadow held between your brother and yourself obscures the face of Christ and memory of God. And would you trade them for an ancient hate?" (T-26.IX.2:2-3)

"What was a place of death has now become a living temple in a world of light. Because of Them. It is Their Presence which has lifted holiness again to take its ancient place upon an ancient throne. Because of Them have miracles sprung up as grass and flowers on the barren ground that hate had scorched and rendered desolate." (T-26.IX.3:2-5)

"When They come, time's purpose is fulfilled. What never was passes to nothingness when They have come." (T-26.IX.4:2-3)

"For They have come to gather in Their Own." (T-26.IX.5:2)

"The holiest of all the spots on earth is where an ancient hatred has become a present love. And They come quickly to the living temple, where a home for Them has been set up. There is no place in Heaven holier." (T-26.IX.6:1-3)

"Your footprints lighten up the world, for where you walk forgiveness gladly goes with you." (T-26.IX.7:2)

"An ancient miracle has come to bless and to replace an ancient enmity that came to kill." (T-26.IX.8:5)

"Now is the Holy Spirit's purpose done. For They have come! For They have come at last!" (T-26.IX.8:7-9)

In summary, Chapter 26 – IX: "For They Have Come" is saying:
Who are "They?" We are told the answer in the first paragraph. "They" are the part of our mind that contains the Voice for God—the Holy Spirit—along with our own spirit, as well as that of our brother's. "They" are the unified part of "Us" Who resides in perfect peace within God's Love. "They" are actually "We." And when "They have come," it is the arrival of our understanding of the truth of our existence within this Holy Trinity—a holy union between ourselves (as part of God's One Son), God and the Holy Spirit. When "They have come," is the moment we see the light of Christ within all our brethren. We will *know* It is there, despite the bodies we may still see with our eyes. It is the time of our realization of Oneness with all people and All Creation. This

CHAPTER 26—THE TRANSITION

is time's purpose; to arrive at this state of awakened knowing. We will at long last be aware of Who lives within us. This state of mind is brought forward through our forgiveness; our overlooking of what we see now as separate from us. And then the ancient hatred—the ancient seeing of separation—will pass. And They will have come, at long last, into our full awareness of Unity.

X. The End of Injustice

"What, then, remains to be undone for you to realize Their Presence? Only this; you have a differential view of when attack is justified, and when you think it is unfair and not to be allowed. When you perceive it as unfair, you think that a response of anger now is just." (T-26.X.1:1-3)

"If it occurs at all it will be total. And in its presence, in whatever form, will hide Their Presence." (T-26.X.1:6-7)

"What does it mean if you perceive attack in certain forms to be unfair to you?" (T-26.X.2:1)

"Unfairness and attack are one mistake, so firmly joined that where one is perceived the other must be seen. You cannot be unfairly treated. The belief you are is but another form of the idea you are deprived by someone not yourself." (T-26.X.3:1-3)

"Beware the temptation to perceive yourself unfairly treated." (T-26.X.4:1)

"You think your brother is unfair to you because you think that one must be unfair to make the other innocent." (T-26.X.5:1)

"The Holy Spirit's purpose is to let the Presence of your holy Guests be known to you." (T-26.X.5:4)

"And each unfairness that the world appears to lay upon you, you have laid on it by rendering it purposeless, without the function that the Holy Spirit sees." (T-26.X.5:7)

"And so you see yourself deprived of light, abandoned to the dark, unfairly left without a purpose in a futile world." (T-26.X.6:3)

"If you perceive injustice anywhere, you need but say:

By this do I deny the Presence of the Father and the Son. And I would rather know of Them than see injustice, which Their Presence shines away." (T-26.X.6:5-7)

X. The End of Injustice

In summary, Chapter 26 – X: "The End of Injustice" is saying:

If God's justice is love, then injustice is a lack of love. When we feel the need to retaliate or act with anger towards anyone, we are reacting to their ego with ours. We are not remembering the truth of Who They Are. In this state of forgetting, we feel slighted, or unfairly treated by them, and then subsequently feel the need to "correct" their ego-based behavior with our own ego-based behavior. This cycle is endless. The only way out is to *choose not to feel unfairly treated*. This will end the injustice of the ego. For how can the ego be just to anyone, when all it sees is the illusion of bodies and what others say and do with them? When you refuse to allow the ego to judge others, you allow the light of truth to shine on them instead. Do not deny the presence of the Father and the Son—a Son with Whom you are a part—as well as everyone else. Remind yourself that you would rather know of Their Presence within anyone your ego finds fault, and They will step forward and shine away all that your ego is using to hide the truth from you. It will be the end of all forms of injustice (lack of love). Then our awareness can make the transition into God's Love.

CHAPTER 27
THE HEALING OF THE DREAM

I. The Picture of the Crucifixion

"The wish to be unfairly treated is a compromise attempt that would combine attack and innocence." (T-27.I.1:1)

"Walk you the gentle way, and you will fear no evil and no shadows in the night." (T-27.I.1:3)

"You cannot crucify yourself alone. And if you are unfairly treated, he must suffer the unfairness that you see. You cannot sacrifice yourself alone. For sacrifice is total." (T-27.I.1:5-8)

"In your release from sacrifice is his made manifest, and shown to be his own. But every pain you suffer do you see as proof that he is guilty of attack." (T-27.I.2:1-2)

"Whenever you consent to suffer pain, to be deprived, unfairly treated or in need of anything, you but accuse your brother of attack upon God's Son. You hold a picture of your crucifixion before his eyes, that he may see his sins are writ in Heaven in your blood and death, and go before him, closing off the gate and damning him to hell." (T-27.I.3:1-2)

"This sick and sorry picture you accept, if only it can serve to punish him." (T-27.I.4:4)

"Now in the hands made gentle by His touch, the Holy Spirit lays a picture of a different you. It is a picture of a body still, for what you really are cannot be seen nor pictured. Yet this one has not been used for purpose of attack, and therefore never suffered pain at all. It witnesses to the eternal truth that you cannot be hurt, and points beyond itself to both your innocence and his." (T-27.I.5:1-4)

"Attest his innocence and not his guilt." (T-27.I.6:1)

"Adornment of the body seeks to show how lovely are the witnesses for guilt. Concerns about the body demonstrate how frail and vulnerable is your life; how easily destroyed is what you love." (T-27.I.6:9-10)

"The strongest witness to futility, that bolsters all the rest and helps them paint the picture in which sin is justified, is sickness in whatever form it takes." (T-27.I.7:1)

"These are not sins, but witnesses unto the strange belief that sin and death are real, and innocence and sin will end alike within the termination of the grave. If this were true, there would be reason to remain content to seek for passing joys and cherish little pleasures where you can. Yet in this picture is the body not perceived as neutral and without a goal inherent in itself." (T-27.I.8:1-3)

"The Holy Spirit's picture changes not the body into something it is not. It only takes away from it all signs of accusation and of blamefulness." (T-27.I.9:3)

"No grounds are offered that it may be judged in any way at all." (T-27.I.9:6)

"Into this empty space, from which the goal of sin has been removed, is Heaven free to be remembered. Here its peace can come, and perfect healing take the place of death." (T-27.I.10:1-2)

"The simple way to let this be achieved is merely this; to let the body have no purpose from the past, when you were sure you knew its purpose was to foster guilt." (T-27.I.11:1)

"You do *not* know its purpose." (T-27.I.11:4)

"Let, then, its purpose and your function both be reconciled at last and seen as one." (T-27.I.11:7)

In summary, Chapter 27 – I: "The Picture of the Crucifixion" is saying:
We do not know what we truly do when we see ourselves as "crucified" or unfairly treated by others. We are upholding a false picture of ourselves and giving it the strength of reality—we are believing in what is untrue about ourself. Why would we do this? Why do we wish to believe we are so frail, that the Son of God (of Whom we are each a part) can be hurt by anything within a world of illusion? It is because we are listening to the ego, and the ego desires to reflect your pain and suffering back upon those whom you accuse of unfair treatment, that they may bear it instead of you. Thus, do you make yourself innocent, and they the "guilty" ones. It is the ego's way of punishing others—of trying to attack God. Yet the Holy Spirit asks us to see the world another way. The body is not for holding another guilty for their "crimes" against you. It is for release from such ego-imprisoning thoughts. Since the body is itself a symbol of our "guilty choice" to be separate from God, then the way to undo

CHAPTER 27 — THE HEALING OF THE DREAM

this choice is to cease to believe it is who we are. Cease to judge what bodies do and say to you, and you release them from your ego—you have forgiven them. You have relinquished your goal of "sin" or separation and allowed God's goal of peace and unity to replace it. Do not see the picture of the crucifixion of yourself, see instead God's Wholeness.

II. The Fear of Healing

"Is healing frightening? To many, yes. For accusation is a bar to love, and damaged bodies are accusers." (T-27.II.1:1-3)

"Who has been injured by his brother, and could love and trust him still?" (T-27.II.1:5)

"To forgive may be an act of charity, but not his due." (T-27.II.1:8)

"The unhealed cannot pardon." (T-27.II.2:1)

"They would retain the consequences of the guilt they overlook." (T-27.II.2:3)

"His pardon and your hurt cannot exist together." (T-27.II.2:9)

"To witness sin and yet forgive it is a paradox that reason cannot see. For it maintains what has been done to you deserves no pardon." (T-27.II.3:1-2)

"The sick remain accusers." (T-27.II.3:4)

"For no one in whom true forgiveness rests can suffer." (T-27.II.3:6)

"Who forgives is healed. And in his healing lies the proof that he has truly pardoned, and retains no trace of condemnation that he still would hold against himself or any living thing." (T-27.II.3:10-11)

"A miracle of healing proves that separation is without effect." (T-27.II.5:2)

"Your body can be a means to teach that it has never suffered pain because of him." (T-27.II.5:6)

"For here is his forgiveness proved to him." (T-27.II.5:9)

"So does your healing show your mind is healed, and has forgiven what he did not do." (T-27.II.6:2)

"Brother, there is no death." (T-27.II.6:8)

"How just are miracles! For they bestow an equal gift of full deliverance from guilt upon your brother and yourself." (T-27.II.7:1-2)

II. The Fear of Healing

"The "cost" of your serenity is his." (T-27.II.8:1)

"Who, then, fears healing? Only those to whom their brother's sacrifice and pain are seen to represent their own serenity." (T-27.II.9:1-2)

"The constant sting of guilt he suffers serves to prove that he is slave, but they are free." (T-27.II.9:4)

"Correction is not your function. It belongs to One Who knows of fairness, not of guilt. If you assume correction's role, you lose the function of forgiveness." (T-27.II.10:1-3)

"Identity and function are the same, and by your function do you know yourself." (T-27.II.10:6)

"In a split mind, identity must seem to be divided." (T-27.II.11:1)

"Correction, to a mind so split, must be a way to punish sins you think are yours in someone else. And thus does he become your victim, not your brother, different from you in that he is more guilty, thus in need of your correction, as the one more innocent than he." (T-27.II.11:3-4)

"Correction you would do must separate, because that is the function given it by you." (T-27.II.12:1)

"Your brother's sins become the central target for correction, lest your errors and his own be seen as one." (T-27.II.13:4)

"In this interpretation of correction, your own mistakes you will not even see. The focus of correction has been placed outside yourself, on one who cannot be a part of you while this perception lasts." (T-27.II.14:1-2)

"This is your brother, focus of your hate, unworthy to be part of you and thus outside yourself; the other half, which is denied." (T-27.II.14:4)

"Correction must be left to One Who knows correction and forgiveness are the same." (T-27.II.16:1)

"In His acceptance of this function lies the means whereby your mind is unified. His single purpose unifies the halves of you that you perceive as separate. And each forgives the other, that he may accept his other half as part of him." (T-27.II.16:5-7)

CHAPTER 27 — THE HEALING OF THE DREAM

In summary, Chapter 27 – II: "The Fear of Healing" is saying:

Healing means the healing of our mind—the healing of our idea of separation—from which all other forms of healing spring. Why would we fear this? Because it means the death of our ego. Think how difficult it is to simply "let someone off the hook" for something you perceive they have done wrong. Yet, it is only our ego that perceives wrongdoing, for the Holy Spirit knows we cannot be harmed. The body may be killed, but our *spirit* can never die. Even so, how do we come to terms with the vilest acts of humanity? The answer lies in our function of forgiveness. If our identity is our function, and our function is forgiveness, and forgiveness is "to overlook" the world of form or "to still our inner thoughts," about the world, then we must be the Stillness. Let go of all ego thoughts; any thoughts that have to do with bodies. Be still. And in that stillness know that God joins both you and all others in His quiet Love—despite what you may see going on outside of you. Let this idea rest in your mind, healing it of all thoughts of separation. You do not have to "like" or "accept" anything the body does. Just let go of your thoughts about it. And in this quiet state of mind, you will cease to fear the idea of letting go of separation. You will cease to fear your healing.

III. Beyond All Symbols

"Power cannot oppose. For opposition would weaken it, and weakened power is a contradiction in ideas." (T-27.III.1:1-2)

"Power is unopposed, to be itself." (T-27.III.1:5)

"Who can understand a double concept, such as "weakened power" or "hateful love?" (T-27.III.1:9)

"You have decided that your brother is a symbol for a "hateful love," a "weakened power," and above all, a "living death. And so he has no meaning to you, for he stands for what is meaningless." (T-27.III.2:1-2)

"Symbols which but represent ideas that cannot be must stand for empty space and nothingness." (T-27.III.2:6)

"The picture of your brother that you see means nothing." (T-27.III.3:1)

"The picture has been wholly canceled out, because it symbolized a contradiction that canceled out the thought it represents. And thus the picture has no cause at all." (T-27.III.3:3-4)

"Let, then, the empty space it occupies be recognized as vacant, and the

III. Beyond All Symbols

time devoted to its seeing be perceived as idly spent, a time unoccupied." (T-27.III.3:8)

"An empty space that is not seen as filled, an unused interval of time not seen as spent and fully occupied, become a silent invitation to the truth to enter, and to make itself at home." (T-27.III.4:1)

"For what you leave as vacant God will fill, and where He is there must the truth abide." (T-27.III.4:3)

"As nothingness cannot be pictured, so there is no symbol for totality. Reality is ultimately known without form, unpictured and unseen. Forgiveness is the means by which the truth is represented temporarily." (T-27.III.5:1-3)

"And what will ultimately take the place of every learning aid will merely be." (T-27.III.6:9)

"Forgiveness vanishes and symbols fade, and nothing that the eyes have ever seen or ears have heard remains to be perceived. A power wholly limitless has come, not to destroy, but to receive its own." (T-27.III.7:1-2)

"Give welcome to the power beyond forgiveness, and beyond the world of symbols and of limitations. He would merely be, and so He merely is." (T-27.III.7:8-9)

In summary, Chapter 27 – III: "Beyond All Symbols" is saying:
When we decided to become bodies, we became a symbol of our separation from God. Yet, such a symbol is a contradiction to the truth; we cannot separate from That Which Sustains us. If we could, we would cease to exist. Therefore, our bodies contradict what God would have us be, and thus such a form cancels itself out. We cannot be two things: separate and One at the same time. Only one can be true. Forgiveness undoes the contradiction of the symbol of our bodies. Forgiveness quietly looks beyond the world and all its forms of separation, knowing only our Unity is true. We are One, despite what our eyes may see. Do not be concerned that your eyes may still see bodies and the world. For forgiveness merely takes us to truth's doorstep. And in this vacant space—the space left open where all ego thoughts are still—God will write His truth upon your heart. Yet the new world that arises from the truth, cannot be seen with bodily eyes, for there is no symbol for Totality. And so, forgiveness is the means we use to go beyond all symbols.

CHAPTER 27 — THE HEALING OF THE DREAM

IV. The Quiet Answer

"In quietness are all things answered, and is every problem quietly resolved. In conflict there can be no answer and no resolution, for its purpose is to make no resolution possible, and to ensure no answer will be plain." (T-27.IV.1:1-2)

"You *are* in conflict." (T-27.IV.1:5)

"Yet if God gave an answer there must be a way in which your problems are resolved, for what He wills already has been done." (T-27.IV.1:7)

"Therefore, God must have given you a way of reaching to another state of mind in which the answer is already there. Such is the holy instant." (T-27.IV.2:3-4)

"Attempt to solve no problems but within the holy instant's surety. For there the problem will be answered and resolved. Outside there will be no solution, for there is no answer there that could be found." (T-27.IV.3:1-3)

"All questions asked within this world are but a way of looking, not a question asked. A question asked in hate cannot be answered, because it is an answer in itself." (T-27.IV.4:1-2)

"It is this: "Of these illusions, which of them is true? Which ones establish peace and offer joy? And which can bring escape from all the pain of which this world is made?" Whatever form the question takes, its purpose is the same. It asks but to establish sin as real, and answers in the form of preference." (T-27.IV.4:5-9)

"What can the body get that you would want the most of all?" (T-27.IV.4:13)

"Thus is all questioning within the world a form of propaganda for itself." (T-27.IV.5:3)

"An honest question is a learning tool that asks for something that you do not know." (T-27.IV.5:6)

"Only within the holy instant can an honest question honestly be asked." (T-27.IV.6:1)

"The questions of the world but ask of whom is sacrifice demanded, asking not if sacrifice is meaningful at all. And so, unless the answer tells "of whom," it will remain unrecognized, unheard, and thus the question is preserved intact because it gave the answer to itself. The holy instant is the interval in which the mind is still enough to hear an answer that is not entailed within the question asked." (T-27.IV.6:7-9)

"In the holy instant, you can bring the question to the answer, and receive the answer that was made for you." (T-27.IV.7:5)

In summary, Chapter 27 – IV: "The Quiet Answer" is saying:
At some point in our lives, we all ask, "Who am I?" The ego will gladly answer for you, making the false assumption that you are a body. And then next it will ask, "And which of the illusions of the world is best for my body?" The holy instant is the interval in which the ego's voice is still and you listen for a new and different answer, to a question not asked of your false self. To do this, you must erase the assumption you are a body. Clear this idea from your mind and allow the Holy Spirit to offer you something new—an answer you never dreamed of. The answer to the question, "Who am I?" is found not in wondering, "How can I make what I *think* I am, happy?" *You are not that thing.* But rather, ask yourself, "How can I learn Who I Am, so that I may know God." For then, the quiet Answer will tell you, "You are One Who is beloved of God Himself." Rejoice that you are not what your ego told you, you were. None of that is true. Only your holy Oneness with Perfection is your Identity. Accept this quiet Answer for everyone, and you are free.

V. The Healing Example

"The only way to heal is to be healed. The miracle extends without your help, but you are needed that it can begin." (T-27.V.1:1-2)

"No one can ask another to be healed. But he can let *himself* be healed, and thus offer the other what he has received." (T-27.V.1:6-7)

"No one is healed through double messages. If you wish only to be healed, you heal. Your single purpose makes this possible. But if you are afraid of healing, then it cannot come through you. The only thing that is required for a healing is a lack of fear." (T-27.V.2:4-8)

"The holy instant is the miracle's abiding place." (T-27.V.3:1)

"There is no sadness where a miracle has come to heal. And nothing more than just one instant of your love without attack is necessary that all this occur." (T-27.V.4:1-2)

"A dying world asks only that you rest an instant from attack upon

CHAPTER 27 — THE HEALING OF THE DREAM

yourself, that it be healed." (T-27.V.5:5)

"The holy instant's radiance will light your eyes, and give them sight to see beyond all suffering and see Christ's face instead." (T-27.V.6:5)

"Thus is your healing everything the world requires, that it may be healed. It needs one lesson that has perfectly been learned." (T-27.V.7:1-2)

"Problems are not specific but they take specific forms, and these specific shapes make up the world. And no one understands the nature of his problem." (T-27.V.8:1-2)

"The total transfer of your learning is not made by you. But that it has been made in spite of all the differences you see, convinces you that they could not be real." (T-27.V.8:10-11)

"Your healing will extend, and will be brought to problems that you thought were not your own." (T-27.V.9:1)

"Fear you not the way that you perceive them. You are wrong, but there is One within you Who is right." (T-27.V.9:5-6)

"Your part is merely to apply what He has taught you to yourself, and He will do the rest." (T-27.V.10:2)

"Peace to you to whom is healing offered. And you will learn that peace is given you when you accept the healing for yourself." (T-27.V.11:1-2)

"What occurred within the instant that love entered in without attack will stay with you forever." (T-27.V.11:4)

"Everywhere you go, will you behold its multiplied effects. Yet all the witnesses that you behold will be far less than all there really are. Infinity cannot be understood by merely counting up its separate parts. God thanks you for your healing, for He knows it is a gift of love unto His Son, and therefore is it given unto Him." (T-27.V.11:6-9)

In summary, Chapter 27 – V: "The Healing Example" is saying:
We are told that the only way we can heal others, is to be healed ourselves. The only thing we need to have healed, is the false idea about who we are. Heal the idea of our separation from one another, and you heal the entire dream. However, total transfer of healing from yourself to the entire illusion of this world is not done by us, but by God. Our part is only to let this idea become truly *believed* by us. Then, everywhere we go, we will behold only Unity with our seemingly separated brethren. And yet, even more than these separate parts

are healed. Our healing will extend into infinity—to all creation—even to that which is currently unknown to us. Therefore, let our "single purpose" be to love one another as Christ has loved us. Do not fear to do this, for in this way, we follow the healing example already given us.

VI. The Witnesses to Sin

"Pain demonstrates the body must be real. It is a loud, obscuring voice whose shrieks would silence what the Holy Spirit says, and keep His words from your awareness. Pain compels attention, drawing it away from Him and focusing upon itself. Its purpose is the same as pleasure, for they both are means to make the body real." (T-27.VI.1:1-4)

"Sin shifts from pain to pleasure, and again to pain. For either witness is the same, and carries but one message: "You are here, within this body, and you can be hurt. You can have pleasure, too, but only at the cost of pain."" (T-27.VI.2:1-3)

"Call pleasure pain, and it will hurt. Call pain a pleasure, and the pain behind the pleasure will be felt no more." (T-27.VI.2:7-8)

"This body, purposeless within itself, holds all your memories and all your hopes. You use its eyes to see, its ears to hear, and let it tell you what it is it feels. *It does not know.*" (T-27.VI.3:1-3)

"God's Witness sees no witnesses against the body." (T-27.VI.4:1)

"He knows it is not real." (T-27.VI.4:3)

"Each miracle He brings is witness that the body is not real. Its pains and pleasures does He heal alike, for all sin's witnesses do His replace." (T-27.VI.4:8-9)

"The miracle makes no distinctions in the names by which sin's witnesses are called. It merely proves that what they represent has no effects." (T-27.VI.5:1-2)

"It matters not the name by which you called your suffering. It is no longer there. The One Who brings the miracle perceives them all as one, and called by name of fear." (T-27.VI.5:4-6)

"Love, too, has symbols in a world of sin. The miracle forgives because it stands for what is past forgiveness and is true." (T-27.VI.6:1-2)

"It is their sameness that the miracle attests. It is their sameness that it proves." (T-27.VI.6:7-8)

CHAPTER 27 — THE HEALING OF THE DREAM

"And God Himself has guaranteed the strength of miracles for what they witness to." (T-27.VI.6:11)

"Be you then witness to the miracle, and not the laws of sin. There is no need to suffer any more. But there is need that you be healed, because the suffering and sorrow of the world have made it deaf to its salvation and deliverance." (T-27.VI.7:1-3)

"What better function could you serve than this? Be you healed that you may heal, and suffer not the laws of sin to be applied to you. And truth will be revealed to you who chose to let love's symbols take the place of sin." (T-27.VI.8:4-6)

In summary, Chapter 27 – VI: "The Witnesses to Sin" is saying:
Everything we see within this world of form, is a witness to sin—or rather, our separation. The body is the loudest voice for proclaiming our separation, in that it is what we are experiencing the world *through*. And yet, it's voice can change, depending on how we want to interpret it. We can feel pleasure, or we can feel pain, yet both feelings attest to the same thing: We are a body that can feel such things here in the world. And we feel through it to the exclusion of all else within us. For within, is another Voice; One Who would tell us otherwise. Let us then, choose not to hear the voice that speaks to us of everything outside our body, and shift our attention to the One within, Who attests to our holiness, our sameness in God. Let us witness to miracles by seeing all the witnesses to sin—separation—as all the same.

VII. The Dreamer of the Dream

"Suffering is an emphasis upon all that the world has done to injure you." (T-27.VII.1:1)

"Like to a dream of punishment, in which the dreamer is unconscious of what brought on the attack against himself, he sees himself attacked unjustly and by something not himself." (T-27.VII.1:3)

"Yet is his own attack upon himself apparent still, for it is he who bears the suffering. And he cannot escape because its source is seen outside himself." (T-27.VII.1:6-7)

"Now you are being shown you *can* escape. All that is needed is you look upon the problem as it is, and not the way that you have set it up." (T-27.VII.2:1-2)

VII. The Dreamer of the Dream

"No one has difficulty making up his mind to let a simple problem be resolved if it is seen as hurting him, and also very easily removed." (T-27.VII.2:6)

"The "reasoning" by which the world is made, on which it rests, by which it is maintained, is simply this: "*You* are the cause of what I do. Your presence justifies my wrath, and you exist and think apart from me." (T-27.VII.3:1-2)

"And so it seems as if there is no need to go beyond the obvious in terms of cause." (T-27.VII.3:7)

"There is indeed need." (T-27.VII.4:1)

"Vengeance must have a focus. Otherwise is the avenger's knife in his own hand, and pointed to himself." (T-27.VII.4:6-7)

"This is the purpose of the world he sees." (T-27.VII.5:1)

"Look, then, beyond effects. It is not here the cause of suffering and sin must lie." (T-27.VII.5:6-7)

"In separation from your brother was the first attack upon yourself begun. And it is this the world bears witness to." (T-27.VII.6:4-5)

"Once you were unaware of what the cause of everything the world appeared to thrust upon you, uninvited and unasked, must really be. Of one thing you were sure: Of all the many causes you perceived as bringing pain and suffering to you, your guilt was not among them. Nor did you in any way request them for yourself. This is how all illusions came about. The one who makes them does not see himself as making them, and their reality does not depend on him." (T-27.VII.7:3-7)

"No one can waken from a dream the world is dreaming for him." (T-27.VII.8:1)

"He cannot choose to waken from a dream he did not make." (T-27.VII.8:3)

"The choice is yours to make between a sleeping death and dreams of evil or a happy wakening and joy of life." (T-27.VII.9:4)

"What could you choose between but life or death, waking or sleeping, peace or war, your dreams or your reality?" (T-27.VII.10:1)

"Yet if the choice is really given you, then you must see the causes of the things you choose between exactly as they are and where they are." (T-27.VII.10:7)

CHAPTER 27 – THE HEALING OF THE DREAM

"The dreaming of the world is but a part of your own dream you gave away, and saw as if it were its start and ending, both." (T-27.VII.11:6)

"The little gap you do not even see, the birthplace of illusions and of fear, the time of terror and of ancient hate, the instant of disaster, all are here. Here is the cause of unreality. And it is here that it will be undone." (T-27.VII.12:4-6)

"You are the dreamer of the world of dreams. No other cause it has, nor ever will." (T-27.VII.13:1-2)

"It is not difficult to change a dream when once the dreamer has been recognized. Rest in the Holy Spirit, and allow His gentle dreams to take the place of those you dreamed in terror and in fear of death." (T-27.VII.14:2-3)

"The sleep is peaceful now, for these are happy dreams." (T-27.VII.14:8)

"Dream softly of your sinless brother, who unites with you in holy innocence. And from this dream the Lord of Heaven will Himself awaken His beloved Son." (T-27.VII.15:1-2)

"Forgive him his illusions, and give thanks to him for all the helpfulness he gave. And do not brush aside his many gifts because he is not perfect in your dreams." (T-27.VII.15:5-6)

"And let no pain disturb your dream of deep appreciation for his gifts to you." (T-27.VII.16:4)

In summary, Chapter 27 – VII: "The Dreamer of the Dream" is saying:

It is our tendency here in this world, to point the finger at someone else as the cause of our suffering. The truth is, we are responsible for how we feel. No one else can control that but us. And we can heal our suffering the instant we take responsibility for it. We do this, through admitting our suffering is our choice and it is caused entirely by our misperception of others. Would you still feel angry if you saw how another was but a part of you; without their body and sharing the same energy of Love from God? Would you still feel vengeance or mistreated by them, if you could see how their negative actions towards you were but a call for Love? We dream this world is real. And the only way to wake is by admitting we have chosen it for our own experience, our own lessons in forgiveness. Each person is simply playing their part perfectly for us, be they villain or lover. All is acted out so that we can learn how to see them differently; to dream a gentler dream of them. To waken then, we only have to see their innocence, their sinless or bodiless Light. As the dreamer of the dream, it is our sole responsibility to do so.

VIII. The "Hero" of the Dream

"The body is the central figure in the dreaming of the world." (T-27.VIII.1:1)

"It takes the central place in every dream, which tells the story of how it was made by other bodies, born into the world outside the body, lives a little while and dies, to be united in the dust with other bodies dying like itself." (T-27.VIII.1:3)

"The dreaming of the world takes many forms, because the body seeks in many ways to prove it is autonomous and real." (T-27.VIII.2:1)

"The body's serial adventures, from the time of birth to dying are the theme of every dream the world has ever had. The "hero" of this dream will never change, nor will its purpose." (T-27.VIII.3:1-2)

"Thus are you not the dreamer, but the dream. And so you wander idly in and out of places and events that it contrives. That this is all the body does is true, for it is but a figure in a dream. But who reacts to figures in a dream unless he sees them as if they were real? The instant that he sees them as they are they have no more effects on him, because he understands he gave them their effects by causing them and making them seem real." (T-27.VIII.4:1-5)

"How willing are you to escape effects of all the dreams the world has ever had?" (T-27.VIII.5:1)

"No one asleep and dreaming in the world remembers his attack upon himself. No one believes there really was a time when he knew nothing of a body, and could never have conceived this world as real." (T-27.VIII.5:4-5)

"How serious they now appear to be! And no one can remember when they would have met with laughter and with disbelief. We can remember this, if we but look directly at their cause. And we will see the grounds for laughter, not a cause for fear." (T-27.VIII.5:7-10)

"Into eternity, where all is one, there crept a tiny, mad idea, at which the Son of God remembered not to laugh. In his forgetting did the thought become a serious idea, and possible of both accomplishment and real

CHAPTER 27—THE HEALING OF THE DREAM

effects. Together, we can laugh them both away, and understand that time cannot intrude upon eternity." (T-27.VIII.6:2-4)

"The world you see depicts exactly what you thought you did." (T-27.VIII.7:2)

"It keeps you narrowly confined within a body, which it punishes because of all the sinful things the body does within its dream." (T-27.VIII.7:6)

"In gentle laughter does the Holy Spirit perceive the cause, and looks not to effects." (T-27.VIII.9:1)

"The secret of salvation is but this: that you are doing this unto yourself." (T-27.VIII.10:1)

"Whatever seems to be the cause of any pain and suffering you feel, this is still true." (T-27.VIII.10:4)

"This single lesson learned will set you free from suffering, whatever form it takes." (T-27.VIII.11:1)

"For this one answer takes away the cause of every form of sorrow and of pain." (T-27.VIII.11:4)

"And you will understand that miracles reflect the simple statement, 'I have done this thing, and it is this I would undo.'" (T-27.VIII.11:6)

"Bring, then, all forms of suffering to Him Who knows that every one is like the rest. He sees no differences where none exists, and He will teach you how each one is caused." (T-27.VIII.12:1-2)

"Salvation is a secret you have kept but from yourself." (T-27.VIII.12:4)

"How differently will you perceive the world when this is recognized! When you forgive the world your guilt, you will be free of it." (T-27.VIII.13:1-2)

"And it is this that has maintained you separate from the world, and kept your brother separate from you. Now need you but to learn that both of you are innocent or guilty. The one thing that is impossible is that you be unlike each other; that they both be true. This is the only secret yet to learn. And it will be no secret you are healed." (T-27.VIII.13:5-9)

VIII. The "Hero" of the Dream

In summary, Chapter 27 – VIII: "The "Hero" of the Dream" is saying:

In this dream we do not know we dream, we cast our bodies as the stars; the main characters we use to act out all our ego desires. Everything we think about, has the body at its center. When have our minds ever ceased to focus on it, or something related to its care and preservation? We think our dream of bodies and separation is real—the seriousness with which we respond to other bodies testifies to this. And yet, the Holy Spirit calls us to relinquish our tight hold on the idea of separation, giving in to a new thought: perhaps none of this is real? Perhaps we are doing this all to ourselves? Perhaps, we can dream a different dream? Once this single lesson is learned, salvation will soon follow. You will know that you have learned it by how you feel, for peace will overtake your mind, replacing all thoughts of attack, fear, and pain. Then you will truly be the "hero" of this dream, for you will have released (forgiven) all bodies you now think are separate from you, seeing them at long last as One with you in God's Love. Then, will the dream be healed.

CHAPTER 28
THE UNDOING OF FEAR

I. The Present Memory

"The miracle does nothing. All it does is to undo. And thus it cancels out the interference to what has been done. It does not add, but merely takes away. And what it takes away is long since gone, but being kept in memory appears to have immediate effects. This world was over long ago. The thoughts that made it are no longer in the mind that thought of them and loved them for a little while. The miracle but shows the past is gone, and what has truly gone has no effects. Remembering a cause can but produce illusions of its presence, not effects." (T-28.I.1:1-9)

"For guilt is over. In its passing went its consequences, left without a cause. Why would you cling to it in memory if you did not desire its effects?" (T-28.I.2:2-4)

"Nothing employed for healing represents an effort to do anything at all. It is a recognition that you have no needs which mean that something must be done. It is an unselective memory, that is not used to interfere with truth." (T-28.I.3:1-3)

"The Holy Spirit can indeed make use of memory, for God Himself is there. Yet this is not a memory of past events, but only of a present state. You are so long accustomed to believe that memory holds only what is past, that it is hard for you to realize it is a skill that can remember *now*." (T-28.I.4:1-3)

"The Holy Spirit's use of memory is quite apart from time. He does not seek to use it as a means to keep the past, but rather as a way to let it go." (T-28.I.5:1-2)

"Time neither takes away nor can restore." (T-28.I.6:3)

"No change can be made in the present if its cause is past. Only the past is held in memory as you make use of it, and so it is a way to hold the past against the now." (T-28.I.6:6-7)

"When ancient memories of hate appear, remember that their cause is gone." (T-28.I.7:3)

I. The Present Memory

"Be glad that it is gone, for this is what you would be pardoned from. And see, instead, the new effects of cause accepted now, with consequences here. They will surprise you with their loveliness. The ancient new ideas they bring will be the happy consequences of a Cause so ancient that It far exceeds the span of memory which your perception sees." (T-28.I.7:6-9)

"This is the Cause the Holy Spirit has remembered for you, when you would forget. It is not past because He let It not be unremembered. It has never changed, because there never was a time in which He did not keep It safely in your mind." (T-28.I.8:1-3)

"What *you* remember never was." (T-28.I.9:1)

"It can deserve but laughter, when you learn you have remembered consequences that were causeless and could never be effects. The miracle reminds you of a Cause forever present, perfectly untouched by time and interference." (T-28.I.9:3-4)

"He has not done the thing you fear. No more have you. And so your innocence has not been lost." (T-28.I.10:5-7)

"The miracle comes quietly into the mind that stops an instant and is still. It reaches gently from that quiet time, and from the mind it healed in quiet then, to other minds to share its quietness." (T-28.I.11:1-2)

"He to Whom time is given offers thanks for every quiet instant given Him. For in that instant is God's memory allowed to offer all its treasures to the Son of God, for whom they have been kept." (T-28.I.12:1-2)

"How instantly the memory of God arises in the mind that has no fear to keep the memory away!" (T-28.I.13:1)

"Now is the Son of God at last aware of present Cause and Its benign Effects." (T-28.I.14:1)

"And where is sacrifice, when memory of God has come to take the place of loss?" (T-28.I.15:2)

"He has built the bridge, and it is He Who will transport His Son across it. Have no fear that He will fail in what He wills. Nor that you be excluded from the Will that is for you." (T-28.I.15:7-9)

CHAPTER 28—THE UNDOING OF FEAR

In summary, Chapter 28 – I: "The Present Memory" is saying:

For us to regain our present memory; the memory of our present state of Union with God and each other—a state that has never changed—we must let go of all our past fears. This is something we can only do *now*, here in the present moment. What our minds are preoccupied with most of the time, are *past events*, those things that happened to us even just a few moments ago, be they "good" or "bad." We also equally fantasize about the future. The Holy Spirit would use our time differently if we simply chose to let Him. We let Him use our mind, when we let our mind be still, emptying it of all thoughts relating to the world, be it past or future. Is it a sacrifice to still our minds? We are not asked to maintain this state for hours or even minutes. All we are asked to do, is practice giving but a single, holy instant of mental quiet. And there, in that clear empty space of stillness, you will *feel* the essence of your own power—your Identity in God's Oneness. For only when your mind is still is the Holy Spirit free at last to restore to you, your present memory of Who You Are.

II. Reversing Effect and Cause

"Without a cause there can be no effects, and yet without effects there is no cause. The cause is made by its effects; the Father *is* a Father by His Son." (T-28.II.1:1-2)

"Fatherhood is creation. Love must be extended." (T-28.II.2:1-2)

"Yet must all healing come about because the mind is recognized as not within the body, and its innocence is quite apart from it, and where all healing is. Where, then, is healing? Only where its cause is given its effects. For sickness is a meaningless attempt to give effects to causelessness, and make it be a cause." (T-28.II.2:8-11)

"Always in sickness does the Son of God attempt to make himself his cause, and not allow himself to be his Father's Son." (T-28.II.3:1)

"The cause of healing is the only Cause of everything. It has but one Effect. And in that recognition, causelessness is given no effects and none is seen." (T-28.II.3:3-5)

"Nothing at all has happened but that you have put yourself to sleep, and dreamed a dream in which you were an alien to yourself, and but a part of someone else's dream. The miracle does not awaken you, but merely shows you who the dreamer is." (T-28.II.4:1-2)

II. Reversing Effect and Cause

"Do you wish for dreams of healing, or for dreams of death?" (T-28.II.4:4)

"But for this change in content of the dream, it must be realized that it is you who dreamed the dreaming that you do not like. It is an effect you have caused, and you would not be cause of this effect." (T-28.II.5:3-4)

"The miracle establishes you dream a dream, and that its content is not true. This is a crucial step in dealing with illusions. No one is afraid of them when he perceives he made them up. The fear was held in place because he did not see that he was the author of the dream, and not a figure in the dream." (T-28.II.7:1-4)

"The miracle does nothing but to show him that he has done nothing. What he fears is cause without the consequences that would make it cause. And so it never was." (T-28.II.7:10-12)

"In the dream, the dreamer made himself." (T-28.II.8:2)

"The miracle is the first step in giving back to cause the function of causation, not effect. For this confusion has produced the dream, and while it lasts will wakening be feared." (T-28.II.9:3-4)

"The miracle returns the cause of fear to you who made it." (T-28.II.11:1)

"The miracle is useless if you learn but that the body can be healed, for this is not the lesson it was sent to teach. The lesson is the mind was sick that thought the body could be sick; projecting out its guilt caused nothing, and had no effects." (T-28.II.11:6-7)

"The world is full of miracles. They stand in shining silence next to every dream of pain and suffering, of sin and guilt. They are the dream's alternative, the choice to be the dreamer, rather than deny the active role in making up the dream." (T-28.II.12:1-3)

"The body is released because the mind acknowledges "this is not done to me, but I am doing this." And thus the mind is free to make another choice instead. Beginning here, salvation will proceed to change the course of every step in the descent to separation, until all the steps have been retraced, the ladder gone, and all the dreaming of the world undone." (T-28.II.12:5-7)

CHAPTER 28—THE UNDOING OF FEAR

In summary, Chapter 28 – II: "Reversing Effect and Cause" is saying:
God is our First Cause, our Creator and Source. We did not create ourselves, yet our ego would have us believe this. Healing comes to our mind when we reverse our thinking. We are not a body, but the mind that invented the dream of being a body rather than an eternal creation of God. With our imagined fallibility as a body, we forgot our Eternal Self as God's Holy Son. When our mind became "sick" with this thought, we manifested physical sickness, the reflection of our new belief, our new identity as a weak, un-eternal body. Therefore, to heal this situation, we must heal it as its source: the mind. *We must change our mind about who we are.* Herein lies the miracle, for to recognize the mind is sick and not the body is the first step to restoring ourselves to our *right* mind. It is as simple as recognizing we are the cause of this dream of bodies, and no one else. Except, it is a false dream; an identity we cannot become in truth, for no one can undo what God has Created. Healing then, is but a mere reversal in thought—God is our Eternal Cause, and we are His Eternal Effect. Nothing else is true about us and we have nothing to fear.

III. The Agreement to Join

"What waits in perfect certainty beyond salvation is not our concern. For you have barely started to allow your first, uncertain steps to be directed up the ladder separation led you down. The miracle alone is your concern at present. Here is where we must begin. And having started, will the way be made serene and simple in the rising up to waking and the ending of the dream." (T-28.III.1:1-5)

"No mind is sick until another mind agrees that they are separate." (T-28.III.2:1)

"If you withhold agreement and accept the part you play in making sickness real, the other mind cannot project its guilt without your aid in letting it perceive itself as separate and apart from you." (T-28.III.2:3)

"Healing is the effect of minds that join, as sickness comes from minds that separate." (T-28.III.2:6)

"The miracle does nothing just *because* the minds are **joined, and cannot separate. Yet in the dreaming has this been reversed, and separate minds are seen as bodies, which are separated and which cannot join."** (T-28.III.3:1-2)

"The end of dreaming is the end of fear, and love was never in the world of dreams. The gap *is* little." (T-28.III.4:1-2)

"The purpose of the gap is all the cause that sickness has. For it was made to keep you separated, in a body which you see as if it were the cause of pain." (T-28.III.4:5-6)

"The cause of pain is separation, not the body, which is only its effect." (T-28.III.5:1)

"God builds the bridge, but only in the space left clean and vacant by the miracle." (T-28.III.6:1)

"And what are you who live within the world except a picture of the Son of God in broken pieces, each concealed within a separate and uncertain bit of clay?" (T-28.III.7:5)

"Be not afraid, my child, but let your world be gently lit by miracles." (T-28.III.8:1)

"The dream of healing in forgiveness lies, and gently shows you that you never sinned." (T-28.III.8:4)

"For love has set its table in the space that seemed to keep your Guests apart from you." (T-28.III.9:8)

In summary, Chapter 28 – III: "The Agreement to Join" is saying:
We "agree to join" with one another and God through the act of true forgiveness. Forgiveness is the act of "overlooking" the world of separate forms, including our bodies, and everything else seemingly outside of us. We do this, not by trying to close our eyes to the world or pretending it is not there, but rather, by going within. We must use our inner eyes to see—not our physical eyes. We do this through *feeling* by changing our *thinking*. When we look with our physical eyes, we first *think about* what we are looking at. But if instead, we first *feel* what we are looking at, we will feel our Oneness without physically seeing it. This is the miracle of knowing the truth without outside proof. "Seeing through feeling" is a way of looking at the world the ego is unable to do. And so, it the is way we give up our ego-projected reality and choose instead to know God's Reality. This is how we clear our inner altar of all thoughts of separation, for no gap is seen where only unity is *felt*. This is how we remember our agreement to join with God.

IV. The Greater Joining

"Accepting the Atonement for yourself means not to give support to someone's dream of sickness and of death. It means that you share not his wish to separate, and let him turn illusions on himself." (T-28.IV.1:1-2)

CHAPTER 28—THE UNDOING OF FEAR

"Refuse to be a part of fearful dreams whatever form they take, for you will lose identity in them." (T-28.IV.2:2)

"Thus you separate the dreamer from the dream, and join in one, but let the other go. The dream is but illusion in the mind. And with the mind you would unite, but never with the dream." (T-28.IV.2:5-7)

"Like you, your brother thinks he is a dream. Share not in his illusion of himself, for your Identity depends on his reality. Think, rather, of him as a mind in which illusions still persist, but as a mind which brother is to you." (T-28.IV.3:1-3)

"Therefore release him, merely by your claim on brotherhood, and not on dreams of fear." (T-28.IV.4:3)

"Be certain, if you do your part, he will do his, for he will join you where you stand. Call not to him to meet you in the gap between you, or you must believe that it is your reality as well as his. You cannot do his part, but this you *do* when you become a passive figure in his dreams, instead of dreamer of your own." (T-28.IV.5:1-3)

"The Holy Spirit is in both your minds, and He is One because there is no gap that separates His Oneness from Itself. The gap between your bodies matters not, for what is joined in Him is always one." (T-28.IV.7:1-2)

"The Holy Spirit's function is to take the broken picture of the Son of God and put the pieces into place again." (T-28.IV.8:1)

"I thank You, Father, knowing You will come to close each little gap that lies between the broken pieces of Your holy son." (T-28.IV.9:1)

"How holy is the smallest grain of sand, when it is recognized as being part of the completed picture of God's Son! The forms the broken pieces seem to take mean nothing. For the whole is in each one." (T-28.IV.9:4-6)

"But miracles are the result when you do not insist on seeing in the gap what is not there. Your willingness to let illusions go is all the Healer of God's Son requires. He will place the miracle of healing where the seeds of sickness were. And there will be no loss, but only gain." (T-28.IV.10:7-10)

V. The Alternate to Dreams of Fear

In summary, Chapter 28 – IV: "The Greater Joining" is saying:
Our greater joining is our realization of our part in God's Greater Whole—the picture of our Oneness. How is this realized? Let us remember we are each like a puzzle piece, a seemingly separate thing in and of ourselves. Yet is any puzzle complete with even one piece missing? And can the function of each piece be fulfilled except by becoming one with the whole picture? We are each ourselves and One at the same time. We have never separated from the greater puzzle picture, but we dream we have. We can only see our individual pieces. The miracle comes when we decide *not* to believe in our separation—even the grains of sand are one with us! There is no gap between *anything*. Know yourself as the dreamer of the dream. Watch it unfold but know that the separation you see in it is not the truth. And when you do this, God will replace what you see with a miracle of feeling Unity where once you thought there was a gap. You will experience the *feeling* of your greater joining with God and All Creation.

V. The Alternate to Dreams of Fear

"What is a sense of sickness but a sense of limitation? Of a splitting *off* and separating *from*? A gap that is perceived between you and your brother, and what is now seen as health? And so the good is seen to be outside; the evil, in." (T-28.V.1:1-4)

"It is the sharing of the evil dreams of hate and malice, bitterness and death, of sin and suffering and pain and loss, that makes them real." (T-28.V.2:1)

"You share no evil dreams if you forgive the dreamer, and perceive that he is not the dream he made." (T-28.V.3:1)

"Forgiveness separates the dreamer from the evil dream, and thus releases him." (T-28.V.3:3)

"What is there God created to be sick? And what that He created not can be? Let not your eyes behold a dream; your ears bear witness to illusion." (T-28.V.5:1-3)

"Yet are there other sounds and other sights that can be seen and heard and understood." (T-28.V.5:5)

"Creation proves reality because it shares the function all creation shares." (T-28.V.6:1)

CHAPTER 28 — THE UNDOING OF FEAR

"For it fills every place and every time, and makes them wholly indivisible." (T-28.V.6:6)

"You who believe there is a little gap between you and your brother, do not see that it is here you are as prisoners in a world perceived to be existing here. The world you see does not exist, because the place where you perceive it is not real." (T-28.V.7:1-2)

"Look at the little gap, and you behold the innocence and emptiness of sin that you will see within yourself, when you have lost the fear of recognizing love." (T-28.V.7:6)

In summary, Chapter 28 – V: "The Alternate to Dreams of Fear" is saying:
There is an alternate reality we can perceive—one not seen through the eyes of the ego, but rather, through the loving heart of the Holy Spirit. This shift in vision takes place through the process of forgiveness. Forgiveness is a state of awakened awareness; awareness of our role as the dreamer of our ego-world. Once we know we are projecting a vision of separation, we can change what we think, and thus change what we see. Do not see yourself as separate. There is no gap! To see a world of separation is considered "sickness" because it stems from a mind that does not know it is whole—at One with All That Is. Heal your mind now, this holy instant, and accept your role as dreamer of the dream. For there is an alternate to dreams of fear, and it is this loving reality we want to recognize above all else.

VI. The Secret Vows

"Who punishes the body is insane." (T-28.VI.1:1)

"It does not victimize, because it has no will, no preferences and no doubts." (T-28.VI.1:6)

"It can be victimized, but cannot feel itself as victim. It accepts no role, but does what it is told, without attack." (T-28.VI.1:9-10)

"It behaves in ways you want, but never makes the choice." (T-28.VI.2:3)

"The thing you hate and fear and loathe and want, the body does not know. You send it forth to seek for separation and be separate. And then you hate it, not for what it is, but for the uses you have made of it." (T-28.VI.3:1-3)

"The body represents the gap between the little bit of mind you call

VI. The Secret Vows

your own and all the rest of what is really yours. You hate it, yet you think it is your self, and that, without it, would your self be lost." (T-28.VI.4:1-2)

"No one can suffer if he does not see himself attacked, and losing by attack." (T-28.VI.4:5)

"Sickness is anger taken out upon the body, so that it will suffer pain." (T-28.VI.5:1)

"Whoever says, "There is no gap between my mind and yours" has kept God's promise, not his tiny oath to be forever faithful unto death. And by his healing is his brother healed." (T-28.VI.5:4-5)

"Let this be your agreement with each one; that you be one with him and not apart." (T-28.VI.6:1)

"In his creation did his Father say, "You are beloved of Me and I of you forever. Be you perfect as Myself, for you can never be apart from Me." His Son remembers not that he replied, "I will," though in that promise he was born. Yet God reminds him of it every time he does not share a promise to be sick, but lets his mind be healed and unified. His secret vows are powerless before the Will of God, Whose promises he shares. And what he substitutes is not his will, who has made promise of himself to God." (T-28.VI.6:4-9)

In summary, Chapter 28 – VI: "The Secret Vows" is saying:
We took a vow when we were brought into creation; we agreed with God that we would be as He created us: perfect in our Oneness with Him and each other. And now here we find ourselves in bodies, appearing imperfect and separate—appearing to have broken our vow, which has caused us endless guilt and sinful feelings, the source of which many of us cannot consciously identify. Yet, God tells us we have not sinned, for we cannot become separate. It is impossible to break our vow, but we can dream that it has happened. The body is not a real thing. It cannot think for itself or do anything without our consent and constant direction. And so, we can choose to disregard it as our identity, for it cannot be who we are in truth. It is pointless to punish, blame, or victimize it. It is nothing but a vehicle we are using to return Home through forgiveness of it. Forgive it by remembering to overlook what we think we are doing with our bodies and remember instead our secret vow; that we remain One as God created us, despite the separation we are dreaming.

CHAPTER 28—THE UNDOING OF FEAR

VII. The Ark of Safety

"God asks for nothing, and His Son, like Him, need ask for nothing. For there is no lack in him." (T-28.VII.1:1-2)

"A space where God is not, a gap between the Father and the Son is not the Will of Either, Who have promised to be one." (T-28.VII.1:5)

"What will can come between what must be one, and in Whose Wholeness there can be no gap?" (T-28.VII.1:8)

"The beautiful relationship you have with all your brothers is a part of you because it is a part of God Himself." (T-28.VII.2:1)

"What could correct for separation but its opposite? There is no middle ground in any aspect of salvation. You accept it wholly or accept it not. What is unseparated must be joined." (T-28.VII.2:6-9)

"Either there is a gap between you and your brother, or you are one." (T-28.VII.3:1)

"Yet who can build his home upon a straw, and count on it as shelter from the wind? The body can be made a home like this, because it lacks foundation in the truth. And yet, because it does, can it be seen as not your home, but merely as an aid to help you reach the home where God abides." (T-28.VII.3:4-6)

"With *this* as the purpose is the body healed." (T-28.VII.4:1)

"All miracles are based upon this choice, and given you the instant it is made. No forms of sickness are immune, because the choice cannot be made in terms of form." (T-28.VII.4:6-7)

"This world is but the dream that you can be alone, and think without affecting those apart from you." (T-28.VII.5.5:2)

"It is like the house set upon straw. It seems to be quite solid and substantial in itself. Yet its stability cannot be judged apart from its foundation." (T-28.VII.5:7-9)

"The wind will topple it, and rain will come and carry it into oblivion." (T-28.VII.5:11)

"What is the sense in seeking to be safe in what was made for danger and for fear?" (T-28.VII.6:1)

"Your home is built upon your brother's health, upon his happiness, his sinlessness, and everything his Father promised him." (T-28.VII.7:1)

"The world will wash away and yet this house will stand forever, for its strength lies not within itself alone. It is an ark of safety, resting on God's promise that His Son is safe forever in Himself." (T-28.VII.7:4-5)

"From here the body can be seen as what it is, and neither less nor more in worth than the extent to which it can be used to liberate God's Son unto his home. And with this holy purpose is it made a home of holiness a little while, because it shares your Father's Will with you." (T-28.VII.7:7-8)

In summary, Chapter 28 – VII: "The Ark of Safety" is saying:
An ark is something that gives you protection and safety; like a home you can go to when you feel yourself in jeopardy. The ego sees us as being in constant danger. We see our bodily home as at risk of death, humiliation, unfair treatment, illness, and victimization. Yet, when we think such things are possible, there is an alternate place we can turn to for rescue from such ego-beliefs. It is the remembering that our body has only one true purpose: to be used to liberate us from all false beliefs in Who We Are. The body does not cause us to have a gap between one another. We are One. And in this Oneness, we are completely safe and at home in God. There is no other truth, for all else in our worldly home will one day wash away into nothingness as changing forms that dissolve in time. Our Eternal Self will never cease to be and believing in this as our ark of safety is the undoing of all fear.

CHAPTER 29
THE AWAKENING

I. The Closing of the Gap

"There is no time, no place, no state where God is absent. There is nothing to be feared. There is no way in which a gap could be conceived of in the Wholeness that is His." (T-29.I.1:3)

"For it would mean His Love could harbor just a hint of hate, His gentleness turn sometimes to attack, and His eternal patience sometimes fail." (T-29.I.1:5)

"Here is the fear of God most plainly seen. For love is treacherous to those who fear, since fear and hate can never be apart. No one who hates but is afraid of love, and therefore must he be afraid of God." (T-29.I.2:1-3)

"The fear of God! The greatest obstacle that peace must flow across has not yet gone." (T-29.I.3:1-2)

"You had decided that your brother is your enemy." (T-29.I.3:4)

"The gap between you and your brother is not one of space between two separate bodies." (T-29.I.4:1)

"The body could not separate your mind from your brother's unless you wanted it to be a cause of separation and of distance seen between you and him." (T-29.I.5:1)

"It will allow but limited indulgences in "love," with intervals of hatred in between." (T-29.I.6:2)

"It will be sick because you do not know what loving means. And so you must misuse each circumstance and everyone you meet, and see in them a purpose not your own." (T-29.I.6:4-5)

"You do not see how limited and weak is your allegiance, and how frequently you have demanded that love go away, and leave you quietly alone in "peace."" (T-29.I.7:5)

"The body, innocent of goals, is your excuse for variable goals you hold, and force the body to maintain." (T-29.I.8:1)

"There is a wariness that is aroused by learning that the body is not real." (T-29.I.8:6)

"Yet all that happens when the gap is gone is peace eternal." (T-29.I.9:1)

"Would you allow the body to say "no" to Heaven's calling, were you not afraid to find a loss of self in finding God? Yet can your self be lost by being found?" (T-29.I.9:5-6)

In summary, Chapter 29 – I: "The Closing of the Gap" is saying:
There is no gap between us and God, for we are eternally One. And yet we dream of a state where it is possible to make an alternate, separate self—the ego—that can experience separation through having a body. And with this dream of separation, we simultaneously developed a fear of God, for God, being Union, is the undeniable "antidote" to our state of separation. The ego fears its own undoing; the undoing of the state of separation; and so, we fear God's Love, which is our Unity. The body cannot separate us unless we want it to, for our minds are eternally joined in God's Love. We have simply forgotten this is so. The way to remember there is no gap between us, is to remind ourselves the body is not real. And then we will find our Self with all creation resting in God's Love, and the imagined gap between us will be closed at last.

II. The Coming of the Guest

"Why would you not perceive it as release from suffering to learn that you are free?" (T-29.II.1:1)

"Why does an easy path, so clearly marked it is impossible to lose the way, seem thorny, rough and far too difficult for you to follow? Is it not because you see it as the road to hell instead of looking on it as a simple way, without a sacrifice or any loss, to find yourself in Heaven and in God? Until you realize you give up nothing, until you understand there is no loss, you will have some regrets about the way that you have chosen." (T-29.II.1:3-5)

"You have accepted healing's cause, and so it must be you are healed. And being healed, the power to heal must also now be yours." (T-29.II.2:1-2)

"It has been hopeless to attempt to find the hope of peace upon a battleground." (T-29.II.3:1)

"Why are you not rejoicing?" (T-29.II.3:5)

"No more is pain your friend and guilt your god, and you should wel-

CHAPTER 29 — THE AWAKENING

come the effects of love." (T-29.II.3:7)

"Your Guest *has* come. You asked Him, and He came. You did not hear Him enter, for you did not wholly welcome Him. And yet His gifts came with Him." (T-29.II.4:1-5)

"He needs your help in giving them to all who walk apart, believing they are separate and alone." (T-29.II.4:6)

"Yet He Who entered in but waits for you to come where you invited Him to be." (T-29.II.5:2)

"And nowhere else His gifts of peace and joy, and all the happiness His Presence brings, can be obtained." (T-29.II.5:4)

"You cannot see your Guest, but you can see the gifts He brought." (T-29.II.5:6)

"The body does not change. It represents the larger dream that change is possible." (T-29.II.7:1-2)

"The body can appear to change with time, with sickness or with health, and with events that seem to alter it. Yet this but means the mind remains unchanged in its belief of what the purpose of the body is." (T-29.II.7:7-8)

"The body that is asked to be a god will be attacked, because its nothingness has not been recognized." (T-29.II.9:1)

"As "something" is the body asked to be God's enemy, replacing what He is with littleness and limit and despair. It is His loss you celebrate when you behold the body as a thing you love, or look upon it as a thing you hate." (T-29.II.10:1-2)

"Your savior is not dead, nor does he dwell in what was built as temple unto death. He lives in God, and it is this that makes him savior unto you, and only this. His body's nothingness releases yours from sickness and from death. For what is yours cannot be more or less than what is his." (T-29.II.10:4-7)

In summary, Chapter 29 – II: "The Coming of the Guest" is saying:
The "Guest" within us, is the Holy Spirit. And we "invite" Him to come forward when we recognize His Presence within another. Therefore, the coming of the Guest, is merely the inner recognition of our shared holy Identity with all others created equal with us in God's Love. We do this by overlooking the

body and sensing His holy Presence instead. Why do we still feel such resistance to this easy path to salvation? Because we refuse to let the body go as our identity. We refuse to recognize the Christ within others above what our bodily eyes can see. And so, the body suffers, because we are forcing it to be who we are not, and it cannot be this. The power to heal this situation is ours. Merely recognize the presence of the Light of God in all, and our Inner Guest will come forward.

III. God's Witnesses

"Condemn your savior not because he thinks he is a body." (T-29.III.1:1)

"But he must learn he is a savior first, before he can remember what he is." (T-29.III.1:3)

"Think you the Father lost Himself when He created you? Was He made weak because He shared His Love?" (T-29.III.2:1-2)

"Deny Him not His witness in the dream His Son prefers to his reality. He must be savior from the dream he made, that he be free of it. He must see someone else as not a body, one with him without the wall the world has built to keep apart all living things who know not that they live." (T-29.III.2:5-7)

"You cannot wake yourself. Yet you can let yourself be wakened. You can overlook your brother's dreams. So perfectly can you forgive him his illusions he becomes your savior from your dreams. And as you see him shining in the space of light where God abides within the darkness, you will see that God Himself is where his body is. Before this light the body disappears, as heavy shadows must give way to light." (T-29.III.3:2-7)

"Whom you forgive is given power to forgive you your illusions. By your gift of freedom is it given unto you." (T-29.III.3:12-13)

"Make way for love, which you did not create, but which you can extend. On earth this means forgive your brother, that the darkness may be lifted from your mind." (T-29.III.4:1-2)

"How holy are you, that the Son of God can be your savior in the midst of dreams of desolation and disaster." (T-29.III.5:1)

"And now the light in you must be as bright as shines in him. This is the spark that shines within the dream; that you can help him waken, and be sure his waking eyes will rest on you. And in his glad salvation you are saved." (T-29.III.5:5-7)

In summary, Chapter 29 – III: "God's Witnesses" is saying:
We are each a witness to God when we choose to overlook the body and instead *feel* the love of Christ within another, joined with us and not separate. This is how each one is savior unto us. We cannot wake ourselves. We need another to reflect the Christ within them, to us. We do this through our recognition of His Light instead of the darkness of the ego. In this way, we extend the Love of God to them, and we are both healed. When you see the Light of God within another, they appear different to you, because you are not using your eyes to see them, but rather your heart. You are *feeling* who they are, rather than *thinking* of who they are. In turn, you will appear different to *them* as well. And so, together, we are all witnesses to God in each other.

IV. Dream Roles

"Do you believe that truth can be but some illusions? They are dreams *because* they are not true. Their equal lack of truth becomes the basis for the miracle, which means that you have understood that dreams are dreams; and that escape depends, not on the dream, but only on awaking." (T-29.IV.1:1-3)

"The dreams you think you like would hold you back as much as those in which the fear is seen. For every dream is but a dream of fear, no matter what the form it seems to take." (T-29.IV.2:1-2)

"Their form can change, but they cannot be made of something else." (T-29.IV.2:6)

"When you are angry, is it not because someone had failed to fill the function you allotted him? And does not this become the "reason" your attack is justified? The dreams you think you like are those in which the functions you have given have been filled; the needs which you ascribe to you are met." (T-29.IV.4:1-3)

"How happy would your dreams become if you were not the one who gave the "proper" role to every figure which the dream contains. No one can fail but your idea of him, and there is no betrayal but of this." (T-29.IV.5:1-2)

"What is your brother for? You do not know, because your function is obscure to you. Do not ascribe a role to him that you imagine would bring happiness to you." (T-29.IV.6:1-3)

"He asks for help in every dream he has, and you have help to give him if you see the function of the dream as He perceives its function, Who can utilize all dreams as means to serve the function given Him. Because He loves the dreamer, not the dream, each dream becomes an offering of love. For at its center is His Love for you, which lights whatever form it takes with love." (T-29.IV.6:5-7)

In summary, Chapter 29 – IV: "Dream Roles" is saying:
In this dream of bodies, we have given each one a role to play. We have imagined roles for our parents, siblings, friends, lovers, and enemies. We have decided in our mind how each role should be played that will make us happy. And if such roles are "failed" according to our own imagined rules, we become unhappy with these people. We may even attack their perceived body for its "wrongdoing" towards us. Is this why we are each here? To spend our lives struggling to fulfill the "dream role" assigned to us by others, while also desiring them to do the same for us? All this is, is ego-drama pain, designed to distract us from the truth: We are here to lay aside all these false ideas about one another and remember the truth of our Oneness. Each person in our dream, needs our help, and we give it by refusing to hold them to an assigned dream role as a body. Free everyone from the dream role you have assigned to them by seeing only the Light of Christ within them and nothing else.

V. The Changeless Dwelling Place

"There is a place in you where this whole world has been forgotten; where no memory of sin and of illusion lingers still. There is a place in you which time has left, and echoes of eternity are heard. There is a place so still no sound except a hymn to Heaven rises up to gladden God the Father and the Son. Where Both abide are They remembered, Both. And where They are is Heaven and is peace." (T-29.V.1:1-5)

"Think not that you can change Their dwelling place. For your Identity abides in Them, and where They are, forever must you be." (T-29.V.2:1-2)

"Here is the role the Holy Spirit gives to you who wait upon the Son of God, and would behold him waken and be glad." (T-29.V.3:1)

"Nothing is asked of you but to accept the changeless and eternal that abide in him, for your Identity is there." (T-29.V.3:3)

CHAPTER 29—THE AWAKENING

"Be very still and hear God's Voice in him, and let It tell you what his function is. He was created that you might be whole, for only the complete can be a part of God's completion, which created you." (T-29.V.4:2-3)

"There is no gift the Father asks of you but that you see in all creation but the shining glory of His gift to you. Behold His Son, His perfect gift, in whom his Father shines forever, and to whom is all creation given as his own." (T-29.V.5:1-2)

"The quiet that surrounds you dwells in him, and from this quiet come the happy dreams in which your hands are joined in innocence." (T-29.V.5:4)

"If you but knew the glorious goal that lies beyond forgiveness, you would not keep hold on any thought, however light the touch of evil on it may appear to be." (T-29.V.6:1)

"Yet nothing in the world of dreams remains without the hope of change and betterment, for here is not where changelessness is found. Let us be glad indeed that this is so, and seek not the eternal in this world. Forgiving dreams are means to step aside from dreaming of a world outside yourself. And leading finally beyond all dreams, unto the peace of everlasting life." (T-29.V.8:3-6)

In summary, Chapter 29 – V: "The Changeless Dwelling Place" is saying:
It has been said that "The Kingdom of Heaven is within us." Yet what do these words really mean? How does one reach this mysterious "inner kingdom?" We reach our inner Kingdom of Heaven through the process of forgiveness. Forgiveness is stillness. Stillness of the mind, which means we have decided to cease to focus on the world of form. We have ceased to think about our outer world and focus on the silence of our inner world—the one we share with All Creation, as One. This is a quiet place, devoid of all noisy thoughts of the world outside. Devoid of all thoughts of separation, anger, unjust treatment, or any thought with even the lightest touch of unlovingness. And in the silence of The Stillness, your mind moves out of dreams and into your inner kingdom: the Changeless Dwelling Place.

VI. Forgiveness and the End of Time

"How willing are you to forgive your brother? How much do you desire peace instead of endless strife and misery and pain?" (T-29.VI.1:1-2)

VI. Forgiveness and the End of Time

"Forgiveness is your peace, for herein lies the end of separation and the dream of danger and destruction, sin and death; of madness and of murder, grief and loss. This is the "sacrifice" salvation asks, and gladly offers peace instead of this." (T-29.VI.1:4-5)

"The Son of Life cannot be killed. He is immortal as his Father. What he is cannot be changed." (T-29.VI.2:3-5)

"What *seems* eternal all will have an end." (T-29.VI.2:7)

"All things that come and go, the tides, the seasons and the lives of men; all things that change with time and bloom and fade will not return." (T-29.VI.2:9)

"God's son can never change by what men made of him." (T-29.VI.2:11)

"Yet time waits upon forgiveness that the things of time may disappear because they have no use." (T-29.VI.2:14)

"Change is the greatest gift God gave to all that you would make eternal, to ensure that only Heaven would not pass away. You were not born to die." (T-29.VI.4:1-2)

"All other goals are set in time and change that time might be preserved, excepting one. Forgiveness does not aim at keeping time, but at its ending, when it has no use." (T-29.VI.4:4-5)

"For even though it was a dream of death, you need not let it stand for this to you. Let *this* be changed, and nothing in the world but must be changed as well." (T-29.VI.5:2-3)

"How lovely is the world whose purpose is forgiveness of God's Son!" (T-29.VI.6:1)

"And what a joyous thing it is to dwell a little while in such a happy place! Nor can it be forgot, in such a world, it is a little while till timelessness comes quietly to take the place of time." (T-29.VI.6:3-4)

In summary, Chapter 29 – VI: "Forgiveness and the End of Time" is saying:
Forgiveness ends the experience of time, because it is a state of mind that reaches beyond it. It is to see with your "inner eyes" what lies beyond our current state of physical separation. Do you desire peace? Then you must forgive (look beyond) the gap your ego sees between yourself and another. Let go of all your painful thoughts regarding other bodies. This may seem difficult, but then ask yourself how badly do you want peace? Is it such a sacrifice to

CHAPTER 29 — THE AWAKENING

overlook a thing we are not, and instead *feel* our Oneness? Vengeance is futile against a body because eventually *all* bodies will one day die. What good does it do to dwell on what it did in the past? Soon enough, it will be no more, whether you hate it or love it. Forgiveness simply skips the waiting process for the passing of the body. It sees it and the world it contains, as already a thing to be disregarded and moves directly to the Love that binds us all. In this inner kingdom, time does not exist because it lies outside of time entirely. And what a lovely place is Love's eternal Home! And the path to It is through forgiveness of all that ends in time, thus ending the experience of time itself.

VII. Seek Not Outside Yourself

"Seek not outside yourself. For it will fail, and you will weep each time an idol falls." (T-29.VII.1:1-2)

"Seek not outside yourself. For all your pain comes simply from a futile search for what you want, insisting where it must be found." (T-29.VII.1:6-7)

"Do you prefer that you be right or happy?" (T-29.VII.1:9)

"You will fail. But it is given you to know the truth, and not to seek for it outside yourself." (T-29.VII.1:11-12)

"No one who comes here but must still have hope, some lingering illusion, or some dream that there is something outside of himself that will bring happiness and peace to him. If everything is in him this cannot be so." (T-29.VII.2:1-2)

"This is the purpose he bestows upon the body; that it seek for what he lacks, and give him what would make himself complete. And thus he wanders aimlessly about, in search of something that he cannot find, believing that he is what he is not." (T-29.VII.2:4-5)

"The lingering illusion will impel him to seek out a thousand idols, and to seek beyond them for a thousand more." (T-29.VII.3:1)

"Yet does he seek to kill God's Son within, and prove that he is victor over him. This is the purpose every idol has, for this the role that is assigned to it, and this the role that cannot be fulfilled." (T-29.VII.3:4-5)

"Whenever you attempt to reach a goal in which the body's betterment is cast as major beneficiary, you try to bring about your death. For you believe that you can suffer lack, and lack is death." (T-29.VII.4:1-2)

VII. Seek Not Outside Yourself

"Seek not outside yourself. The search implies you are not whole within and fear to look upon your devastation, but prefer to seek outside yourself for what you are." (T-29.VII.4:5-6)

"Idols must fall *because* they have no life, and what is lifeless is a sign of death. You came to die, and what would you expect but to perceive the signs of death you seek?" (T-29.VII.5:1-2)

"All idols of this world were made to keep the truth within from being known to you, and to maintain allegiance to the dream that you must find what is outside yourself to be complete and happy." (T-29.VII.6:1)

"God dwells within, and your completion lies in Him. No idol takes His place. Look not to idols. Do not seek outside yourself." (T-29.VII.6:3-6)

"To change all this, and open up a road of hope and of release in what appeared to be an endless circle of despair, you need but to decide you do not know the purpose of the world. You give it goals it does not have, and thus do you decide what it is for." (T-29.VII.8:1-2)

"Save time, my brother; learn what time is for. And speed the end of idols in a world made sad and sick by seeing idols there." (T-29.VII.9:3-4)

"The fear of God is but the fear of loss of idols." (T-29.VII.9:6)

"An idol cannot take the place of God." (T-29.VII.10:4)

"Seek not outside your Father for your hope. For hope of happiness is not despair." (T-29.VII.10:6-7)

In summary, Chapter 29 – VII: "Seek Not Outside Yourself" is saying:

Why is it so difficult for us to cease attempting what always fails? At the root, it seems the ego has convinced us we need a multitude of things. Yet, none of those things will bring us what we truly desire. We seem to have an undefined lack we do not know how to fill. It is but our seeming separation from Source. Deep down, we know we lack the awareness of God's Presence. The ego knows that if you accomplished re-joining your mind to God's it would disappear, because all sense of lack in us would disappear. And so, the ego scrambles to distract us with one worldly goal after another, and yet we know from experience that this is a bottomless pit. We are satisfied for but a moment, and then move on to the next goal. Let us stop the insanity of this unending, exhausting cycle. Let us seek instead to let go of such striving through forgiveness of the world—the stillness of our thoughts about it—and seek not outside ourselves, but rather, turn within instead.

VIII. The Anti-Christ

"What is an idol? Do you think you know? For idols are unrecognizable as such, and never seen for what they really are." (T-29.VIII.1:1-2)

"An idol is an image of your brother that you would value more than what he is." (T-29.VIII.1:6)

"Be it a body or a thing, a place, a situation or a circumstance, an object owned or wanted, or a right demanded or achieved, it is the same." (T-29.VIII.1:9)

"Let not their form deceive you. Idols are but substitutes for your reality." (T-29.VIII.2:1-2)

"No one believes in idols who has not enslaved himself to littleness and loss." (T-29.VIII.2:5)

"An idol is a false impression, or a false belief; some form of anti-Christ, that constitutes a gap between the Christ and what you see. An idol is a wish, made tangible and given form, and thus perceived as real and seen outside the mind." (T-29.VIII.3:1-2)

"All forms of anti-Christ oppose the Christ." (T-29.VIII.3:5)

"This world of idols is a veil across the face of Christ, because its purpose is to separate your brother from yourself." (T-29.VIII.4:1)

"Christ's enemy is nowhere. He can take no form in which he ever will be real." (T-29.VIII.4:8-9)

"What is an idol? Nothing!" (T-29.VIII.5:1-2)

"An idol is established by belief, and when it is withdrawn the idol "dies." This is the anti-Christ; the strange idea there is a power past omnipotence, a place beyond the infinite, a time transcending the eternal." (T-29.VIII.6:1-2)

"Where is an idol? Nowhere! Can there be a gap in what is infinite, a place where time can interrupt eternity?" (T-29.VIII.7:1-3)

"Nothing and nowhere must an idol be, while God is everything and everywhere." (T-29.VIII.7:6)

"What purpose has an idol, then? What is it for?" (T-29.VIII.8:1-2)

"The world believes in idols. No one comes unless he worshiped them, and still attempts to seek for one that yet might offer him a gift reality does not contain." (T-29.VIII.8:4-5)

"But more of something is an idol for." (T-29.VIII.8:9)

"Be not deceived by forms the "something" takes. An idol is a means for getting more. And it is this that is against God's Will." (T-29.VIII.8:11-13)

"God has not many Sons, but only One. Who can have more, and who be given less?" (T-29.VIII.9:1-2)

"For more in Heaven can you never have." (T-29.VIII.9:5)

"God gave you all there is." (T-29.VIII.9:7)

"And thus is every living thing a part of you, as of Himself. No idol can establish you as more than God. But you will never be content with being less." (T-29.VIII.9:9-11)

In summary, Chapter 29 – VIII: "The Anti-Christ" is saying:
The anti-Christ is any idea or form that goes in the opposite direction of our Unity. It is anything that draws our mind and heart towards separation. The world outside of us is filled then, with idols representing the anti-Christ, or anti-Unity. We each have an inexhaustible list of wants, needs, goals and desires in this world—all in the hopes of making our stay here a little less miserable. We seek our peace through attainment in the world. ACIM states, "An idol is a means for getting more. And it is this that is against God's Will." So, does this mean God does not want us to have anything in the world and we are to get rid of all our possessions and live homeless and penniless? No, that is not what God wants. His Will is merely that we know our true abundance in Him, and nothing greater can be found outside of us in this world. All we need do, is give up our *emotional attachment* to the seeking of such things; give up the idea that attainments in this world are what brings us joy. Make God your only goal, and you will learn how to live joyfully in this world but be not of it. Your mind must cease to be obsessed with anything that lies without. The only other place to turn, then, is within. In this way, you turn away from the anti-Christ (separation without), and towards the Christ (Unity within).

IX. The Forgiving Dream

"The slave of idols is a willing slave. For willing he must be to let himself bow down in worship to what has no life, and seek for power in the powerless." (T-29.IX.1:1-2)

"A dream of judgment came into the mind that God created perfect as Himself. And in that dream was Heaven changed to hell, and God

CHAPTER 29—THE AWAKENING

made enemy unto His Son. How can God's Son awaken from the dream? It is a dream of judgment. So must he judge not, and he will waken." (T-29.IX.2:1-5)

"But in the dream of judgment you attack and are condemned; and wish to be the slave of idols, which are interposed between your judgment and the penalty it brings." (T-29.IX.3:7)

"Little child, the light is there. You do but dream, and idols are the toys you dream you play with. Who has need of toys but children? They pretend they rule the world, and give their toys the power to move about, and talk and think and feel and speak for them." (T-29.IX.4:3-6)

"But they are eager to forget that they made up the dream in which their toys are real, nor recognize their wishes are their own." (T-29.IX.4:8)

"Nightmares are childish dreams." (T-29.IX.5:1)

"There is a time when childhood should be passed and gone forever. Seek not to retain the toys of children." (T-29.IX.6:1-2)

"The dream of judgment is a children's game, in which the child becomes the father, powerful, but with the little wisdom of a child." (T-29.IX.6:4)

"Yet is the real world unaffected by the world he thinks is real." (T-29.IX.6:8)

"The real world still is but a dream. Except the figures have been changed." (T-29.IX.7:1-2)

"No one is used for something he is not, for childish things have all been put away. And what was once a dream of judgment now has changed into a dream where all is joy, because that is the purpose that it has. Only forgiving dreams can enter here, for time is almost over." (T-29.IX.7:5-7)

"Forgiveness, once complete, bring timelessness so close the song of Heaven can be heard, not with the ears, but with the holiness that never left the altar that abides forever deep within the Son of God." (T-29.IX.8:5)

"Whenever you feel fear in any form, - and you are fearful if you do not feel a deep content, a certainty of help, a calm assurance Heaven goes with you, - be sure you made an idol, and believe it will betray you." (T-29.IX.9:1)

IX. The Forgiving Dream

"Forgiving dreams remind you that you live in safety and have not attacked yourself." (T-29.IX.10:1)

"Forgiving dreams are kind to everyone who figures in the dream." (T-29.IX.10:3)

"He does not fear his judgment for he has judged no one, nor has sought to be released through judgment from what judgment must impose. And all the while he is remembering what he forgot, when judgment seemed to be the way to save him from its penalty." (T-29.IX.10:5-6)

In summary, Chapter 29 – IX: "The Forgiving Dream" is saying:
To waken from this dream of suffering, we must let go of all judgment. Judgment makes illusion, for we have judged the world and see what we have decided *must* be there: separation. Idols are merely the specific things within the illusionary dream of our separation that we "play with." These "things" are our childish toys, our bodily roles, and our bodily needs. We end these childish games through forgiveness. We forgive by allowing our thoughts about the world to become still. In this stillness, we enter a sacred timeless space. It is here we *feel* the holiness and Unity that never left us. The stillness of forgiveness is felt, not seen. And in this stillness, we remember Heaven's song, that sings to our tired hearts we need not strive against God any longer. Feel the truth of our Oneness; suspend all judgment of what your eyes see and know instead that you are safe and healed and whole. And through this forgiving dream, you will experience the Great Awakening.

CHAPTER 30
THE NEW BEGINNING

Introduction

"The new beginning now becomes the focus of the curriculum. The goal is clear, but now you need specific methods for attaining it. The speed by which it can be reached depends on this one thing alone; your willingness to practice every step. Each one will help a little, every time it is attempted. And together will these steps lead you from dreams of judgment to forgiving dreams and out of pain and fear. They are not new to you, but they are more ideas than rules of thought to you as yet. So now we need to practice them awhile, until they are the rules by which you live. We seek to make them habits now, so you will have them ready for whatever need." (T-30.in.1:1-8)

In summary, Chapter 30 – "Introduction" is saying:
We are now taking this course seriously and will give our full commitment to what we are about to do. We are going from mere words to real practice of the type of forgiveness this course has set forth, thus bringing us the healing and peace we so desperately seek.

I. Rules for Decision

"Decisions are continuous. You do not always know when you are making them. But with a little practice with the ones you recognize, a set begins to form which sees you through the rest." (T-30.I.1:1-3)

"And if you find resistance strong and dedication weak, you are not ready. *Do not fight yourself.* But think about the kind of day you want, and tell yourself there is a way in which this very day can happen just like that. Then try again to have the day you want." (T-30.I.1:6-9)

"The outlook starts with this:

Today I will make no decisions by myself.

This means that you are choosing not to be the judge of what to do. But it must also mean you will not judge the situations where you will be called upon to make response." (T-30.I.2:1-4)

"This is your major problem now. You still make up your mind,

I. Rules for Decision

and then decide to ask what you should do." (T-30.I.3:1-2)

"Throughout the day, at any time you think of it and have a quiet moment for reflection, tell yourself again the kind of day you want; the feelings you would have, the things you want to happen to you, and the things you would experience, and say:

If I make no decisions by myself, this is the day that will be given me.

These two procedures, practiced well, will serve to let you be directed without fear, for opposition will not first arise and then become a problem in itself." (T-30.I.4:1-3)

"But there will still be times when you have judged already." (T-30.I.5:1)

"Then realize that you have asked a question by yourself, and must have set an answer in your terms. Then say:

I have no question. I forgot what to decide.

This cancels out the terms that you have set, and lets the answer show you what the question must have really been." (T-30.I.6:2-6)

"Try to observe this rule without delay, despite your opposition. For you have already gotten angry." (T-30.I.7:1-2)

"If you are so unwilling to receive you cannot even let your question go, you can begin to change your mind with this:

At least I can decide I do not like what I feel now.

This much is obvious, and paves the way for the next easy step." (T-30.I.8:1-3)

"Having decided that you do not like the way you feel, what could be easier than to continue with:

And so I hope I have been wrong. (T-30.I.9:1-2)

"Until this point is reached, you will believe your happiness depends on being right. But this much reason have you now attained; you would be better off if you were wrong." (T-30.I.10:2-3)

"And you can say in perfect honesty:

I want another way to look at this.

Now you have changed your mind about the day, and have remembered what you really want." (T-30.I.11:3-5)

"This final step is but acknowledgment of lack of opposition to be

CHAPTER 30 — THE NEW BEGINNING

helped. It is a statement of an open mind, not certain yet, but willing to be shown:

> *Perhaps there is another way to look at this.*
> *What can I lose by asking?" (T-30.I.12:1-4)*

"It must be clear that it is easier to have a happy day if you prevent unhappiness from entering at all. But this takes practice in the rules that will protect you from the ravages of fear." (T-30.I.13:1-2)

"We said you can begin a happy day with the determination not to make decisions by yourself." (T-30.I.14:1)

"You will not make decisions by yourself whatever you decide. For they are made with idols or with God." (T-30.I.14:7-8)

"Your day is not at random. It is set by what you choose to live it with, and how the friend whose counsel you have sought perceives your happiness." (T-30.I.15:1-2)

"The second rule as well is but a fact. For you and your adviser must agree on what you want before it can occur." (T-30.I.16:1-2)

"Nothing can be caused without some form of union, be it with a dream of judgment or the Voice for God." (T-30.I.16:4)

"It needs but two who would have happiness this day to promise it to all the world." (T-30.I.17:1)

"It needs but two. These two are joined before there can be a decision. Let this be the one reminder that you keep in mind, and you will have the day you want, and give it to the world by having it yourself. Your judgment has been lifted from the world by your decision for a happy day. And as you have received, so must you give." (T-30.I.17:4-8)

In summary, Chapter 30 – I: "Rules for Decision" is saying:
We all want a happy, peaceful day, every day. How is it possible to achieve this? It all depends on which voice we listen to when responding to our surroundings; what inner dialogue we are feeding into. Are we listening to the ego or the Holy Spirit? We are constantly joined with one or the other. It is impossible that we think alone. Our day can be reset at any time—even if it is moments before falling asleep; we can still turn around our thoughts and rejoin the Holy Spirit in our thinking. We have only to admit first that we have listened to the wrong voice. Second, we stop our negative thoughts in recognition that they

are causing us to feel the opposite of what we want. Third we decide we do not like how we feel. Fourth we realize that perhaps we are wrong in listening to the ego, because we are not happy and at peace. Then our mind is open to listening to the Holy Spirit, and we are ready to see things another way—a way that moves us in the opposite direction of the ego. You will remember your Union with all things instead of your separation. The rules for decision will always lead you to a peaceful, happy day, so long as you release all judgment as to how such a day should happen.

II. Freedom of Will

"Do you not understand that to oppose the Holy Spirit is to fight yourself?" (T-30.II.1:1)

"In His Divinity is but your own." (T-30.II.1:3)

"God asks you do your will. He joins with you. He did not set His Kingdom up alone." (T-30.II.1:5-7)

"No spark of life but was created with your glad consent, as you would have it be. And not one Thought that God has ever had but waited for your blessing to be born. God is no enemy to you." (T-30.II.1:9-11)

"How wonderful it is to do your will! For that is freedom. There is nothing else that ever should be called by freedom's name." (T-30.II.2:1-3)

"God would not have His Son made prisoner to what he does not want. He joins with you in willing you be free." (T-30.II.2:8-9)

"Look once again upon your enemy, the one you chose to hate instead of love." (T-30.II.3:1)

"Now hear God speak to you, through Him Who is His Voice and yours as well, reminding you that it is not your will to hate and be a prisoner to fear, a slave to death, a little creature with a little life." (T-30.II.3:3)

"What cause have you for anger in a world that merely waits your blessing to be free? If you be prisoner, then God Himself could not be free. For what is done to him whom God so loves is done to God Himself." (T-30.II.4:1-3)

"He would but keep your will forever and forever limitless. This world awaits the freedom you will give when you have recognized that you are free. But you will not forgive the world until you have forgiven Him Who gave your will to you." (T-30.II.4:5-7)

CHAPTER 30—THE NEW BEGINNING

"God turns to you to ask the world be saved, for by your own salvation is it healed. And no one walks upon the earth but must depend on your decision, that he learn death has no power over him, because he shares your freedom as he shares your will. It is your will to heal him, and because you have decided with him, he is healed. And now is God forgiven, for you chose to look upon your brother as a friend." (T-30.II.5:1-4)

In summary, Chapter 30 – II: "Freedom of Will" is saying:
By the very nature of our creation, we are free-willed beings. We can choose whether or not to join with God's Thoughts or be oblivious to Them. What are God's Thoughts? We are each a Thought of God. And we have the freedom to decide for, or against, the experience of our unity in God—but we cannot truly separate. What we choose is expressed through how we think and feel towards one another. If we see an "enemy" we are choosing against God's Thoughts. If we call them friend, we join God's Thoughts in seeing only our Oneness as part of His Son. This seeing is healing, for it joins what once was thought to be separate. Let us each recognize we are free, and not bound to these separate bodies; let us give up all cause for anger against each other, for we but fight against our One Self. Our freedom lies in our will to know ourselves as whole once again.

III. Beyond All Idols

"Idols are quite specific." (T-30.III.1:1)

"Idols are limits. They are the belief that there are forms that will bring happiness, and that, by limiting, is all attained." (T-30.III.1:4-5)

"It is not form you seek. What form can be a substitute for God the Father's Love?" (T-30.III.2:1-2)

"Behind the search for every idol lies the yearning for completion. Wholeness has no form because it is unlimited. To seek a special person or a thing to add to you to make yourself complete, can only mean that you believe some form is missing." (T-30.III.3:1-3)

"This is the purpose of an idol; that you will not look beyond it, to the source of the belief that you are incomplete." (T-30.III.3:5)

"It never is the idol that you want. But what you think it offers you, you want indeed and have the right to ask for." (T-30.III.4:1-2)

"What idol can be called upon to give the Son of God what he already has?" (T-30.III.4:10)

III. Beyond All Idols

"Completion is the *function* of God's Son. He has no need to seek for it at all." (T-30.III.5:1-2)

"For thoughts endure as long as does the mind that thought of them. And in the Mind of God there is no ending, nor a time in which His Thoughts were absent or could offer change." (T-30.III.6:3-4)

"The thoughts you think are in your mind, as you are in the Mind which thought of you. And so there are no separate parts in what exists within God's Mind. It is forever One, eternally united and at peace." (T-30.III.6:7-9)

"Thoughts seem to come and go. Yet all this means is that you are sometimes aware of them, and sometimes not." (T-30.III.7:1-2)

"The Thought God holds of you is perfectly unchanged by your forgetting." (T-30.III.7:6)

"Beyond all idols is the Thought God holds of you. Completely unaffected by the turmoil and the terror of the world, the dreams of birth and death that here are dreamed, the myriad of forms that fear can take; quite undisturbed, the Thought God holds of you remains exactly as it always was. Surrounded by a stillness so complete no sound of battle comes remotely near, it rests in certainty and perfect peace." (T-30.III.10:1-3)

"Where could the Thought God holds of you exist but where you are?" (T-30.III.11:1)

"Outside you there is no eternal sky, no changeless star and no reality." (T-30.III.11:3)

"You have not two realities, but one. Nor can you be aware of more than one. An idol or the Thought God holds of you is your reality. Forget not, then, that idols must keep hidden what you are, not from the Mind of God, but from your own. The star shines still; the sky has never changed. But you, the holy Son of God Himself, are unaware of your reality." (T-30.III.11:5-10)

In summary, Chapter 30 – III: "Beyond All Idols" is saying:
Idols are everything and anything outside of our minds—all physical things we can see with our bodily eyes. What lies beyond them? We cannot see this eternal world with physical eyes because it is unlike our physical world; it is

an eternal realm. The eternal realm is where we exist in truth, but we seem to think we live in the physical because it is all we can see. What if, what we see now is a false reality, not unlike having goggles over our eyes, projecting a make-believe world? This is indeed what the Course is suggesting here. We can either see this false world of idols, or the Eternal Reality of God beyond it. True reality is held in God's Mind, and we are one with Him as part of His Thoughts. And it is here we exist in truth, whether we see it or not and whether we believe in it or not. Fulfill your function of completion in God then, by forgiving the reality you see now. You do this, by looking beyond all idols, and knowing the truth our Oneness instead.

IV. The Truth Behind Illusions

"You will attack what does not satisfy, and thus you will not see you made it up. You always fight illusions. For the truth behind them is so lovely and so still in loving gentleness, were you aware of it you would forget defensiveness entirely, and rush to its embrace." (T-30.IV.1:1-3)

"All idols are the false ideas you made to fill the gap you think arose between yourself and what is true." (T-30.IV.1:8)

"The wearying, dissatisfying gods you made are blown-up children's toys." (T-30.IV.2:1)

"The gap that is not there is filled with toys in countless forms." (T-30.IV.3:1)

"You can laugh at popping heads and squeaking toys, as does the child who learns they are no threat to him." (T-30.IV.3:6)

"Yet is he at the mercy of his toys? And can they represent a threat to him?" (T-30.IV.3:9-10)

"Reality observes the laws of God, and not the rules you set. It is His laws that guarantee your safety. All illusions that you believe about yourself obey no laws." (T-30.IV.4:1-3)

"Appearances deceive because they are appearances and not reality. Dwell not on them in any form." (T-30.IV.5:1-2)

"Do not attack what you have made to let you be deceived, for thus you prove that you have been deceived." (T-30.IV.5:4)

"Look calmly at its toys, and understand that they are idols which but dance to vain desires. Give them not your worship, for they are not there." (T-30.IV.5:9-10)

"Appearances can but deceive the mind that wants to be deceived. And you can make a simple choice that will forever place you far beyond deception. You need not concern yourself with how this will be done, for this you cannot understand. But you will understand that mighty changes have been quickly brought about, when you decide one very simple thing; you do not want whatever you believe an idol gives. For thus the Son of God declares that he is free of idols. And thus *is* he free." (T-30.IV.6:1-6)

"Salvation is a paradox indeed!" (T-30.IV.7:1)

"It asks you but that you forgive all things that no one ever did; to overlook what is not there, and not to look upon the unreal as reality." (T-30.IV.7:3)

"No more than this is asked. Be glad indeed salvation asks so little, not so much." (T-30.IV.8:3-4)

"Such is the only rule for happy dreams. The gap is emptied of the toys of fear, and then its unreality is plain." (T-30.IV.8:7-8)

"He is delivered from illusions by his will, and but restored to what he is. What could God's plan for his salvation be, except a means to give him to Himself?" (T-30.IV.8:12-13)

In summary, Chapter 30 – IV: "The Truth Behind Illusions" is saying: Everything we think we cherish in this world is merely an illusion; a child's toy we are temporarily playing pretend with. We are all pretending to be bodies we are not. And like a child's game, we can be vicious and cruel to each other with our toys—and yet, when the playtime is done everyone goes home and all is well. So it is when we leave these bodies and return to God. Toys may be damaged, but the one who plays, is not. We have decided we are the toy, and not the one who plays. We have thus placed a barrier between us, and our truth as part of God—our true Identity as one who cannot be harmed. This is the truth behind all illusions we must come to understand that will deliver us from all illusions and be restored to what we are.

V. The Only Purpose

"The real world is the state of mind in which the only purpose of the world is seen to be forgiveness." (T-30.V.1:1)

"The value of forgiveness is perceived and takes the place of idols, which are sought no longer, for their "gifts" are not held dear." (T-30.V.1:3)

CHAPTER 30—THE NEW BEGINNING

"Instead, there is a wish to understand all things created as they really are. And it is recognized that all things must be first forgiven, and then understood." (T-30.V.1:5-6)

"Here, it is thought that understanding is acquired by attack. There, it is clear that by attack is understanding lost." (T-30.V.2:1-2)

"The world becomes a place of hope, because its only purpose is to be a place where hope of happiness can be fulfilled." (T-30.V.2:7)

"Not yet is Heaven quite remembered, for the purpose of forgiveness still remains. Yet everyone is certain he will go beyond forgiveness, and he but remains until it is made perfect in himself. He has no wish for anything but this." (T-30.V.3:1-3)

"Yet is he glad to wait till every hand is joined, and every heart made ready to arise and go with him. For thus is he made ready for the step in which is all forgiveness left behind." (T-30.V.3:6-7)

"The final step is God's, because it is but God Who could create a perfect Son and share His Fatherhood with him. No one outside of Heaven knows how this can be, for understanding this is Heaven itself." (T-30.V.4:1-2)

"The real world is a state in which the mind has learned how easily do idols go when they are still perceived but wanted not." (T-30.V.5:2)

"Thus is the real world's purpose gently brought into awareness, to replace the goal of sin and guilt. And all that stood between your image of yourself and what you are, forgiveness washes joyfully away." (T-30.V.6:1-2)

"When brothers join in purpose in the world of fear, they stand already at the edge of the real world." (T-30.V.7:1)

"How light and easy is the step across the narrow boundaries of the world of fear when you have recognized Whose hand you hold!" (T-30.V.8:1)

"An ancient hate is passing from the world." (T-30.V.9:1)

"Look back no longer, for what lies ahead is all you ever wanted in your heart. Give up the world! But not to sacrifice. You never wanted it. What happiness have you sought here that did not bring you pain?" (T-30.V.9:3-7)

VI. The Justification for Forgiveness

"Do not look back except in honesty. And when an idol tempts you, think of this:

There never was a time an idol brought you anything except the "gift" of guilt. Not one was bought except at cost of pain, nor was it ever paid by you alone." (T-30.V.10:1-4)

"Look forward, then; in confidence walk with a happy heart that beats in hope and does not pound in fear." (T-30.V.10:8)

"And thus the Will of God must reach to their awareness. Nor can they forget for long that it is but their own." (T-30.V.11:4-5)

In summary, Chapter 30 – V: "The Only Purpose" is saying:
We think we are here in this world for many purposes, and yet there is only one: to let it go completely. Why bother coming here then? The reason is, because we still think there is something here, we want. And it is not until we learn there is nothing the world can give us that will fill the void of separation, that we will understand we need come here no more. And so, we must learn to forgive the world; to look beyond all forms of separation before understanding of our unity can be returned to our awareness. Therefore, walk away from the world and all its empty promises and do not look back with regret. You never wanted what it gave you anyway. This—forgiveness—is the only purpose you have in the world.

VI. The Justification for Forgiveness

"Anger is *never* justified. Attack has no foundation. It is here escape from fear begins, and will be made complete." (T-30.VI.1:1-3)

"You are not asked to offer pardon where attack is due, and would be justified. For that would mean that you forgive a sin by overlooking what is really there. This is not pardon." (T-30.VI.1:6-8)

"You do not forgive the unforgivable, nor overlook a real attack that calls for punishment. Salvation does not lie in being asked to make unnatural responses which are inappropriate to what is real. Instead, it merely asks that you respond appropriately to what is not real by not perceiving what has not occurred." (T-30.VI.2:3-5)

"But you are merely asked to see forgiveness as the natural reaction to distress that rests on error, and thus calls for help. Forgiveness is the only sane response." (T-30.VI.2:7-8)

CHAPTER 30—THE NEW BEGINNING

"This understanding is the only change that lets the real world rise to take the place of dreams of terror." (T-30.VI.3:1)

"If you can see your brother merits pardon, you learned forgiveness is your right as much as his. Nor will you think that God intends for you a fearful judgment that your brother does not merit." (T-30.VI.4:7-8)

"Forgiveness recognized as merited will heal. It gives the miracle its strength to overlook illusions. This is how you learn that you must be forgiven too. There can be no appearance that can not be overlooked." (T-30.VI.5:1-4)

"There is no surer proof idolatry is what you wish, than a belief there are some forms of sickness and of joylessness, forgiveness cannot heal. This means that you prefer to keep some idols, and are not prepared, as yet, to let all idols go." (T-30.VI.6:1-2)

"It always means you think forgiveness must be limited." (T-30.VI.6:5)

"It must be true the miracle can heal all forms of sickness, or it cannot heal." (T-30.VI.7:1)

"You must forgive God's Son entirely. Or you will keep an image of yourself that is not whole, and will remain afraid to look within and find escape from every idol there. Salvation rests on faith there cannot be some forms of guilt that you cannot forgive." (T-30.VI.7:5-7)

"Look on your brother with the willingness to see him as he is." (T-30.VI.T-30.VI.8:1)

"To heal is to make whole." (T-30.VI.8:3)

"There is no way to think of him but this, if you would know the truth about yourself.

I thank you Father, for Your perfect Son,
And in his glory will I see my own.

Here is the joyful statement that there are no forms of evil that can overcome the Will of God; the glad acknowledgement that guilt has not succeeded by your wish to make illusions real." (T-30.VI.9:3-5)

"Look on your brother with this hope in you, and you will understand he could not make an error that could change the truth in him." (T-30.VI.10:1)

"Is his Father wrong about His Son? Or have you been deceived in him who has been given you to heal, for your salvation and deliverance?" (T-30.VI.10:6-7)

In summary, Chapter 30 – VI: "The Justification for Forgiveness" is saying:
We understand that true forgiveness is to overlook the body, knowing it is not who we are in truth. We know in truth, we are One in God, as part of His Sonship, and nothing the body's eyes see is real. However, how do we justify true forgiveness for the most heinous, hateful acts of humanity? How do we "overlook" what appears to be unforgivable? When we think of such acts, remember one thing: forgiveness is not *seen*, but *felt*. No one else must change in order for *you* to be happy. In fact, this is the opposite of how happiness works. Change your perception and you change how you feel. Ask then, how you can see only Love and this is what you will feel. So, if we are not our bodies, then what are we? We are The Stillness within the body. The Stillness is what lies beyond the body and all its perceived deeds. Let your mind be still then, of all other thoughts but this, and you will feel your Oneness with all others—even the perceived worst of us. You must overlook the body to do this, and when you do, you will *feel* the justification for your forgiveness—you will know it is your One Self you are healing, and no one else.

VII. The New Interpretation

"Would God have left the meaning of the world to your interpretation? If He had, it has no meaning." (T-30.VII.1:1-2)

"The Holy Spirit looks upon the world as with one purpose, changelessly established." (T-30.VII.1:4)

"You add an element into the script you write for every minute in the day, and all that happens now means something else. You take away another element, and every meaning shifts accordingly." (T-30.VII.1:7-8)

"What do your scripts reflect except your plans for what the day should be? And thus you judge disaster and success, advance, retreat, and gain and loss. These judgments all are made according to the roles the script assigns." (T-30.VII.2:1-3)

"And then, in looking back, you think you see another meaning in what went before. What have you really done, except to show there was no meaning there?" (T-30.VII.2:5-6)

CHAPTER 30 — THE NEW BEGINNING

"Only a constant purpose can endow events with stable meaning. But it must accord one meaning to them all." (T-30.VII.3:1-2)

"Perception cannot be in constant flux, and make allowance for stability of meaning anywhere." (T-30.VII.3:7)

"A common purpose is the only means whereby perception can be stabilized, and one interpretation given to the world and all experiences here. In this shared purpose is one judgment shared by everyone and everything you see. You do not have to judge, for you have learned one meaning has been given everything, and you are glad to see it everywhere." (T-30.VII.4:1-3)

"Escape from judgment simply lies in this; all things have but one purpose, which you share with all the world." (T-30.VII.5:1)

"Look not to separate dreams for meaning. Only dreams of pardon can be shared. They mean the same to both of you." (T-30.VII.6:16-18)

"We have one Interpreter. And through His use of symbols are we joined, so that they mean the same to all of us. Our common language lets us speak to all our brothers, and to understand with them forgiveness has been given to us all, and thus we can communicate again." (T-30.VII.7:6-8)

In summary, Chapter 30 – VII: "The New Interpretation" is saying:
Our ego interprets this world in ever changing ways. One day we can be happy with a situation, and the next, we despair over that very same situation, though it has not changed a bit. We can be fine one minute, and in anguish the next, simply because our ego changed its mind. There is but one interpretation that remains constant though the world is in a rolling state of change all around us; it is the Holy Spirit's interpretation of our reality. He interprets but one thing: we are One. There can be no change in this because what God has joined can never be separated. And though we may seem to have separate dreams, this still is true. Let us join in purpose to know this one truth as our One Reality. The Holy Spirit will use all forms of separation we see, as opportunities for forgiveness if we let Him. Opportunities to see our Oneness instead of separation. We have defined this world through the eyes of separation. Let us embrace a new interpretation of reality and see only our Unity and stillness in the Mind of God.

VIII. Changeless Reality

"Appearances deceive, but can be changed. Reality is changeless. It does not deceive at all, and if you fail to see beyond appearances you *are* deceived." (T-30.VIII.1:1-3)

"Your brother has a changelessness in him beyond appearance and deception, both. It is obscured by changing views of him that you perceive as his reality. The happy dream about him takes the form of the appearance of his perfect health, his perfect freedom from all forms of lack, and safety from disaster of all kinds. The miracle is proof he is not bound by loss or suffering in any form, because it can so easily be changed." (T-30.VIII.2:3-6)

"What is temptation but a wish to make illusions real?" (T-30.VIII.1:1)

"Temptation, then, is nothing more than this; a prayer the miracle touch not some dreams, but keep their unreality obscure and give to them reality instead. And Heaven gives no answer to the prayer, nor can a miracle be given you to heal appearances you do not like. You have established limits." (T-30.VIII.3:4-6)

"Miracles but show what you have interposed between reality and your awareness is unreal, and does not interfere at all." (T-30.VIII.4:2)

"*Because* reality is changeless is a miracle already there to heal all things that change, and offer them to you to see in happy form, devoid of fear. It will be given you to look upon your brother thus." (T-30.VIII.5:1-2)

"The Christ in him is perfect. Is it this that you would look upon?" (T-30.VIII.5:5-6)

"This will you look upon when you decide there is not one appearance you would hold in place of what your brother really is." (T-30.VIII.6:1)

"There is no false appearance but will fade, if you request a miracle instead." (T-30.VIII.6:5)

"Why should you fear to see the Christ in him? You but behold yourself in what you see. As he is healed are you made free of guilt, for his appearance is your own to you." (T-30.VIII.6:7-9)

CHAPTER 30—THE NEW BEGINNING

In summary, Chapter 30 – VIII: "Changeless Reality" is saying:

Only what is changeless, is real. Everything in the world outside of us, changes, and therefore is not part of our eternal reality. We want to become aware of our eternal reality and shift our perception away from the ego's temporary reality. Therefore, do not let appearances deceive you. What you see is not the truth of our eternal existence. In fact, it is the direct opposite. It is a miracle to remember the changelessness that exists within each and every one of us as we move through this temporal reality. This miraculous remembrance is what brings forth our eternal reality into our awareness, and thus our *experience*. Practice this all day, every day, in every interaction with every human being, be it in thought or deed. Do we not want to experience God's changeless Reality? Then do not fear to see the changeless Christ in all who walk this world with you, and you will be made free of guilt—the body. And the miracles you extend will usher in a new beginning for us all.

CHAPTER 31
THE FINAL VISION

I. The Simplicity of Salvation

"How simple is salvation! All it says is what was never true is not true now, and never will be. The impossible has not occurred, and can have no effects. And that is all. Can this be hard to learn by anyone who wants it to be true?" (T-31.I.1:1-5)

"You can no longer say that you perceive no differences in false and true. You have been told exactly how to tell one from the other, and just what to do if you become confused. Why, then, do you persist in learning not such simple things?" (T-31.I.1:8-10)

"There is a reason." (T-31.I.2:1)

"What you have taught yourself is such a giant learning feat it is indeed incredible. But you accomplished it because you wanted to, and did not pause in diligence to judge it hard to learn or too complex to grasp." (T-31.I.2:7-8)

"No one who understands what you have learned, how carefully you learned it, and the pains to which you went to practice and repeat the lessons endlessly, in every form you could conceive of them, could ever doubt the power of your learning skill." (T-31.I.3:1)

"For your power to learn is strong enough to teach you that your will is not your own, your thoughts do not belong to you, and even you are someone else." (T-31.I.3:6)

"You who have taught yourself the Son of God is guilty, say not that you cannot learn the simple things salvation teaches you!" (T-31.I.4:6)

"His simple lessons in forgiveness have a power mightier than yours, because they call from God and from your Self to you." (T-31.I.5:6)

"Is this a little Voice, so small and still It cannot rise above the senseless noise of sounds that have no meaning? God willed not His Son forget Him." (T-31.I.6:1-2)

"Which lesson will you learn?" (T-31.I.6:4)

"The lessons to be learned are only two. Each has its outcome in a different world." (T-31.I.7:1-2)

CHAPTER 31 — THE FINAL VISION

"The certain outcome of the lesson that God's Son is guilty is the world you see. It is a world of terror and despair." (T-31.I.7:4-5)

"The outcome of the lesson that God's Son is guiltless is a world in which there is no fear, and everything is lit with hope and sparkles with a gentle friendliness. Nothing but calls to you in soft appeal to be your friend, and let it join with you. And never does a call remain unheard, misunderstood, nor left unanswered in the selfsame tongue in which the call was made. And you will understand it was this call that everyone and everything within the world has always made, but you had not perceived it as it was. And now you see you were mistaken. You had been deceived by forms the call was hidden in. And so you did not hear it, and had lost a friend who always wanted to be part of you. The soft eternal calling of each part of God's creation to the whole is heard throughout the world this second lesson brings." (T-31.I.8:1-8)

"There is no living thing that does not share the universal Will that it be whole, and that you do not leave its call unheard." (T-31.I.9:1)

"God's perfect Son remembers his creation. But in guilt he has forgotten what he really is." (T-31.I.9:6-7)

"He will appear when you have answered Him, and you will know in Him that God is Love." (T-31.I.10:6)

"You are deceived if you believe you want disaster and disunity and pain." (T-31.I.11:3)

"Its outcome is the world you look upon." (T-31.I.11:10)

"Let us be still an instant, and forget all things we ever learned, all thoughts we had, and every preconception that we hold of what things mean and what their purpose is. Let us remember not our own ideas of what the world is for. We do not know. Let every image held of everyone be loosened from our minds and swept away." (T-31.I.12:1-4)

"Be innocent of judgment, unaware of any thoughts of evil or of good that ever crossed your mind of anyone. Now do you know him not. But you are free to learn of him, and learn of him anew. Now is he born again to you, and you are born again to him, without the past that sentenced him to die, and you with him. Now is he free to live as you are free, because an ancient learning passed away, and left a place for truth to be reborn." (T-31.I.13:1-5)

In summary, Chapter 31 – I: "The Simplicity of Salvation" is saying:
Salvation is simple because it comes down to only two choices. A choice between two voices we can listen to, guiding our thoughts: God or the ego. Our thoughts create our reality, and whichever voice we listen to, is the reality we will experience. How can such a choice be hard? Because we have overlearned from the ego and believe wholeheartedly in what it shows us. We believe we are bodies and that this physical world and all the forms within it are the truth. We know we believe in this reality based upon our reactions to it. We covet things, people, and places—sometimes so ferociously it turns to violence. We cannot let go of the physical things our ego holds dear. And yet, salvation begs that we share, not covet. What are we to share? Our love. We share our love through the inner recognition that nothing in this world is separate from us, but is in truth, One in God. To see in this way, we must forgive all forms we see. To forgive, we must undo guilt. To be "guilty" is to believe you are a body. The guiltless are those who believe they are bodiless and are thus forgiven. And with forgiveness, you will see a bodiless, "guiltless," world. To forgive then, we must remember to simply still our thoughts about the world. We do not know what the bodiless look like, nor how to see anything as it is in truth, as God created it eternally. Let all things be born again in your mind as you wipe it clean of all judgments, and in this purified place, truth will be reborn. The simplicity of salvation is the simplicity of your choice between God or the ego; the choice between guiltlessness—believing you are bodiless—and guilt—believing you are a body.

II. Walking with Christ

"An ancient lesson is not overcome by the opposing of the new and old." (T-31.II.1:1)

"There is an ancient battle being waged against the truth, but truth does not respond." (T-31.II.1:4)

"He has no enemy in truth." (T-31.II.1:6)

"Let us review again what seems to stand between you and the truth of what you are. For there are steps in its relinquishment. The first is a decision that you make." (T-31.II.2:1-3)

"What you would choose between is not a choice and gives but the illusion it is free, for it will have one outcome either way." (T-31.II.3:1)

"The leader and the follower emerge as separate roles, each seeming to

CHAPTER 31 — THE FINAL VISION

possess advantages you would not want to lose." (T-31.II.3:3)

"You see yourself divided into both these roles, forever split between the two. And every friend or enemy becomes a means to help you save yourself from this." (T-31.II.3:5-6)

"Perhaps you call it love. Perhaps you think that it is murder justified at last." (T-31.II.4:1-2)

"And what of him? What does he want of you? What could he want, but what you want of him? Herein is life as easily as death, for what you choose you choose as well for him. Two calls you make to him, as he to you. Between these two is choice, because from them there is a different outcome." (T-31.II.5:1-6)

"The voice you hear in him is but your own." (T-31.II.5:11)

"For he is asking what will come to you, because you see an image of yourself and hear your voice requesting what you want." (T-31.II.5:14)

"Before you answer, pause to think of this:

The answer that I give my brother is what I am asking for. And what I learn of him is what I learn about myself.

Then let us wait an instant and be still, forgetting everything we thought we heard; remembering how much we do not know." (T-31.II.6:1-4)

"Because he is your equal in God's Love, you will be saved from all appearances and answer to the Christ Who calls to you. Be still and listen. Think not ancient thoughts. Forget the dismal lessons that you learned about the Son of God who calls to you." (T-31.II.7:1-4)

"Be very still an instant. Come without all thought of what you ever learned before, and put aside all images you made. The old will fall away before the new without your opposition or intent." (T-31.II.8:1-3)

"Nothing will hurt you in this holy place, to which you come to listen silently and learn the truth of what you really want." (T-31.II.8:6)

"Forgive your brother all appearances, that are but ancient lessons you have taught yourself about the sinfulness in you. Hear but his call for mercy and release from all the fearful images he holds of what he is and of what you must be." (T-31.II.9:1-2)

"And in this choice is learning's outcome changed, for Christ has been reborn to both of you." (T-31.II.9:7)

"An instant spent without your old ideas of who your great companion is and what he should be asking for, will be enough to let this happen." (T-31.II.10:1)

"He asks and you receive, for you have come with but one purpose; that you learn you love your brother with a brother's love." (T-31.II.10:5)

"Together is your joint inheritance remembered and accepted by you both." (T-31.II.11:1)

"For next to you is One Who holds the light before you, so that every step is made in certainty and sureness of the road. A blindfold can indeed obscure your sight, but cannot make the way itself grow dark. And He Who travels with you *has* the light." (T-31.II.11:7-9)

In summary, Chapter 31 – II: "Walking with Christ" is saying:
Because we have forgotten we are One with each other in God, we have forgotten Who walks with us. We are always walking with Christ, for He is part of our One Self. There are steps to remembering this. The first is to remember you have only one choice: who do I want to listen to; God or the ego? If you listen to the ego, you will forget your Oneness and see only a body and react to it as such. Thus, damning yourself to a bodily identity, for what you see in another, you are seeing in yourself. If you listen to God, you will see one who is need of your help in remembering Who They Are, same as you. How you answer this question, "Who do I want to listen to?" determines the world you will see. The second step then, is to stop, be still and listen within. Hold still all thoughts of the ego that scream, "They are a body! React to them in an unloving way! They are wrong and I am right!" Remember that the ego is always wrong in what it sees, and therefore you are always wrong whenever you see a body. So, forget all such nonsense for an instant and be still. Then the third step will come; sanity returns to your mind. For by the simple act of recognizing you do not want to choose to see the body you welcome God. He then, will take care of all that needs healing, for you have chosen to walk with Christ.

III. The Self-Accused

"Only the self-accused condemn. As you prepare to make a choice that will result in different outcomes, there is first one thing that must be overlearned." (T-31.III.1:1-2)

"Learn this, and learn it well, for it is here delay of happiness is short-

CHAPTER 31 — THE FINAL VISION

ened by a span of time you cannot realize. You never hate your brother for his sins, but only for your own. Whatever form his sins appear to take, it but obscures the fact that you believe them to be yours, and therefore meriting a "just" attack." (T-31.III.1:4-6)

"Why should his sins be sins, if you did not believe they could not be forgiven in you? Why are they real in him, if you did not believe that they are your reality?" (T-31.III.2:1-2)

"If you did not believe that you deserved attack, it never would occur to you to give attack to anyone at all." (T-31.III.2:7)

"And how could murder bring you benefit?" (T-31.III.2:11)

"Sins are in bodies. They are not perceived in minds. They are not seen as purposes, but actions. Bodies act, and minds do not. And therefore must the body be at fault for what it does. It is not seen to be a passive thing, obeying your commands, and doing nothing of itself at all." (T-31.III.3:1-6)

"Yet is the *body* prisoner, and not the mind. The body thinks no thoughts." (T-31.III.4:1-2)

"The mind that thinks it is a sin has but one purpose; that the body be the source of sin, to keep it in the prison house it chose and guards and hold itself at bay, a sleeping prisoner to the snarling dogs of hate and evil, sickness and attack; of pain and age, of grief and suffering." (T-31.III.5:1)

"Let us be glad that you will see what you believe, and that it has been given you to change what you believe. The body will but follow." (T-31.III.6:1-2)

"Release your body from imprisonment, and you will see no one as prisoner to what you have escaped. You will not want to hold in guilt your chosen enemies, nor keep in chains, to the illusion of a changing love, the ones you think are friends." (T-31.III.6:5-6)

"The innocent release in gratitude for their release." (T-31.III.7:1)

"Open your mind to change, and there will be no ancient penalty exacted from your brother or yourself. For God has said there is no sacrifice that can be asked; there is no sacrifice that can be made." (T-31.III.7:3-4)

In summary, Chapter 31 – III: "The Self-Accused" is saying:

Guilt is the belief we are bodies and innocence is the relinquishment of this belief. When we see bodies, our Innocent Identity as One stands accused of "sin" or separation. To bear witness to our innocence then, we must release everyone from the bodies we see. For we never hate anyone for *their* body, but only for how we interact with them through our *own*. Whatever form a body or "sin" appears to take, it but obscures the fact that you believe yourself to be a body as well, and therefore meriting a "just" attack against theirs. Without the body, it would never occur to you to attack at all. Separation or "sin" is acted out through bodies. Yet this is not the true state of our minds. Be glad you can change your mind about bodies! Release everyone in your mind from the belief they are a separate body from your own, and you will feel your own release as well. And you will stand in innocence, no longer feeling the pain of the self-accused.

IV. The Real Alternative

"There is a tendency to think the world can offer consolation and escape from problems that its purpose is to keep. Why should this be? Because it is a place where choice among illusions seems to be the only choice." (T-31.IV.1:1-3)

"Real choice is no illusion. But the world has none to offer. All its roads but lead to disappointment, nothingness and death." (T-31.IV.2:1-3)

"Seek not escape from problems here. The world was made that problems could not be escaped." (T-31.IV.2:5-6)

"There is no choice where every end is sure. Perhaps you would prefer to try them all, before you really learn they are but one. The roads this world can offer seem to be quite large in number, but the time must come when everyone begins to see how like they are to one another. Men have died on seeing this, because they saw no way except the pathways offered by the world. And learning they led nowhere, lost their hope. And yet this was the time they could have learned their greatest lesson. All must reach this point, and go beyond it." (T-31.IV.3:1-7)

"Learn now, without despair, there is no hope of answer in the world." (T-31.IV.4:3)

"Who would be willing to be turned away from all the roadways of the world, unless he understood their real futility?" (T-31.IV.5:1)

CHAPTER 31 — THE FINAL VISION

"The learning that the world can offer but one choice, no matter what its form may be, is the beginning of acceptance that there is a real alternative instead. To fight against this step is to defeat your purpose here." (T-31.IV.6:1-2)

"There is a choice that you have power to make when you have seen the real alternatives. Until that point is reached you have no choice, and you can but decide how you would choose the better to deceive yourself again." (T-31.IV.8:1-2)

"He has not left His Thoughts! But you forgot His Presence and remembered not His Love. No pathway in the world can lead to Him, nor any worldly goal be one with His. What road in all the world will lead within, when every road was made to separate the journey from the purpose it must have unless it be but futile wandering?" (T-31.IV.9:1-4)

"He has not left His Thoughts! He could no more depart from them than they could keep Him out. In unity with Him do they abide, and in Their Oneness Both are kept complete. There is no road that leads away from Him. A journey from yourself does not exist." (T-31.IV.10:1-5)

"Forgive yourself your madness, and forget all senseless journeys and all goal-less aims. They have no meaning. You can not escape from what you are." (T-31.IV.11:1-3)

"Nowhere but where He is can you be found. There is no path that does not lead to Him." (T-31.IV.11:7)

In summary, Chapter 31 – IV: "The Real Alternative" is saying:
We have but two choices; we can either choose to move towards God or away. Except we cannot truly ever leave Him, or we would cease to exist. We are each one of God's Thoughts and can no more leave His Mind than He can "unthink" us. We are eternally created as His. And yet, in this world, we think we have an untold number of choices in what will bring us happiness. And all this time, we have simply forgotten we are unhappy because of our imagined separation from God. Once we realize this world will never fulfill the void left by our mistaken choice, the futility of all we have tried to accomplish hits some people with devastation. This is what brings some to suicide. They suddenly see the truth of the nothingness of the world and with no understanding of the truth to replace such thoughts, their heart moves into utter despair. Yet here is the moment of one's highest achievement, your greatest glory. *You can make*

another choice! Let the world go! Become still as you stand on the precipice of knowing God—for He is within you and all roads outside of you will only lead you back to this realization. This choice—the choice to turn within—is the only real alternative you have to suffering in the world.

V. Self-Concept versus Self

"The learning of the world is built upon a concept of the self adjusted to the world's reality." (T-31.V.1:1)

"The building of a concept of the self is what the learning of the world is for. This is its purpose; that you come without a self, and make one as you go along." (T-31.V.1:5-6)

"A concept of the self is made by you. It bears no likeness to yourself at all. It is an idol, made to take the place of your reality as Son of God." (T-31.V.2:1-3)

"This aspect can grow angry, for the world is wicked and unable to provide the love and shelter innocence deserves. And so this face is often wet with tears at the injustices the world accords to those who would be generous and good." (T-31.V.3:1-2)

"Beneath the face of innocence there is a lesson that the concept of the self was made to teach. It is a lesson in a terrible displacement, and a fear so devastating that the face that smiles above it must forever look away, lest it perceive the treachery it hides. The lesson teaches this: "I am the thing you made of me, and as you look on me, you stand condemned because of what I am." On this conception of the self the world smiles with approval, for it guarantees the pathways of the world are safely kept, and those who walk on them will not escape." (T-31.V.5:1-4)

"Your brother then is symbol of your sins to you who are but silently, and yet with ceaseless urgency, condemning still your brother for the hated thing you are." (T-31.V.6:8)

"Concepts are learned. They are not natural." (T-31.V.7:1-2)

"What is a concept but a thought to which its maker gives a meaning of his own?" (T-31.V.7:6)

"They are ideas of idols, painted with the brushes of the world, which cannot make a single picture representing truth." (T-31.V.7:10)

"Yet is all learning that the world directs begun and ended with the

CHAPTER 31 — THE FINAL VISION

single aim of teaching you this concept of yourself, that you will choose to follow this world's laws, and never seek to go beyond its roads nor realize the way you see yourself. Now must the Holy Spirit find a way to help you see this concept of the self must be undone, if any peace of mind is to be given you." (T-31.V.8:2-3)

"Thus are the Holy Spirit's lesson plans arranged in easy steps, that though there be some lack of ease at times and some distress, there is no shattering of what was learned, but just a re-translation of what seems to be the evidence on its behalf." (T-31.V.9:1)

"Let us forget the concept's foolishness, and merely think of this; there are two parts to what you think yourself to be. If one were generated by your brother, who was there to make the other?" (T-31.V.10:6-7)

"Perhaps the reason why this concept must be kept in darkness is that, in the light, the one who would not think it true is you. And what would happen to the world you see, if all its underpinnings were removed? Your concept of the world depends upon this concept of the self. And both would go, if either one were ever raised to doubt." (T-31.V.11:1-4)

"There are alternatives about the thing that you must be." (T-31.V.12:1)

"There is some understanding that you chose for both of you, and what he represents has meaning that was given it by you." (T-31.V.12:4)

"Yet who was it that did the choosing first?" (T-31.V.12:6)

"Something must have gone before these concepts of the self. And something must have done the learning which gave rise to them." (T-31.V.13:2-3)

"But this gain is paid in almost equal loss, for now you stand accused of guilt for what your brother is. And you must share his guilt, because you chose it for him in the image of your own." (T-31.V.13:6-7)

"The concept of the self has always been the great preoccupation of the world. And everyone believes that he must find the answer to the riddle of himself. Salvation can be seen as nothing more than the escape from concepts." (T-31.V.14:1-3)

"Seek not your Self in symbols. There can be no concept that can stand for what you are." (T-31.V.15:1-2)

"If you can be hurt by anything, you see a picture of your secret wishes.

V. Self-Concept versus Self

Nothing more than this." (T-31.V.15:8-9)

"You will make many concepts of the self as learning goes along." (T-31.V.16:1)

"There will be some confusion every time there is a shift, but be you thankful that the learning of the world is loosening its grasp upon your mind. And be you sure and happy in the confidence that it will go at last, and leave your mind at peace. The role of accuser will appear in many places and in many forms." (T-31.V.16:3-5)

"Yet have no fear it will not be undone." (T-31.V.16:7)

"There will come a time when images have all gone by, and you will see you know not what you are. It is to this unsealed and open mind that truth returns, unhindered and unbound." (T-31.V.17:2-3)

"There is no statement that the world is more afraid to hear than this:
I do not know the thing I am, and therefore do not know what I am doing, where I am, or how to look upon the world or myself.
Yet in this learning is salvation born. And What you are will tell you of Itself." (T-31.V.17:6-9)

In summary, Chapter 31 – V: "Self-Concept versus Self" is saying:
By our decision to come into an experience of separation from God, we had to become a different "self." For we could not retain the Identity of being One if we were to experience separation. And thus, the ego was born, and with it, a body through which we could see ourselves as separate. And so it was, that we seemingly became two "selves." One is merely a self-concept and not real, while the other is our true Self. As we relearn Who We Are, we will return many times, making many different "selves." Each one bringing us closer to the truth as each one fails to bring us the peace we seek. When we come to the point in our learning where we discover that *we have done this to ourselves*, great guilt may be experienced. It is often painful to hear that by judging our brethren to be bodies, we hold them in that small, painful identity and ourselves as well. For what they are, so must we also be. The ego never wants you to realize this. It wants you to be endlessly preoccupied with searching for "who you are," yet never finding it. For if you understood you held the power to undo your own self-concept, both the ego (and therefore the body) along with all the world you see now, would go. This is why the most powerful statement, the most powerful self-concept you can ever have, is that you do

CHAPTER 31—THE FINAL VISION

not know who you are. With belief in these words, you effectively wipe your mind clean of all ego self-concepts and allow the truth to enter and replace your own self-concept with your Self.

VI. Recognizing the Spirit

"You see the flesh or recognize the spirit. There is no compromise between the two. If one is real the other must be false, for what is real denies its opposite. There is no other choice in vision but this one. What you decide in this determines all you see and think is real and hold as true. On this one choice does all your world depend, for here have you established what you are, as flesh or spirit in your own belief. If you choose flesh, you never will escape the body as your own reality, for you have chosen that you want it so. But choose the spirit, and all Heaven bends to touch your eyes and bless your holy sight, that you may see the world of flesh no more except to heal and comfort and to bless." (T-31.VI.1:1-8)

"Salvation is undoing. If you choose to see the body, you behold a world of separation, unrelated things, and happenings that make no sense at all." (T-31.VI.1:1-2)

"Salvation is undoing of all this. For constancy arises in the sight of those whose eyes salvation has released from looking at the cost of keeping guilt, because they chose to let it go instead." (T-31.VI.2:6-7)

"Salvation does not ask that you behold the spirit and perceive the body not. It merely asks that this should be your choice. For you can see the body without help, but do not understand how to behold a world apart from it." (T-31.VI.3:1-3)

"Be not concerned how this could ever be. You do not understand how what you see arose to meet your sight. For if you did, it would be gone." (T-31.VI.3:5-7)

"Only in arrogance could you conceive that you must make the way to Heaven plain. The means are given you by which to see the world that will replace the one you made. Your will be done!" (T-31.VI.4:1-3)

"For God Himself has said, "Your will be done." And it is done to you accordingly." (T-31.VI.4:7-8)

"Are you a body? So is all the world perceived as treacherous, and out to kill." (T-31.VI.6:5-6)

"Are you a spirit, deathless, and without the promise of corruption and the stain of sin upon you? So the world is seen as stable, fully worthy of your trust; a happy place to rest in for a while, where nothing need be feared, but only loved." (T-31.VI.6:7-8)

"Your will be done, you holy child of God. It does not matter if you think you are in earth or Heaven. What your Father wills of you can never change. The truth in you remains as radiant as a star, as pure as light, as innocent as love itself. And you are worthy that your will be done!" (T-31.VI.7:1-5)

In summary, Chapter 31 – VI: "Recognizing the Spirit" is saying:
We are told that we either see the body or recognize the spirit within the body. We see either one or the other; in this, our seeing is uncompromising. And what we decide determines our reality. We will experience either this world or Heaven. Salvation is the only way to ensure that we consistently make the choice for Heaven by seeing only Spirit in others. Salvation is undoing and to undo this world we must forgive it. Forgiveness is merely the stillness of our thoughts about the world—cease to give what you see a second thought! This does not mean we go about pretending we do not see the world, but merely that we know that it is not the truth. In truth all is One. There is no separation. And all we have to do to heal our mind is recognize when we are suffering and choose against it. Remember that you are wrong about what you see as all forms of form, and you will be on the path to Light. This is how your will is done! For Who You Are in truth shines on regardless of what your ego sees. Remember this always, and you will always recognize the Spirit.

VII. The Savior's Vision

"Learning is change. Salvation does not seek to use a means as yet too alien to your thinking to be helpful, nor to make the kinds of change you could not recognize. Concepts are needed while perception lasts, and changing concepts is salvation's task." (T-31.VII.1:1-3)

"You could not recognize your "evil" thoughts as long as you see value in attack. You will perceive them sometimes, but will not see them as meaningless." (T-31.VII.2:1-2)

"But should *one* brother dawn upon your sight as wholly worthy of forgiveness, then your concept of yourself is wholly changed. Your "evil" thoughts have been forgiven with his, because you let them all affect you not." (T-31.VII.2:5-6)

CHAPTER 31 — THE FINAL VISION

"In terms of concepts, it is thus you see him more than just a body, for the good is never what the body seems to be." (T-31.VII.3:1)

"By focusing upon the good in him, the body grows decreasingly persistent in your sight, and will at length be seen as little more than just a shadow circling round the good." (T-31.VII.3:3)

"Have faith in him who walks with you, so that your fearful concept of yourself may change. And look upon the good in him, that you may not be frightened by your "evil" thoughts because they do not cloud your view of him. And all this shift requires is that you be willing that this happy change occur. No more than this is asked." (T-31.VII.5:1-4)

"The concept of yourself that now you hold would guarantee your function here remain forever unaccomplished and undone." (T-31.VII.6:1)

"The concept of the self stands like a shield, a silent barricade before the truth, and hides it from your sight. All things you see are images, because you look on them as through a barrier that dims your sight and warps your vision, so that you behold nothing with clarity." (T-31.VII.7:1-2)

"Behold your role within the universe!" (T-31.VII.8:1)

"And this he learns when first he looks upon one brother as he looks upon himself, and sees the mirror of himself in him." (T-31.VII.8:4)

"And in this single vision does he see the face of Christ, and understands he looks on everyone as he beholds this one." (T-31.VII.8:6)

"The veil across the face of Christ, the fear of God and of salvation, and the love of guilt and death, they all are different names for just one error; that there is a space between you and your brother, kept apart by an illusion of yourself that holds him off from you, and you away from him." (T-31.VII.9:1)

"What is temptation but the wish to stay in hell and misery? And what could this give rise to but an image of yourself that can be miserable, and remain in hell and torment? Who has learned to see his brother not as this has saved himself, and thus is he a savior to the rest." (T-31.VII.10:1-3)

"The holy ones whom God has given you to save are but everyone you meet or look upon, not knowing who they are; all those you saw an

VII. The Savior's Vision

instant and forgot, and those you knew a long while since, and those you will yet meet; the unremembered and the not yet born. For God has given you His Son to save from every concept that he ever held." (T-31.VII.10:5-6)

"For holiness is seen through holy eyes that look upon the innocence within, and thus expect to see it everywhere. And so they call it forth in everyone they look upon, that he may be what they expect of him." (T-31.VII.11:3-4)

"Whatever form temptation seems to take, it always but reflects a wish to be a self that you are not." (T-31.VII.12:1)

"The savior's vision is as innocent of what your brother is as it is free of any judgment made upon yourself." (T-31.VII.13:1)

"Be vigilant against temptation, then, remembering that it is but a wish, insane and meaningless, to make yourself a thing that you are not. And think as well upon the thing that you would be instead." (T-31.VII.14:1-2)

"Let not the world's light, given unto you, be hidden from the world. It needs the light, for it is dark indeed, and men despair because the savior's vision is withheld and what they see is death." (T-31.VII.15:1-2)

"Can you to whom God says, "Release My Son!" be tempted not to listen, when you learn that it is you for whom He asks release? And what but this is what this course would teach? And what but this is there for you to learn?" (T-31.VII.15:5-7)

In summary, Chapter 31 – VII: "The Savior's Vision" is saying:
To change what we see, we must change what we have learned. In this world, we are taught we are bodies. This must be unlearned and replaced with the knowledge we are spirit, and the body is but a vehicle for communicating God's Love to one another while we imagine ourselves as separate. Learning is change. Learn this, and you change what you experience. Therefore, forgive all bodies you see. The Course states that "To forgive is to overlook." (T-9.IV.1:2) To overlook all bodies then, we must quiet our thoughts about what those bodies are saying and doing. We know not who they are in truth. The Savior's Vision understands this, knowing that we are not our ego and what it does with the body. The Savior's Vison knows that without a body, we would only know the Love that binds us all in God and all else would be forgotten. Be vigilant then, against all thoughts of separation—any thought that causes you

CHAPTER 31 — THE FINAL VISION

to lose your peace, even a fraction. And once you catch such a thought, banish it with the understanding that you do not want it. Then replace the thought with what you know to be true—that we are beings of Light and all else is false. God asks us to release Christ from the bodily visions our ego holds so dear. We do this through forgiveness, looking beyond the body and using our Savior's Vision instead.

VIII. Choose Once Again

"Temptation has one lesson it would teach, in all its forms, wherever it occurs. It would persuade the holy Son of God he is a body, born in what must die, unable to escape its frailty, and bound by what it orders him to feel." (T-31.VIII.1:1-2)

"Would you be this, if Christ appeared to you in all His glory, asking you but this:
Choose once again if you would take your place among the saviors of the world, or would remain in hell, and hold your brothers there. For He has come, and He is asking this." (T-31.VIII.1:4-6)

"How do you make the choice? How easily is this explained! You always choose between your weakness and the strength of Christ in you. And what you choose is what you think is real." (T-31.VIII.2:1-4)

"Trials are but lessons that you failed to learn presented once again, so where you made a faulty choice before you now can make a better one, and thus escape all pain that what you chose before has brought to you. In every difficulty, all distress, and each perplexity Christ calls to you and gently says, "My brother, choose again." He would not leave one source of pain unhealed, nor any image left to veil the truth." (T-31.VIII.3:1-3)

"The images you make cannot prevail against what God Himself would have you be. Be never fearful of temptation, then, but see it as it is; another chance to choose again, and let Christ's strength prevail in every circumstance and every place you raised an image of yourself before." (T-31.VIII.4:1-2)

"Learn, then, the happy habit of response to all temptation to perceive yourself as weak and miserable with these words:
I am as God created me. His Son can suffer nothing. And I am His Son.
Thus is Christ's strength invited to prevail, replacing all your weakness

VIII. Choose Once Again

with the strength that comes from God and that can never fail." (T-31.VIII.5:1-5)

"You *are* as God created you, and so is every living thing you look upon, regardless of the images you see." (T-31.VIII.6:1)

"A miracle has come to heal God's Son, and close the door upon his dreams of weakness, opening the way to his salvation and release. Choose once again what you would have him be, remembering that every choice you make establishes your own identity as you will see it and believe it is." (T-31.VIII.6:4-5)

"My brothers in salvation, do not fail to hear my voice and listen to my words. I ask for nothing but your own release." (T-31.VIII.8:1-2)

"Let us be glad that we can walk the world, and find so many chances to perceive another situation where God's gift can once again be recognized as ours!" (T-31.VIII.9:1)

"In joyous welcome is my hand outstretched to every brother who would join with me in reaching past temptation, and who looks with fixed determination toward the light that shines beyond in perfect constancy." (T-31.VIII.11:1)

"And now we say "Amen." For Christ has come to dwell in the abode You set for Him before time was, in calm eternity. The journey closes, ending at the place where it began. No trace of it remains. Not one illusion is accorded faith, and not one spot of darkness still remains to hide the face of Christ from anyone. Thy Will is done, complete and perfectly, and all creation recognizes You, and knows You as the only Source it has. Clear in Your likeness does the light shine forth from everything that lives and moves in You. For we have reached where all of us are one, and we are home, where You would have us be." (T-31.VIII.12:1-8)

In summary, Chapter 31 – VIII: "Choose Once Again" is saying:
Always, we are making a choice with our thoughts—we are either choosing to think with the ego or the Holy Spirit. We know with whom we are choosing to think, by how we feel. All forms of suffering felt stem from our choice to join with the ego. And all peace and love come from joining our thoughts with the Holy Spirit. Temptation then, is nothing more than being fooled by the forms we see and falling for the temptation to believe they are real. We know we have been fooled, by how we feel. When you are tempted to believe that

CHAPTER 31 — THE FINAL VISION

you or anyone else is a body and are tempted to feel suffering in response to bodies in any form, simply remember: *You remain as God created you. And nothing you imagine can undo the Love that you are. If anything but Love is perceived, then remember that you are listening to the ego and you are wrong.* Then choose once again. Choose to step among the saviors of the world, by choosing to overlook, or forgive, what you see. With this choice, the journey to Love comes to an end, for illusions no longer tempt us to believe in anything but the truth of our Oneness. With these thoughts, we choose once again, allowing God to step forward to restore our true sight—the final vision of a world transformed into Unity.

AUTHOR BIOGRAPHY

Beth Geer's spiritual background is rich and diverse. She has had a multitude of psychic, paranormal, and deeply profound spiritual experiences—including extraterrestrial contact—throughout her life. She comes from a strong, traditional Catholic upbringing, although she no longer attends or identifies with any religious group. If asked what religion she belongs to she simply states that she is "self-taught," meaning that she prefers to seek guidance from her own Inner Teacher or higher Self, rather than follow any organized religious institution.

Beth has been a student of *A Course in Miracles* since 2004 and now actively teaches its principles to others through her online writings, videos and books. She has also practiced tarot reading since 1993, is a Reiki Master and has enthusiastically studied astrology, numerology, and many other psychic, paranormal and spiritual arenas.

Though her religious and spiritual background may appear to be contradictory, it is this very contrast that has given her an open-mindedness towards God and life.

Beth is the author of *Awakening To One Love: Uncover The Inner Peace and Joy Hidden Within You*, a compilation of inner conversations with the Holy Spirit surrounding the Workbook lessons and many questions she had from "*A Course In Miracles*. Her second book is *Awakening Humanity: Our Place Among Extraterrestrials and Angels*, which recounts the story of an extraterrestrial contact Beth had with an individual she calls "Martha" who not only shared information about her home world, but also had much spiritual information to impart to our world.

Beth regularly posts her current miraculous experiences, deep insights, and latest adventures with other beings from the unseen realms—nature spirits, fairies, and sasquatch, to name a few—on her blog, YouTube channel, and newsletter. She frequently is a contributor to Miracles Magazine, The Embrace, and the Miracle Worker magazines, and has been a keynote, guest speaker on "Miracle Network" and the "Miracle Café." In 2019 Beth was a speaker at the "Miracles in the Mountains" weekend conference in Boone, SC. She has enjoyed interviews on various podcasts, including "Sunday with Mundy," by author Jon Mundy as well as being a repeat guest speaker at the Lake Harriet Spiritual Community Church in Minneapolis, MN.

Beth is a pharmacist by day, and in her free time, when not tending to family, animals, or plants, she works on extending a message of healing and love to the world through many avenues, including her monthly newsletter "Miracle Minded Messages," which she turns into YouTube videos. In these videos, rather than sitting in front of the camera herself, she often uses footage from the beautiful countryside landscape surrounding her farm—which she feels is far more interesting to watch rather than her "talking head." She thoroughly enjoys creating these videos, using her own nature photography and videography.

Beth lives in a log home on a 40-acre hobby farm in rural Minnesota, with her husband Paul, their two children, Miranda, and Samuel, along with three beautiful horses and varying numbers of outdoor cats. They also have one special six-toed (polydactyl) indoor cat named Toby and a rottweiler named Freya—who both appear to be animals, but she feels they are actually just very hairy people with four legs.

A video series of *The Light Has Come!* can now be found on YouTube under the channel handle name: @BethGeer. The videos are grouped together under the "Playlists" heading titled: "ACIM Text Chapter Summaries." In addition, an ebook will soon be made available on Amazon.com and Kobo.com.

You can find more from Beth on her website at: www.bethgeer.com and on YouTube under the channel handle name: @BethGeer.

ACKNOWLEDGMENTS

Thank you, beloved Creator, for in your infinite wisdom You sent me exactly the right people, blessings, and challenges I needed to complete this work. As your Creations, we are at your service and deeply grateful to work together with Your Will for the peace and union of humanity.

My grateful heart also goes out to my beloved husband Paul, and children Miranda and Samuel. Thank you for being the loving, supportive people that you are.

I extend my infinite gratitude to my dear friends and publishers, Ronnie, and Ivor Whitson at Cogent Publishing. This book would not exist without you.

I am also deeply grateful to you, dear reader. For without you my One Self is not complete, and I thank you for your Presence and your Light. You are an essential part of All Creation. We are all in this together, striving to do God's Will—to love one another as He loves us—unconditionally, as One. Thank you for your willingness to be here and do this work of loving.

Made in the USA
Middletown, DE
08 November 2024